VERTIGO
DC COMICS

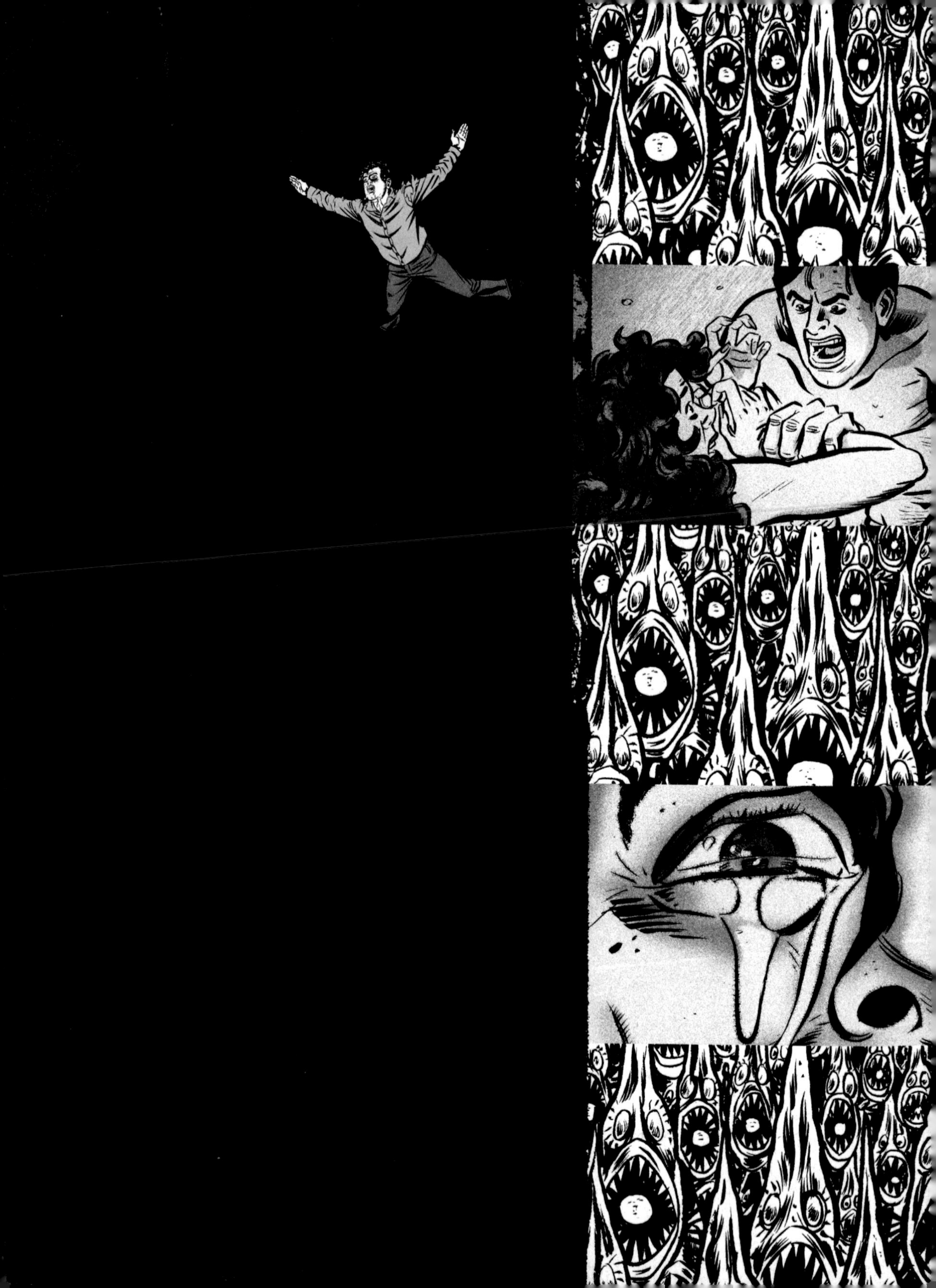

LOP
CLOP

SILVERFISH

DAVID LAPHAM

Greytones by Dom Ramos   Lettering by Jared K. Fletcher

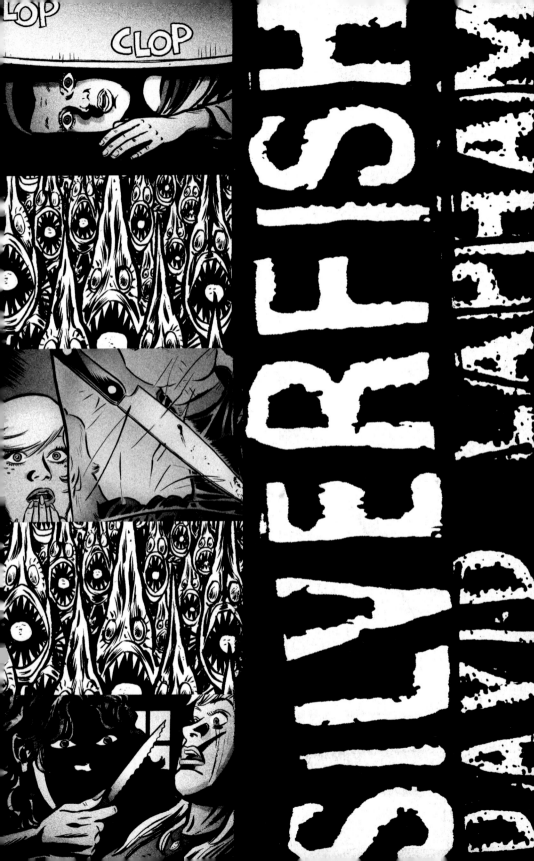

Karen Berger Sr. VP-Executive Editor
Shelly Bond Editor
Angela Rufino Assistant Editor
Louis Prandi Art Director
Paul Levitz President & Publisher
Georg Brewer VP-Design & DC Direct Creative
Richard Bruning Sr. VP-Creative Director
Patrick Caldon Exec. VP-Finance & Operations
Chris Caramalis VP-Finance
John Cunningham VP-Marketing
Terri Cunningham VP-Managing Editor
Alison Gill VP-Manufacturing
Hank Kanalz VP-General Manager, WildStorm
Jim Lee Editorial Director-WildStorm
Paula Lowitt Sr. VP-Business & Legal Affairs
MaryEllen McLaughlin VP-Advertising & Custom Publishing
John Nee VP-Business Development
Gregory Noveck Sr. VP-Creative Affairs
Sue Pohja VP-Book Trade Sales
Cheryl Rubin Sr. VP-Brand Management
Jeff Trojan VP-Business Development, DC Direct
Bob Wayne VP-Sales

COVER BY DAVID LAPHAM

SILVERFISH Published by DC Comics, 1700 Broadway, New York, NY
10019. Copyright © 2007 Lapham, Inc. All rights reserved. All
characters featured in this publication, the distinctive likenesses
thereof and related elements are trademarks of Lapham, Inc.
The stories, characters and incidents mentioned in this publication are
entirely fictional. Printed in Canada. DC Comics,
a Warner Bros. Entertainment Company.
SC ISBN: 1-4012-1049-X
SC ISBN13: 978-1-4012-1049-6
HC ISBN 1-4012-1048-1
HC ISBN13: 978-1-4012-1048-9

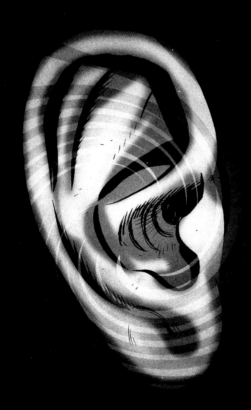

"TO HAVE THE EAR OF MAN
IS TO HEAR THE WORD OF GOD."

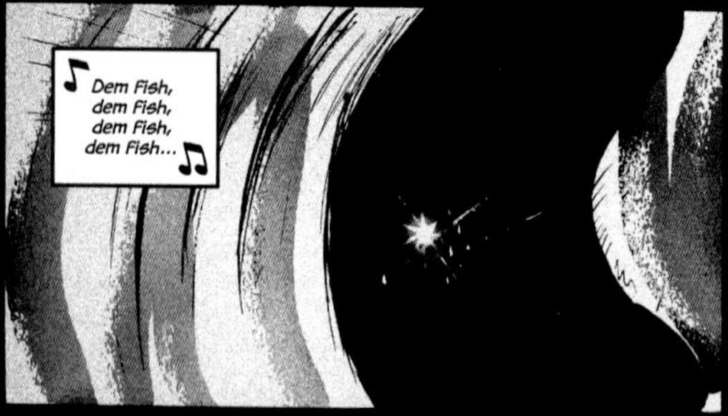
Dem Fish, dem Fish, dem Fish, dem Fish...

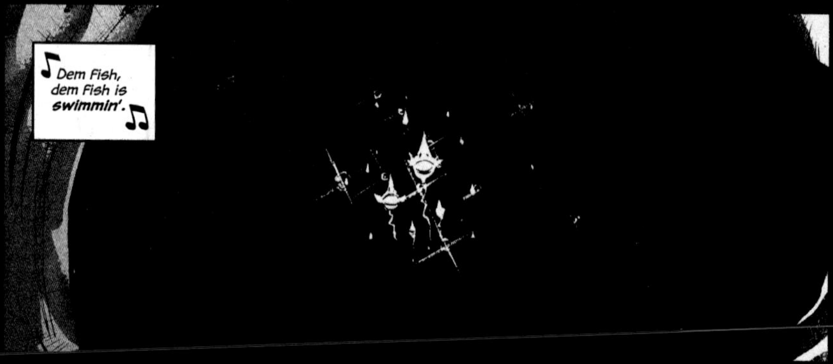
Dem Fish, dem Fish is swimmin'.

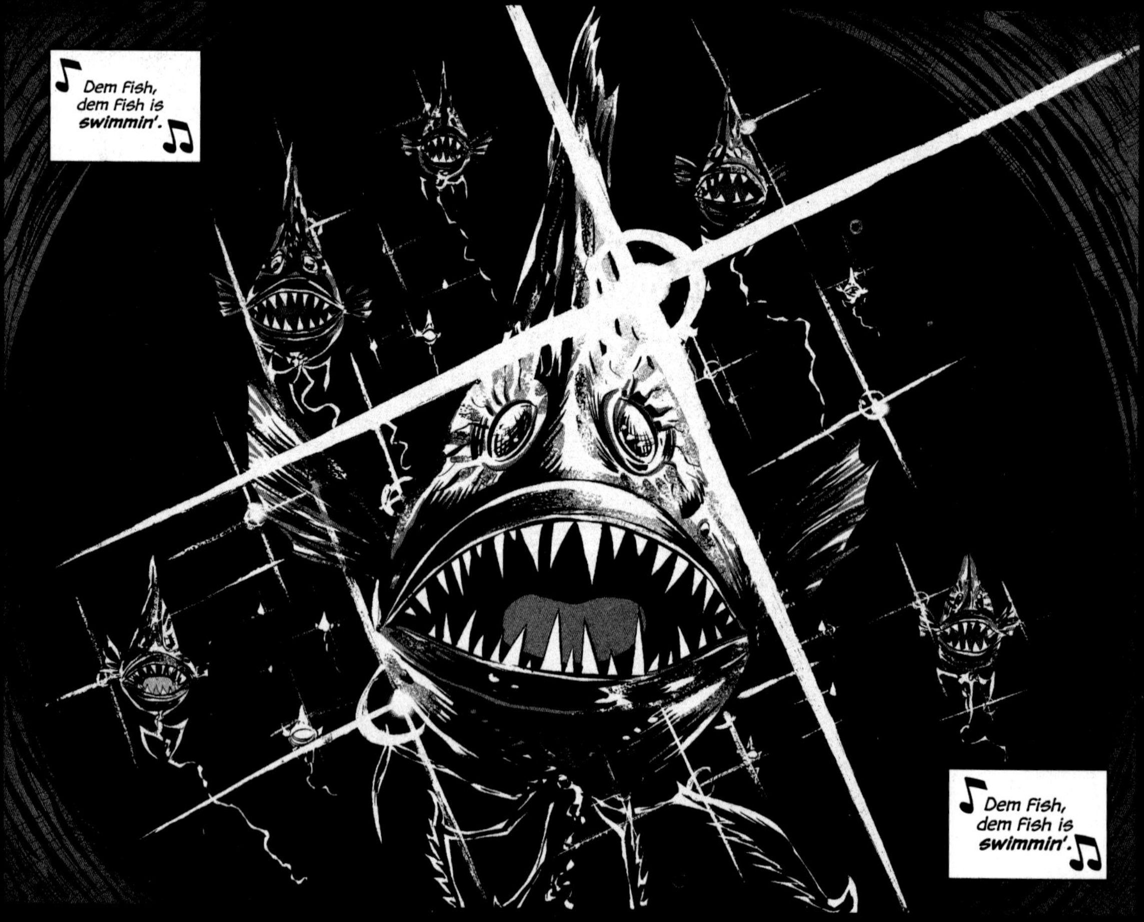
Dem Fish, dem Fish is swimmin'.
Dem Fish, dem Fish is swimmin'.

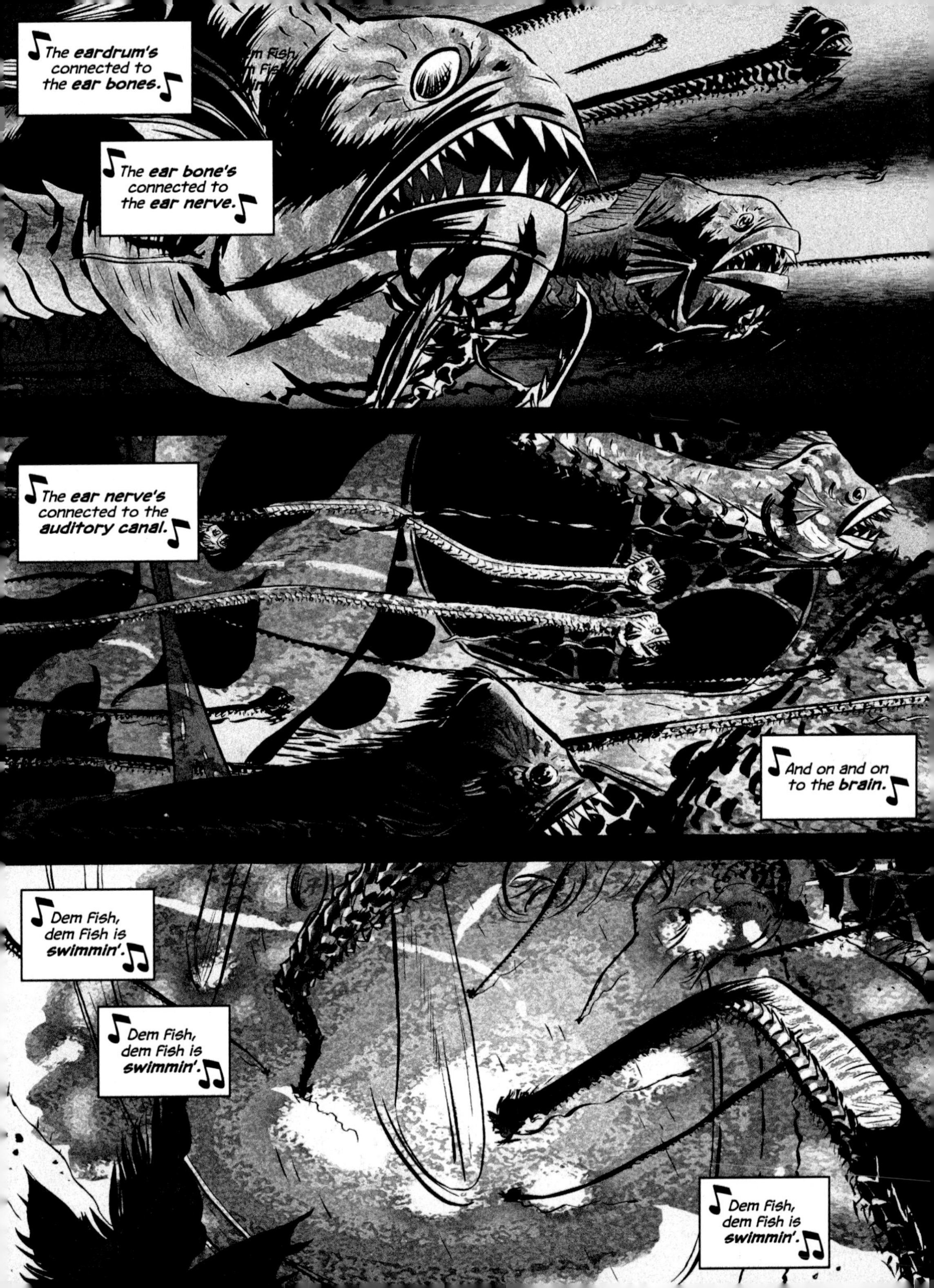
The eardrum's connected to the ear bones.
The ear bone's connected to the ear nerve.
The ear nerve's connected to the auditory canal.
And on and on to the brain.
Dem Fish, dem Fish is swimmin'.
Dem Fish, dem Fish is swimmin'.
Dem Fish, dem Fish is swimmin'.

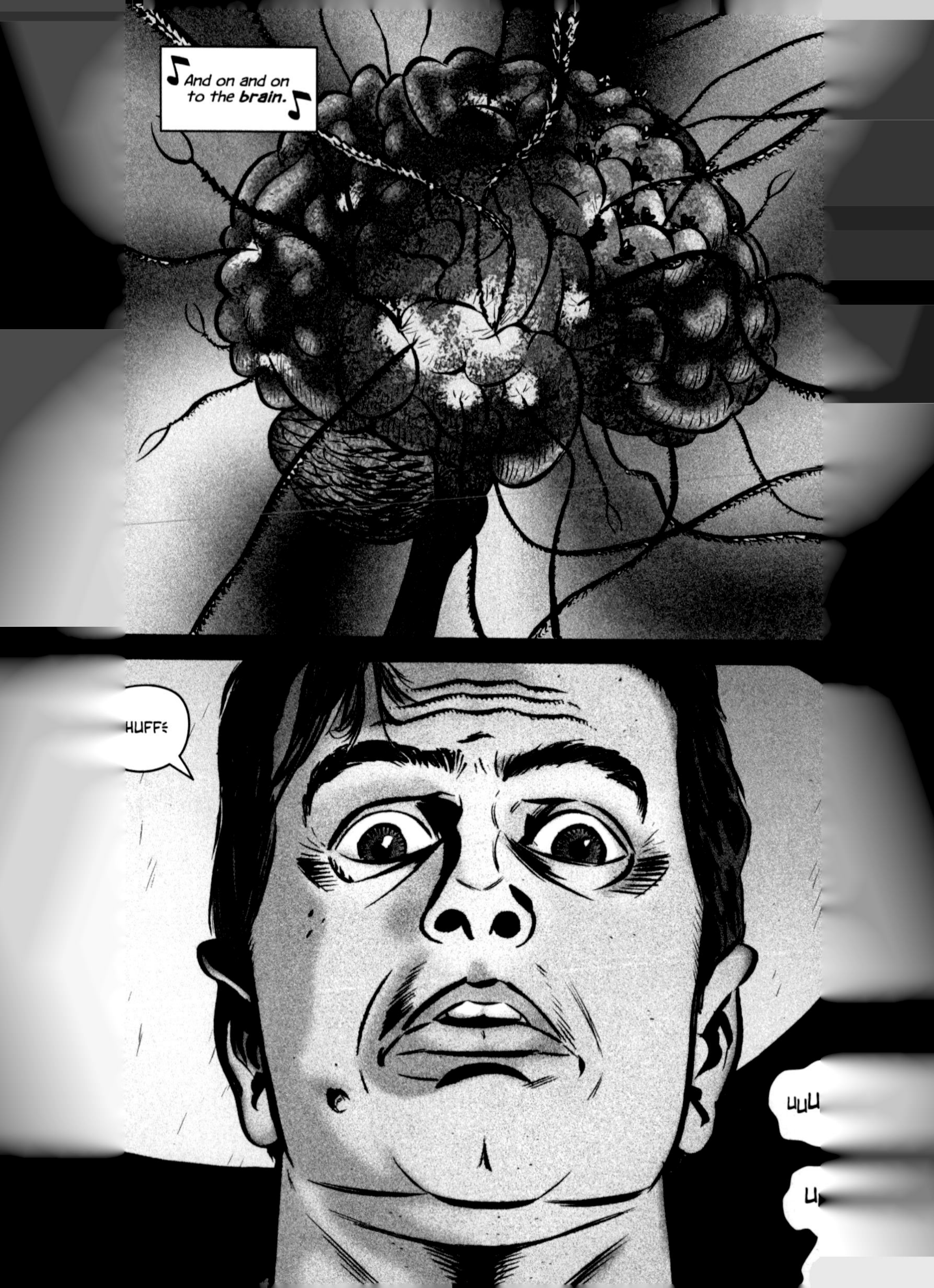
And on and on to the brain.
HUFF
UUU
U

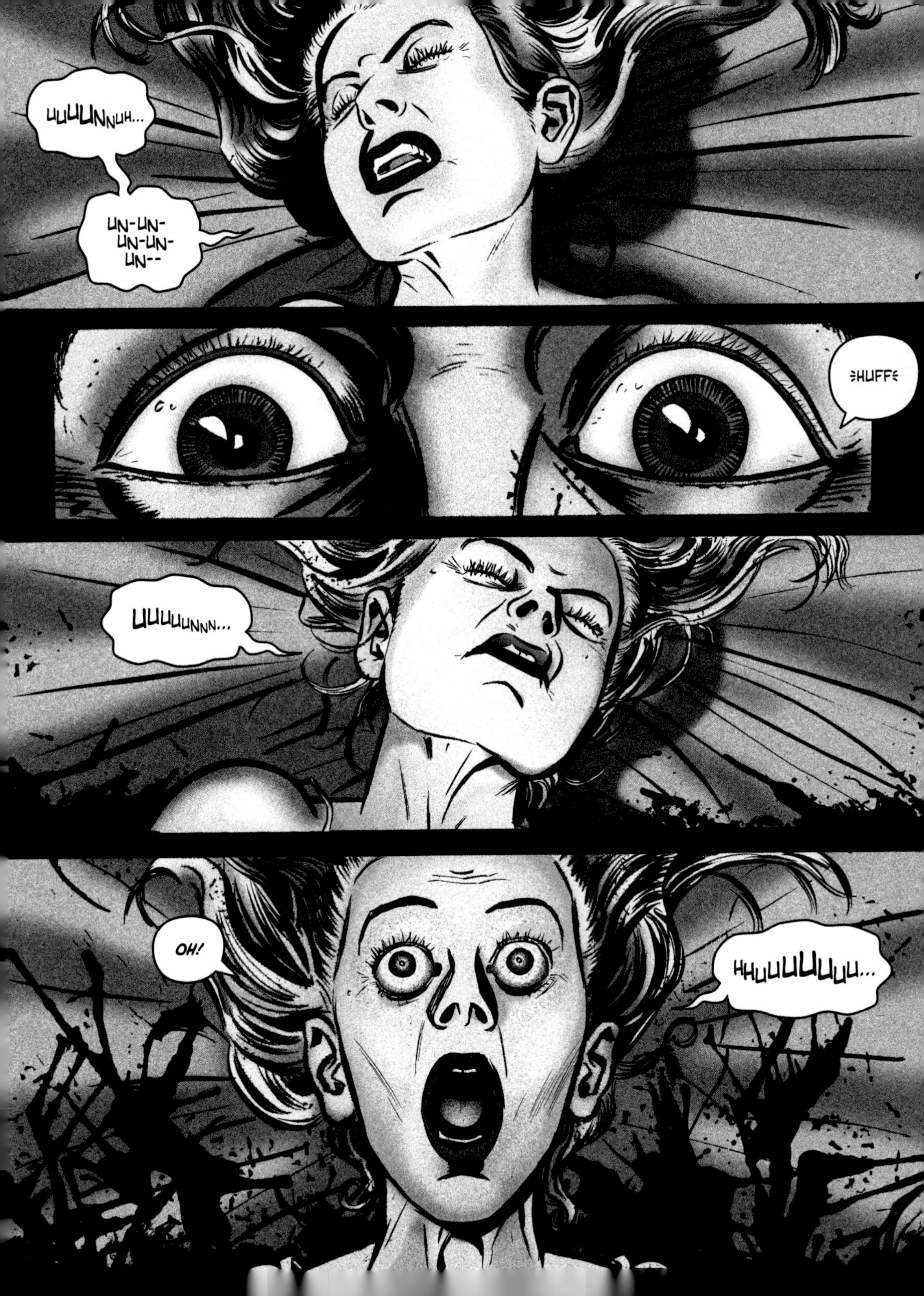
uuUUNnuh...
UN-UN-
UN-UN-
UN--
HUFF
UUUuunnn...
OH!
HHuuUUUuuu...

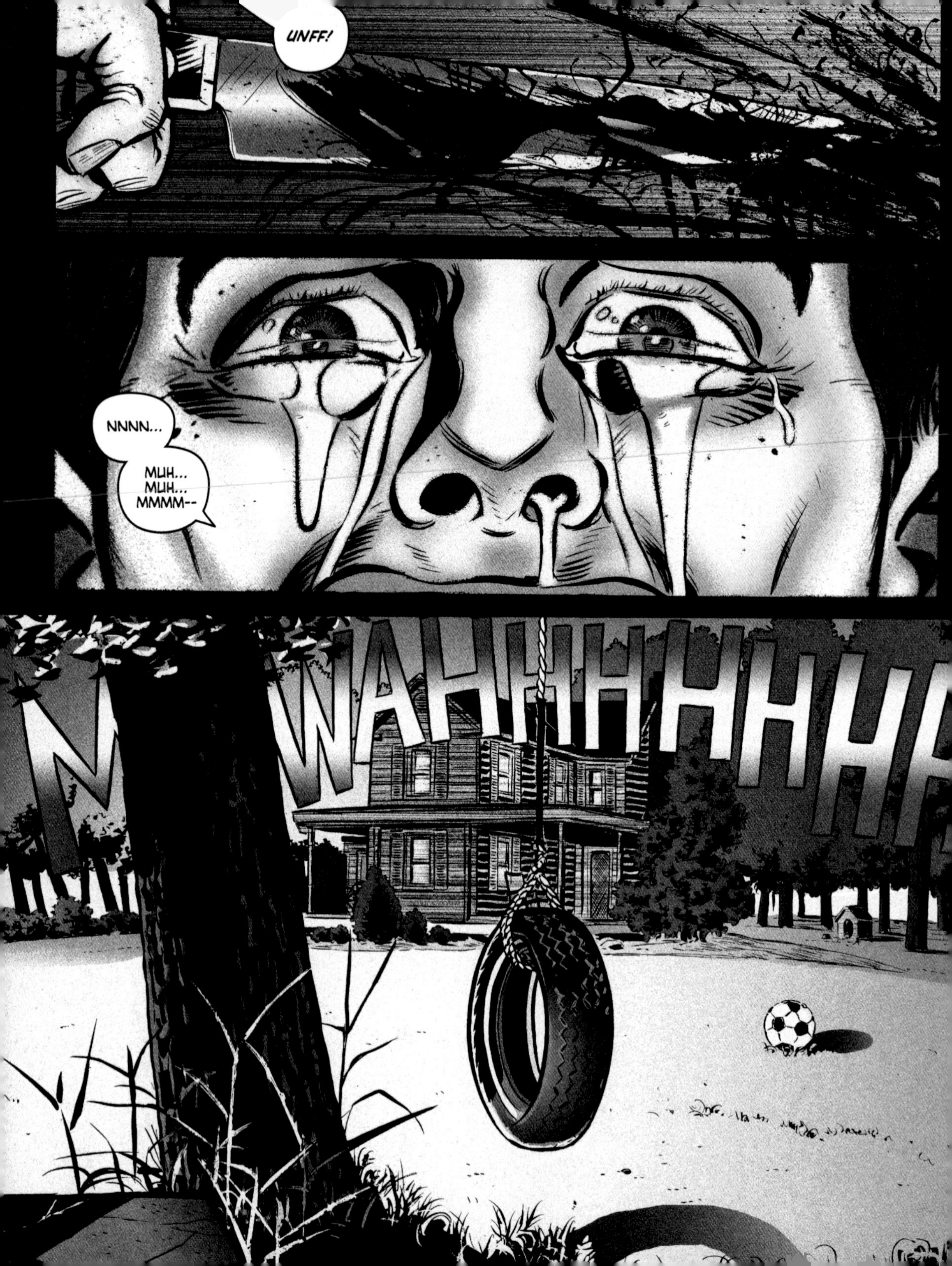
UNFF!
NNNN...
MUH... MUH... MMMM--
NWAHHHHHHH

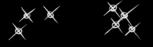

SILVERFISH

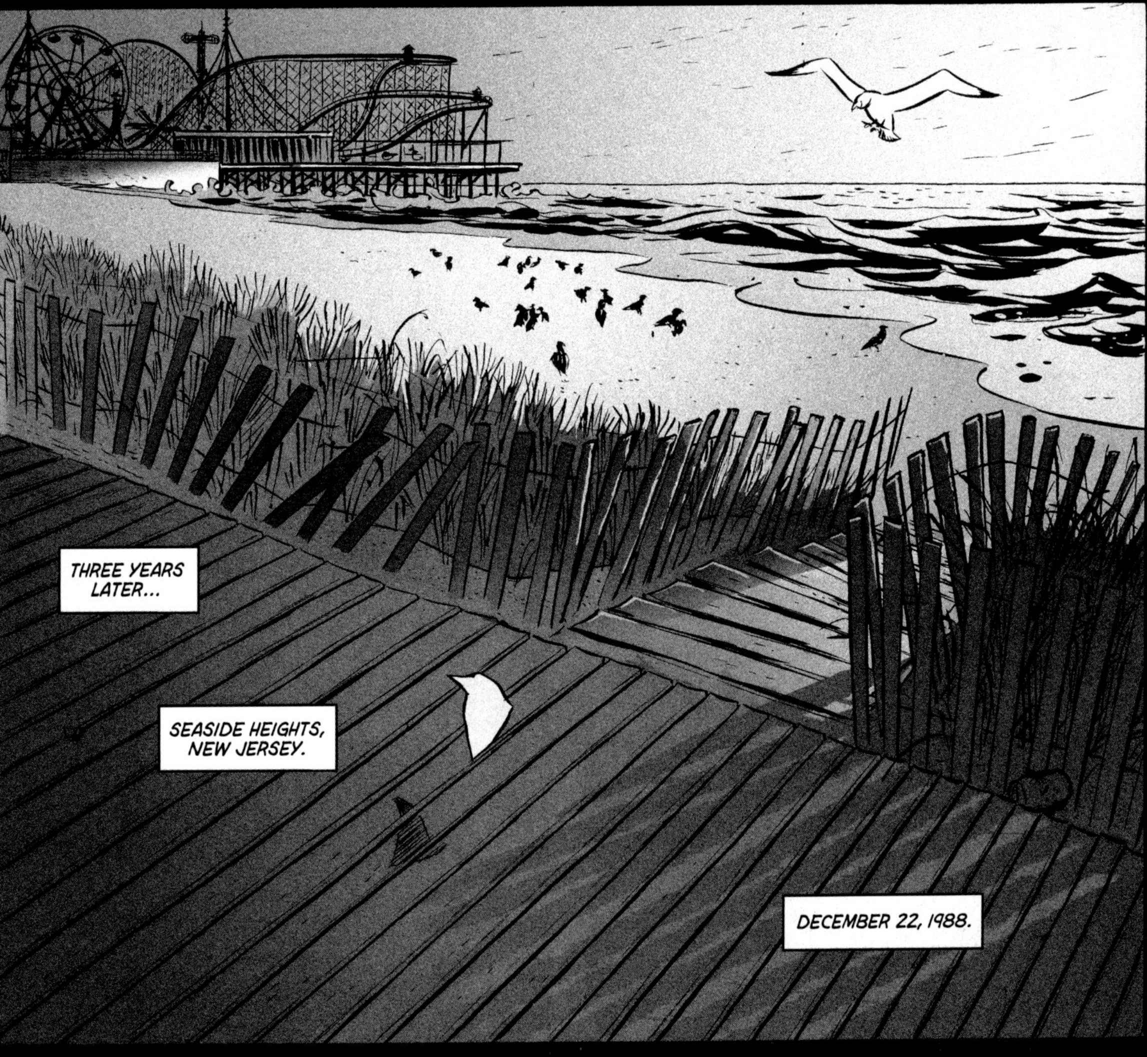

THREE YEARS LATER...
SEASIDE HEIGHTS, NEW JERSEY.
DECEMBER 22, 1988.

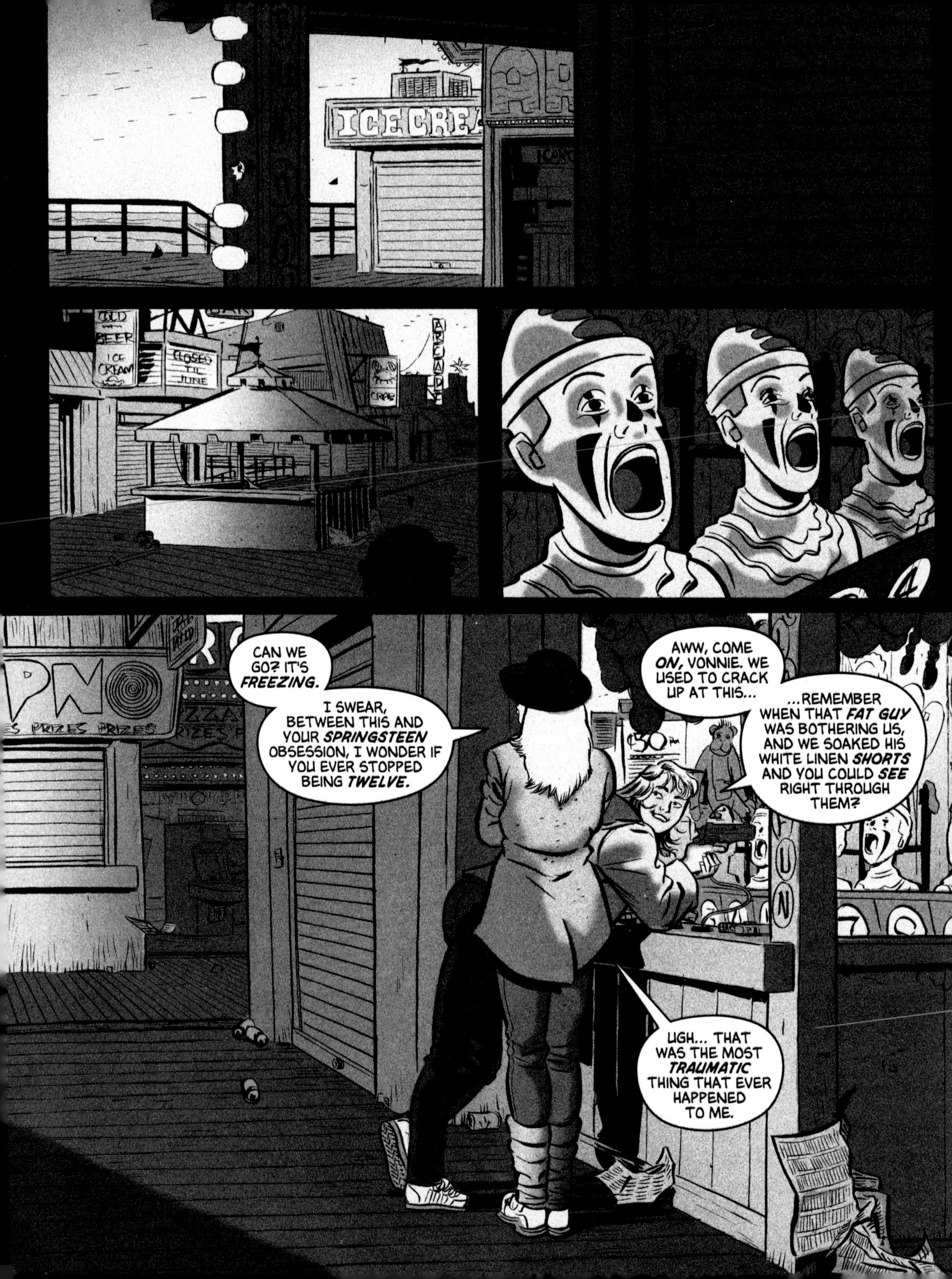
ICE CREA
COLD BEER
ICE CREAM
CLOSED TIL JUNE
ARCADE
PRIZES PRIZES
CAN WE GO? IT'S FREEZING.
I SWEAR, BETWEEN THIS AND YOUR SPRINGSTEEN OBSESSION, I WONDER IF YOU EVER STOPPED BEING TWELVE.
AWW, COME ON, VONNIE. WE USED TO CRACK UP AT THIS...
...REMEMBER WHEN THAT FAT GUY WAS BOTHERING US, AND WE SOAKED HIS WHITE LINEN SHORTS AND YOU COULD SEE RIGHT THROUGH THEM?
UGH... THAT WAS THE MOST TRAUMATIC THING THAT EVER HAPPENED TO ME.

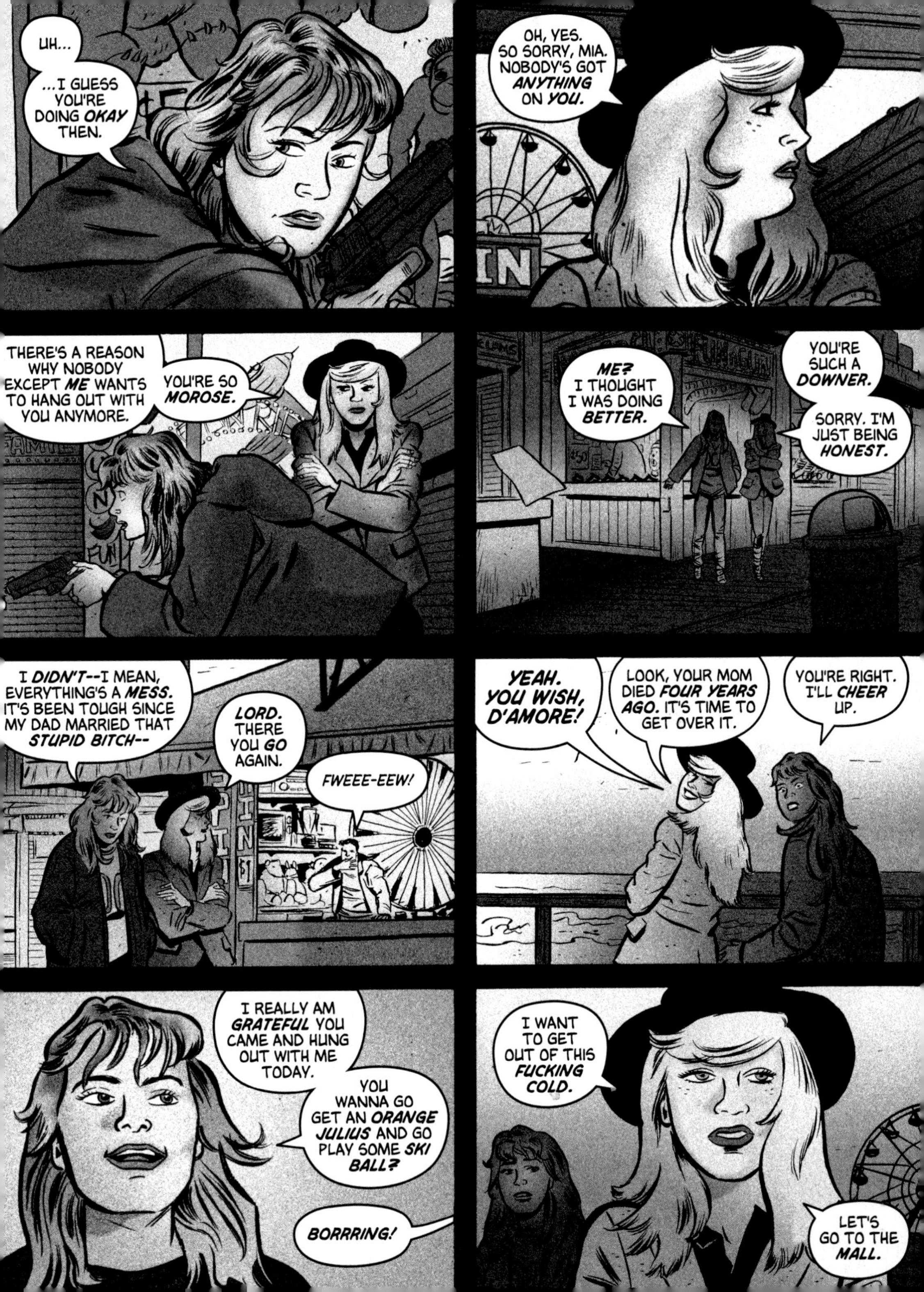
UH...
...I GUESS YOU'RE DOING OKAY THEN.
OH, YES. SO SORRY, MIA. NOBODY'S GOT ANYTHING ON YOU.
THERE'S A REASON WHY NOBODY EXCEPT ME WANTS TO HANG OUT WITH YOU ANYMORE.
YOU'RE SO MOROSE.
ME? I THOUGHT I WAS DOING BETTER.
YOU'RE SUCH A DOWNER.
SORRY. I'M JUST BEING HONEST.
I DIDN'T--I MEAN, EVERYTHING'S A MESS. IT'S BEEN TOUGH SINCE MY DAD MARRIED THAT STUPID BITCH--
LORD. THERE YOU GO AGAIN.
FWEEE-EEW!
YEAH. YOU WISH, D'AMORE!
LOOK, YOUR MOM DIED FOUR YEARS AGO. IT'S TIME TO GET OVER IT.
YOU'RE RIGHT. I'LL CHEER UP.
I REALLY AM GRATEFUL YOU CAME AND HUNG OUT WITH ME TODAY.
YOU WANNA GO GET AN ORANGE JULIUS AND GO PLAY SOME SKI BALL?
BORRRING!
I WANT TO GET OUT OF THIS FUCKING COLD.
LET'S GO TO THE MALL.

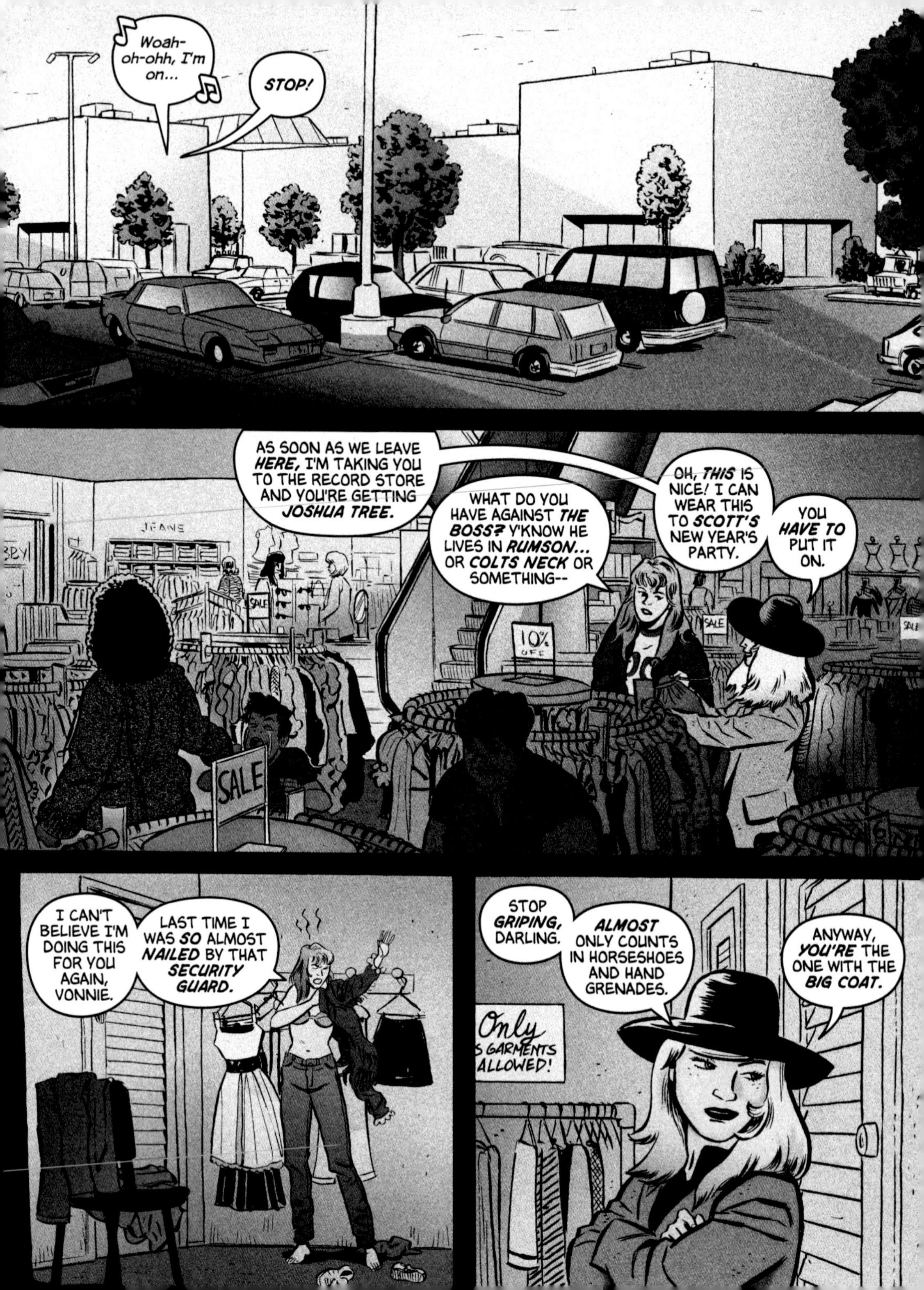
Woah-oh-ohh, I'm on...
STOP!
AS SOON AS WE LEAVE HERE, I'M TAKING YOU TO THE RECORD STORE AND YOU'RE GETTING JOSHUA TREE.
WHAT DO YOU HAVE AGAINST THE BOSS? Y'KNOW HE LIVES IN RUMSON... OR COLTS NECK OR SOMETHING--
OH, THIS IS NICE! I CAN WEAR THIS TO SCOTT'S NEW YEAR'S PARTY.
YOU HAVE TO PUT IT ON.
JEANS
SALE
10% OFF
SALE
I CAN'T BELIEVE I'M DOING THIS FOR YOU AGAIN, VONNIE.
LAST TIME I WAS SO ALMOST NAILED BY THAT SECURITY GUARD.
STOP GRIPING, DARLING.
ALMOST ONLY COUNTS IN HORSESHOES AND HAND GRENADES.
ANYWAY, YOU'RE THE ONE WITH THE BIG COAT.
Only
S GARMENTS
ALLOWED!

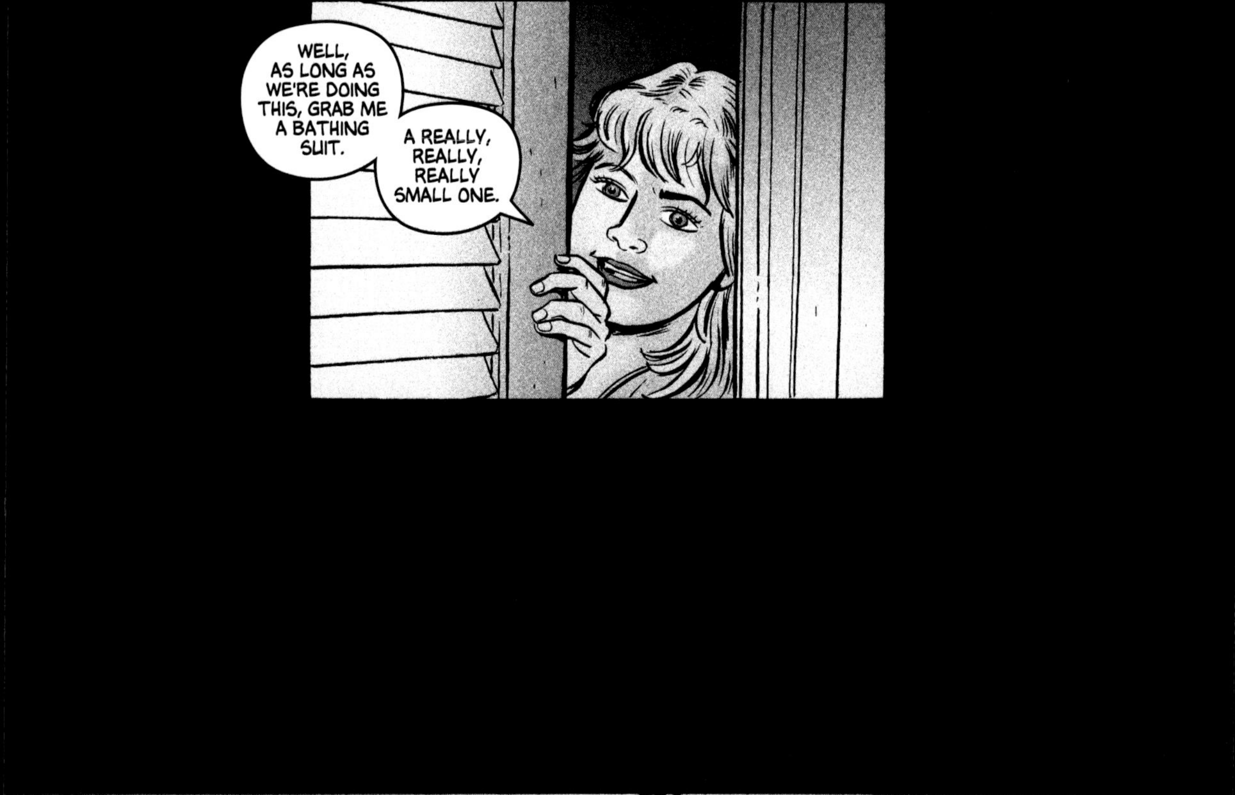
WELL, AS LONG AS WE'RE DOING THIS, GRAB ME A BATHING SUIT.
A REALLY, REALLY, REALLY SMALL ONE.

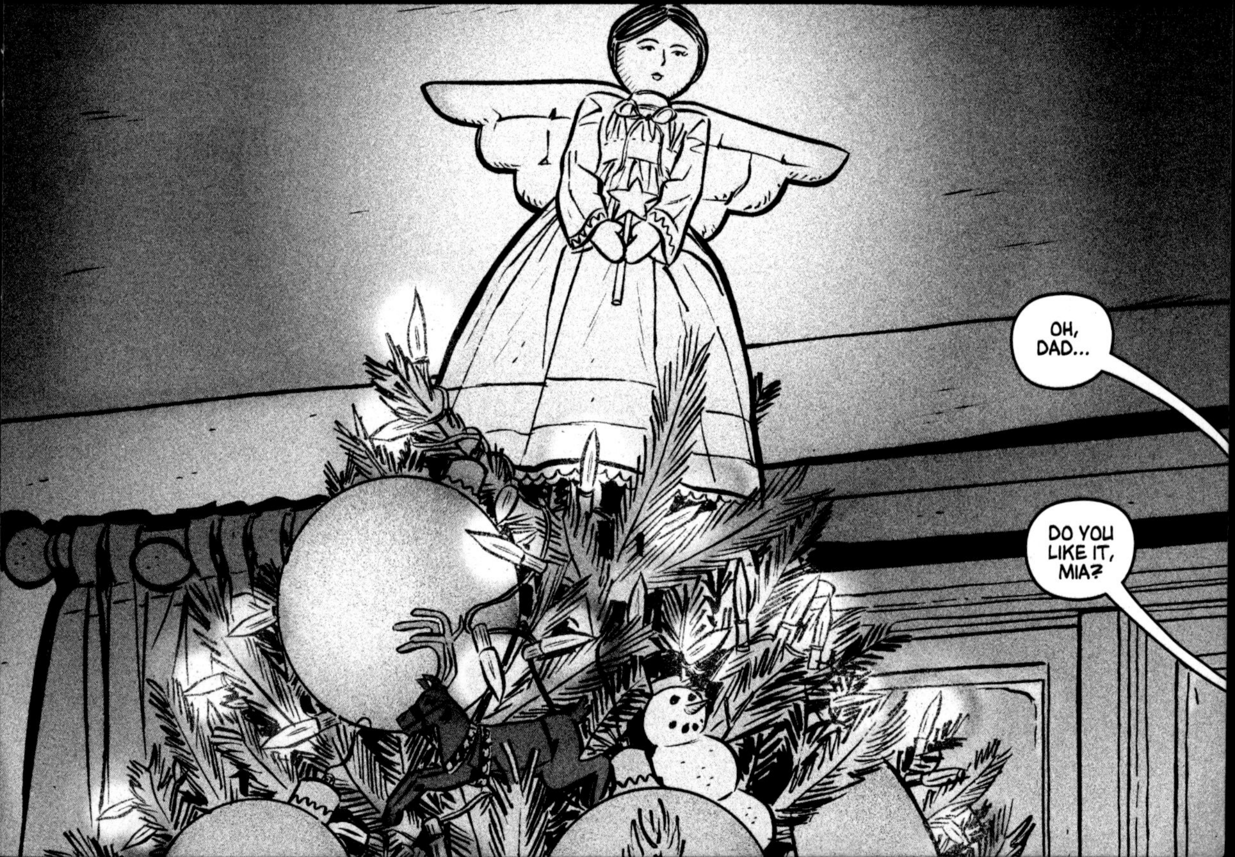
OH, DAD...
DO YOU LIKE IT, MIA?

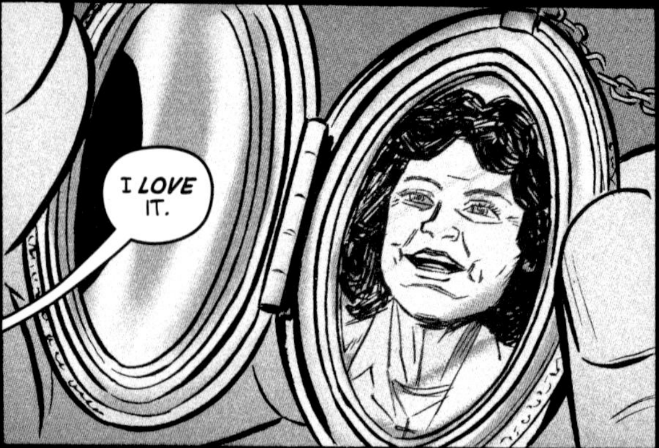
I LOVE IT.

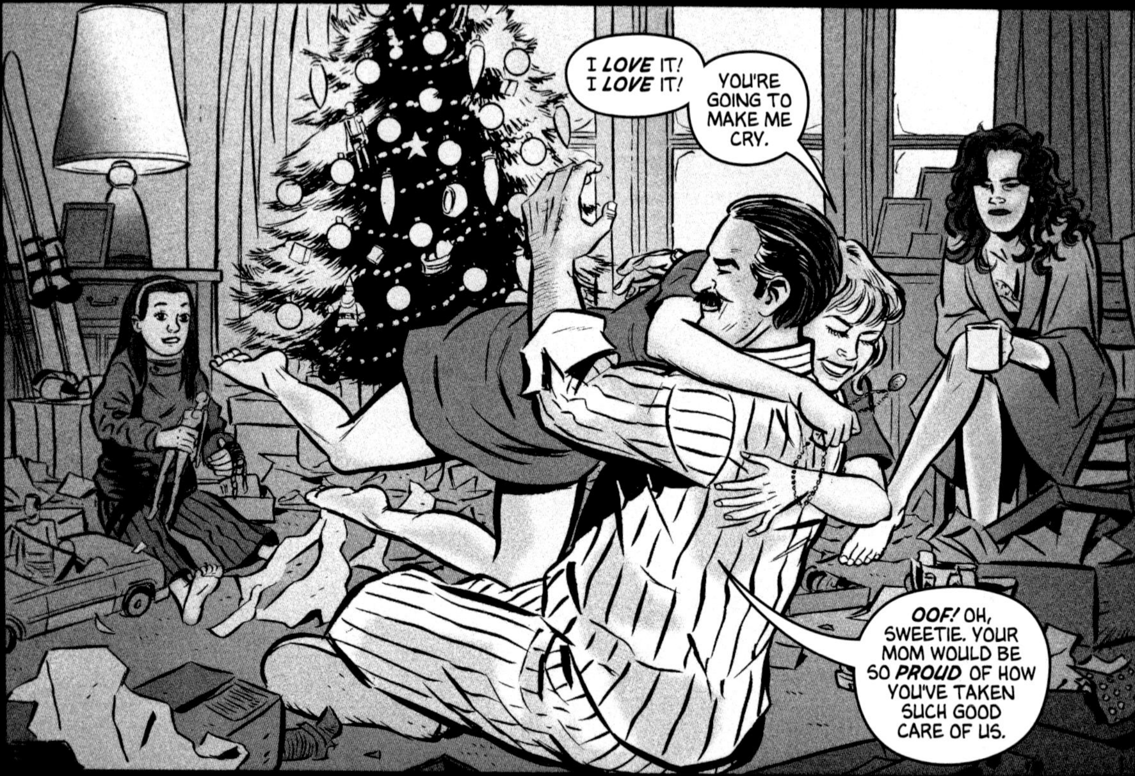
I LOVE IT! I LOVE IT!
YOU'RE GOING TO MAKE ME CRY.
OOF! OH, SWEETIE. YOUR MOM WOULD BE SO PROUD OF HOW YOU'VE TAKEN SUCH GOOD CARE OF US.

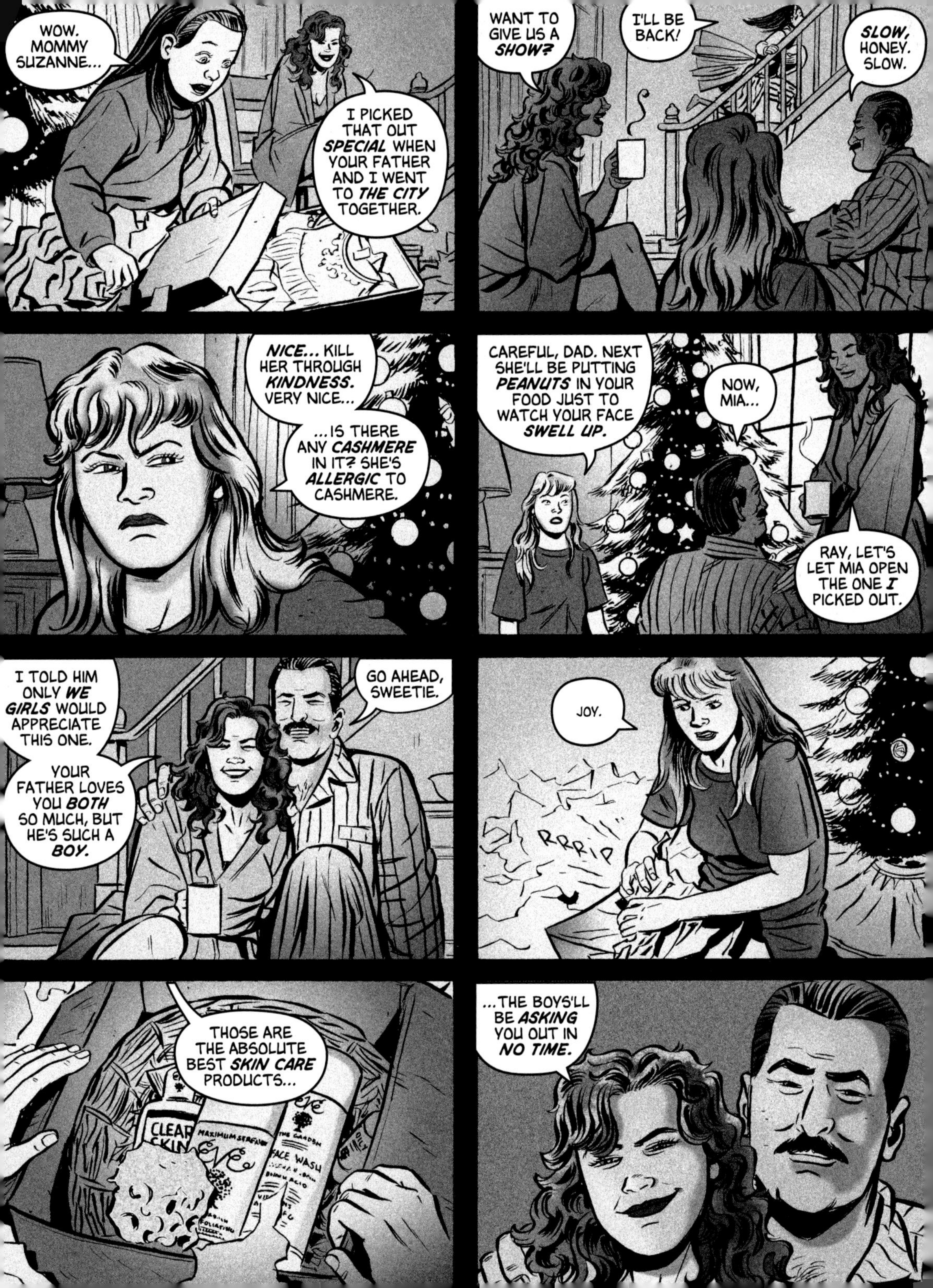
WOW. MOMMY SUZANNE...
I PICKED THAT OUT SPECIAL WHEN YOUR FATHER AND I WENT TO THE CITY TOGETHER.
WANT TO GIVE US A SHOW?
I'LL BE BACK!
SLOW, HONEY. SLOW.
NICE... KILL HER THROUGH KINDNESS. VERY NICE...
...IS THERE ANY CASHMERE IN IT? SHE'S ALLERGIC TO CASHMERE.
CAREFUL, DAD. NEXT SHE'LL BE PUTTING PEANUTS IN YOUR FOOD JUST TO WATCH YOUR FACE SWELL UP.
NOW, MIA...
RAY, LET'S LET MIA OPEN THE ONE I PICKED OUT.
I TOLD HIM ONLY WE GIRLS WOULD APPRECIATE THIS ONE.
YOUR FATHER LOVES YOU BOTH SO MUCH, BUT HE'S SUCH A BOY.
GO AHEAD, SWEETIE.
JOY.
RRRIP
THOSE ARE THE ABSOLUTE BEST SKIN CARE PRODUCTS...
CLEAR SKIN
EVE
FACE WASH
...THE BOYS'LL BE ASKING YOU OUT IN NO TIME.

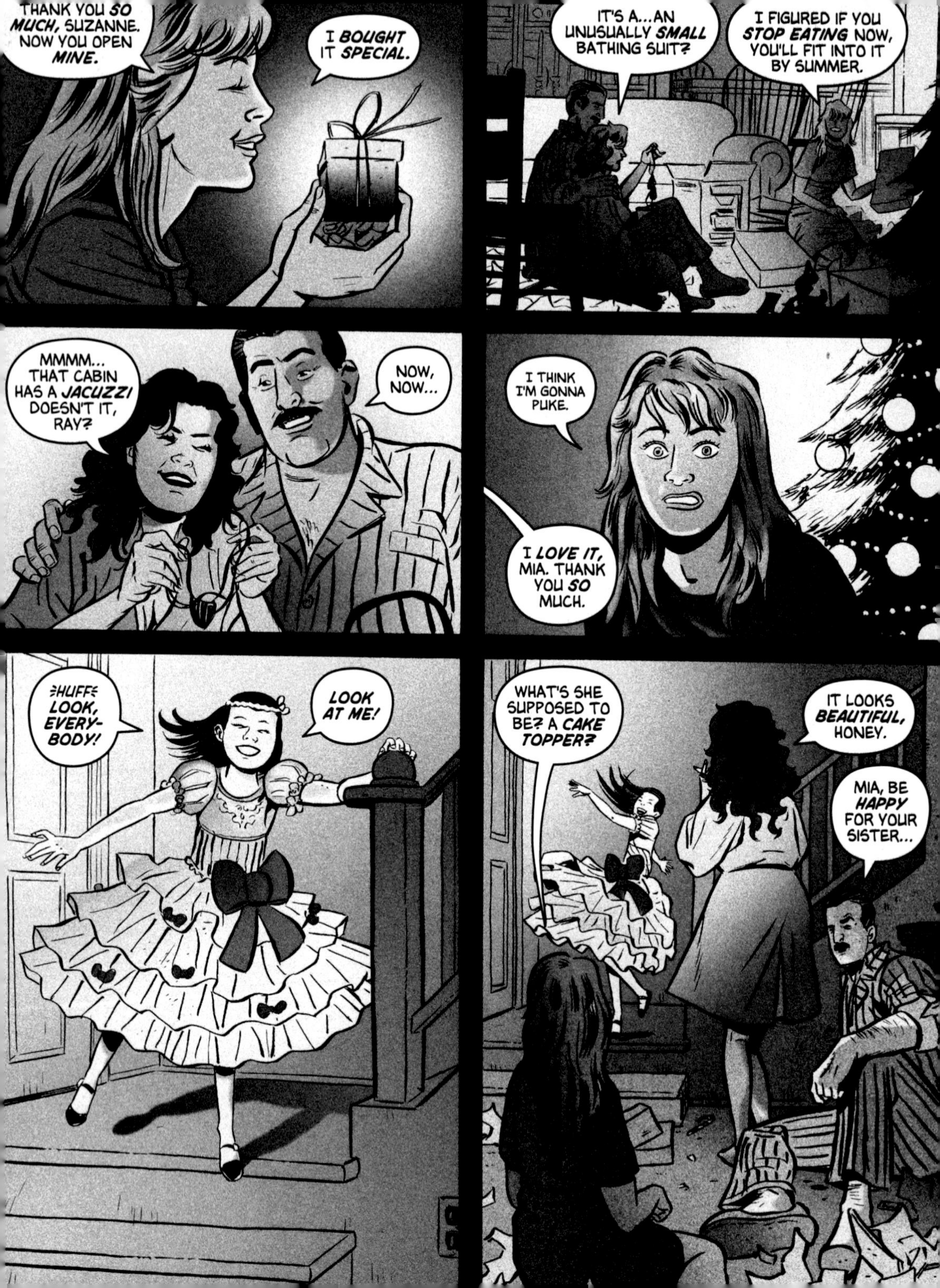

THANK YOU SO MUCH, SUZANNE. NOW YOU OPEN MINE.
I BOUGHT IT SPECIAL.
IT'S A...AN UNUSUALLY SMALL BATHING SUIT?
I FIGURED IF YOU STOP EATING NOW, YOU'LL FIT INTO IT BY SUMMER.
MMMM... THAT CABIN HAS A JACUZZI DOESN'T IT, RAY?
NOW, NOW...
I THINK I'M GONNA PUKE.
I LOVE IT, MIA. THANK YOU SO MUCH.
HUFF LOOK, EVERY-BODY!
LOOK AT ME!
WHAT'S SHE SUPPOSED TO BE? A CAKE TOPPER?
IT LOOKS BEAUTIFUL, HONEY.
MIA, BE HAPPY FOR YOUR SISTER...

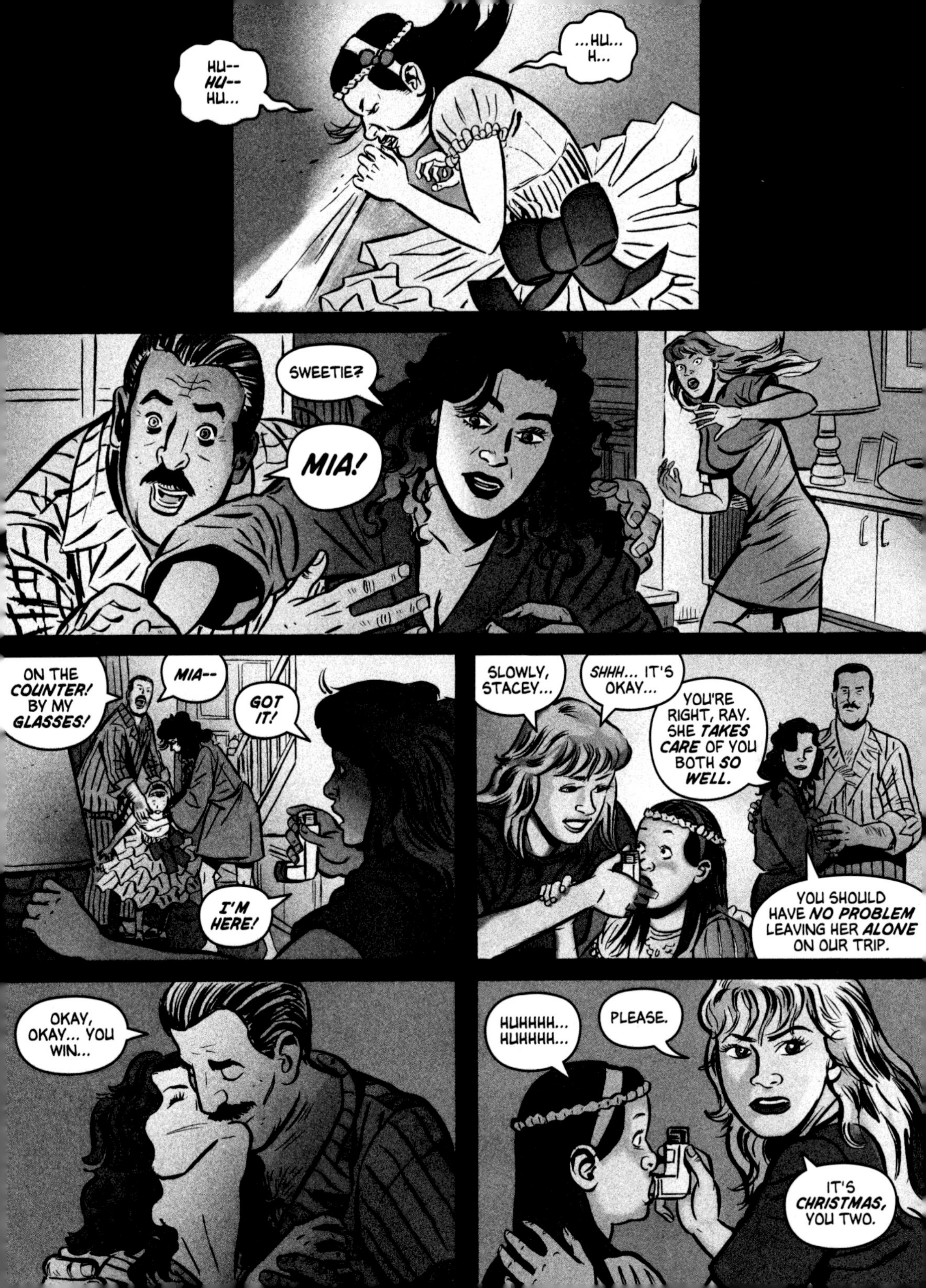
HU--
HU--
HU...
...HU...
H...
SWEETIE?
MIA!
ON THE COUNTER! BY MY GLASSES!
MIA--
GOT IT!
I'M HERE!
SLOWLY, STACEY...
SHHH... IT'S OKAY...
YOU'RE RIGHT, RAY. SHE TAKES CARE OF YOU BOTH SO WELL.
YOU SHOULD HAVE NO PROBLEM LEAVING HER ALONE ON OUR TRIP.
OKAY, OKAY... YOU WIN...
HUHHHH... HUHHHH...
PLEASE.
IT'S CHRISTMAS, YOU TWO.

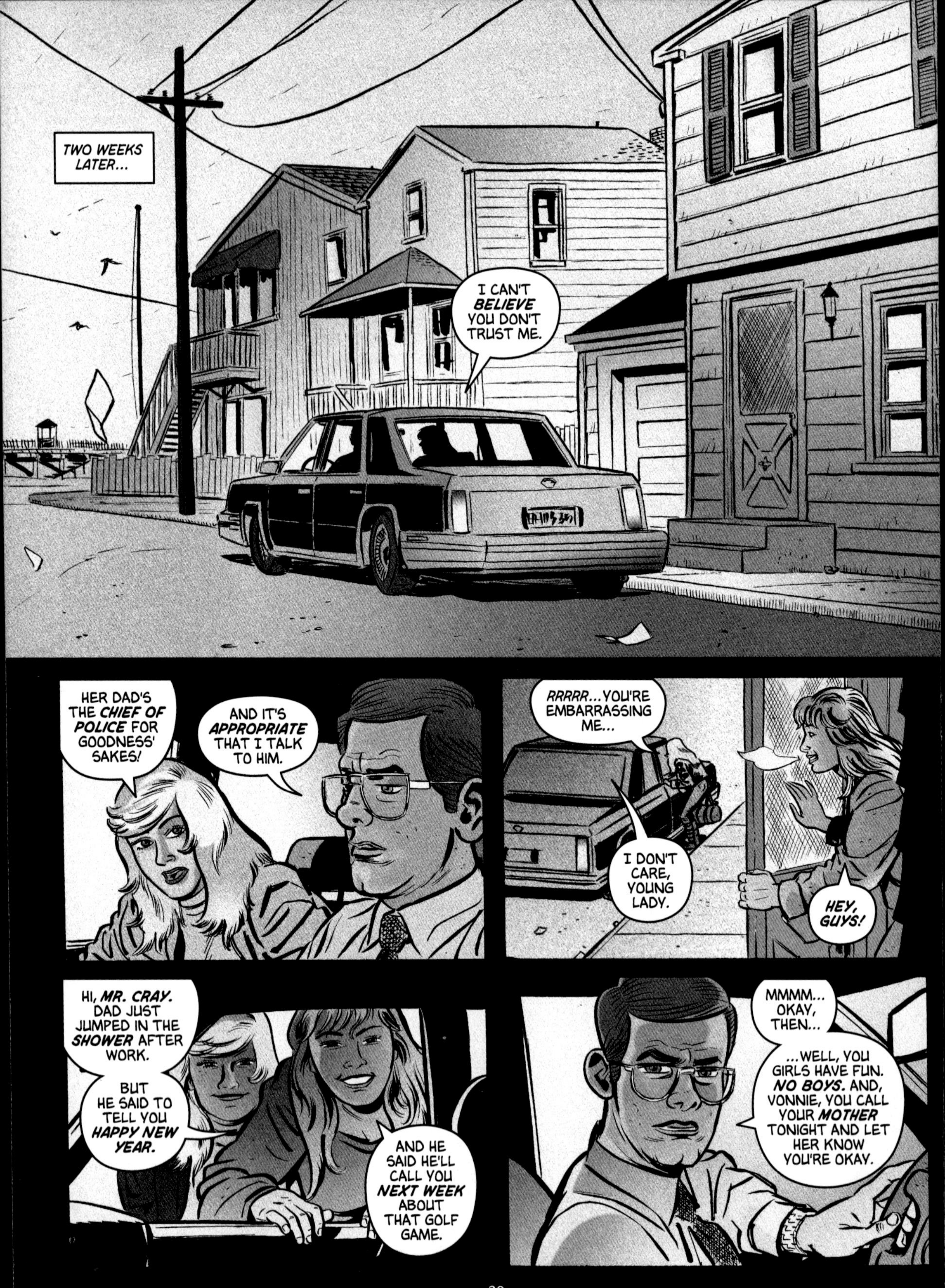
TWO WEEKS LATER...
I CAN'T BELIEVE YOU DON'T TRUST ME.
HER DAD'S THE CHIEF OF POLICE FOR GOODNESS' SAKES!
AND IT'S APPROPRIATE THAT I TALK TO HIM.
RRRRR... YOU'RE EMBARRASSING ME...
I DON'T CARE, YOUNG LADY.
HEY, GUYS!
HI, MR. CRAY. DAD JUST JUMPED IN THE SHOWER AFTER WORK.
BUT HE SAID TO TELL YOU HAPPY NEW YEAR.
AND HE SAID HE'LL CALL YOU NEXT WEEK ABOUT THAT GOLF GAME.
MMMM... OKAY, THEN...
...WELL, YOU GIRLS HAVE FUN. NO BOYS. AND, VONNIE, YOU CALL YOUR MOTHER TONIGHT AND LET HER KNOW YOU'RE OKAY.

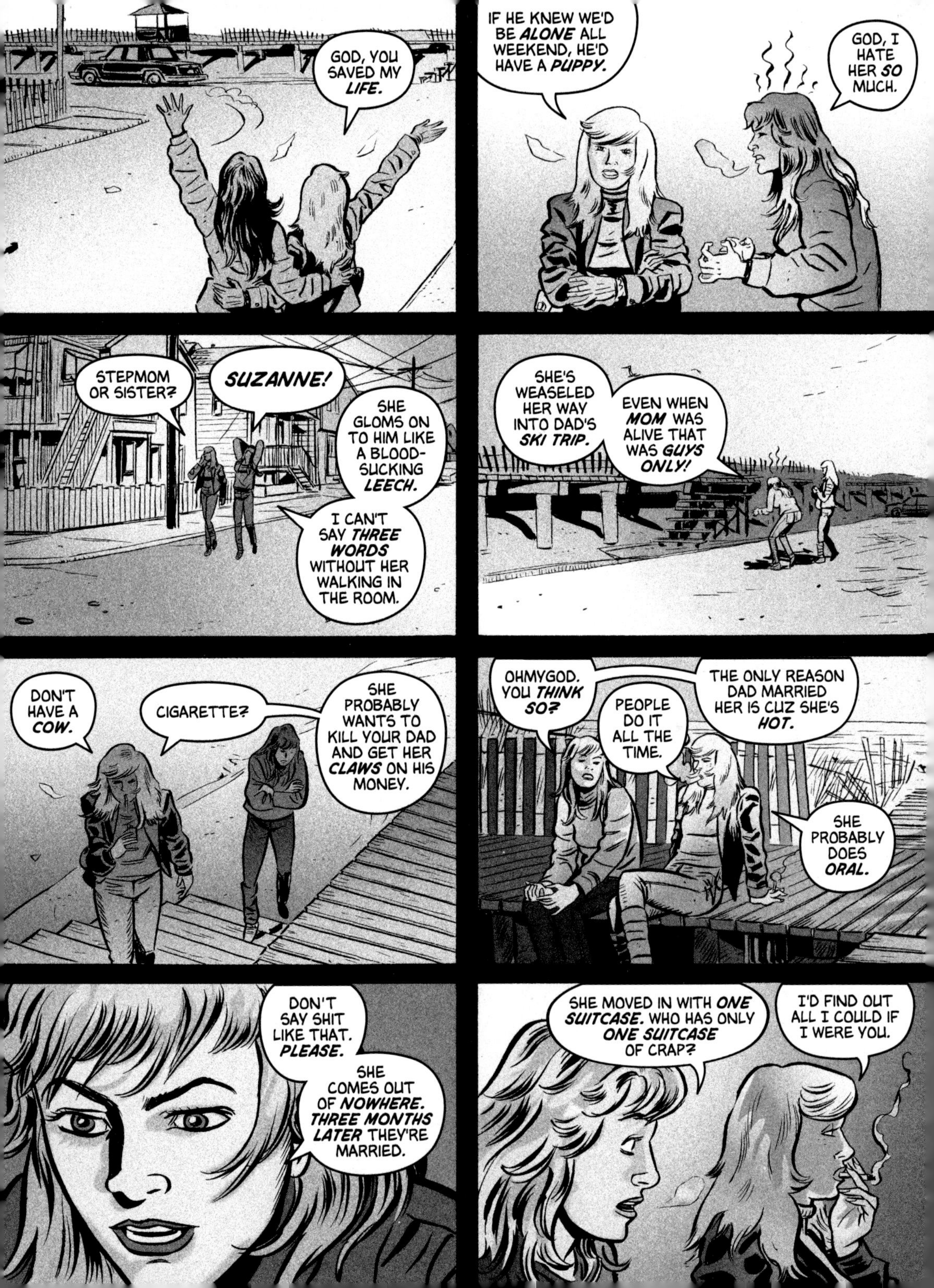
GOD, YOU SAVED MY LIFE.
IF HE KNEW WE'D BE ALONE ALL WEEKEND, HE'D HAVE A PUPPY.
GOD, I HATE HER SO MUCH.
STEPMOM OR SISTER?
SUZANNE!
SHE GLOMS ON TO HIM LIKE A BLOOD-SUCKING LEECH.
I CAN'T SAY THREE WORDS WITHOUT HER WALKING IN THE ROOM.
SHE'S WEASELED HER WAY INTO DAD'S SKI TRIP.
EVEN WHEN MOM WAS ALIVE THAT WAS GUYS ONLY!
DON'T HAVE A COW.
CIGARETTE?
SHE PROBABLY WANTS TO KILL YOUR DAD AND GET HER CLAWS ON HIS MONEY.
OHMYGOD. YOU THINK SO?
THE ONLY REASON DAD MARRIED HER IS CUZ SHE'S HOT.
PEOPLE DO IT ALL THE TIME.
SHE PROBABLY DOES ORAL.
DON'T SAY SHIT LIKE THAT. PLEASE.
SHE COMES OUT OF NOWHERE. THREE MONTHS LATER THEY'RE MARRIED.
SHE MOVED IN WITH ONE SUITCASE. WHO HAS ONLY ONE SUITCASE OF CRAP?
I'D FIND OUT ALL I COULD IF I WERE YOU.

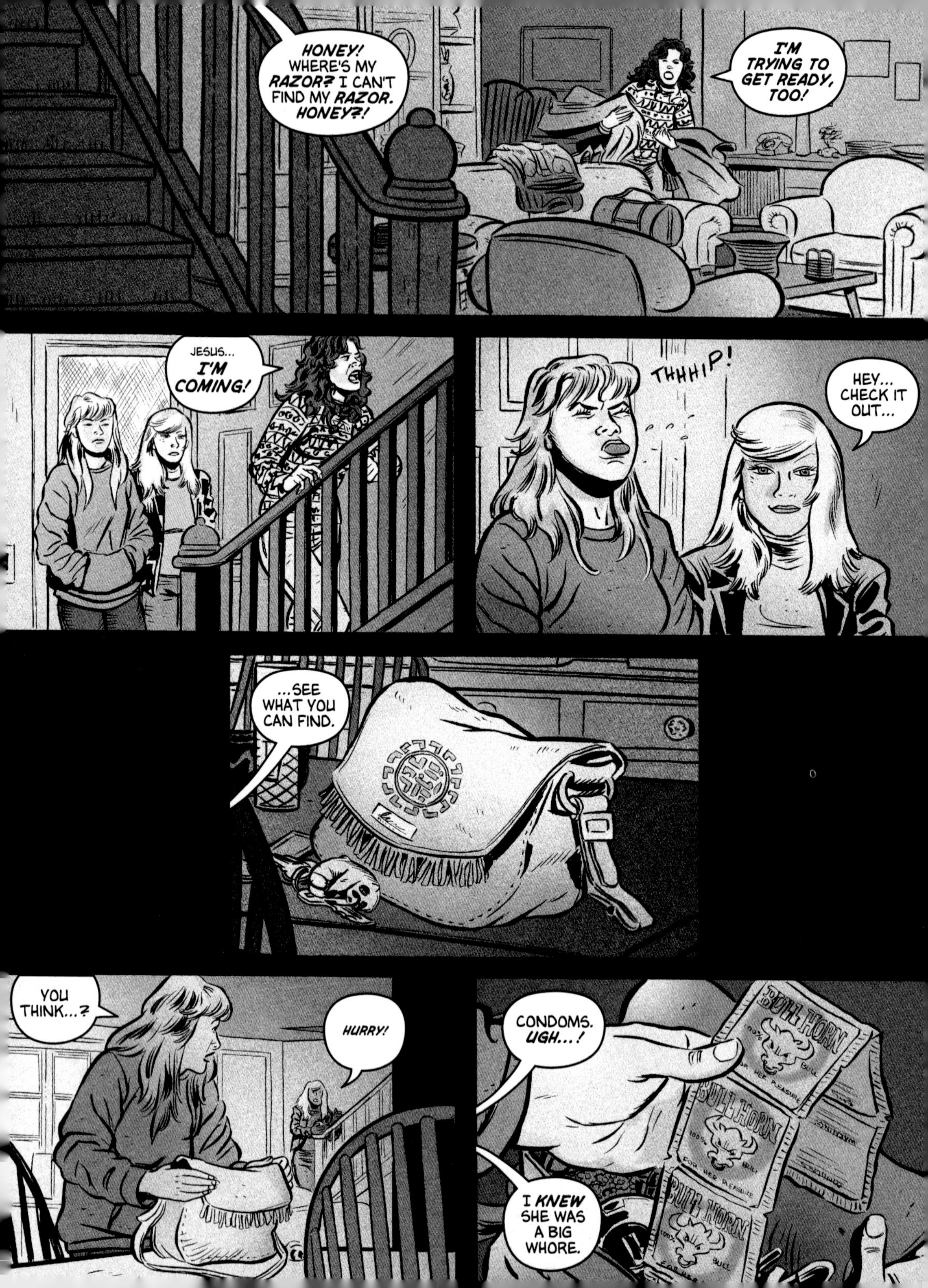
HONEY! WHERE'S MY RAZOR? I CAN'T FIND MY RAZOR. HONEY?!
I'M TRYING TO GET READY, TOO!
JESUS... I'M COMING!
THHHIP!
HEY... CHECK IT OUT...
...SEE WHAT YOU CAN FIND.
YOU THINK...?
HURRY!
CONDOMS. UGH...!
I KNEW SHE WAS A BIG WHORE.
BULL HORN

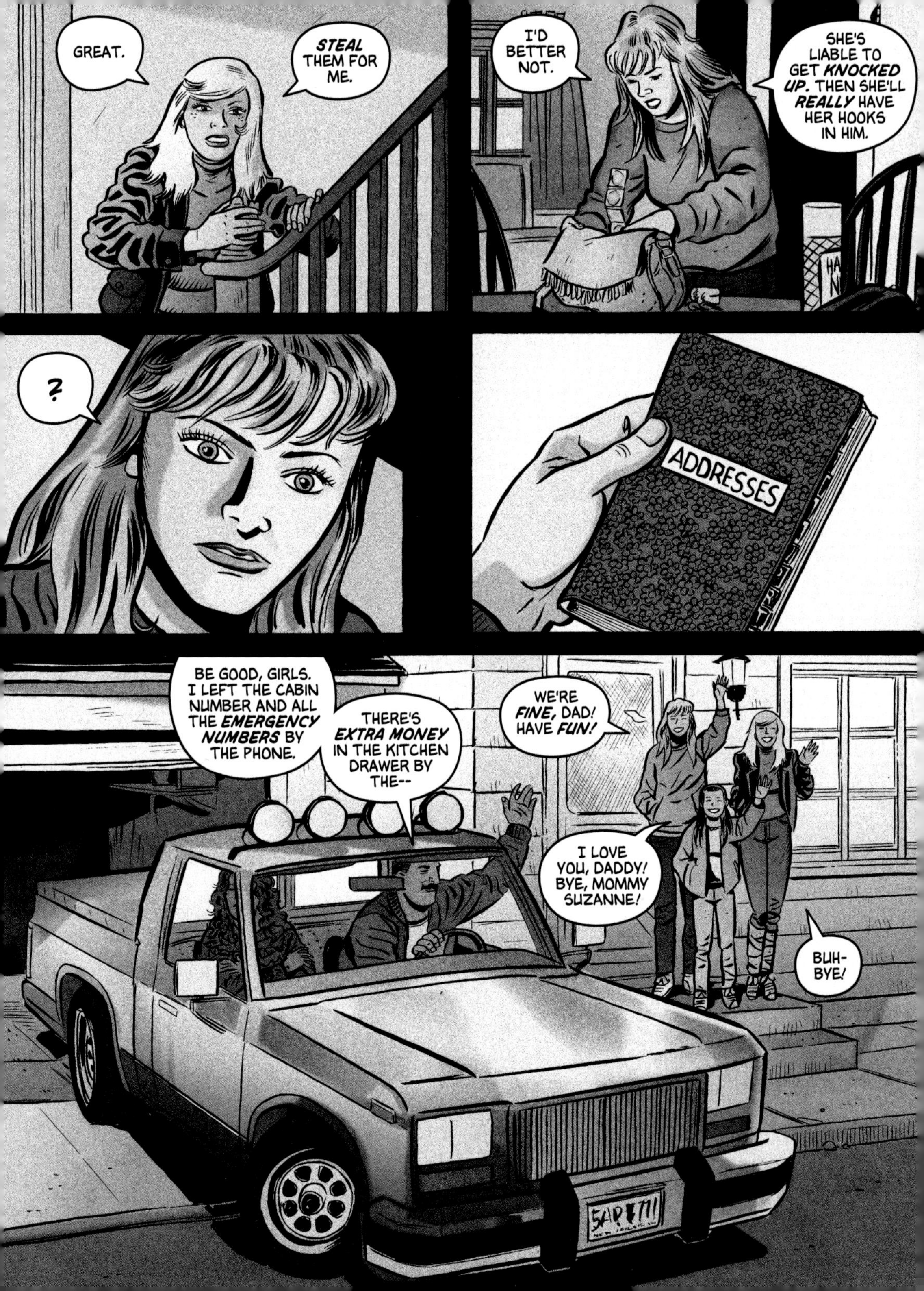
GREAT.
STEAL THEM FOR ME.
I'D BETTER NOT.
SHE'S LIABLE TO GET KNOCKED UP. THEN SHE'LL REALLY HAVE HER HOOKS IN HIM.
?
ADDRESSES
BE GOOD, GIRLS. I LEFT THE CABIN NUMBER AND ALL THE EMERGENCY NUMBERS BY THE PHONE.
THERE'S EXTRA MONEY IN THE KITCHEN DRAWER BY THE--
WE'RE FINE, DAD! HAVE FUN!
I LOVE YOU, DADDY! BYE, MOMMY SUZANNE!
BUH-BYE!

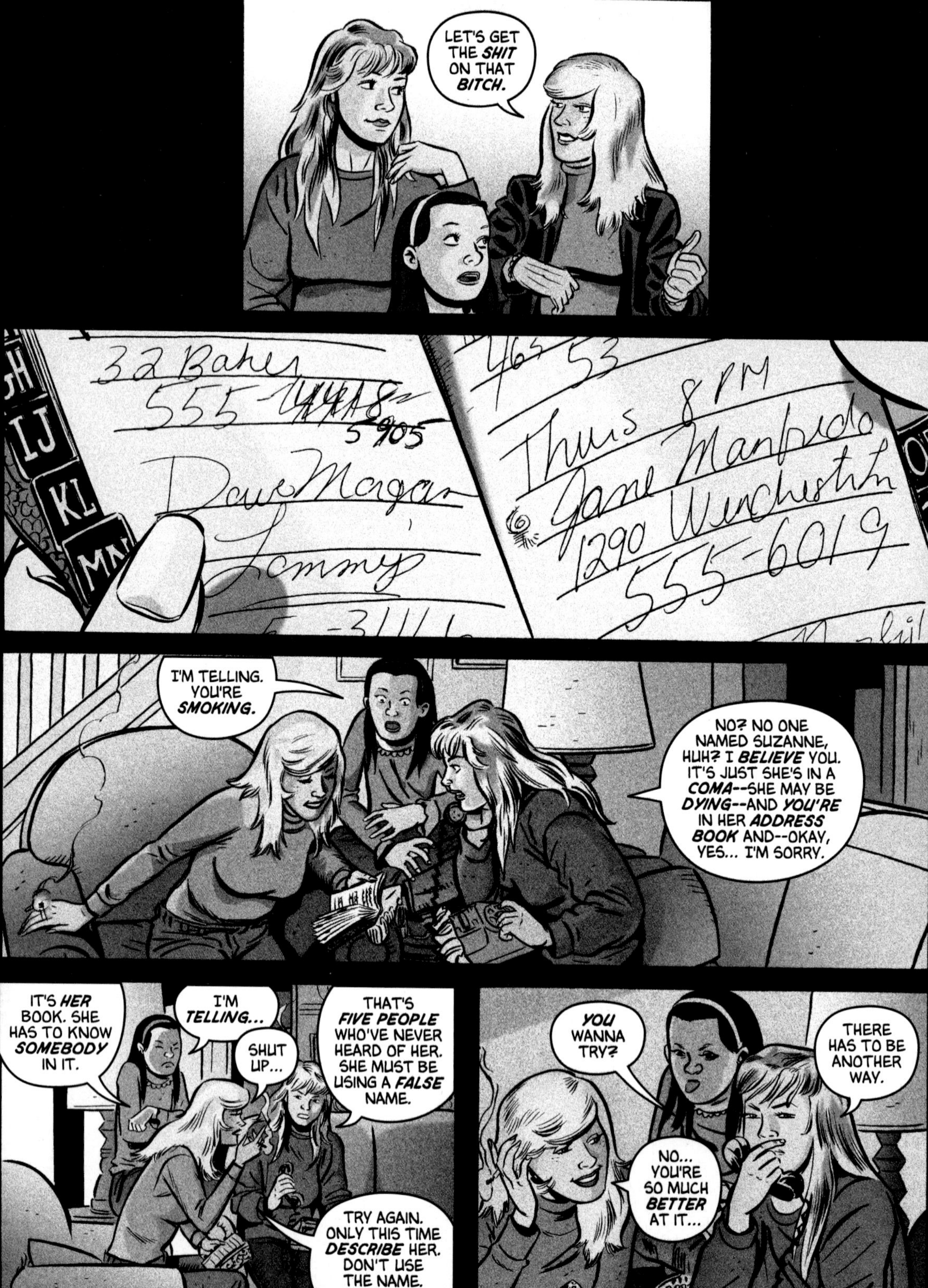

LET'S GET THE *SHIT* ON THAT *BITCH.*
Thurs 8 PM
1290 Winchester
555-6019
I'M TELLING. YOU'RE *SMOKING.*
NO? NO ONE NAMED SUZANNE, HUH? I *BELIEVE* YOU. IT'S JUST SHE'S IN A *COMA*--SHE MAY BE *DYING*--AND *YOU'RE* IN HER *ADDRESS BOOK* AND--OKAY, YES... I'M SORRY.
IT'S *HER* BOOK. SHE HAS TO KNOW *SOMEBODY* IN IT.
I'M *TELLING...*
SHUT UP...
THAT'S *FIVE PEOPLE* WHO'VE NEVER HEARD OF HER. SHE MUST BE USING A *FALSE* NAME.
TRY AGAIN. ONLY THIS TIME *DESCRIBE* HER. DON'T USE THE NAME.
YOU WANNA TRY?
THERE HAS TO BE ANOTHER WAY.
NO... YOU'RE SO MUCH *BETTER* AT IT...

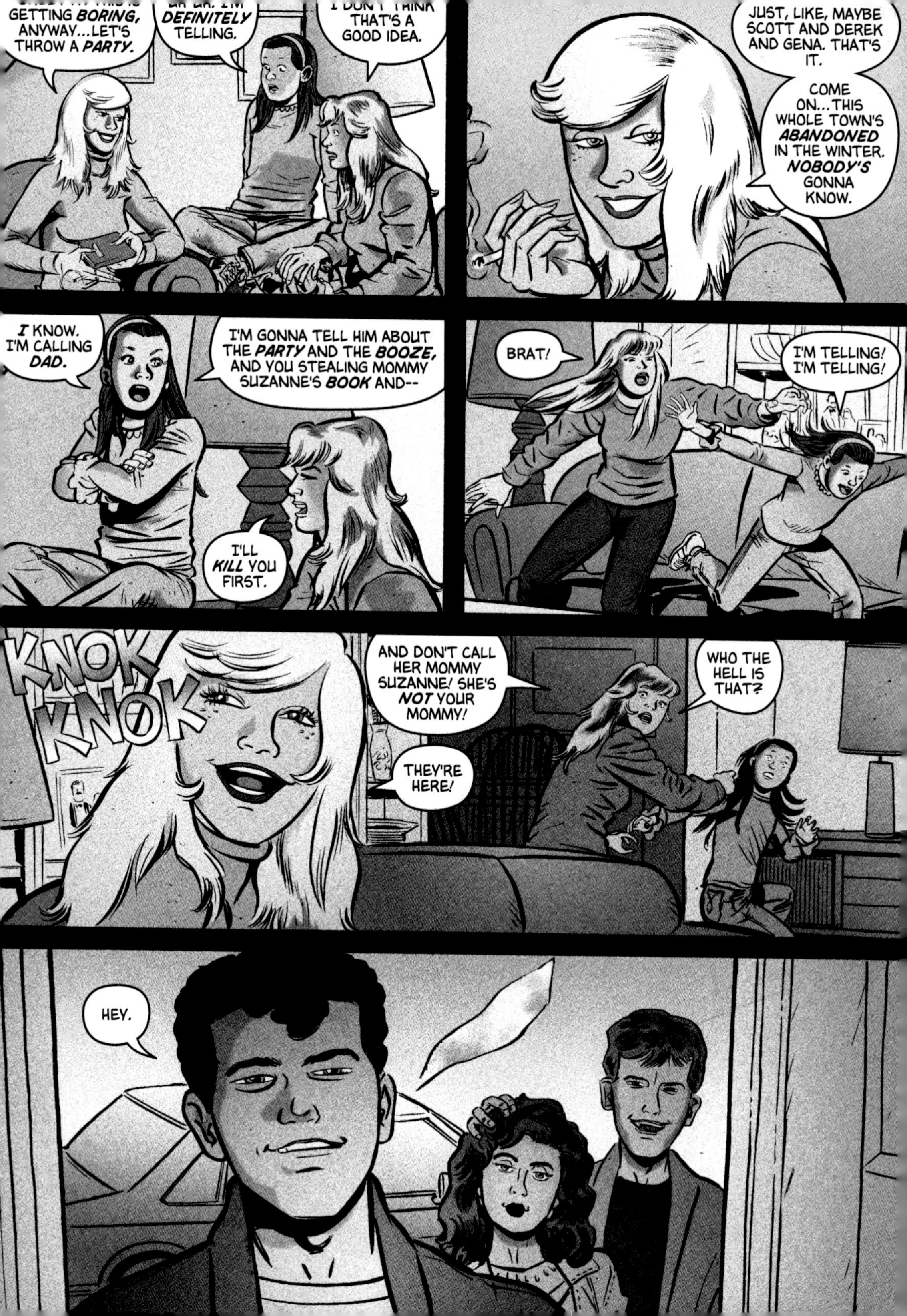
GETTING BORING, ANYWAY...LET'S THROW A PARTY.
DEFINITELY TELLING.
THAT'S A GOOD IDEA.
JUST, LIKE, MAYBE SCOTT AND DEREK AND GENA. THAT'S IT.
COME ON...THIS WHOLE TOWN'S ABANDONED IN THE WINTER. NOBODY'S GONNA KNOW.
I KNOW. I'M CALLING DAD.
I'M GONNA TELL HIM ABOUT THE PARTY AND THE BOOZE, AND YOU STEALING MOMMY SUZANNE'S BOOK AND--
I'LL KILL YOU FIRST.
BRAT!
I'M TELLING! I'M TELLING!
KNOK KNOK
AND DON'T CALL HER MOMMY SUZANNE! SHE'S NOT YOUR MOMMY!
WHO THE HELL IS THAT?
THEY'RE HERE!
HEY.

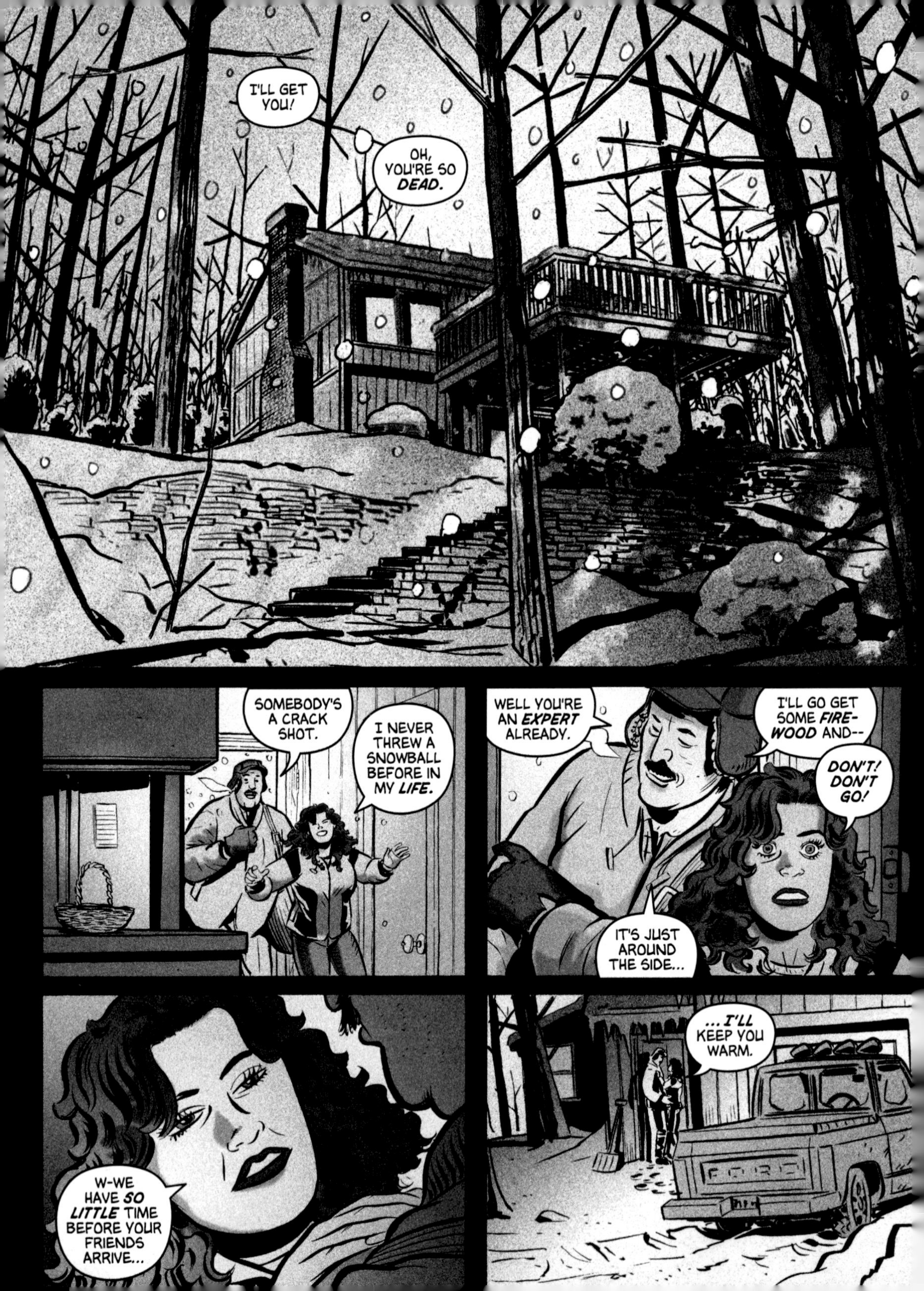
I'LL GET YOU!
OH, YOU'RE SO DEAD.
SOMEBODY'S A CRACK SHOT.
I NEVER THREW A SNOWBALL BEFORE IN MY LIFE.
WELL YOU'RE AN EXPERT ALREADY.
I'LL GO GET SOME FIRE-WOOD AND--
DON'T! DON'T GO!
IT'S JUST AROUND THE SIDE...
W-WE HAVE SO LITTLE TIME BEFORE YOUR FRIENDS ARRIVE...
...I'LL KEEP YOU WARM.

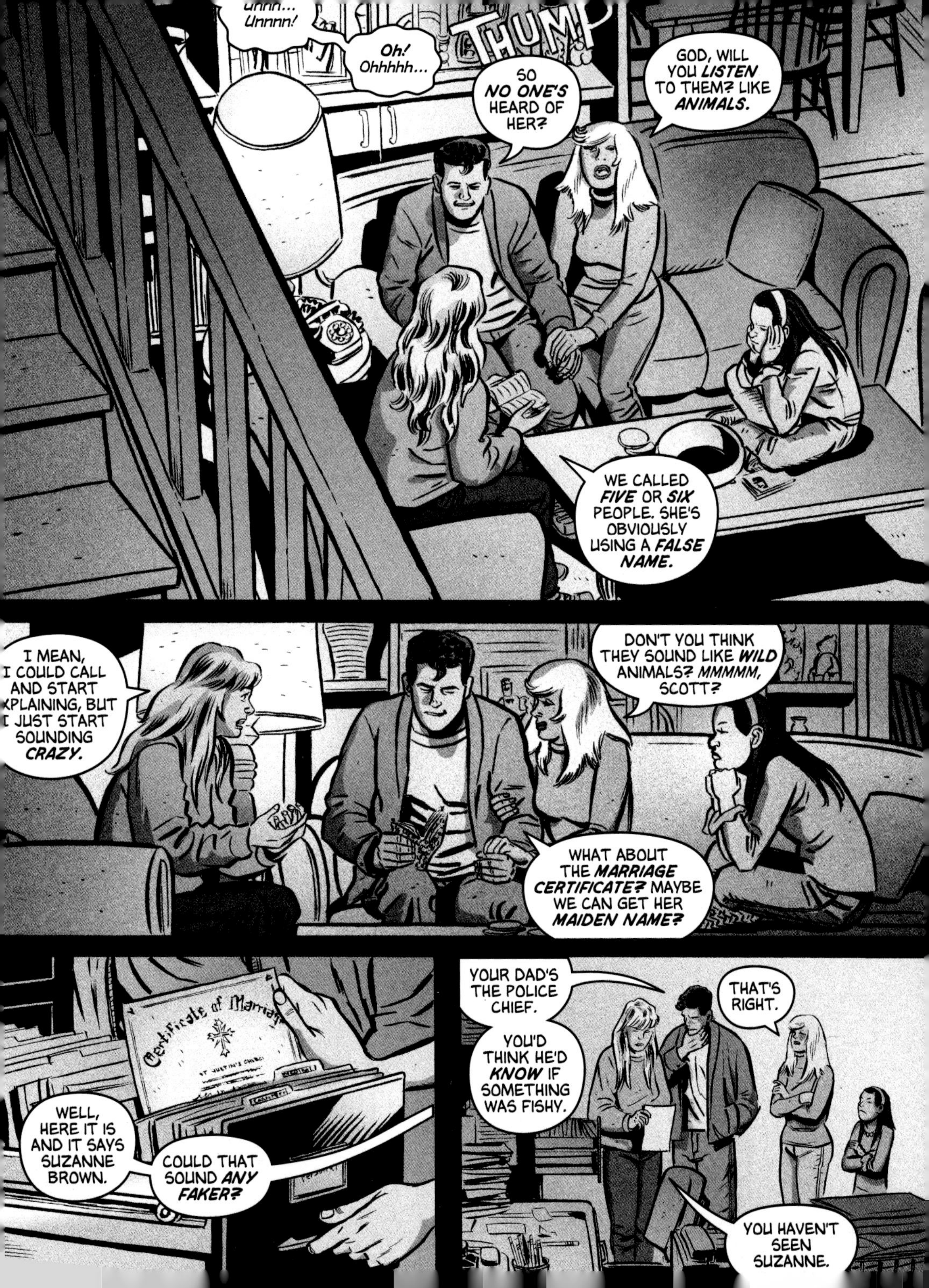
Unnnn!
Oh! Ohhhhh...
THUMP
SO NO ONE'S HEARD OF HER?
GOD, WILL YOU LISTEN TO THEM? LIKE ANIMALS.
WE CALLED FIVE OR SIX PEOPLE. SHE'S OBVIOUSLY USING A FALSE NAME.
I MEAN, I COULD CALL AND START XPLAINING, BUT I JUST START SOUNDING CRAZY.
DON'T YOU THINK THEY SOUND LIKE WILD ANIMALS? MMMMM, SCOTT?
WHAT ABOUT THE MARRIAGE CERTIFICATE? MAYBE WE CAN GET HER MAIDEN NAME?
Certificate of Marriage
WELL, HERE IT IS AND IT SAYS SUZANNE BROWN.
COULD THAT SOUND ANY FAKER?
YOUR DAD'S THE POLICE CHIEF.
YOU'D THINK HE'D KNOW IF SOMETHING WAS FISHY.
THAT'S RIGHT.
YOU HAVEN'T SEEN SUZANNE.

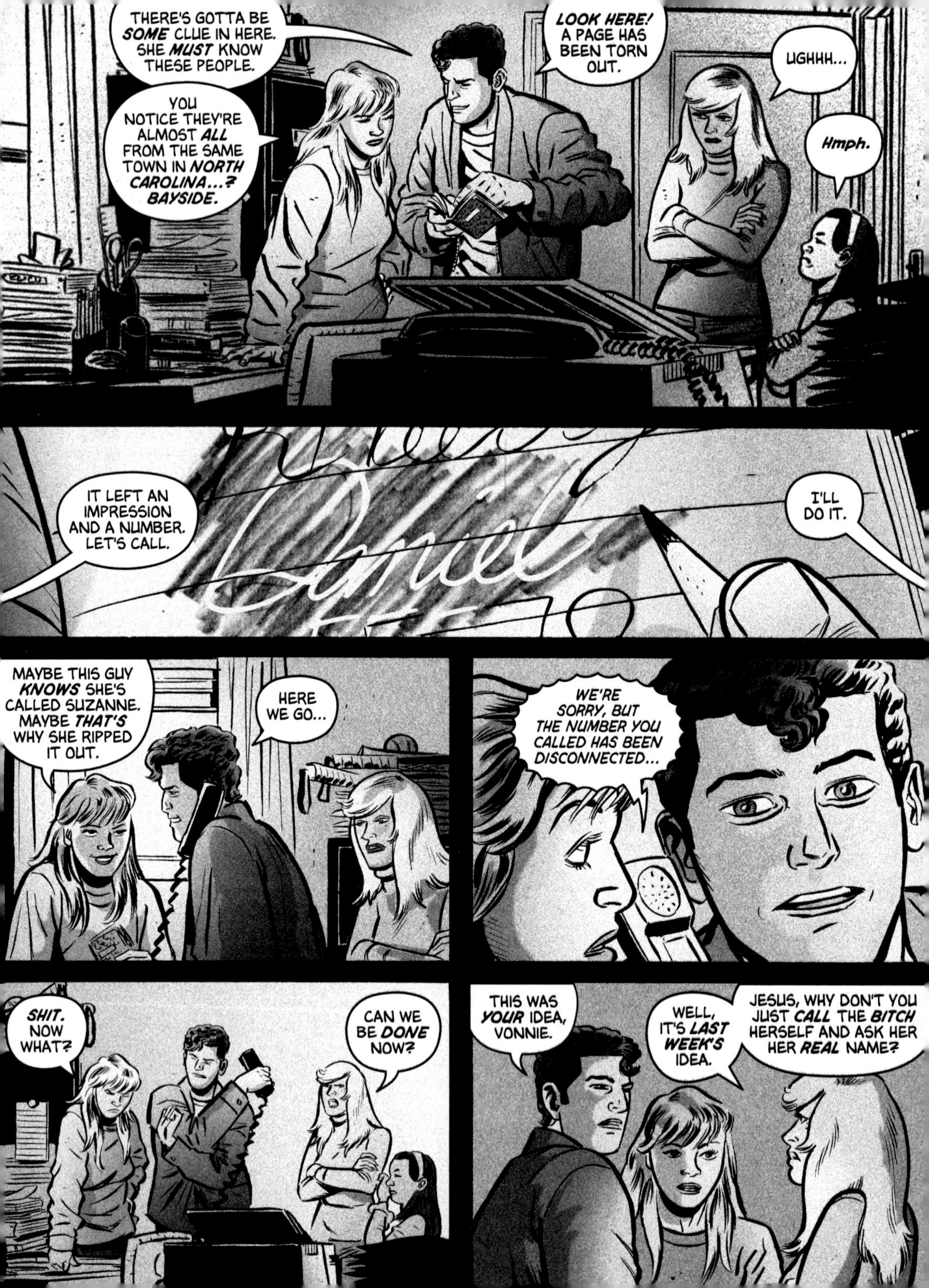
THERE'S GOTTA BE SOME CLUE IN HERE. SHE MUST KNOW THESE PEOPLE.
YOU NOTICE THEY'RE ALMOST ALL FROM THE SAME TOWN IN NORTH CAROLINA...? BAYSIDE.
LOOK HERE! A PAGE HAS BEEN TORN OUT.
UGHHH...
Hmph.
IT LEFT AN IMPRESSION AND A NUMBER. LET'S CALL.
I'LL DO IT.
MAYBE THIS GUY KNOWS SHE'S CALLED SUZANNE. MAYBE THAT'S WHY SHE RIPPED IT OUT.
HERE WE GO...
WE'RE SORRY, BUT THE NUMBER YOU CALLED HAS BEEN DISCONNECTED...
SHIT. NOW WHAT?
CAN WE BE DONE NOW?
THIS WAS YOUR IDEA, VONNIE.
WELL, IT'S LAST WEEK'S IDEA.
JESUS, WHY DON'T YOU JUST CALL THE BITCH HERSELF AND ASK HER HER REAL NAME?

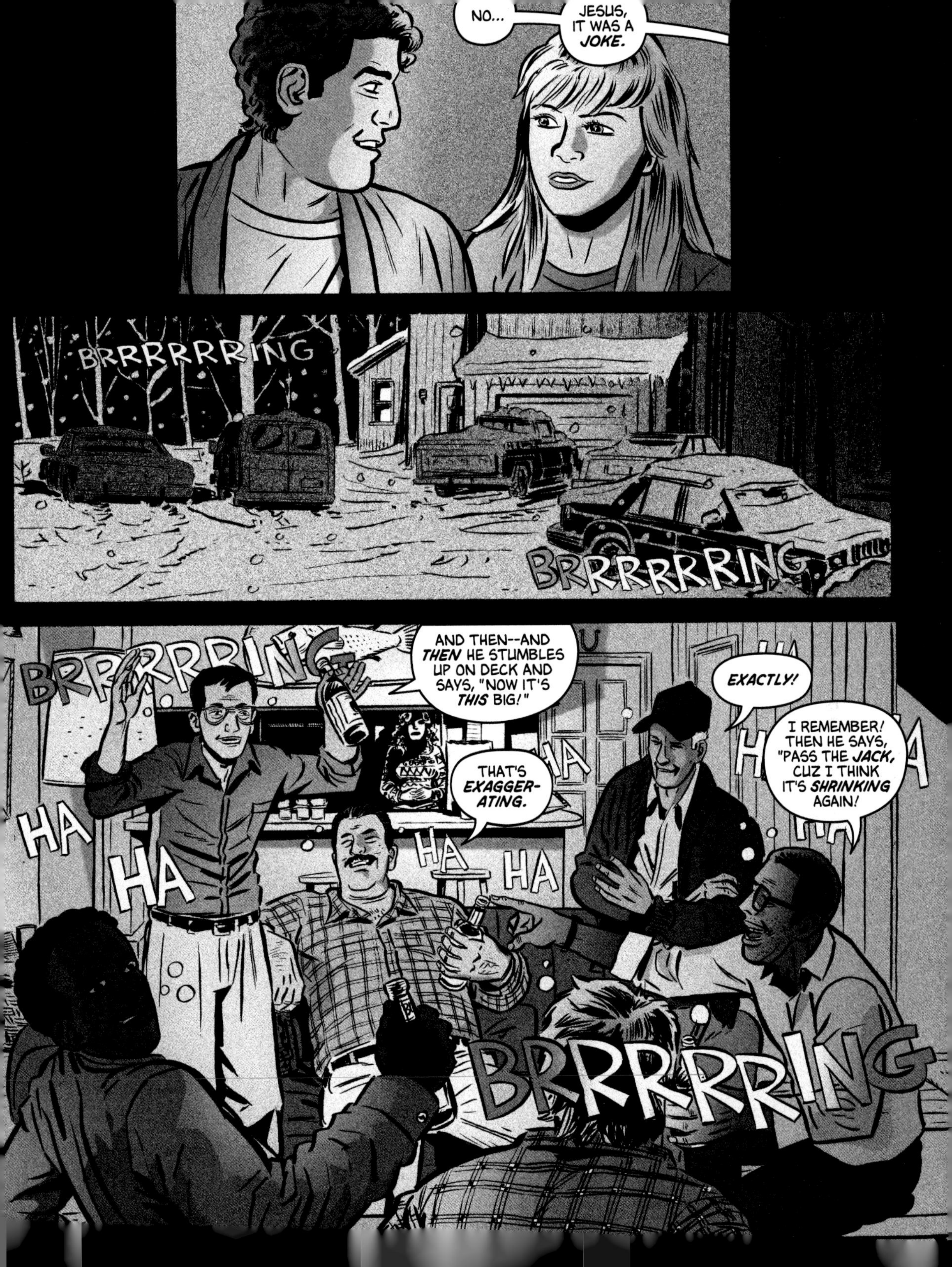
NO...
JESUS, IT WAS A *JOKE.*
BRRRRRRRING
BRRRRRRRING
BRRRRRRING
AND THEN--AND *THEN* HE STUMBLES UP ON DECK AND SAYS, "NOW IT'S *THIS* BIG!"
EXACTLY!
THAT'S *EXAGGER-ATING.*
I REMEMBER! THEN HE SAYS, "PASS THE *JACK,* CUZ I THINK IT'S *SHRINKING* AGAIN!"
HA
HA
HA
HA
BRRRRRRING

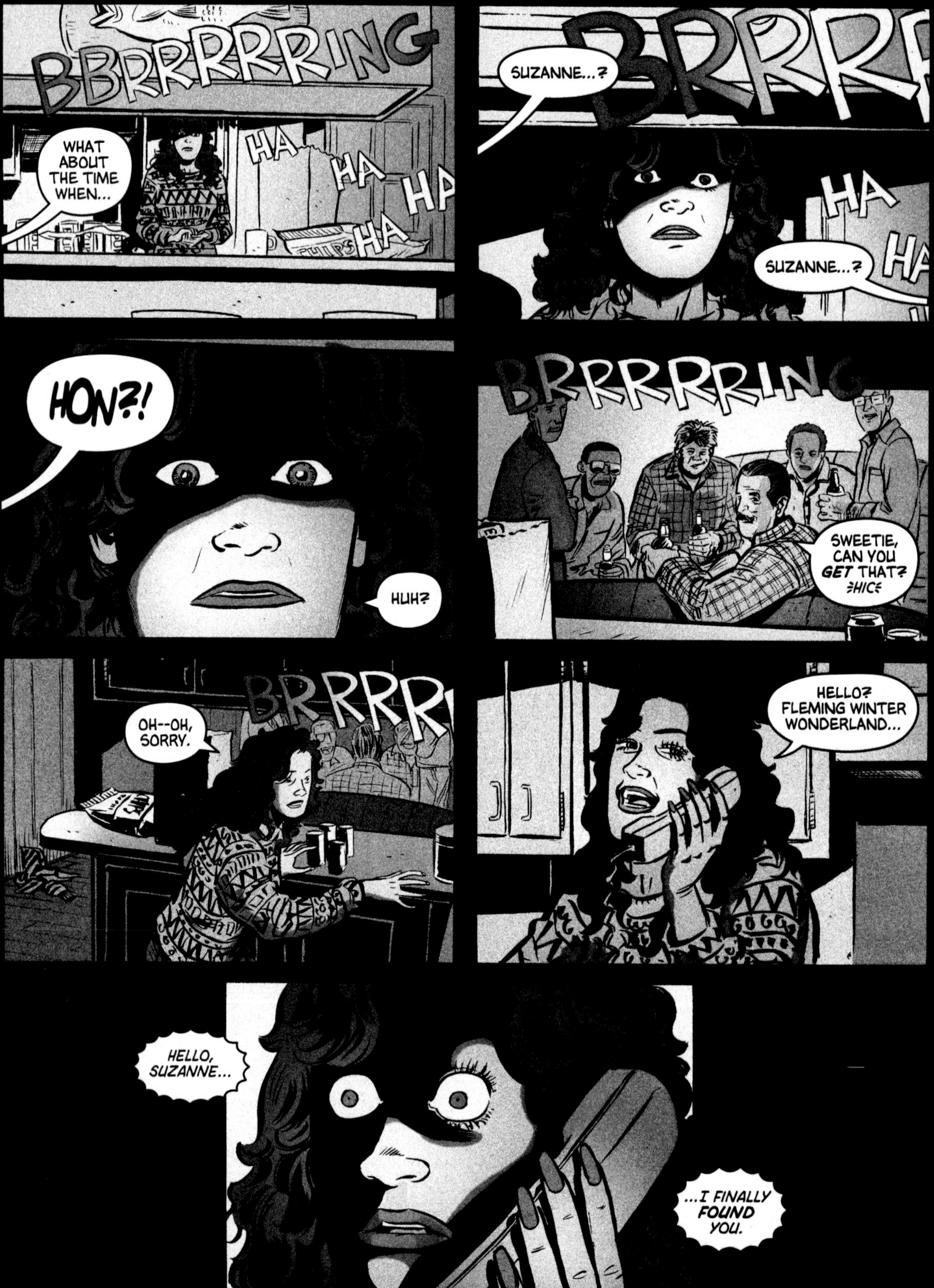
BBRRRRRRING
WHAT ABOUT THE TIME WHEN...
HA HA HA HA
CHIPS
SUZANNE...?
BRRRR
HA HA
SUZANNE...?
HON?!
HUH?
BRRRRRRING
SWEETIE, CAN YOU GET THAT? HIC
BRRRR
OH--OH, SORRY.
HELLO? FLEMING WINTER WONDERLAND...
HELLO, SUZANNE...
...I FINALLY FOUND YOU.

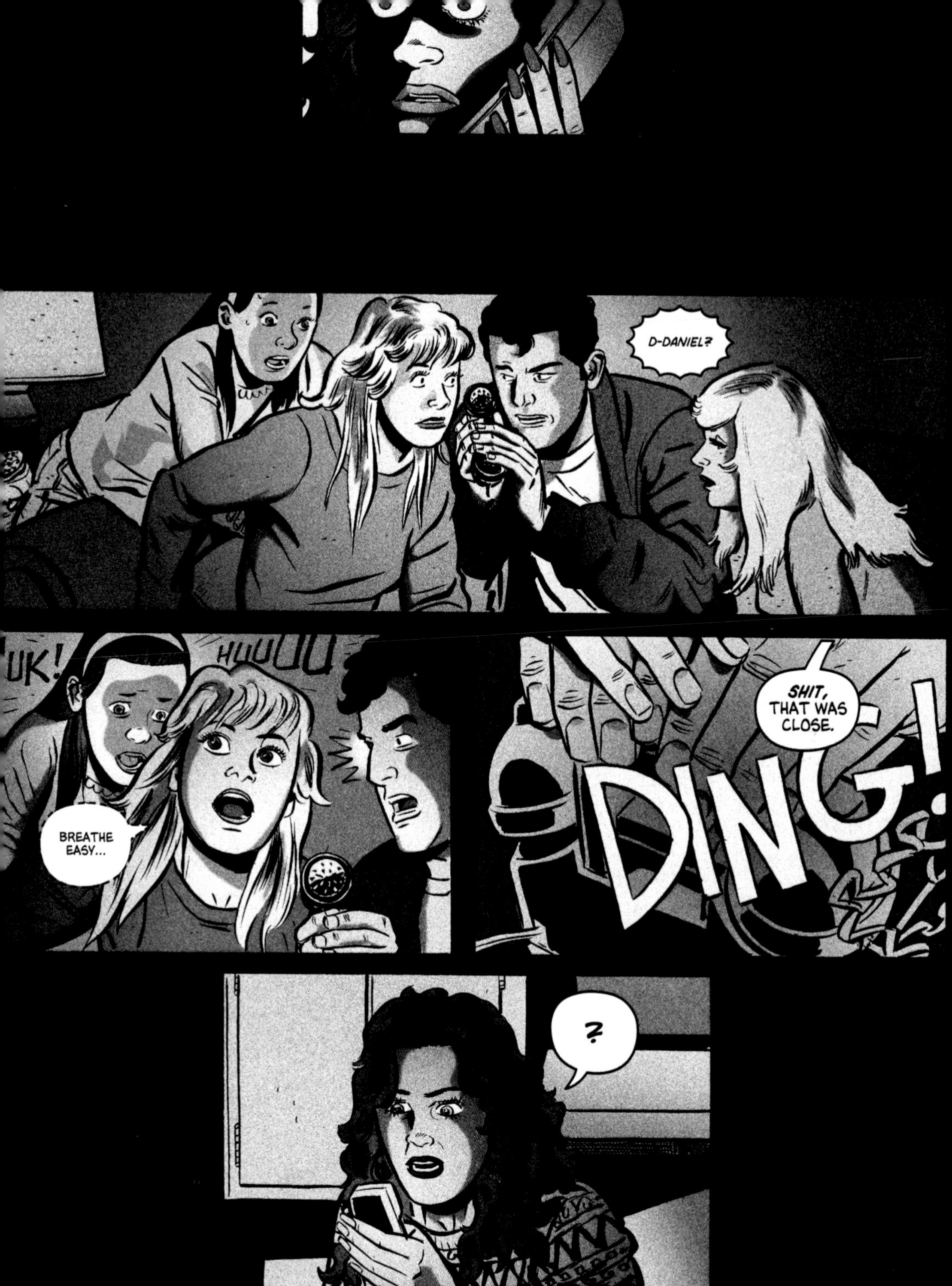
D-DANIEL?
UK!
HUUUU
BREATHE EASY...
SHIT, THAT WAS CLOSE.
DING!
?

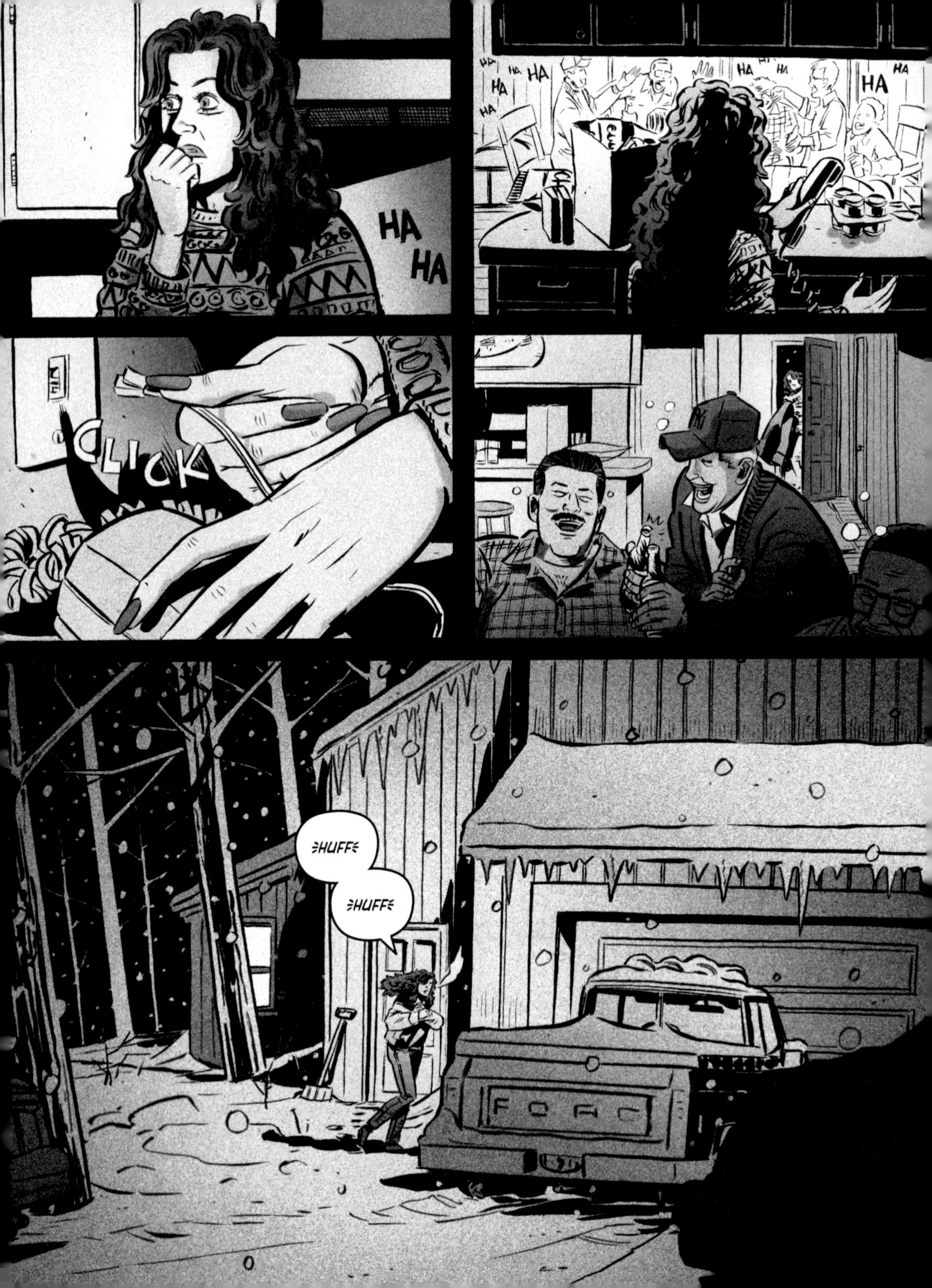
HA
HA
HA HA HA HA HA HA HA HA HA
CLICK
HUFF
HUFF
FORD

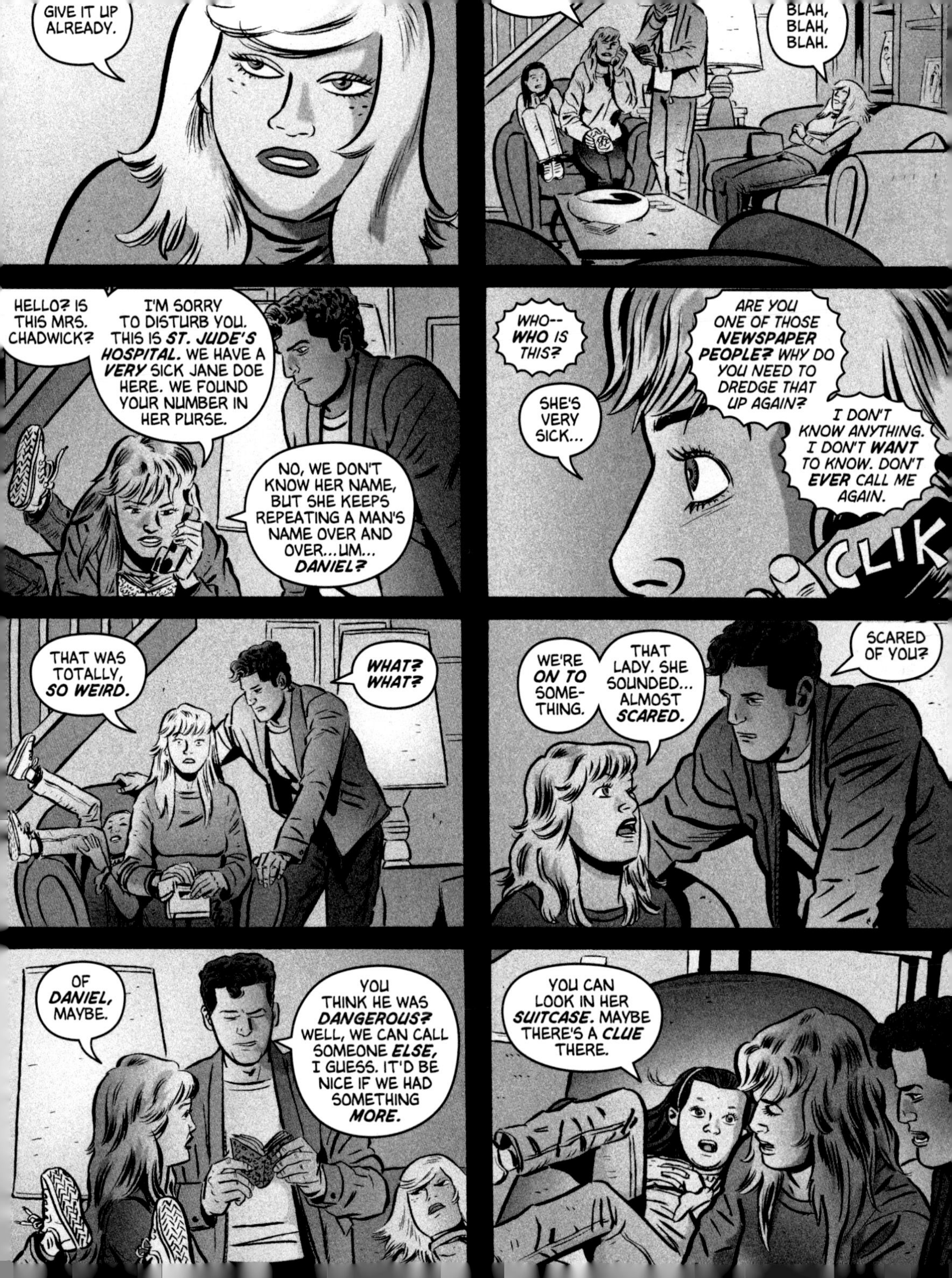
GIVE IT UP ALREADY.
BLAH, BLAH, BLAH.
HELLO? IS THIS MRS. CHADWICK?
I'M SORRY TO DISTURB YOU. THIS IS ST. JUDE'S HOSPITAL. WE HAVE A VERY SICK JANE DOE HERE. WE FOUND YOUR NUMBER IN HER PURSE.
NO, WE DON'T KNOW HER NAME, BUT SHE KEEPS REPEATING A MAN'S NAME OVER AND OVER... UM... DANIEL?
WHO-- WHO IS THIS?
SHE'S VERY SICK...
ARE YOU ONE OF THOSE NEWSPAPER PEOPLE? WHY DO YOU NEED TO DREDGE THAT UP AGAIN?
I DON'T KNOW ANYTHING. I DON'T WANT TO KNOW. DON'T EVER CALL ME AGAIN.
CLIK
THAT WAS TOTALLY, SO WEIRD.
WHAT? WHAT?
WE'RE ON TO SOME-THING.
THAT LADY. SHE SOUNDED... ALMOST SCARED.
SCARED OF YOU?
OF DANIEL, MAYBE.
YOU THINK HE WAS DANGEROUS? WELL, WE CAN CALL SOMEONE ELSE, I GUESS. IT'D BE NICE IF WE HAD SOMETHING MORE.
YOU CAN LOOK IN HER SUITCASE. MAYBE THERE'S A CLUE THERE.

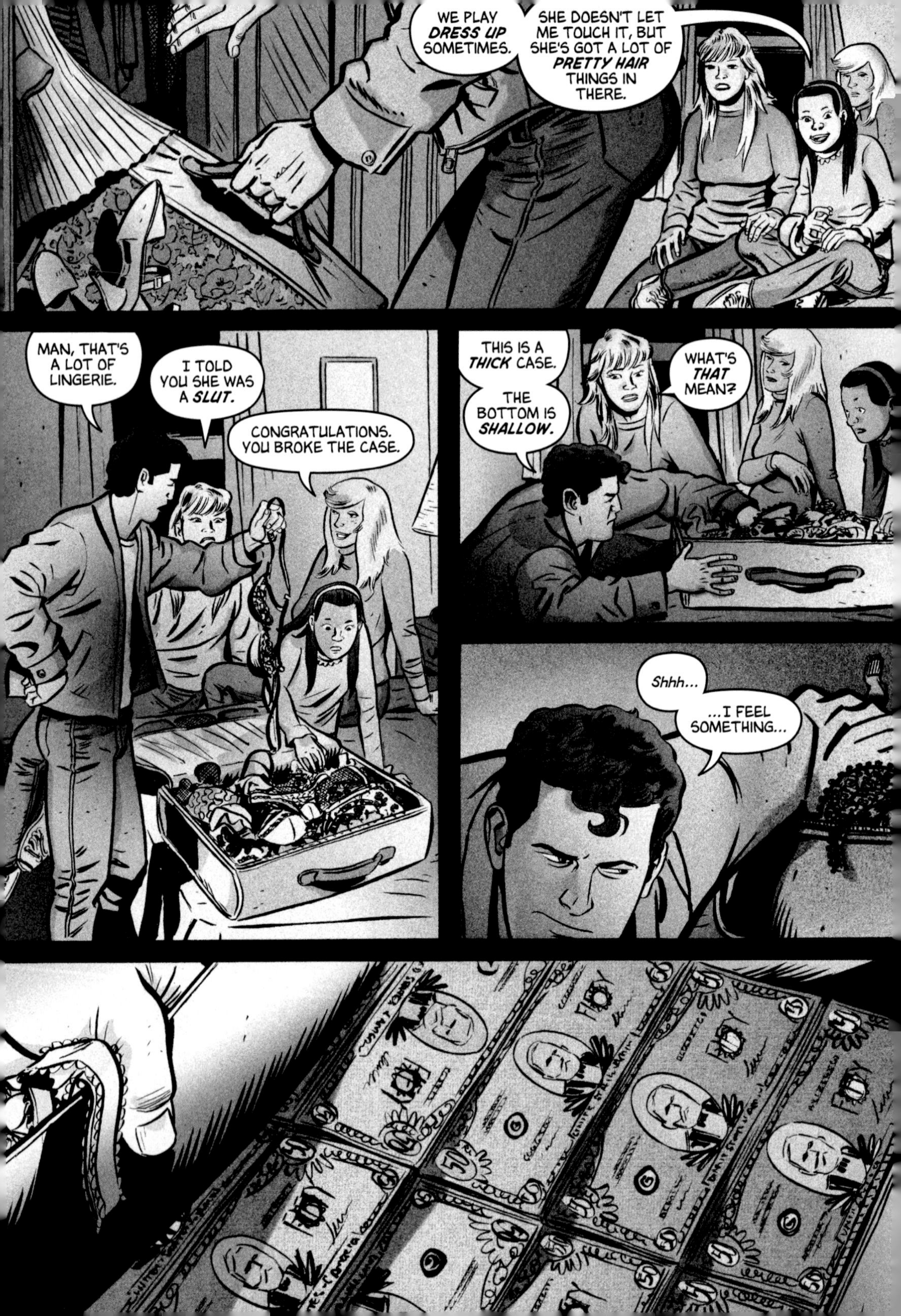
WE PLAY DRESS UP SOMETIMES.
SHE DOESN'T LET ME TOUCH IT, BUT SHE'S GOT A LOT OF PRETTY HAIR THINGS IN THERE.
MAN, THAT'S A LOT OF LINGERIE.
I TOLD YOU SHE WAS A SLUT.
CONGRATULATIONS. YOU BROKE THE CASE.
THIS IS A THICK CASE.
THE BOTTOM IS SHALLOW.
WHAT'S THAT MEAN?
Shhh...
...I FEEL SOMETHING...

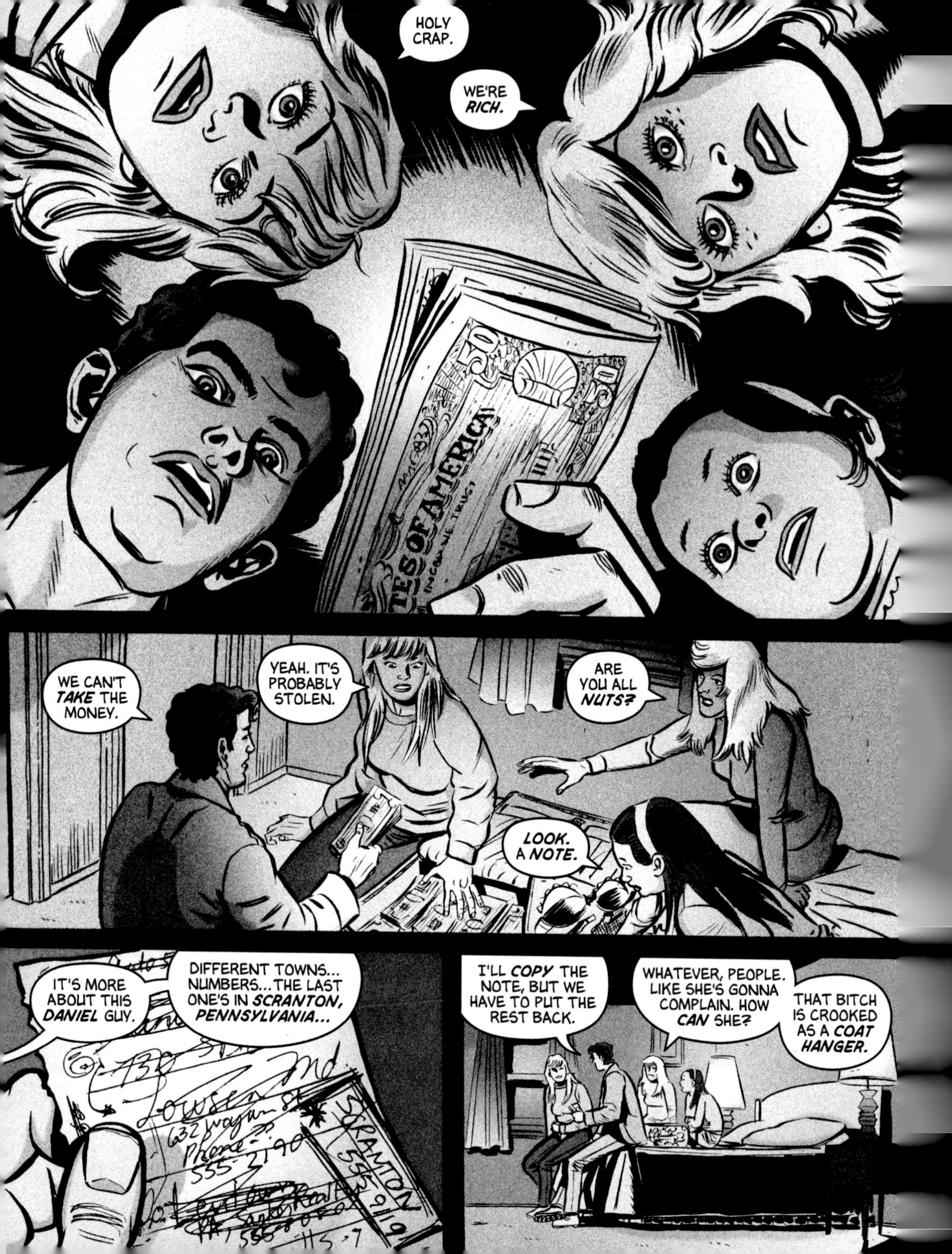
HOLY CRAP.
WE'RE RICH.
WE CAN'T TAKE THE MONEY.
YEAH. IT'S PROBABLY STOLEN.
ARE YOU ALL NUTS?
LOOK. A NOTE.
IT'S MORE ABOUT THIS DANIEL GUY.
DIFFERENT TOWNS... NUMBERS... THE LAST ONE'S IN SCRANTON, PENNSYLVANIA...
I'LL COPY THE NOTE, BUT WE HAVE TO PUT THE REST BACK.
WHATEVER, PEOPLE. LIKE SHE'S GONNA COMPLAIN. HOW CAN SHE?
THAT BITCH IS CROOKED AS A COAT HANGER.

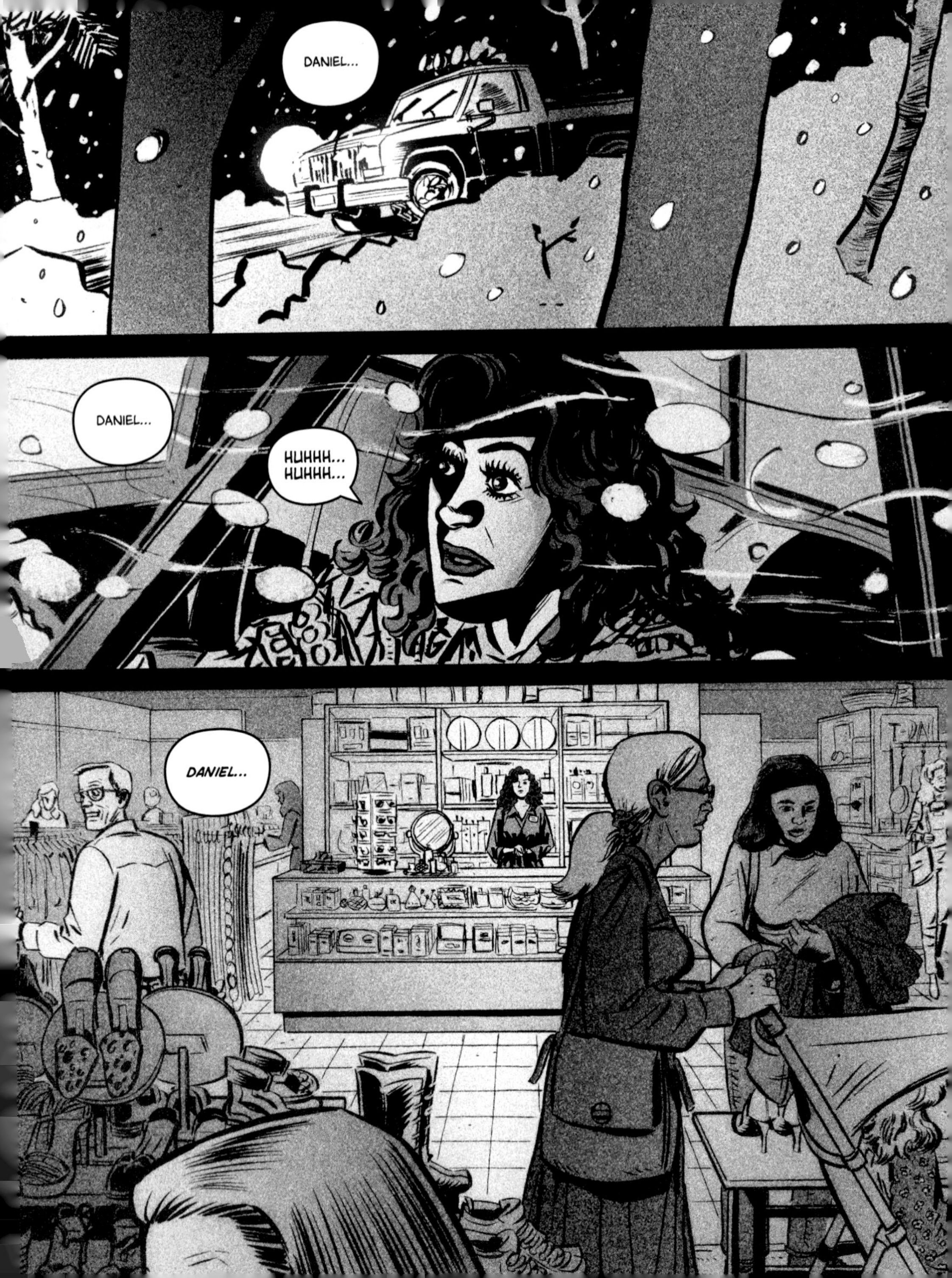
DANIEL...
DANIEL...
HUHHH... HUHHH...
DANIEL...

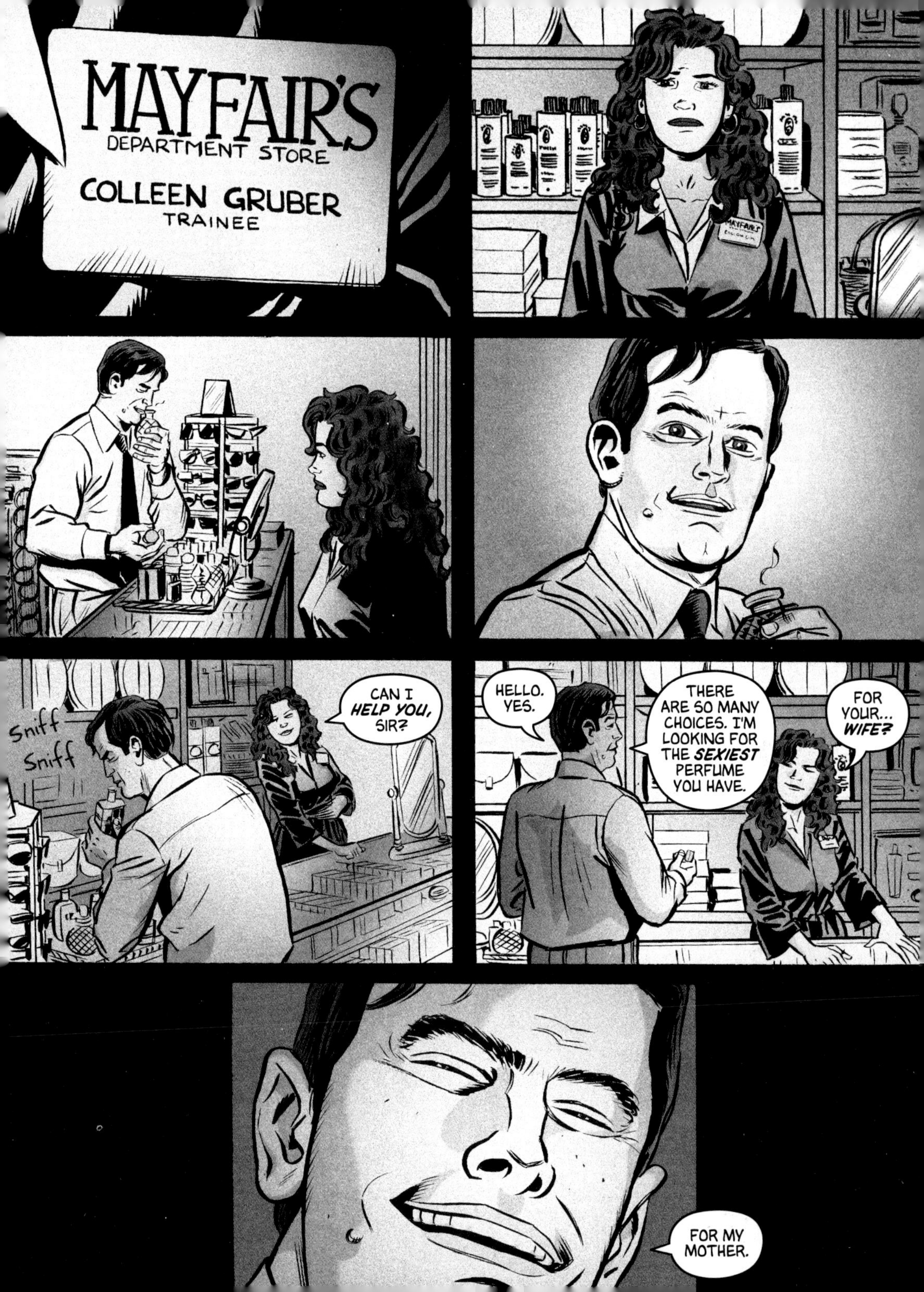
MAYFAIR'S
DEPARTMENT STORE
COLLEEN GRUBER
TRAINEE
Sniff Sniff
CAN I HELP YOU, SIR?
HELLO. YES.
THERE ARE SO MANY CHOICES. I'M LOOKING FOR THE SEXIEST PERFUME YOU HAVE.
FOR YOUR... WIFE?
FOR MY MOTHER.

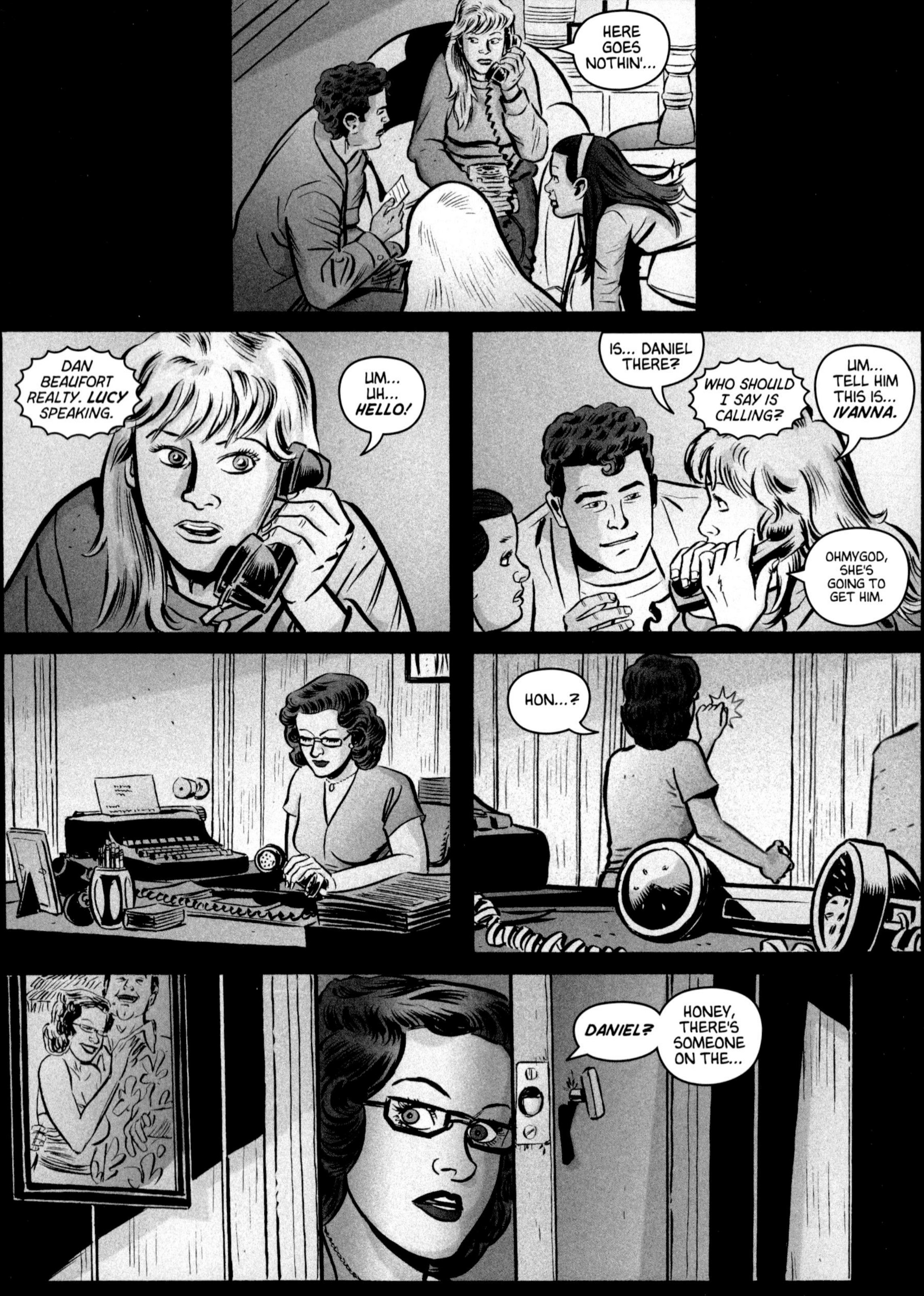

HERE GOES NOTHIN'...
DAN BEAUFORT REALTY. LUCY SPEAKING.
UM... UH... HELLO!
IS... DANIEL THERE?
WHO SHOULD I SAY IS CALLING?
UM... TELL HIM THIS IS... IVANNA.
OHMYGOD, SHE'S GOING TO GET HIM.
HON...?
DANIEL?
HONEY, THERE'S SOMEONE ON THE...

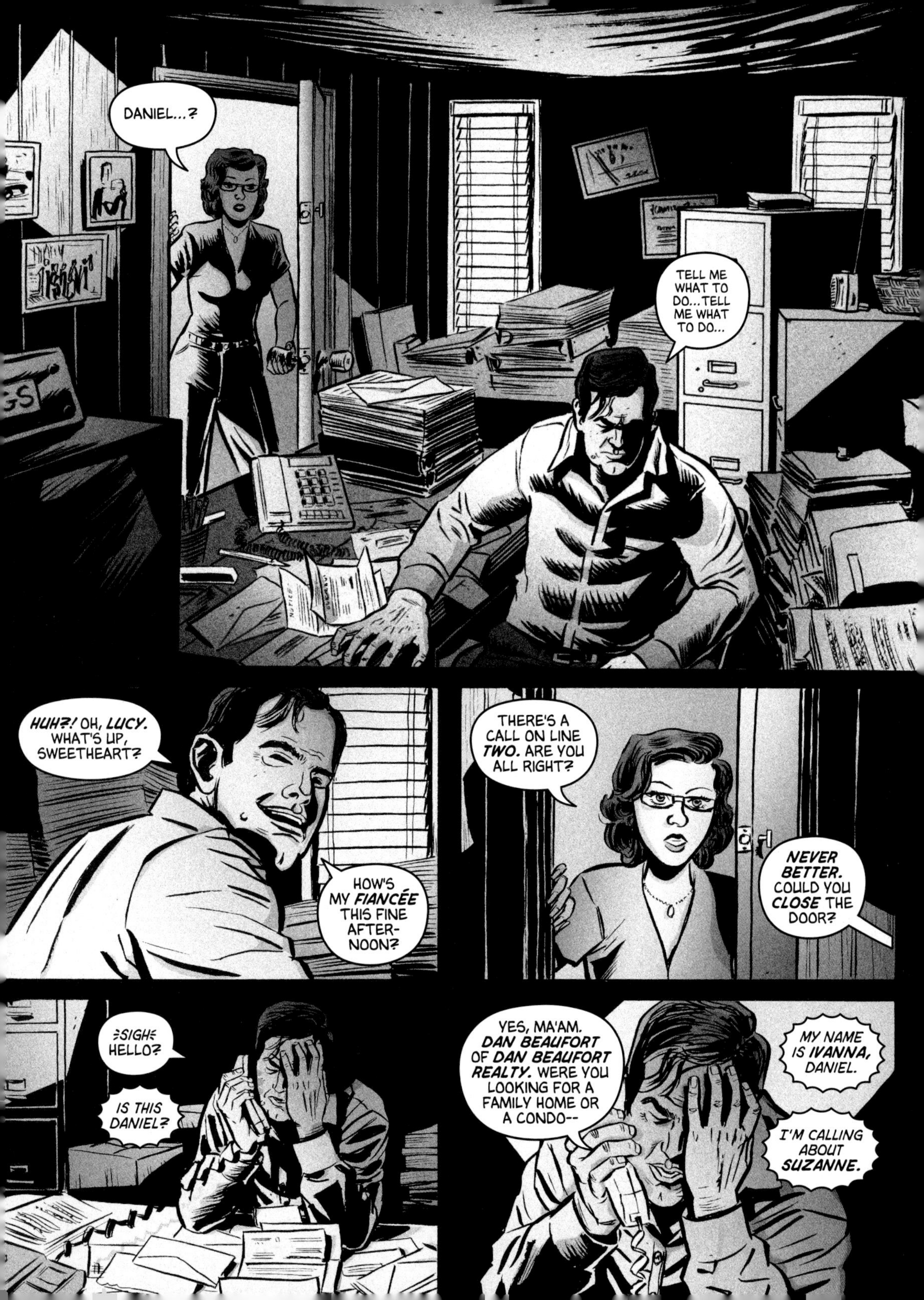
DANIEL...?
TELL ME WHAT TO DO...TELL ME WHAT TO DO...
HUH?! OH, LUCY. WHAT'S UP, SWEETHEART?
HOW'S MY FIANCÉE THIS FINE AFTER-NOON?
THERE'S A CALL ON LINE TWO. ARE YOU ALL RIGHT?
NEVER BETTER. COULD YOU CLOSE THE DOOR?
SIGH HELLO?
IS THIS DANIEL?
YES, MA'AM. DAN BEAUFORT OF DAN BEAUFORT REALTY. WERE YOU LOOKING FOR A FAMILY HOME OR A CONDO--
MY NAME IS IVANNA, DANIEL.
I'M CALLING ABOUT SUZANNE.

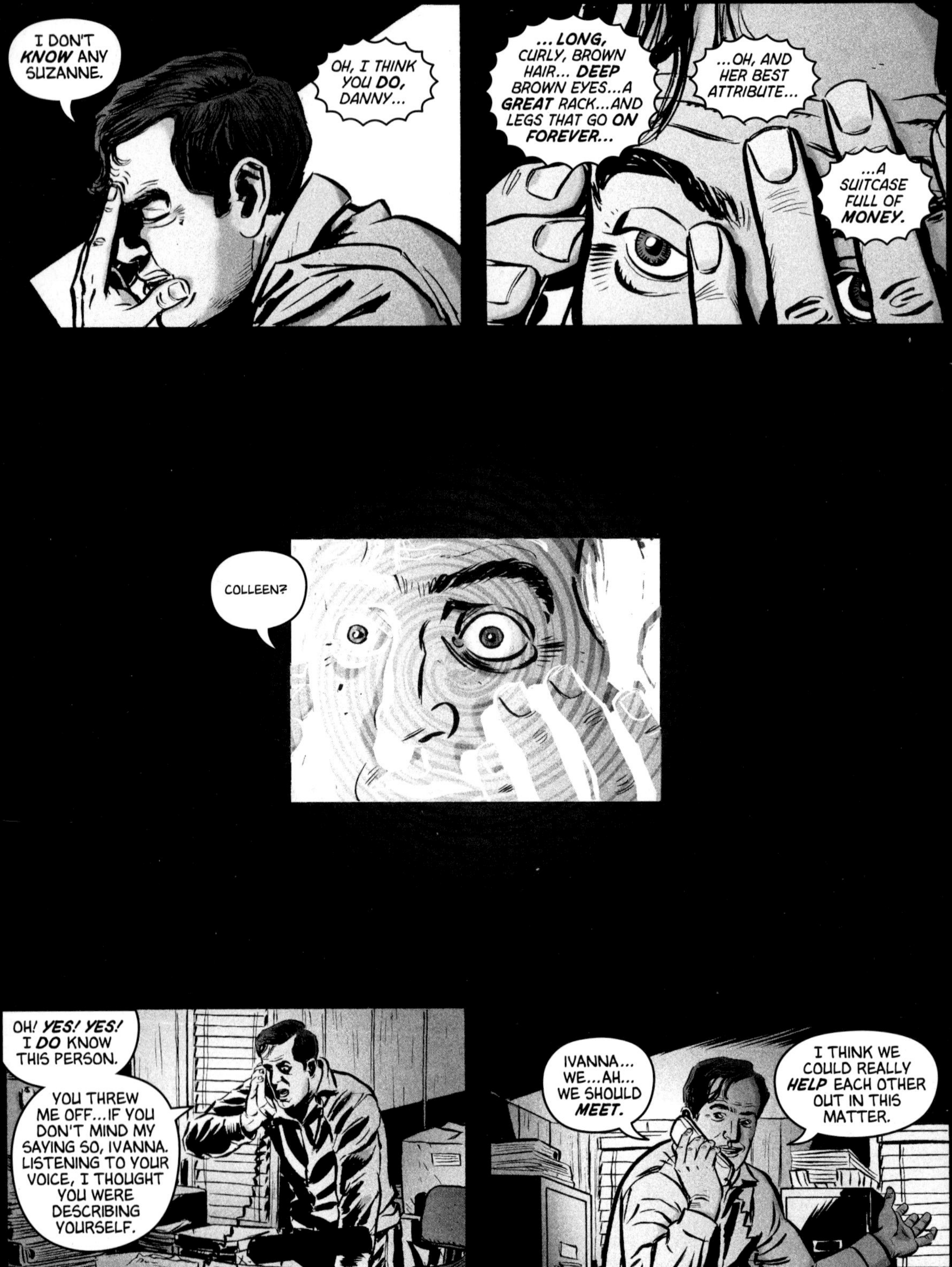
I DON'T KNOW ANY SUZANNE.
OH, I THINK YOU DO, DANNY...
...LONG, CURLY, BROWN HAIR... DEEP BROWN EYES...A GREAT RACK...AND LEGS THAT GO ON FOREVER...
...OH, AND HER BEST ATTRIBUTE...
...A SUITCASE FULL OF MONEY.
COLLEEN?
OH! YES! YES! I DO KNOW THIS PERSON.
YOU THREW ME OFF...IF YOU DON'T MIND MY SAYING SO, IVANNA. LISTENING TO YOUR VOICE, I THOUGHT YOU WERE DESCRIBING YOURSELF.
IVANNA... WE...AH... WE SHOULD MEET.
I THINK WE COULD REALLY HELP EACH OTHER OUT IN THIS MATTER.

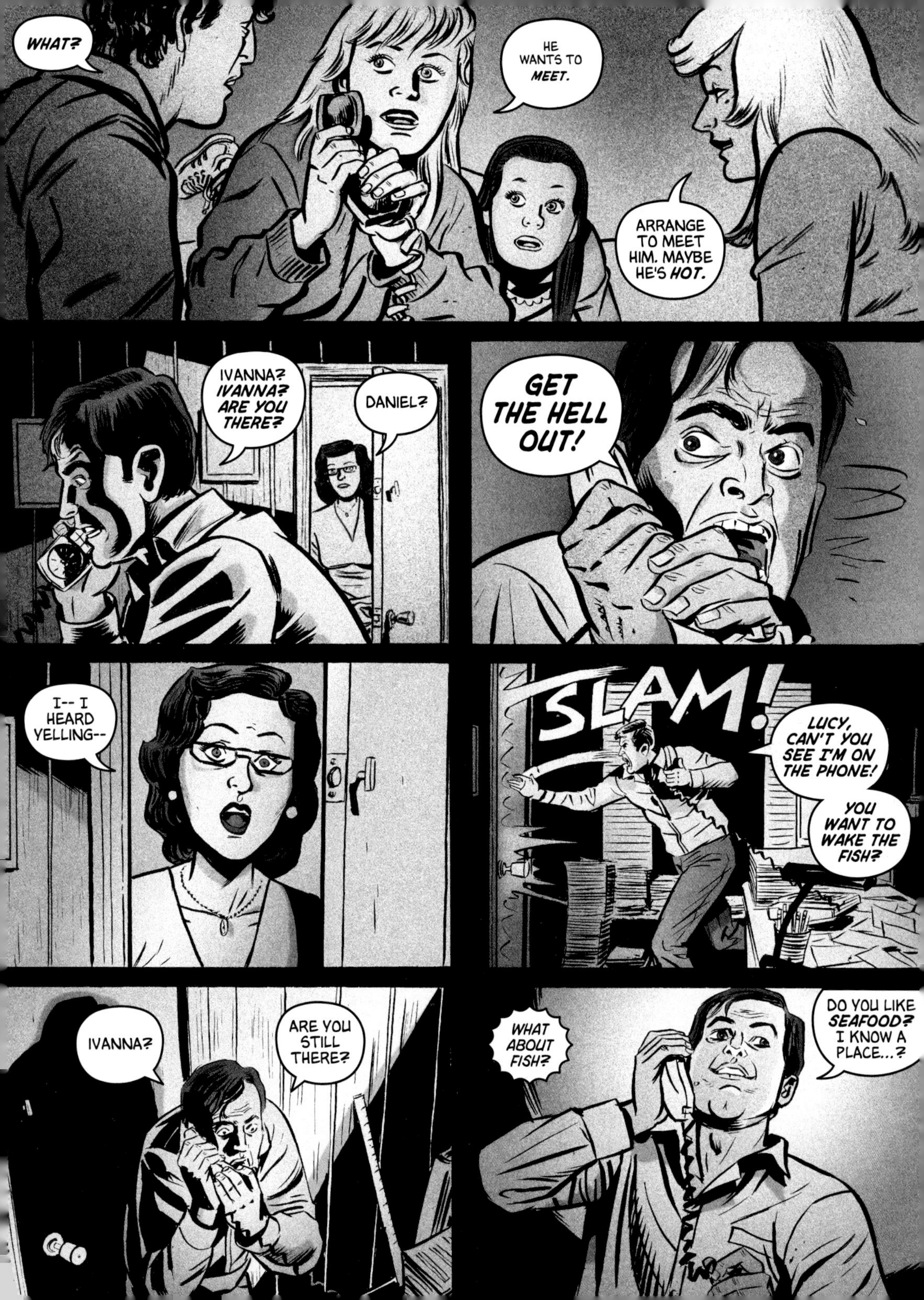
WHAT?
HE WANTS TO MEET.
ARRANGE TO MEET HIM. MAYBE HE'S HOT.
IVANNA? IVANNA? ARE YOU THERE?
DANIEL?
GET THE HELL OUT!
I-- I HEARD YELLING--
SLAM!
LUCY, CAN'T YOU SEE I'M ON THE PHONE!
YOU WANT TO WAKE THE FISH?
IVANNA?
ARE YOU STILL THERE?
WHAT ABOUT FISH?
DO YOU LIKE SEAFOOD? I KNOW A PLACE...?

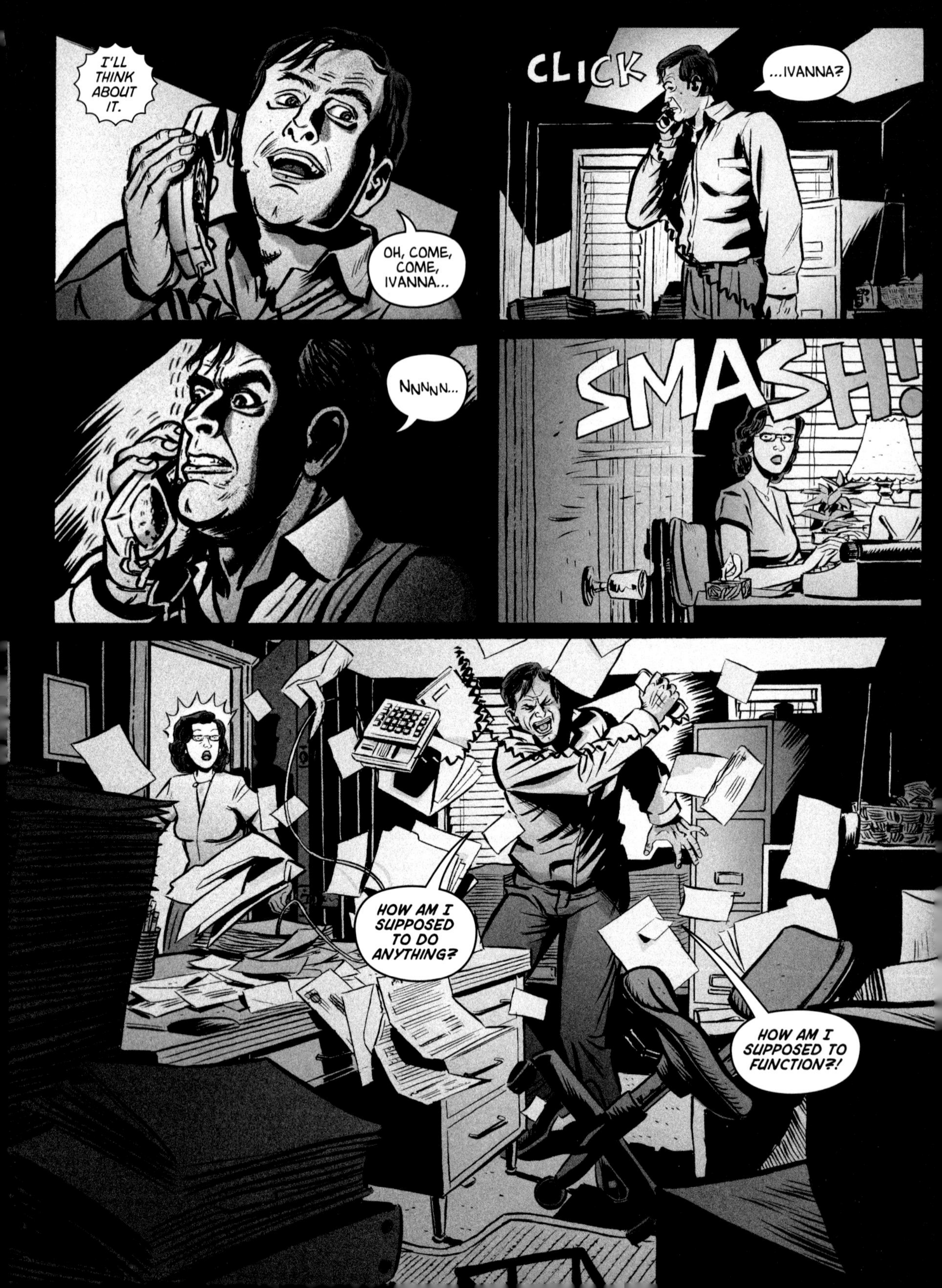
I'LL THINK ABOUT IT.
OH, COME, COME, IVANNA...
CLICK
...IVANNA?
NNNNN...
SMASH!
HOW AM I SUPPOSED TO DO ANYTHING?
HOW AM I SUPPOSED TO FUNCTION?!

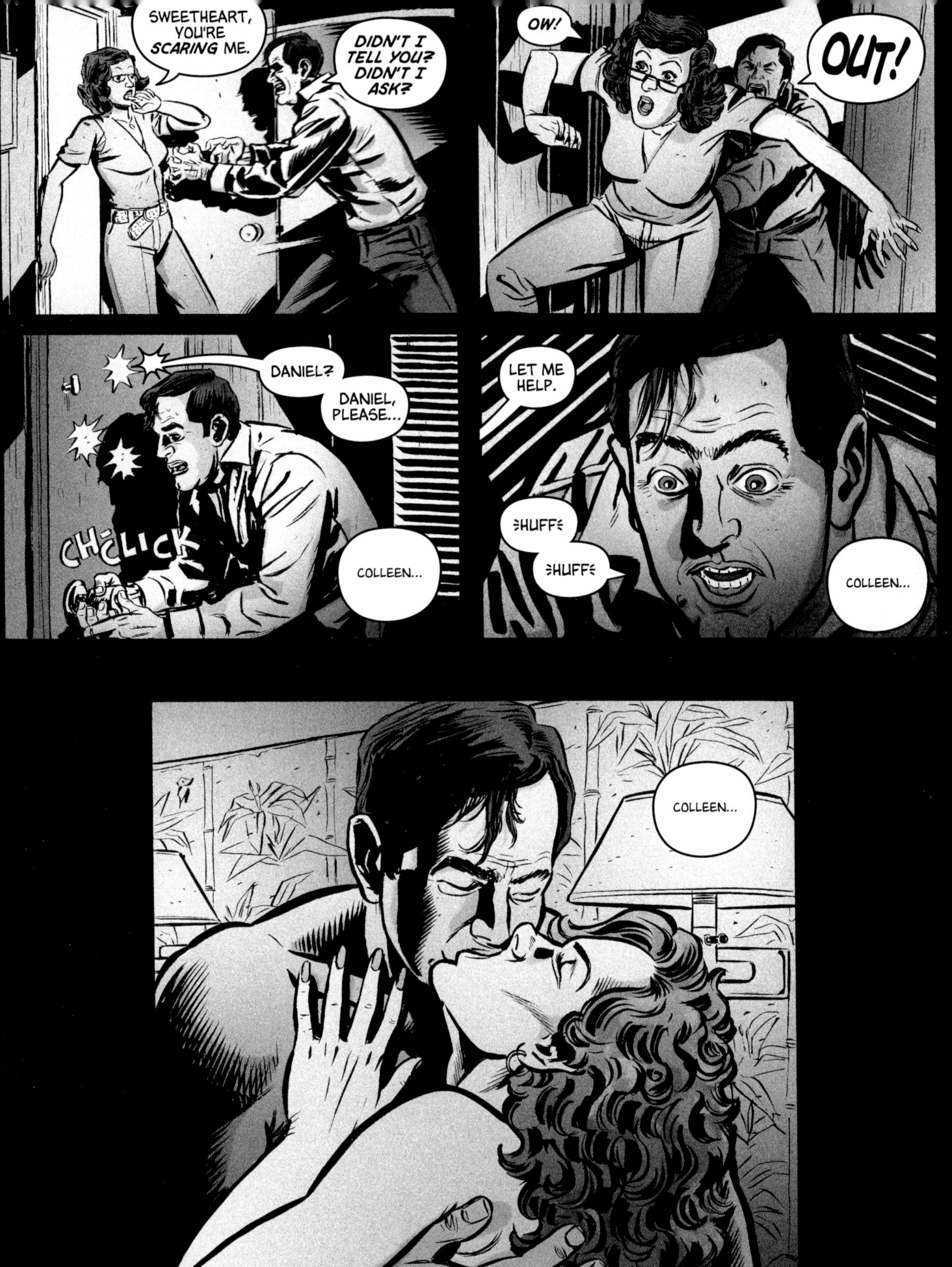
SWEETHEART, YOU'RE SCARING ME.
DIDN'T I TELL YOU? DIDN'T I ASK?
OW!
OUT!
DANIEL?
DANIEL, PLEASE...
CH-CLICK
COLLEEN...
LET ME HELP.
HUFF
HUFF
COLLEEN...
COLLEEN...

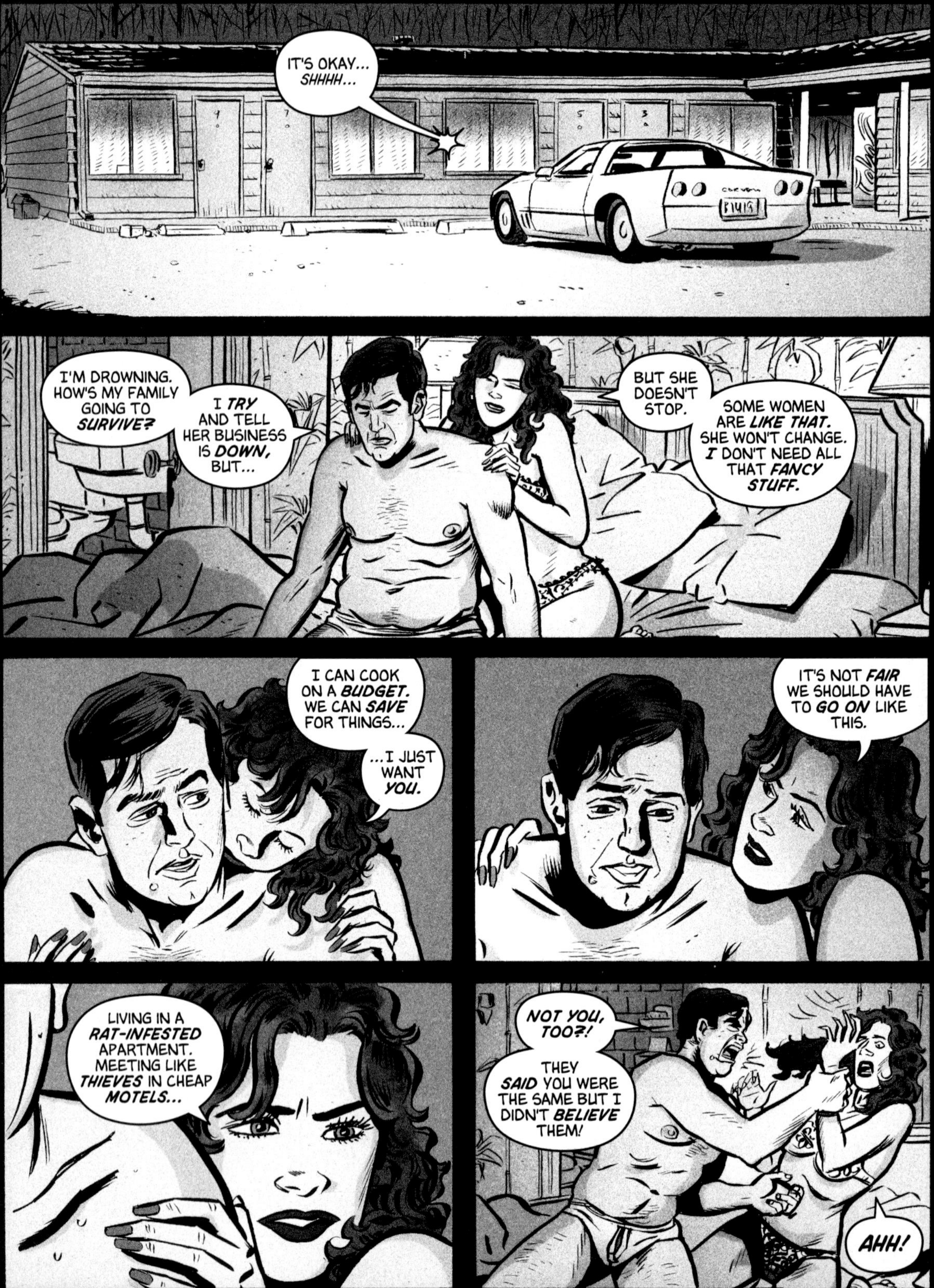
IT'S OKAY... SHHHH...
I'M DROWNING. HOW'S MY FAMILY GOING TO SURVIVE?
I TRY AND TELL HER BUSINESS IS DOWN, BUT...
BUT SHE DOESN'T STOP.
SOME WOMEN ARE LIKE THAT. SHE WON'T CHANGE. I DON'T NEED ALL THAT FANCY STUFF.
I CAN COOK ON A BUDGET. WE CAN SAVE FOR THINGS...
...I JUST WANT YOU.
IT'S NOT FAIR WE SHOULD HAVE TO GO ON LIKE THIS.
LIVING IN A RAT-INFESTED APARTMENT. MEETING LIKE THIEVES IN CHEAP MOTELS...
NOT YOU, TOO?!
THEY SAID YOU WERE THE SAME BUT I DIDN'T BELIEVE THEM!
AHH!

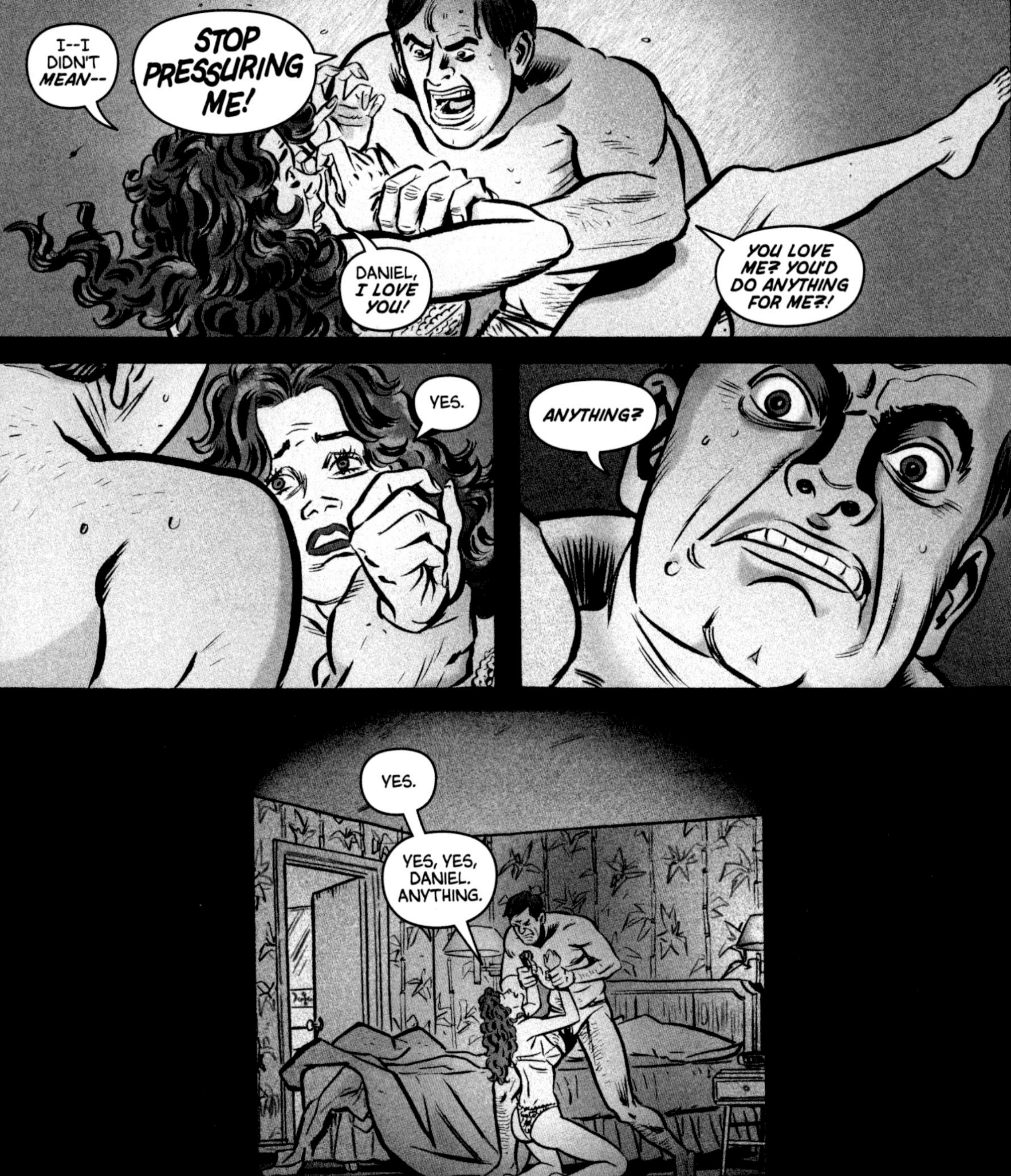
I--I DIDN'T MEAN--
STOP PRESSURING ME!
DANIEL, I LOVE YOU!
YOU LOVE ME? YOU'D DO ANYTHING FOR ME?!
YES.
ANYTHING?
YES.
YES, YES, DANIEL. ANYTHING.

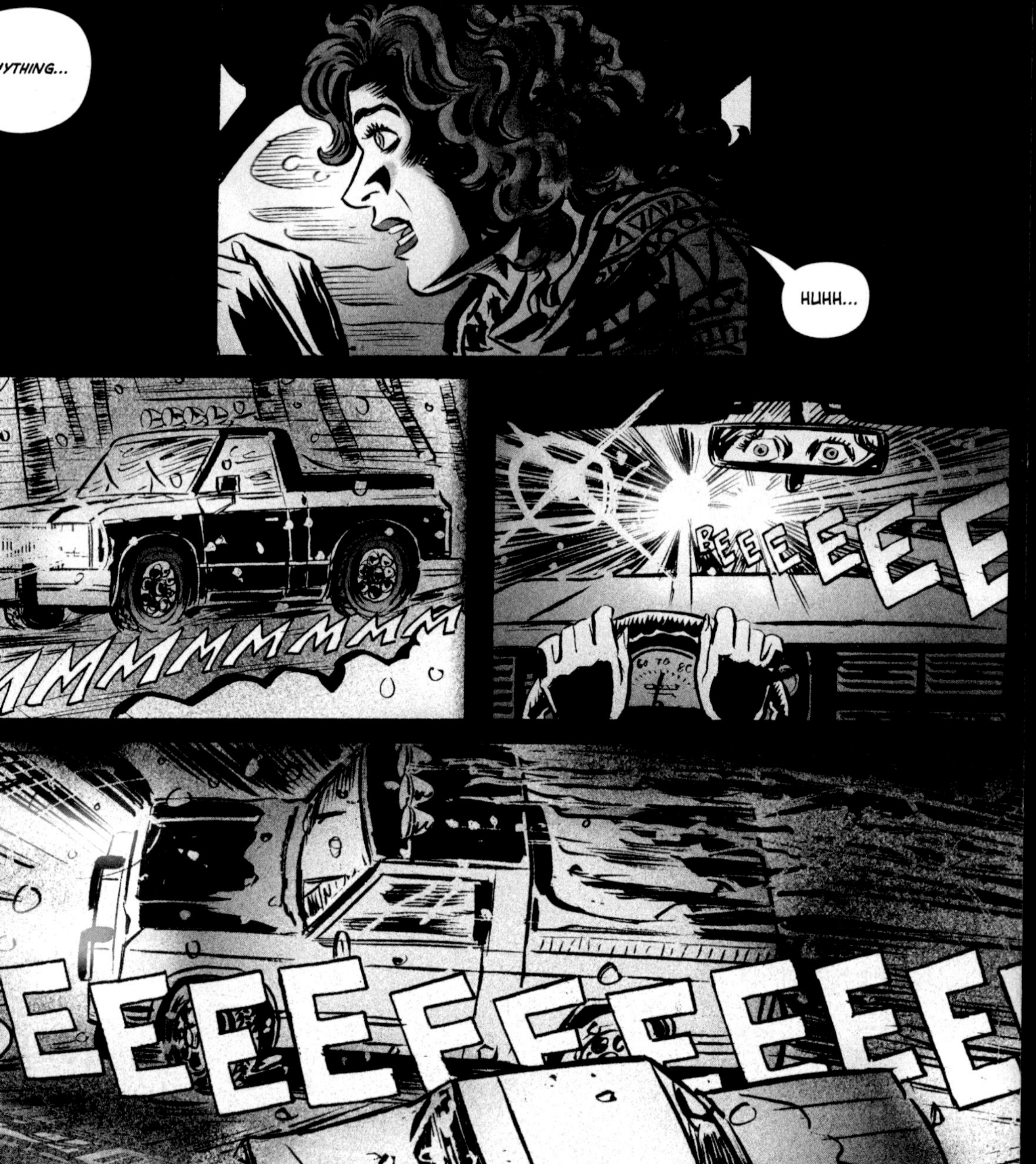

YTHING...
HUHH...
MMMMMMMMM
BEEEEEE
EEEEEEEEEE

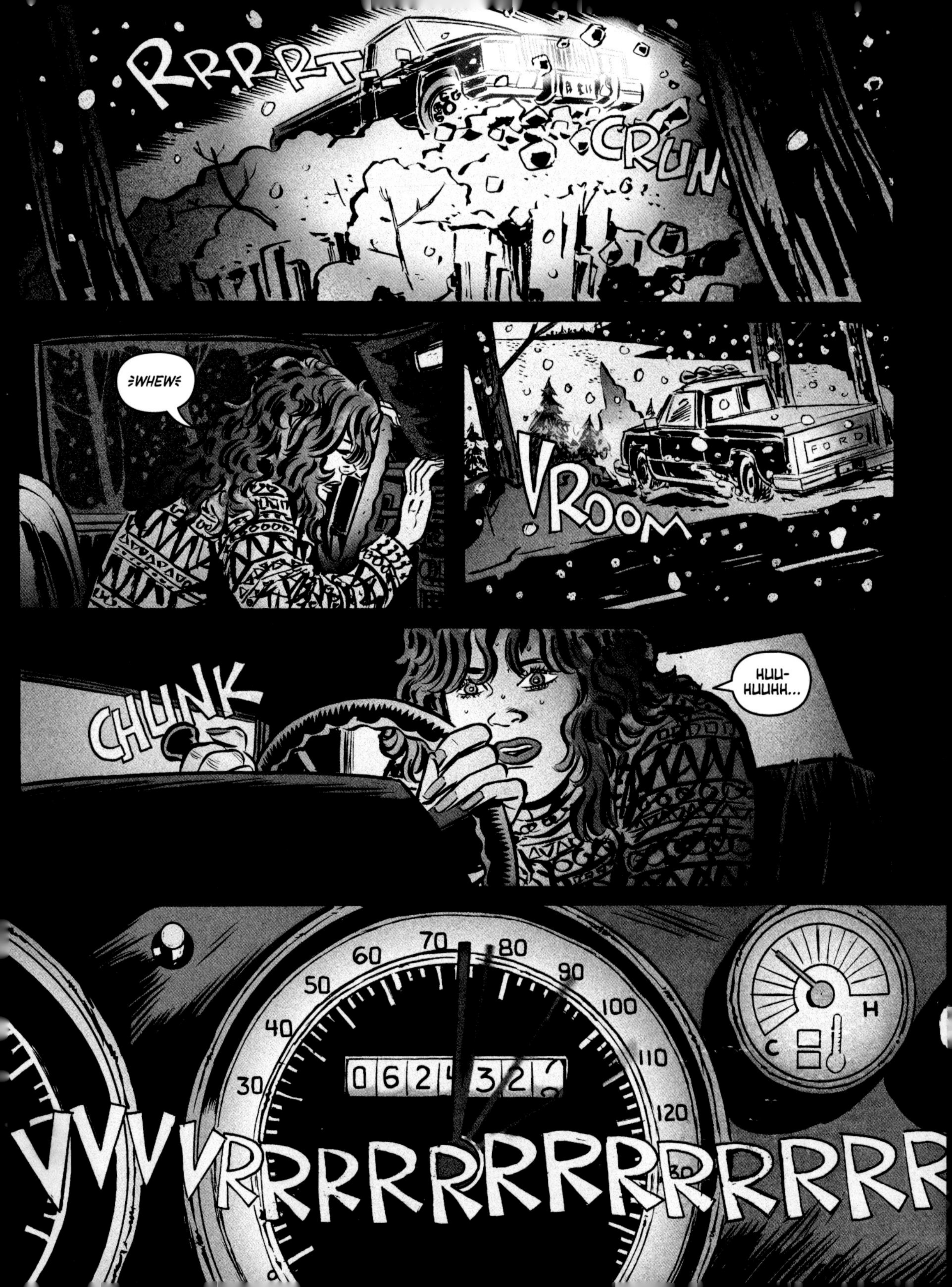
RRRRT-
CRUNC
WHEW
VROOM
FORD
CHUNK
HUU-HUUHH...
VVVVRRRRRRRRRRRR

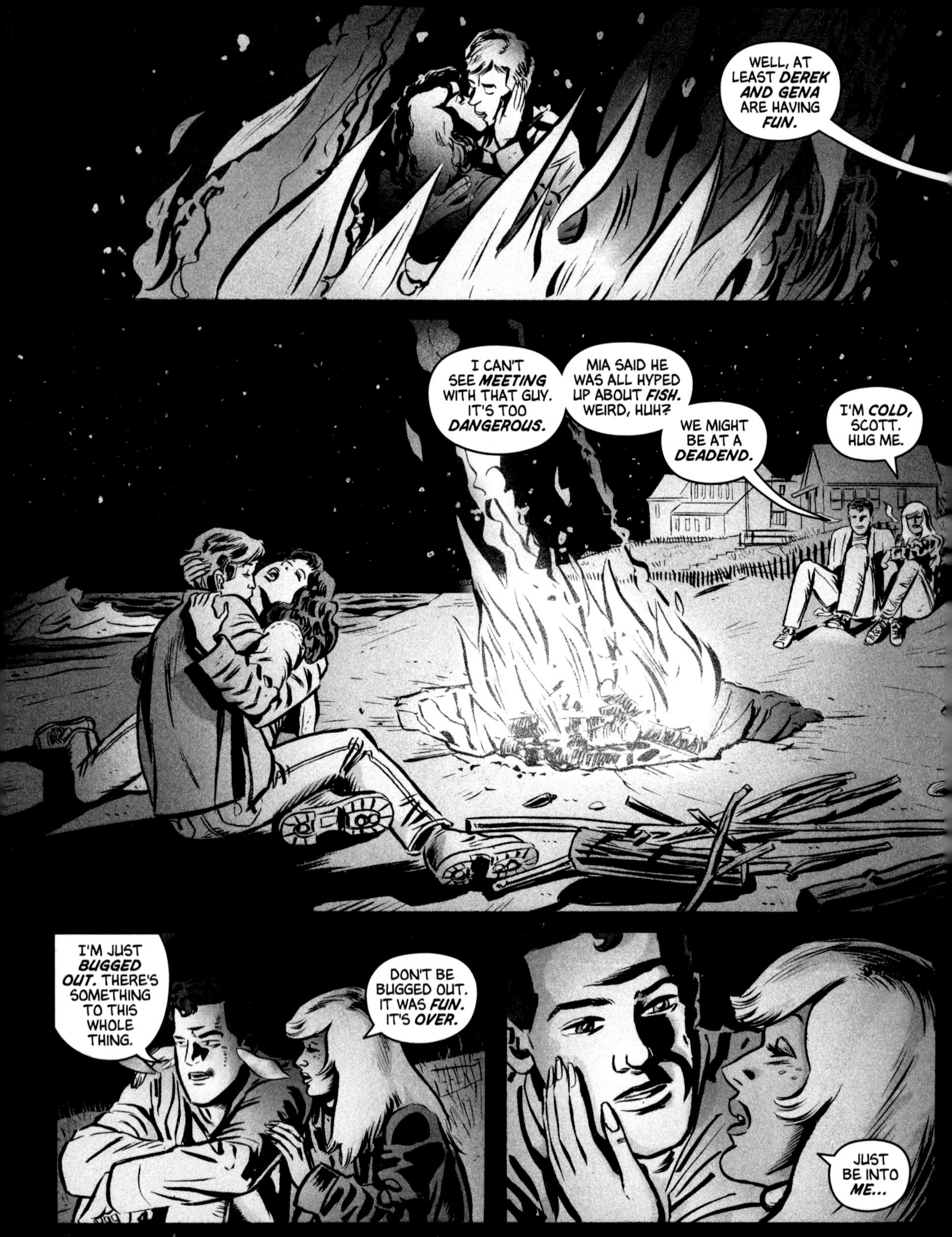
WELL, AT LEAST *DEREK AND GENA* ARE HAVING *FUN.*
I CAN'T SEE *MEETING* WITH THAT GUY. IT'S TOO *DANGEROUS.*
MIA SAID HE WAS ALL HYPED UP ABOUT *FISH.* WEIRD, HUH?
WE MIGHT BE AT A *DEADEND.*
I'M *COLD,* SCOTT. HUG ME.
I'M JUST *BUGGED OUT.* THERE'S SOMETHING TO THIS WHOLE THING.
DON'T BE BUGGED OUT. IT WAS *FUN.* IT'S *OVER.*
JUST BE INTO *ME...*

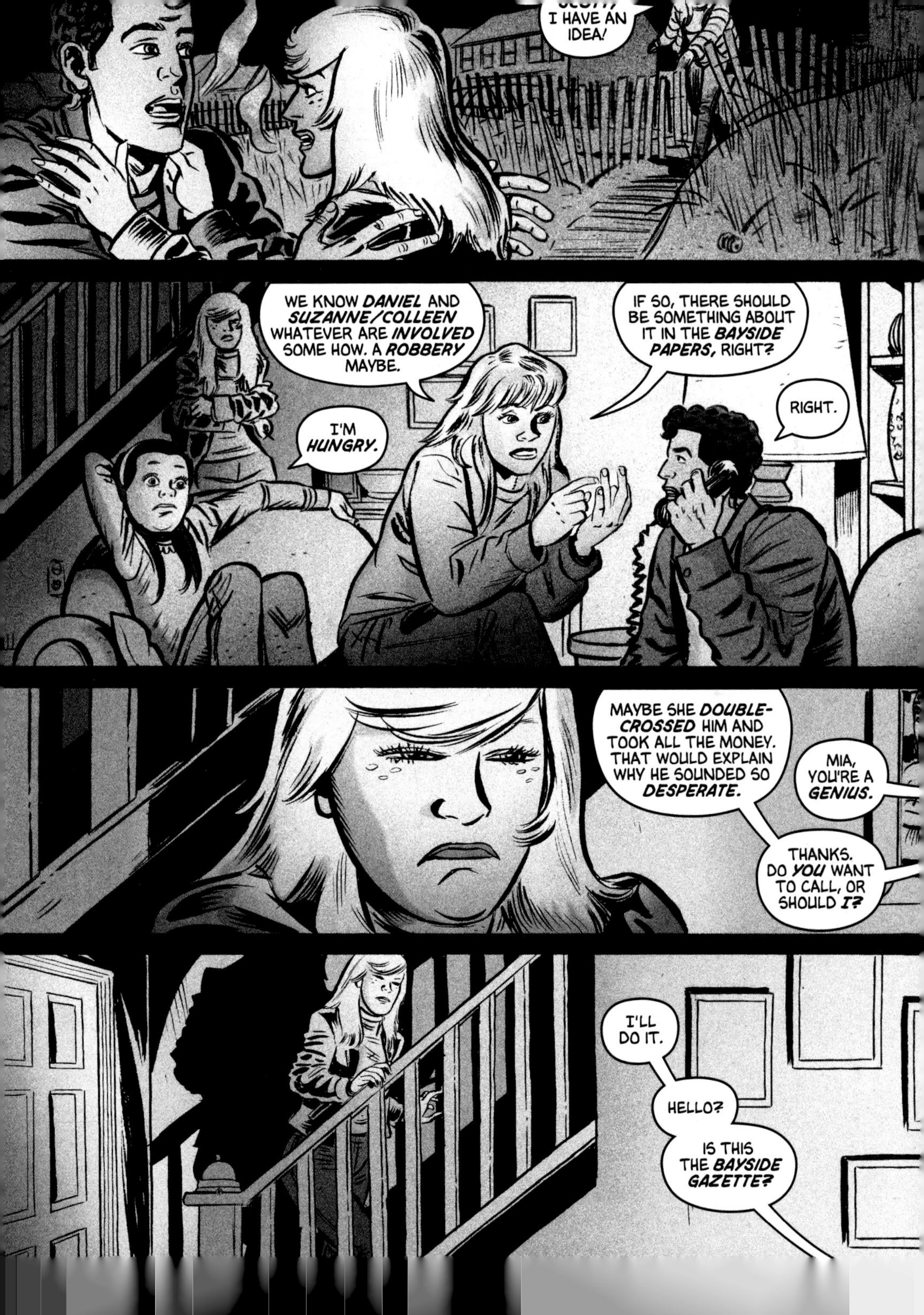

I HAVE AN IDEA!
WE KNOW *DANIEL* AND *SUZANNE/COLLEEN* WHATEVER ARE *INVOLVED* SOME HOW. A *ROBBERY* MAYBE.
IF SO, THERE SHOULD BE SOMETHING ABOUT IT IN THE *BAYSIDE PAPERS,* RIGHT?
I'M *HUNGRY.*
RIGHT.
MAYBE SHE *DOUBLE-CROSSED* HIM AND TOOK ALL THE MONEY. THAT WOULD EXPLAIN WHY HE SOUNDED SO *DESPERATE.*
MIA, YOU'RE A *GENIUS.*
THANKS. DO *YOU* WANT TO CALL, OR SHOULD *I?*
I'LL DO IT.
HELLO?
IS THIS THE *BAYSIDE GAZETTE?*

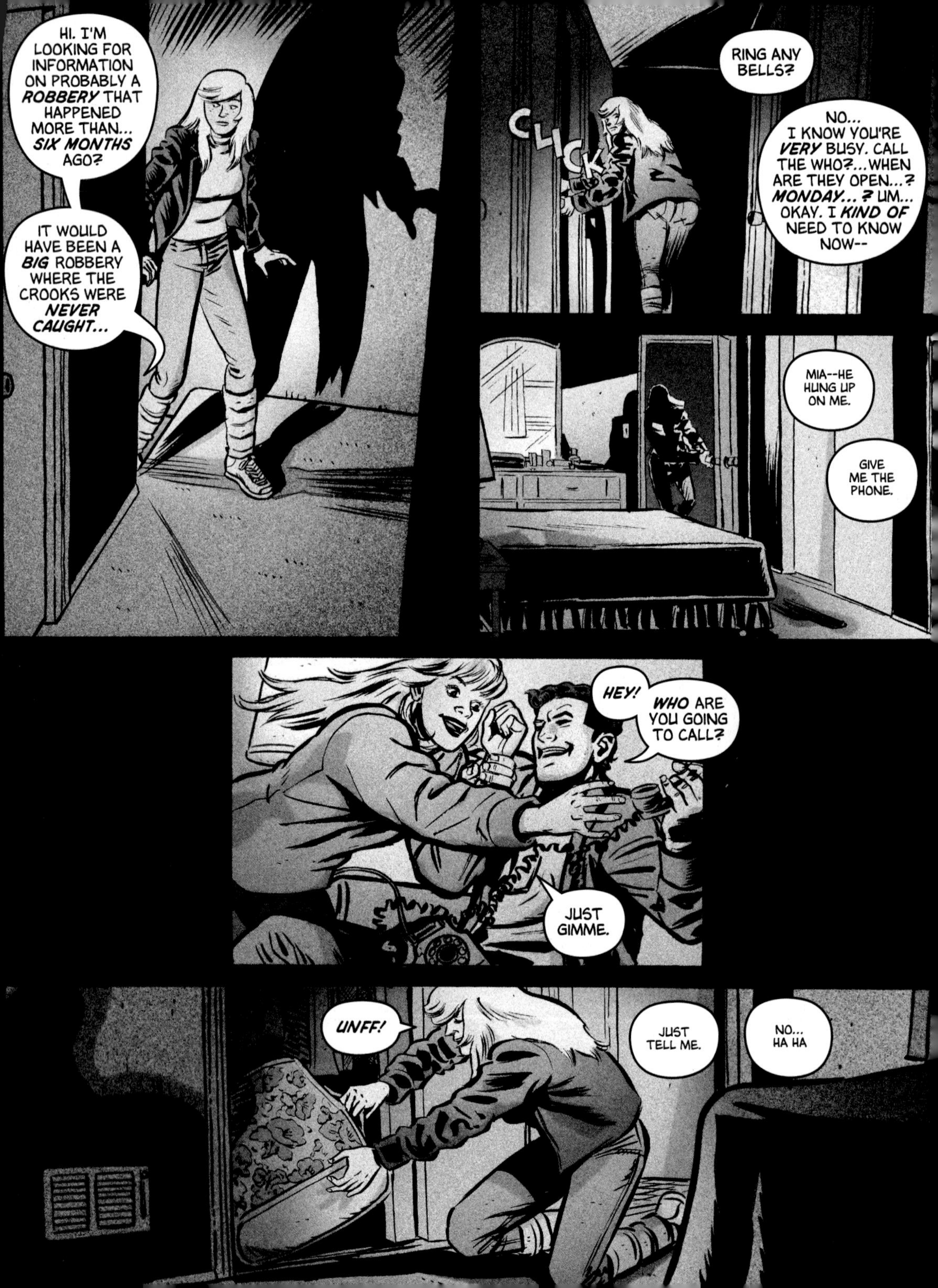
HI. I'M LOOKING FOR INFORMATION ON PROBABLY A ROBBERY THAT HAPPENED MORE THAN... SIX MONTHS AGO?
IT WOULD HAVE BEEN A BIG ROBBERY WHERE THE CROOKS WERE NEVER CAUGHT...
RING ANY BELLS?
CLICK
NO... I KNOW YOU'RE VERY BUSY. CALL THE WHO?...WHEN ARE THEY OPEN...? MONDAY...? UM... OKAY. I KIND OF NEED TO KNOW NOW--
MIA--HE HUNG UP ON ME.
GIVE ME THE PHONE.
HEY!
WHO ARE YOU GOING TO CALL?
JUST GIMME.
UNFF!
JUST TELL ME.
NO... HA HA

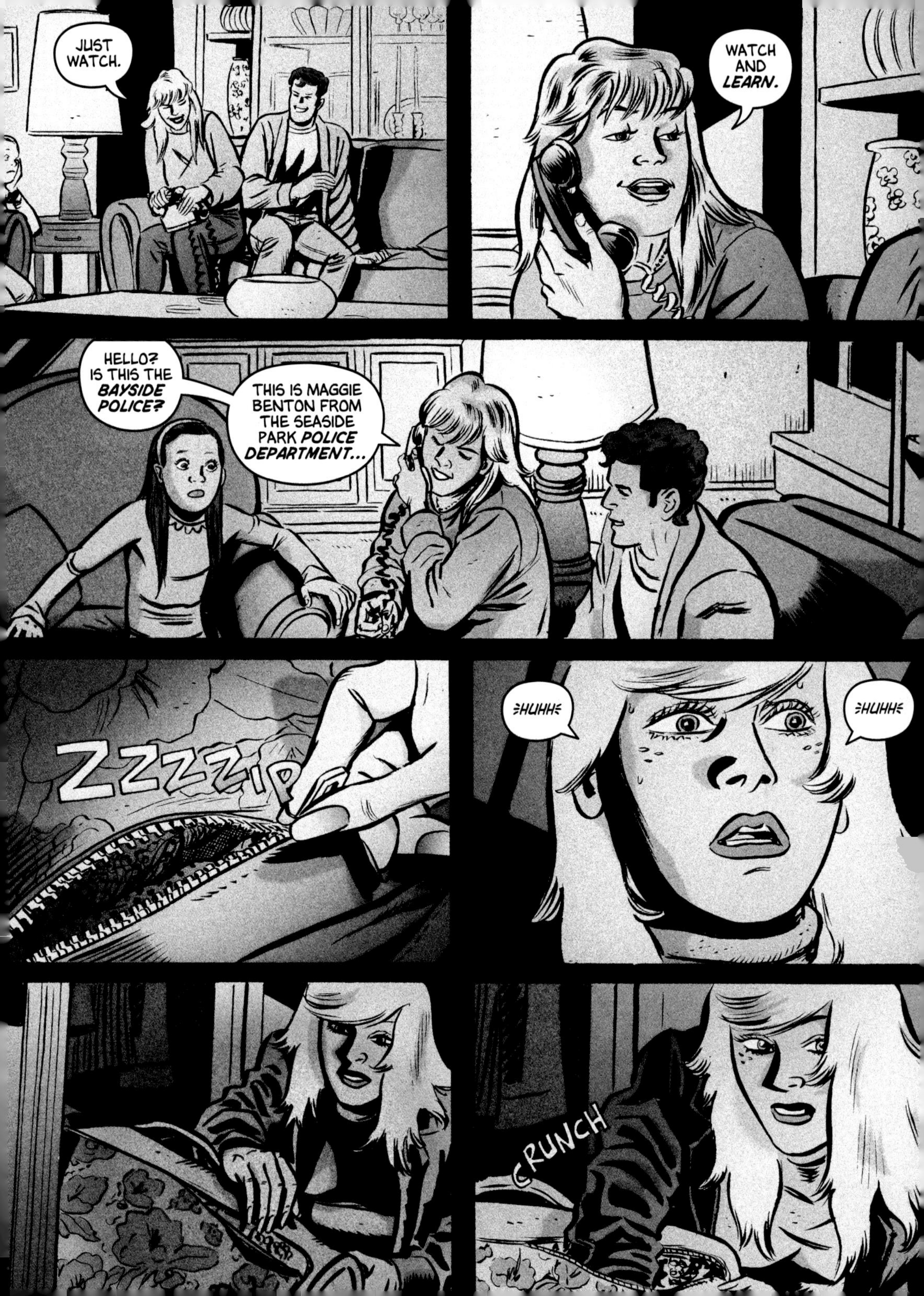
JUST WATCH.
WATCH AND LEARN.
HELLO? IS THIS THE BAYSIDE POLICE?
THIS IS MAGGIE BENTON FROM THE SEASIDE PARK POLICE DEPARTMENT...
ZZZZIP
HUHH
HUHH
CRUNCH

OWW!

SHIT!

MAGGIE *WORKS* FOR MY DAD. SHE DOES *ALL* THIS CALLING AND COORDINATING STUFF.

ANYWAY, SOMETHING *DID* HAPPEN. THEY'RE *FAXING* US THE POLICE REPORT.

≋MMMF≋

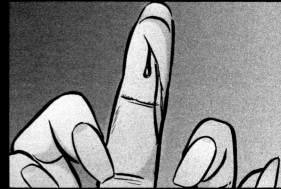

KRINK

FUCK.

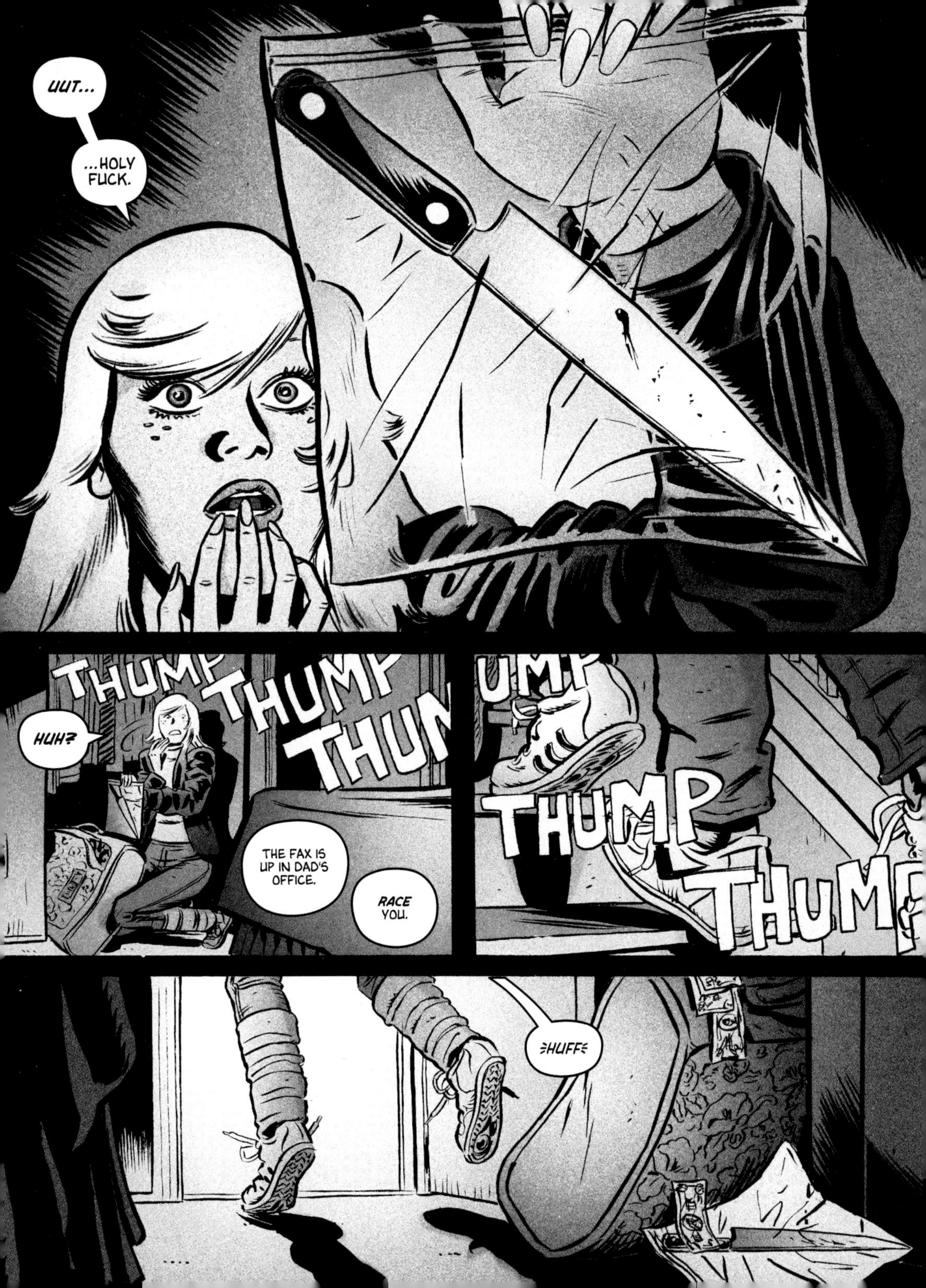
UUT...
...HOLY FUCK.
THUMP THUMP THUMP
HUH?
THE FAX IS UP IN DAD'S OFFICE.
RACE YOU.
THUMP THUMP
THUMP
THUMP
HUFF
...

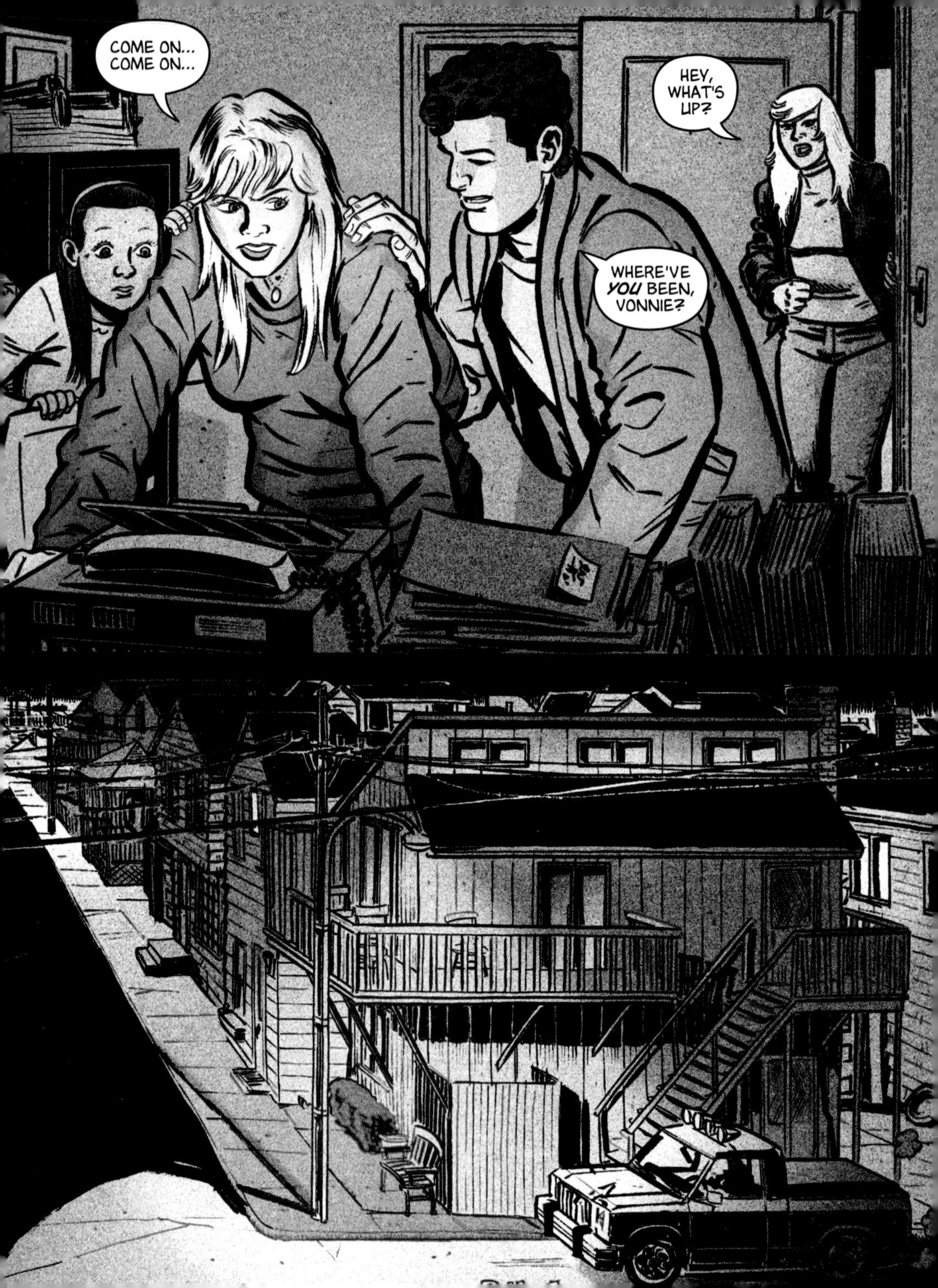
COME ON... COME ON...
HEY, WHAT'S UP?
WHERE'VE *YOU* BEEN, VONNIE?

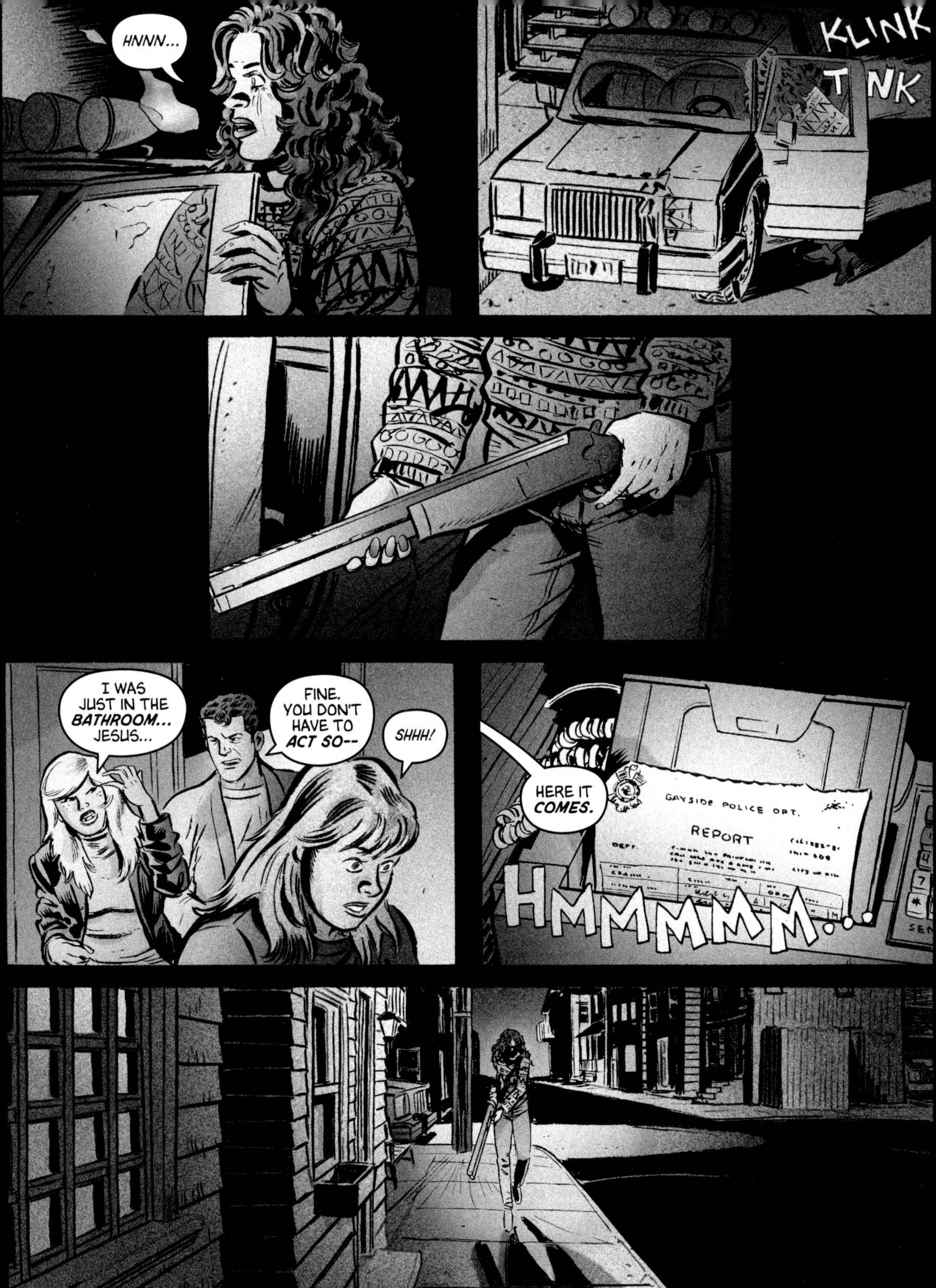
HNNN...
KLINK
TINK
I WAS JUST IN THE BATHROOM... JESUS...
FINE. YOU DON'T HAVE TO ACT SO--
SHHH!
HERE IT COMES.
GAYSIDE POLICE DPT.
REPORT
HMMMMM...

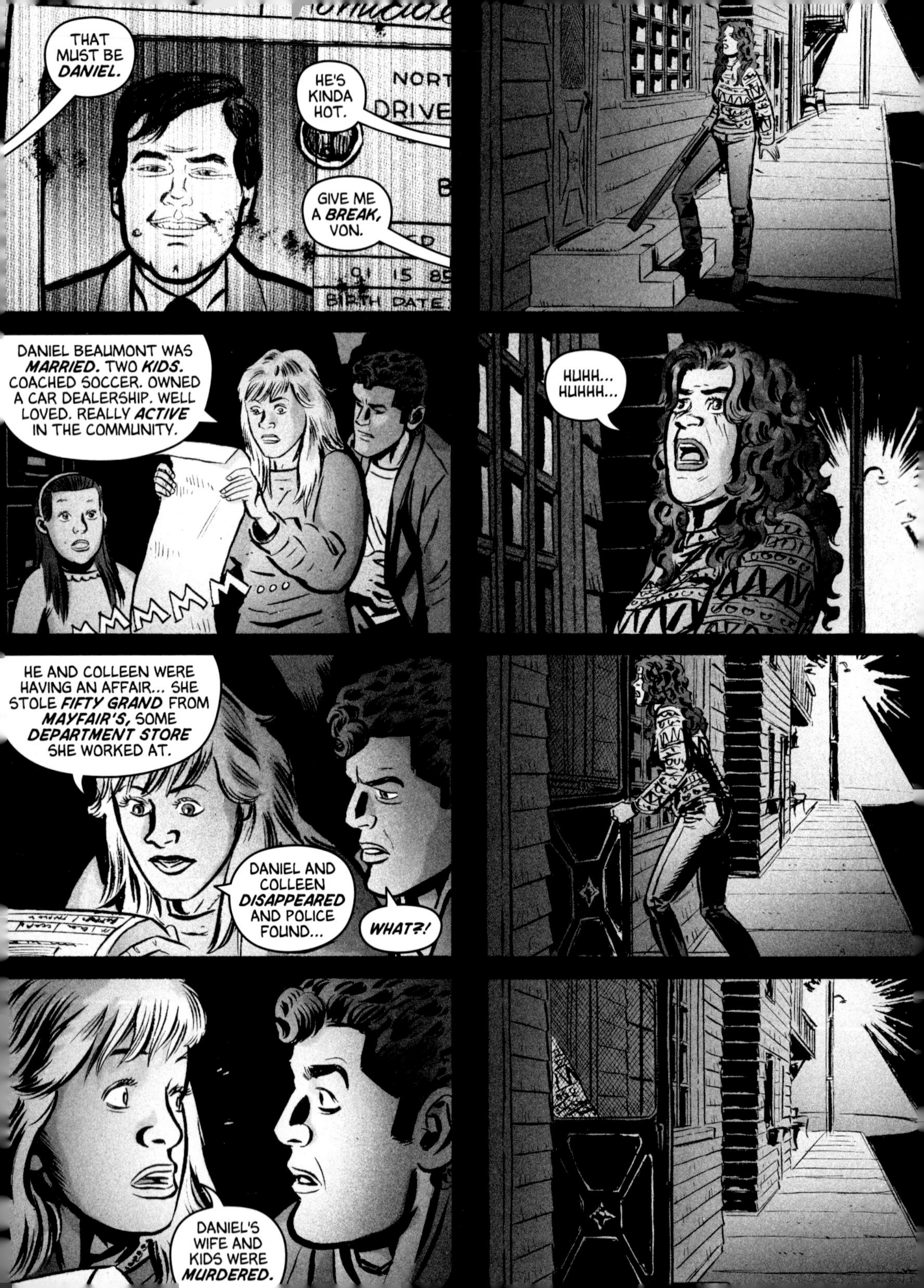

THAT MUST BE DANIEL.
HE'S KINDA HOT.
GIVE ME A BREAK, VON.
NORT
DRIVE
91 15 85
BIRTH DATE
DANIEL BEAUMONT WAS MARRIED. TWO KIDS. COACHED SOCCER. OWNED A CAR DEALERSHIP. WELL LOVED. REALLY ACTIVE IN THE COMMUNITY.
HUHH... HUHHH...
HE AND COLLEEN WERE HAVING AN AFFAIR... SHE STOLE FIFTY GRAND FROM MAYFAIR'S, SOME DEPARTMENT STORE SHE WORKED AT.
DANIEL AND COLLEEN DISAPPEARED AND POLICE FOUND...
WHAT?!
DANIEL'S WIFE AND KIDS WERE MURDERED.

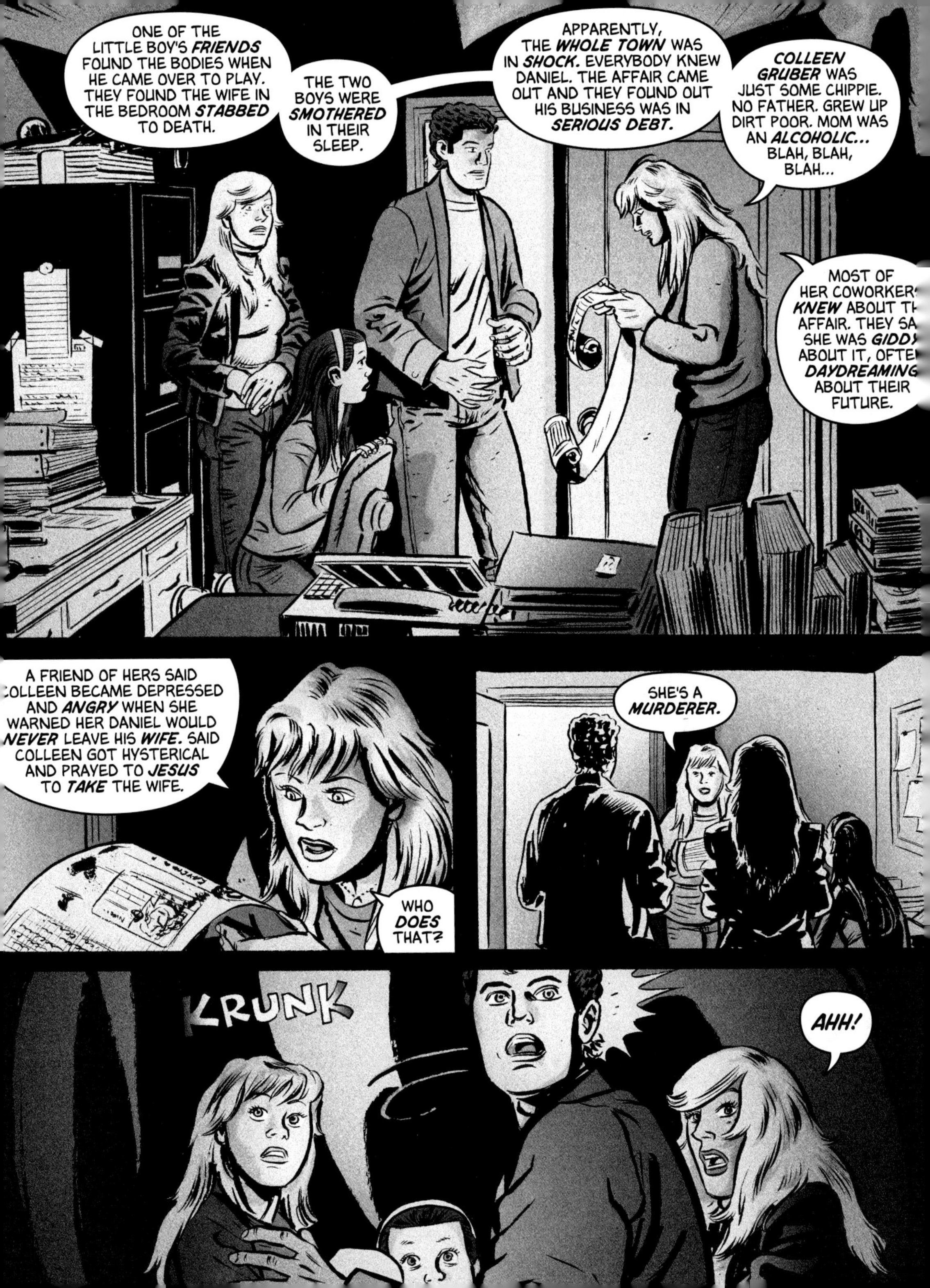
ONE OF THE LITTLE BOY'S FRIENDS FOUND THE BODIES WHEN HE CAME OVER TO PLAY. THEY FOUND THE WIFE IN THE BEDROOM STABBED TO DEATH.
THE TWO BOYS WERE SMOTHERED IN THEIR SLEEP.
APPARENTLY, THE WHOLE TOWN WAS IN SHOCK. EVERYBODY KNEW DANIEL. THE AFFAIR CAME OUT AND THEY FOUND OUT HIS BUSINESS WAS IN SERIOUS DEBT.
COLLEEN GRUBER WAS JUST SOME CHIPPIE. NO FATHER. GREW UP DIRT POOR. MOM WAS AN ALCOHOLIC... BLAH, BLAH, BLAH...
MOST OF HER COWORKERS KNEW ABOUT TH AFFAIR. THEY SA SHE WAS GIDDY ABOUT IT, OFTE DAYDREAMING ABOUT THEIR FUTURE.
A FRIEND OF HERS SAID COLLEEN BECAME DEPRESSED AND ANGRY WHEN SHE WARNED HER DANIEL WOULD NEVER LEAVE HIS WIFE. SAID COLLEEN GOT HYSTERICAL AND PRAYED TO JESUS TO TAKE THE WIFE.
WHO DOES THAT?
SHE'S A MURDERER.
KRUNK
AHH!

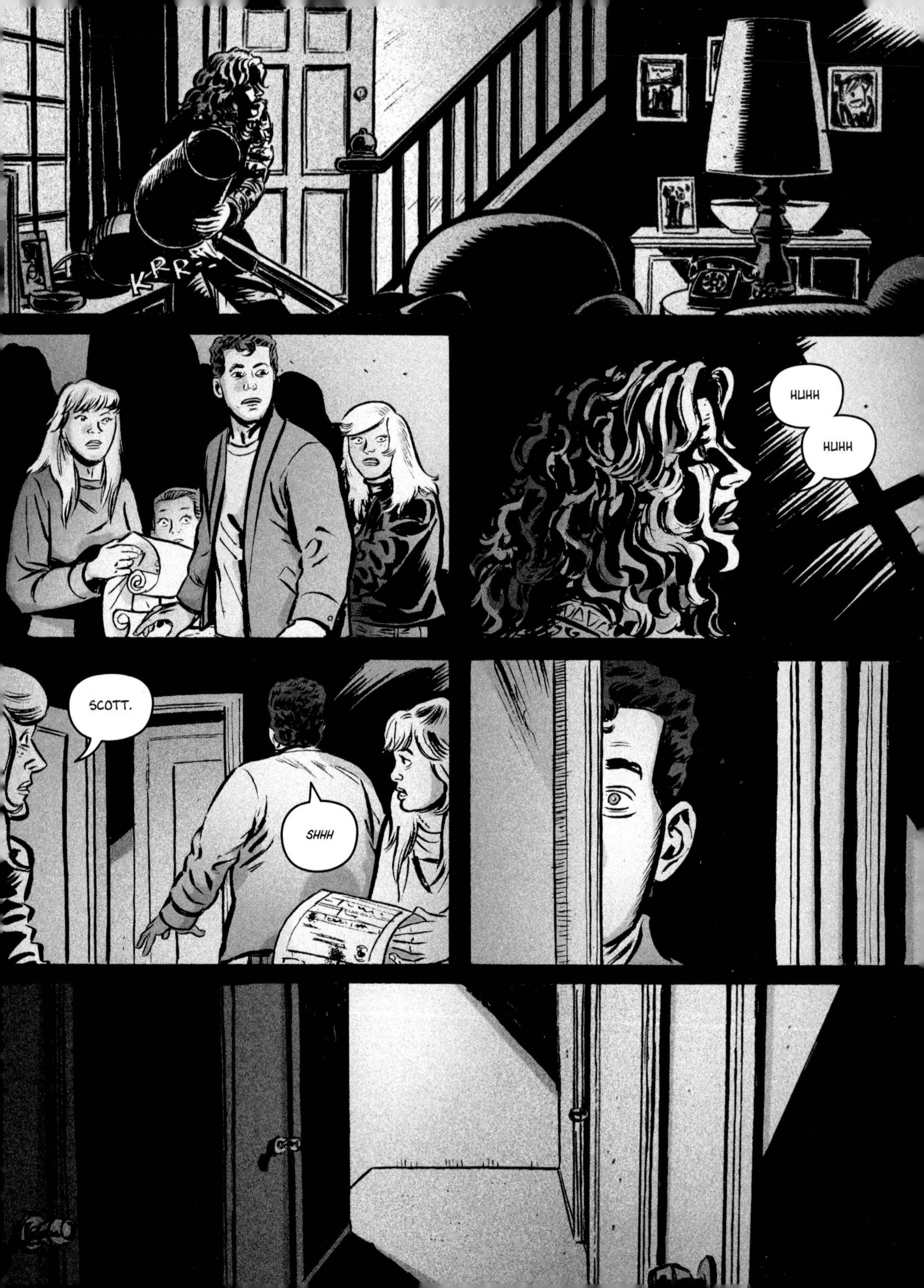
KRR--
HUHH
HUHH
SCOTT.
SHHH

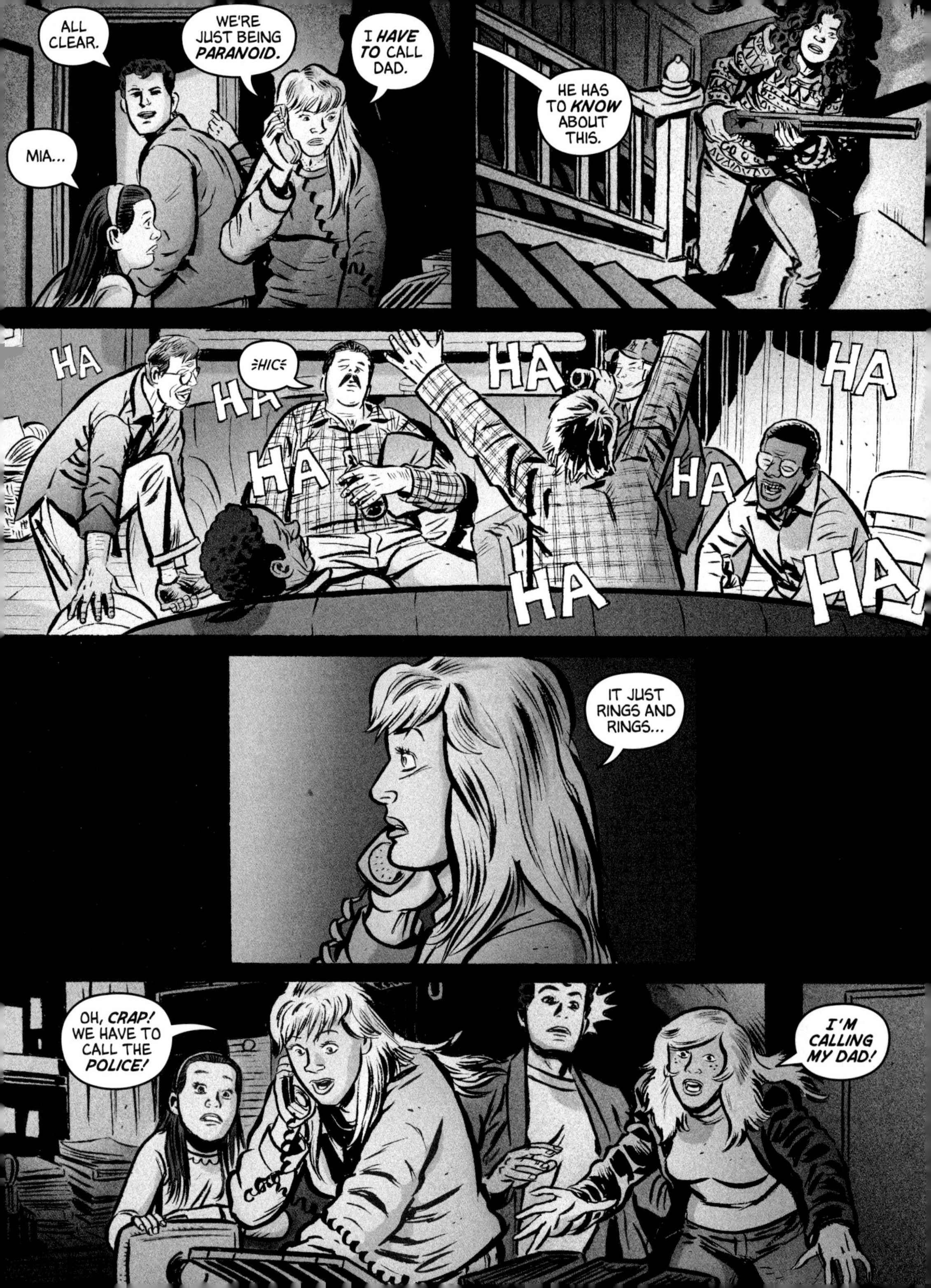

ALL CLEAR.
MIA...
WE'RE JUST BEING *PARANOID.*
I *HAVE TO* CALL DAD.
HE HAS TO *KNOW* ABOUT THIS.
HA
HA
HA
HIC
HA
HA
HA
HA
HA
IT JUST RINGS AND RINGS...
OH, *CRAP!* WE HAVE TO CALL THE *POLICE!*
I'M CALLING MY DAD!

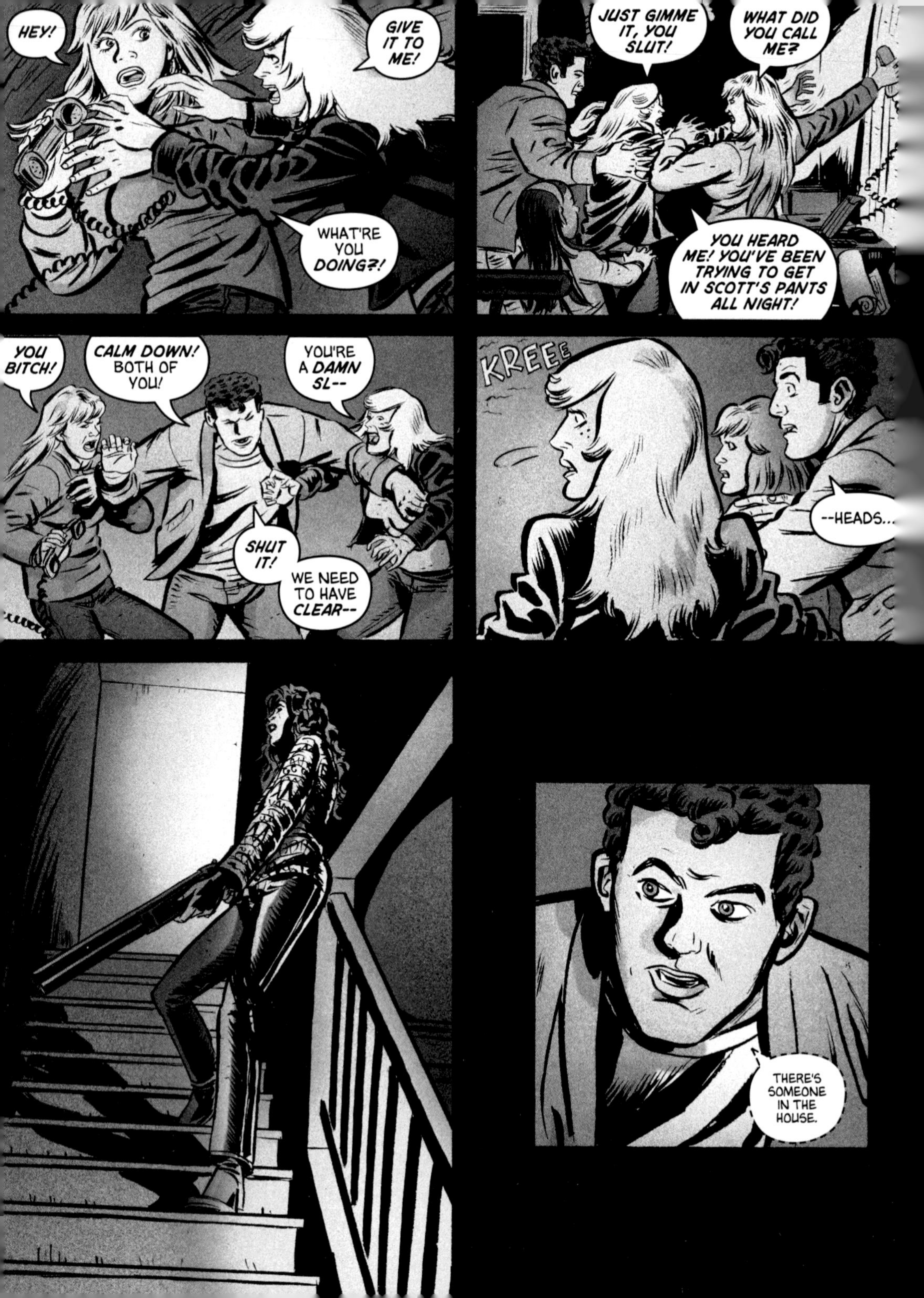
HEY!
GIVE IT TO ME!
WHAT'RE YOU DOING?!
JUST GIMME IT, YOU SLUT!
WHAT DID YOU CALL ME?
YOU HEARD ME! YOU'VE BEEN TRYING TO GET IN SCOTT'S PANTS ALL NIGHT!
YOU BITCH!
CALM DOWN! BOTH OF YOU!
YOU'RE A DAMN SL--
SHUT IT!
WE NEED TO HAVE CLEAR--
KREEE
--HEADS...
THERE'S SOMEONE IN THE HOUSE.

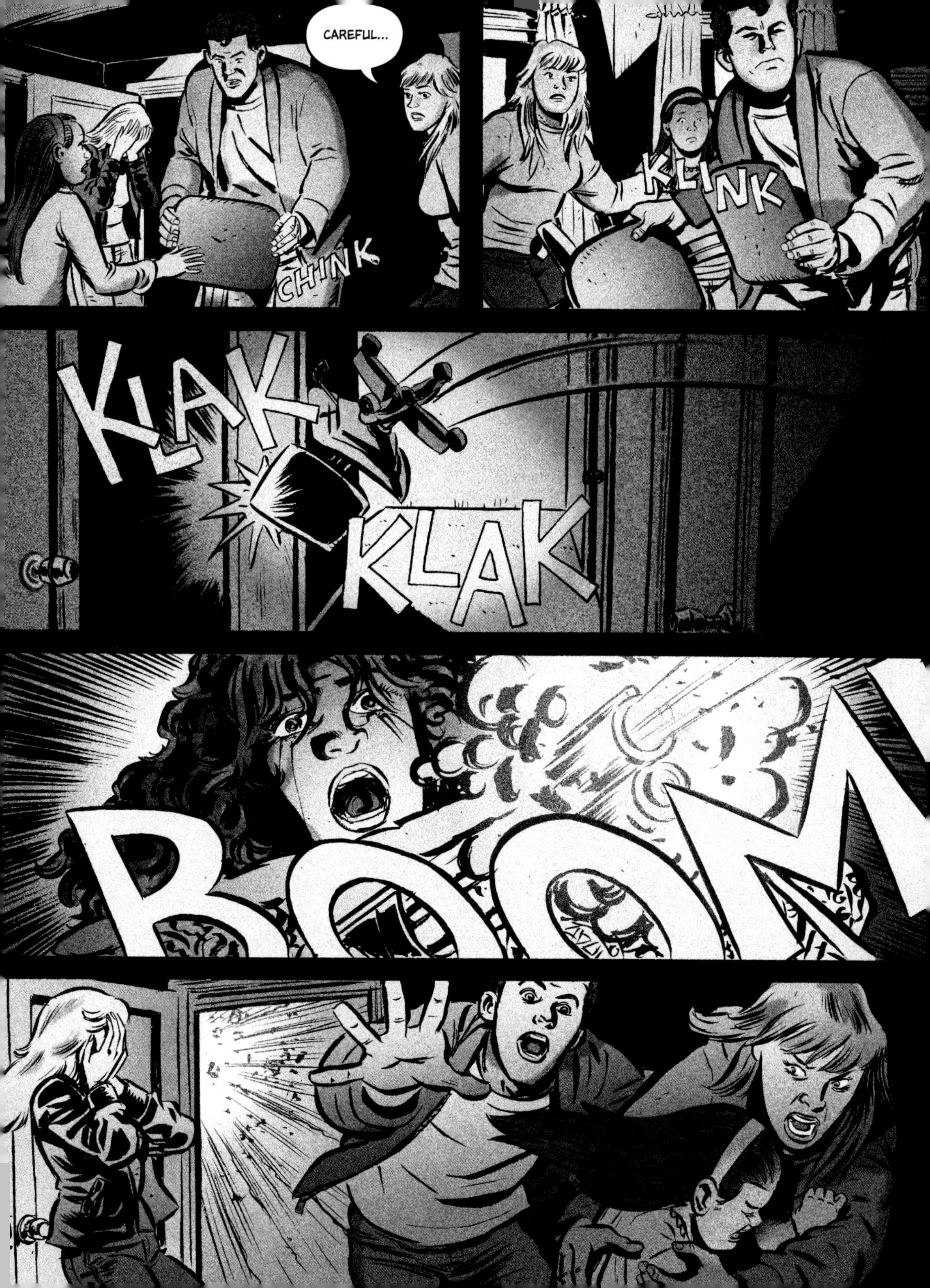
CAREFUL...
CHINK
KLINK
KLAK
KLAK
BOOM

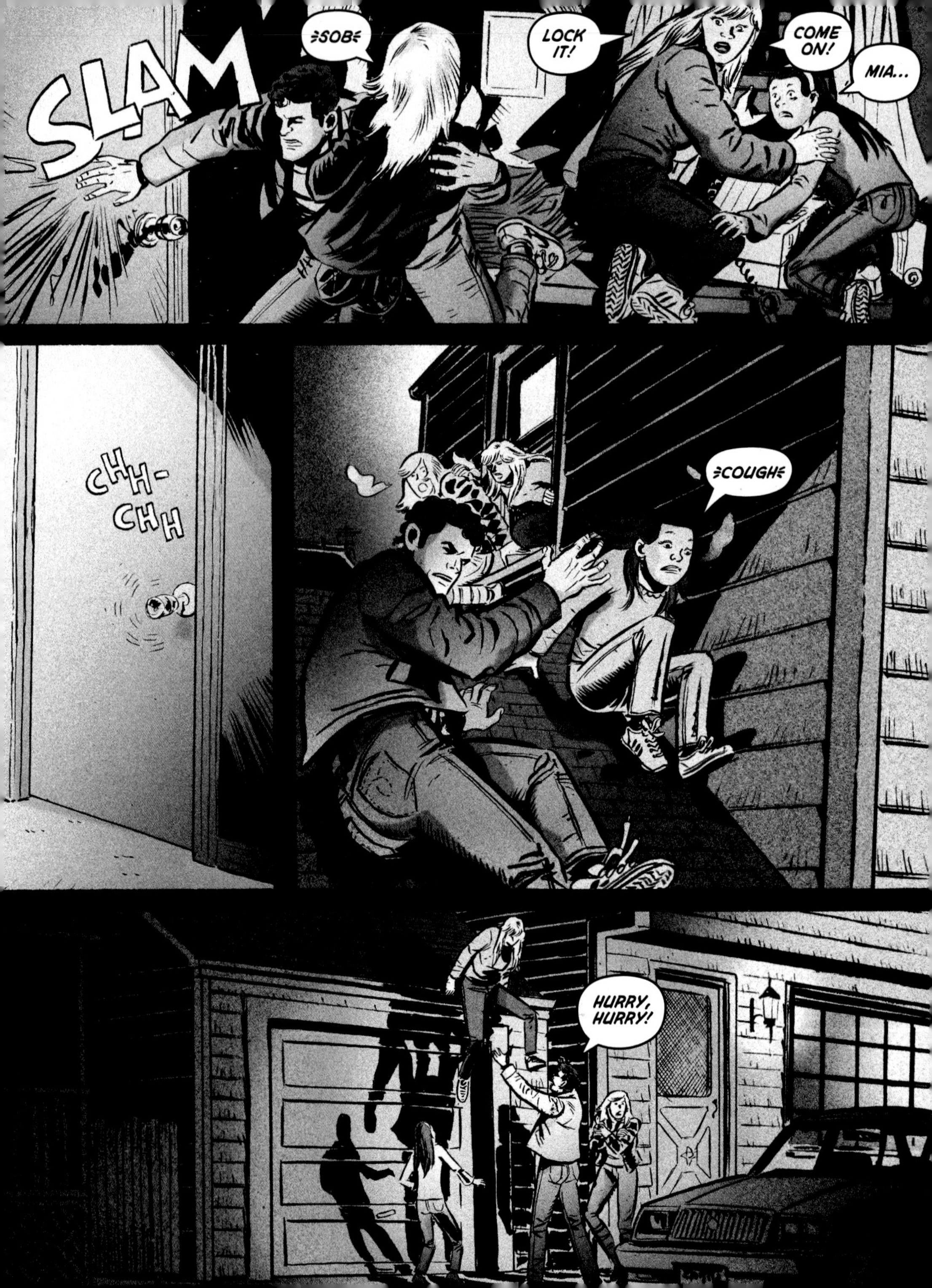
SLAM
SOB
LOCK IT!
COME ON!
MIA...
CHH-CHH
COUGH
HURRY, HURRY!

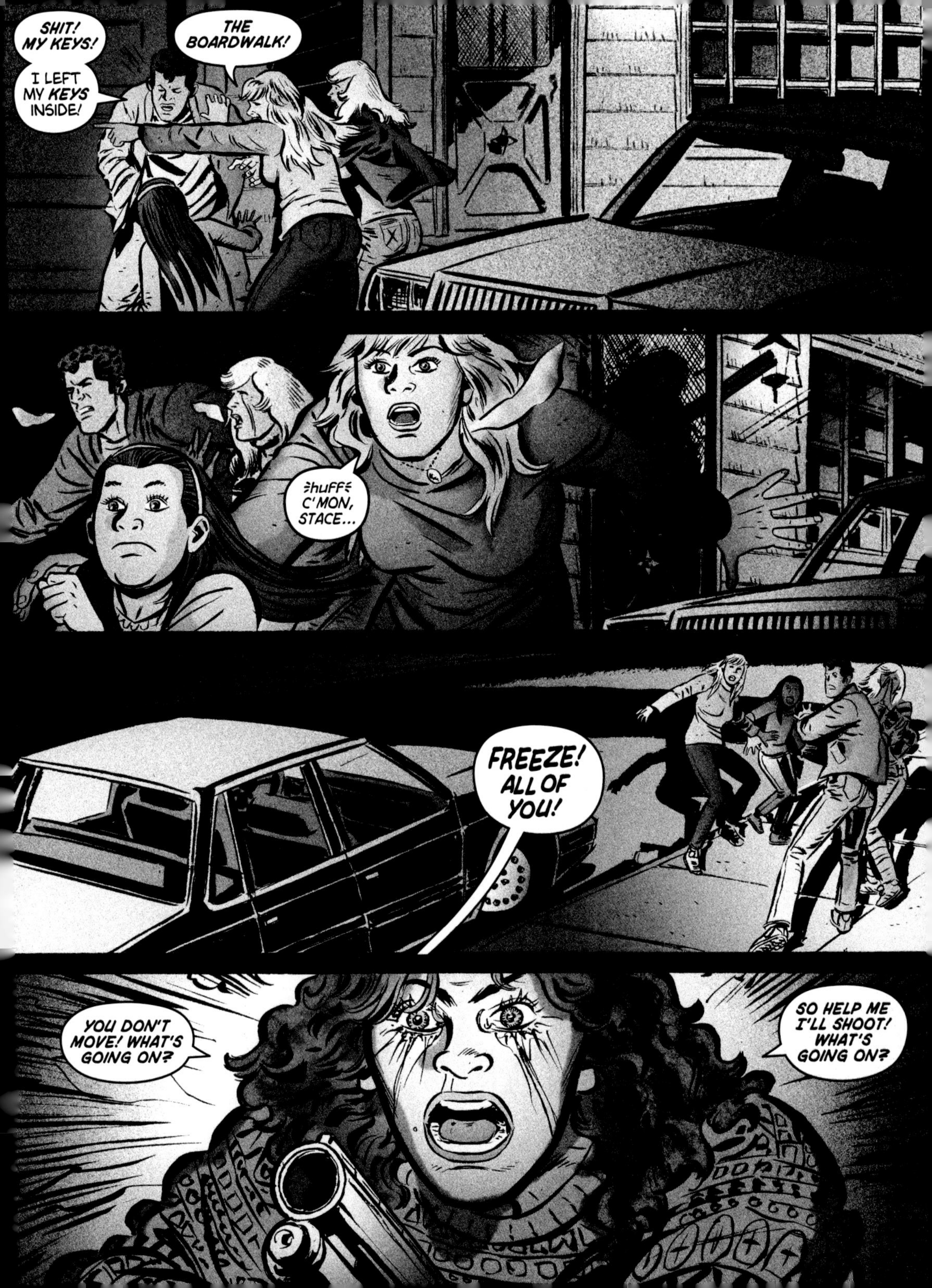
SHIT! MY KEYS!
I LEFT MY KEYS INSIDE!
THE BOARDWALK!
huff C'MON, STACE...
FREEZE! ALL OF YOU!
YOU DON'T MOVE! WHAT'S GOING ON?
SO HELP ME I'LL SHOOT! WHAT'S GOING ON?

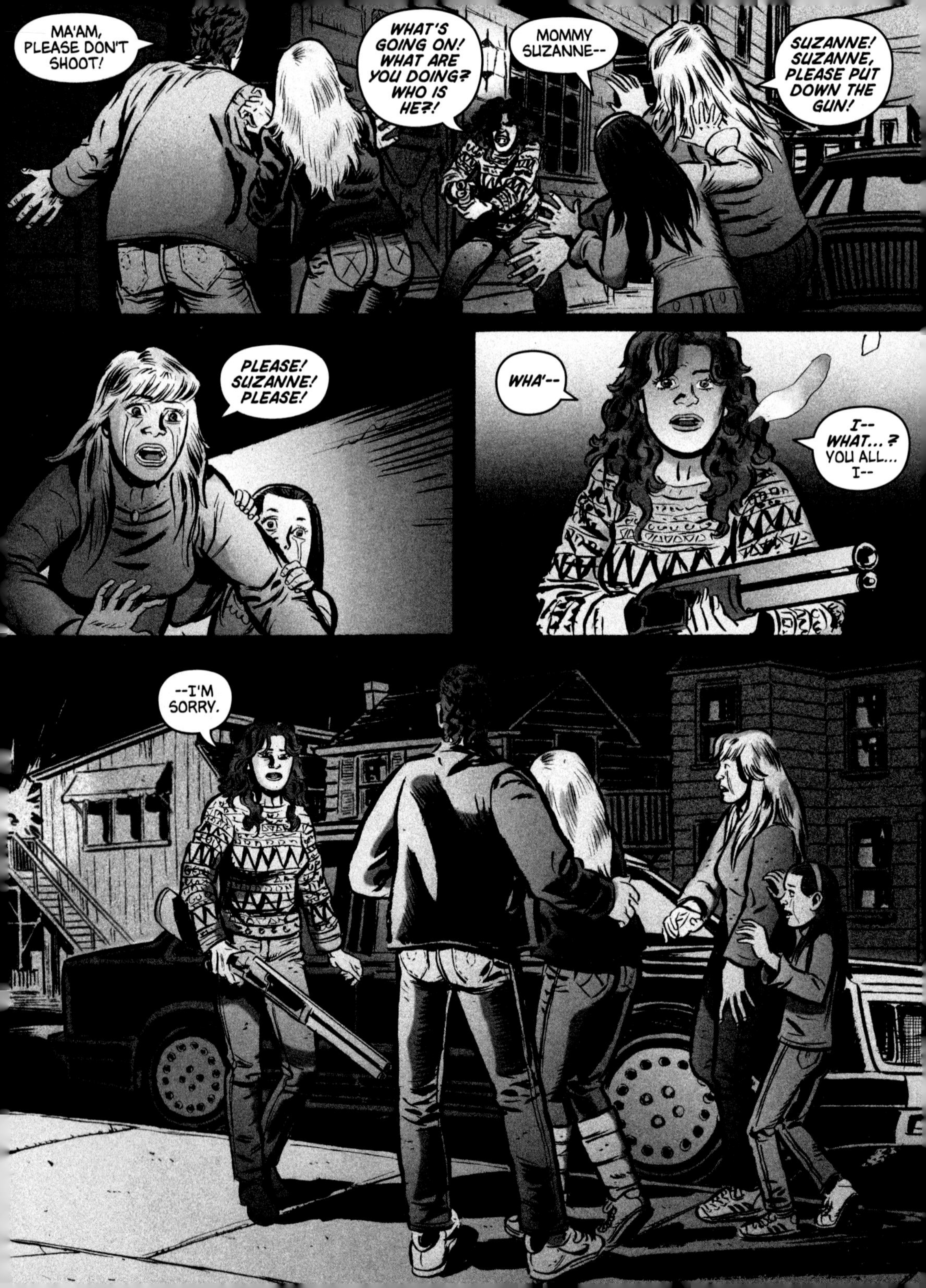
MA'AM, PLEASE DON'T SHOOT!
WHAT'S GOING ON! WHAT ARE YOU DOING? WHO IS HE?!
MOMMY SUZANNE--
SUZANNE! SUZANNE, PLEASE PUT DOWN THE GUN!
PLEASE! SUZANNE! PLEASE!
WHA'--
I-- WHAT...? YOU ALL... I--
--I'M SORRY.

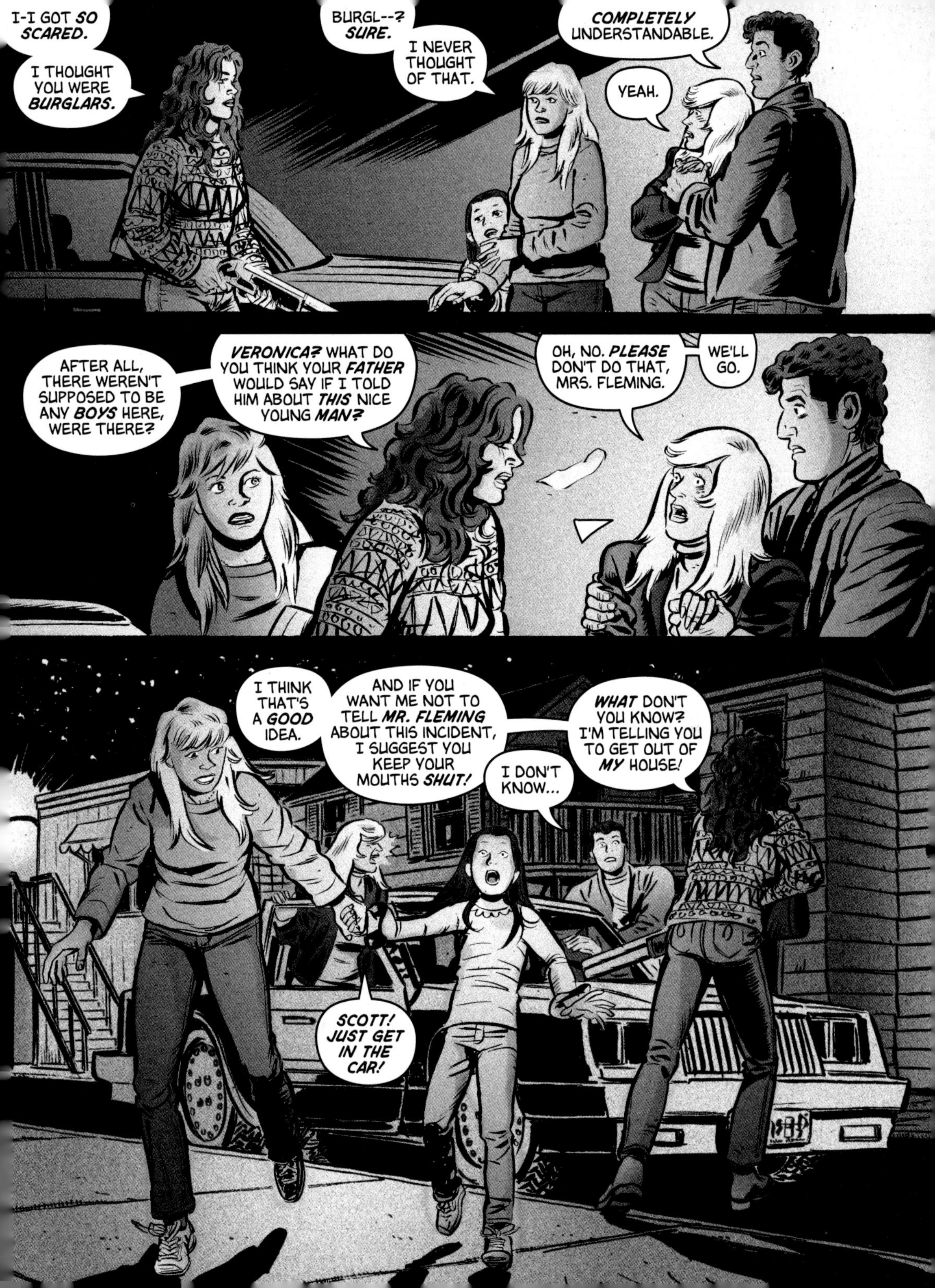
I-I GOT SO SCARED.
I THOUGHT YOU WERE BURGLARS.
BURGL--? SURE.
I NEVER THOUGHT OF THAT.
COMPLETELY UNDERSTANDABLE.
YEAH.
AFTER ALL, THERE WEREN'T SUPPOSED TO BE ANY BOYS HERE, WERE THERE?
VERONICA? WHAT DO YOU THINK YOUR FATHER WOULD SAY IF I TOLD HIM ABOUT THIS NICE YOUNG MAN?
OH, NO. PLEASE DON'T DO THAT, MRS. FLEMING.
WE'LL GO.
I THINK THAT'S A GOOD IDEA.
AND IF YOU WANT ME NOT TO TELL MR. FLEMING ABOUT THIS INCIDENT, I SUGGEST YOU KEEP YOUR MOUTHS SHUT!
I DON'T KNOW...
WHAT DON'T YOU KNOW? I'M TELLING YOU TO GET OUT OF MY HOUSE!
SCOTT! JUST GET IN THE CAR!

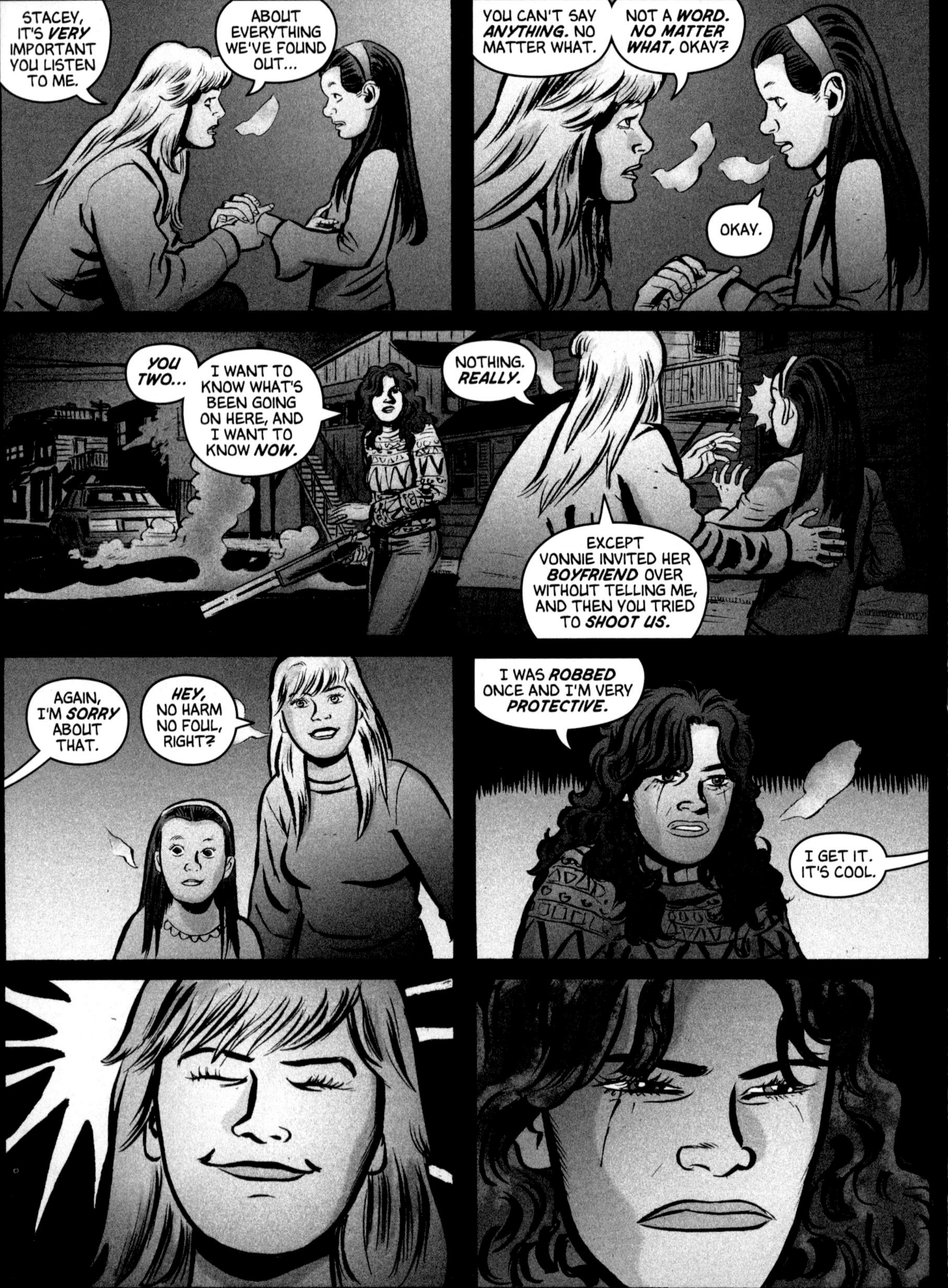
STACEY, IT'S VERY IMPORTANT YOU LISTEN TO ME.
ABOUT EVERYTHING WE'VE FOUND OUT...
YOU CAN'T SAY ANYTHING. NO MATTER WHAT.
NOT A WORD. NO MATTER WHAT, OKAY?
OKAY.
YOU TWO...
I WANT TO KNOW WHAT'S BEEN GOING ON HERE, AND I WANT TO KNOW NOW.
NOTHING. REALLY.
EXCEPT VONNIE INVITED HER BOYFRIEND OVER WITHOUT TELLING ME, AND THEN YOU TRIED TO SHOOT US.
AGAIN, I'M SORRY ABOUT THAT.
HEY, NO HARM NO FOUL, RIGHT?
I WAS ROBBED ONCE AND I'M VERY PROTECTIVE.
I GET IT. IT'S COOL.

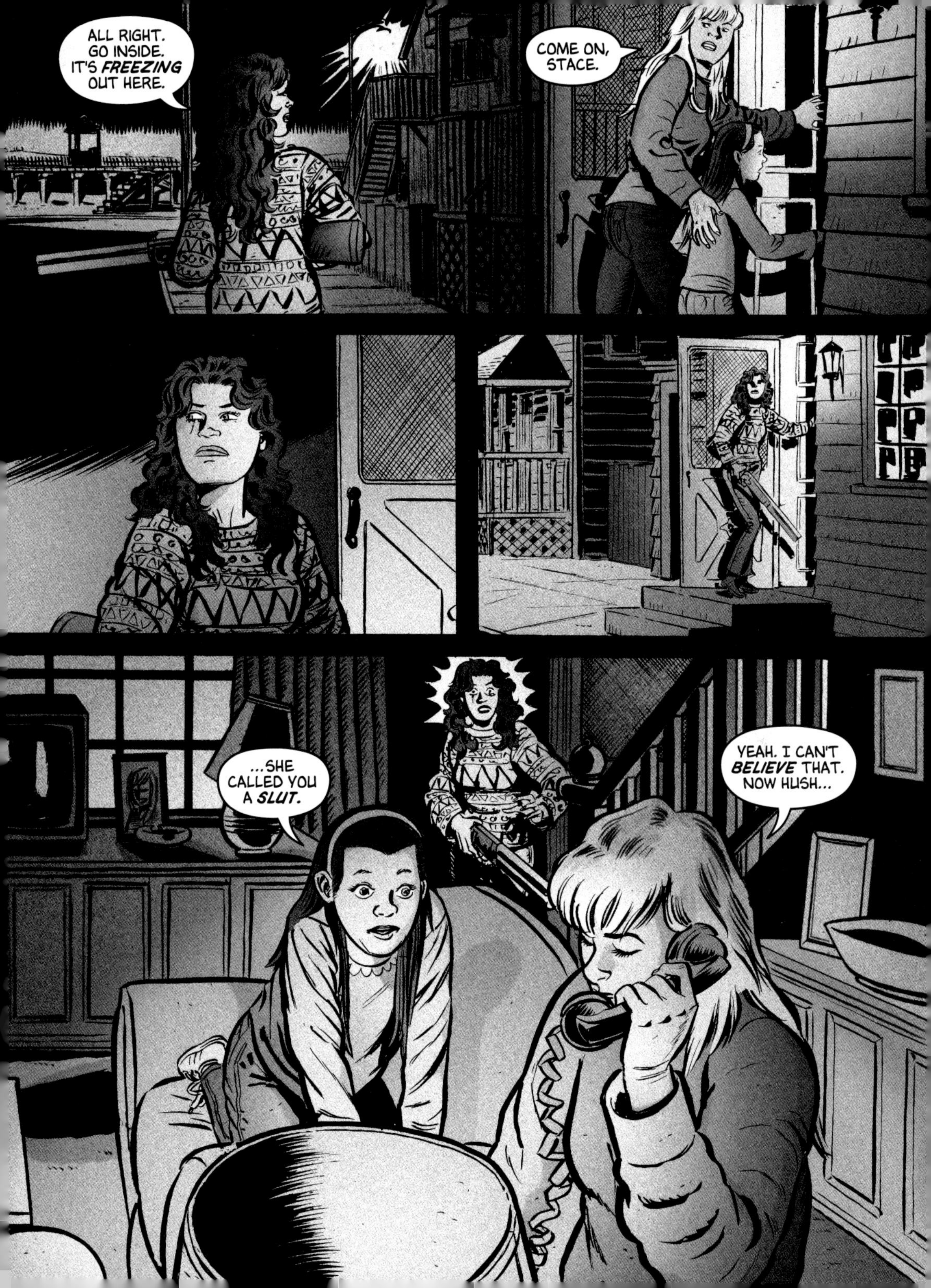
ALL RIGHT. GO INSIDE. IT'S *FREEZING* OUT HERE.
COME ON, STACE.
...SHE CALLED YOU A *SLUT.*
YEAH. I CAN'T *BELIEVE* THAT. NOW HUSH...

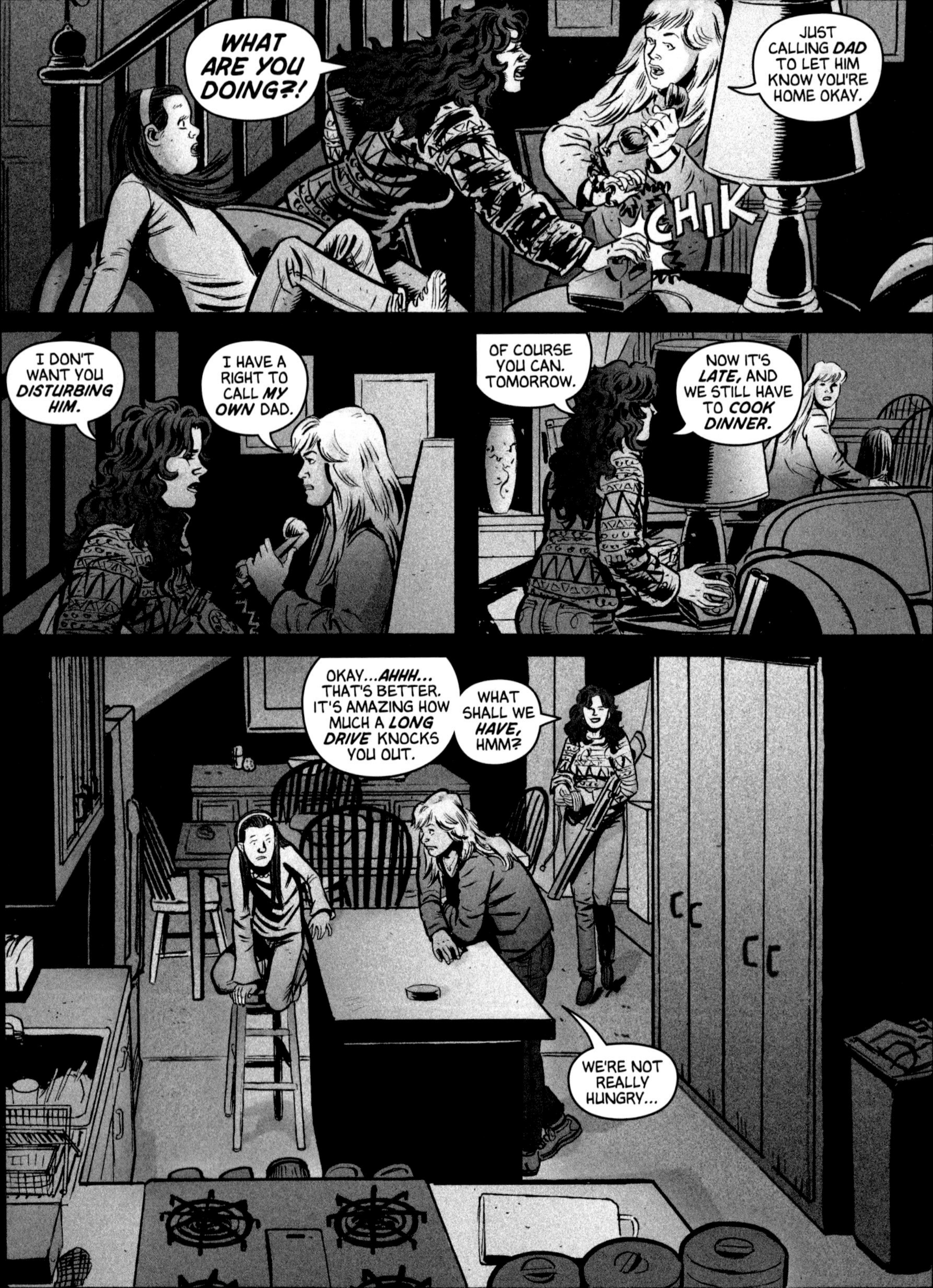
WHAT ARE YOU DOING?!
JUST CALLING DAD TO LET HIM KNOW YOU'RE HOME OKAY.
CHIK
I DON'T WANT YOU DISTURBING HIM.
I HAVE A RIGHT TO CALL MY OWN DAD.
OF COURSE YOU CAN. TOMORROW.
NOW IT'S LATE, AND WE STILL HAVE TO COOK DINNER.
OKAY...AHHH... THAT'S BETTER. IT'S AMAZING HOW MUCH A LONG DRIVE KNOCKS YOU OUT.
WHAT SHALL WE HAVE, HMM?
WE'RE NOT REALLY HUNGRY...

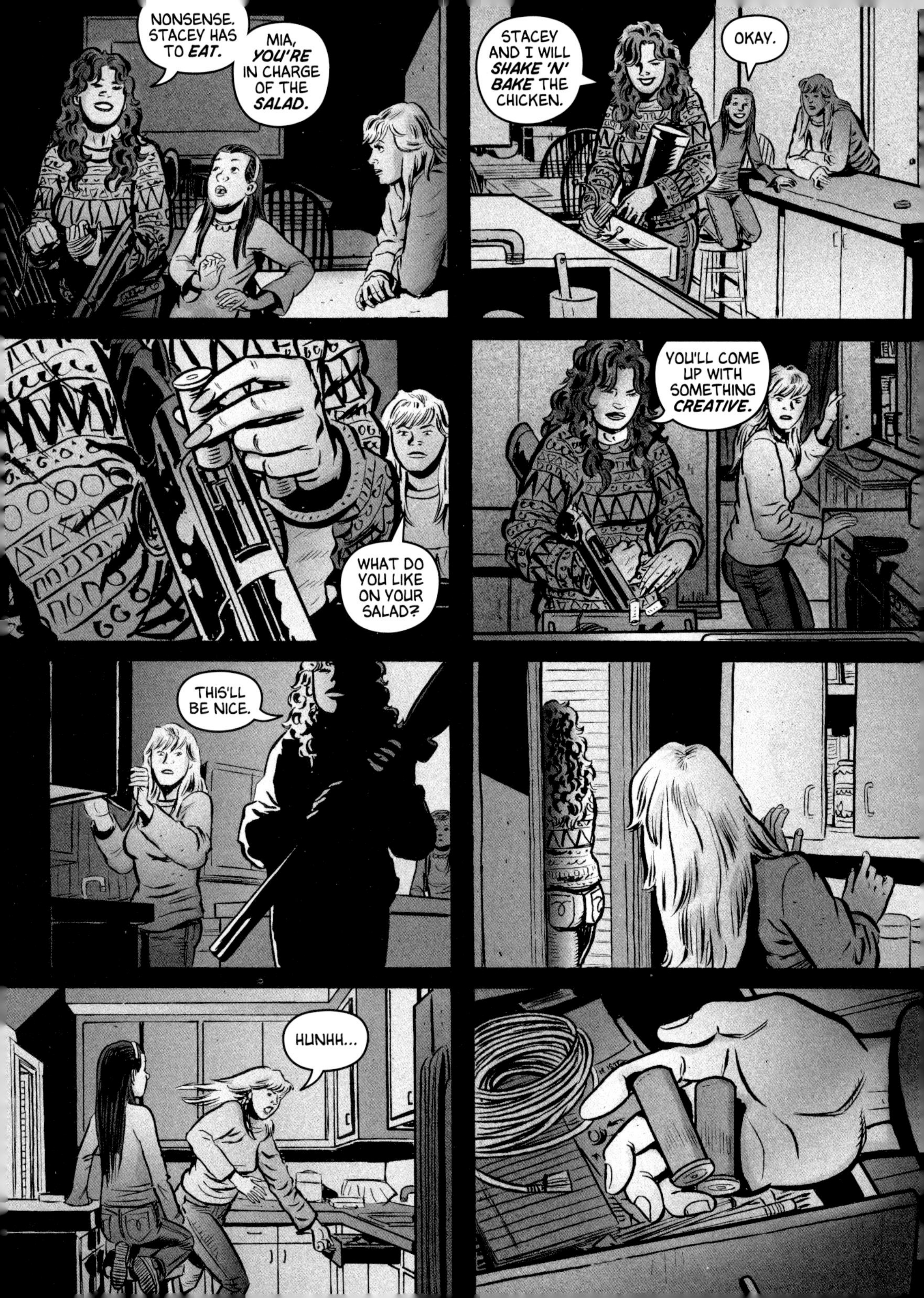
NONSENSE. STACEY HAS TO EAT.
MIA, YOU'RE IN CHARGE OF THE SALAD.
STACEY AND I WILL SHAKE 'N' BAKE THE CHICKEN.
OKAY.
WHAT DO YOU LIKE ON YOUR SALAD?
YOU'LL COME UP WITH SOMETHING CREATIVE.
THIS'LL BE NICE.
HUNHH...

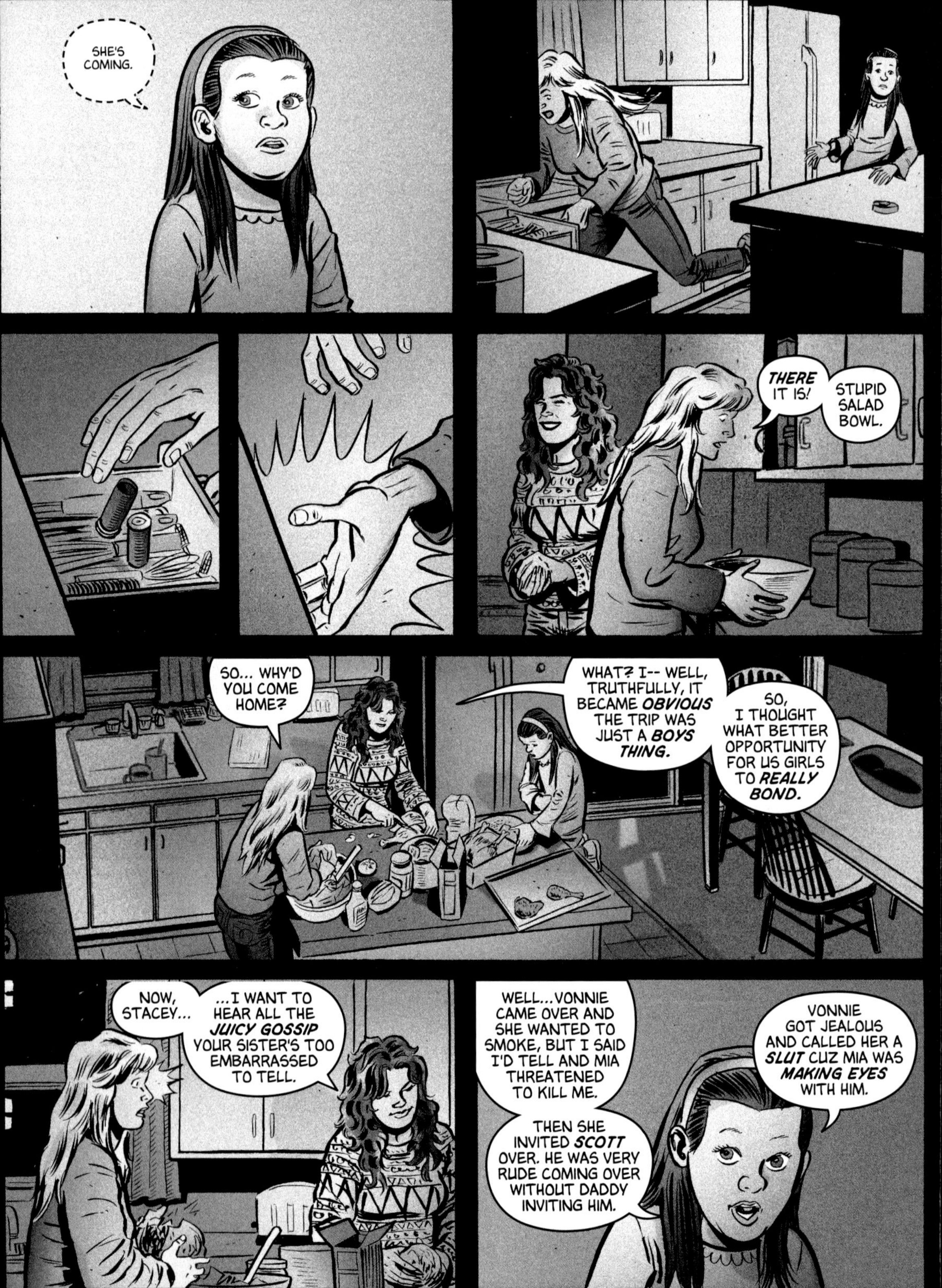
SHE'S COMING.
THERE IT IS!
STUPID SALAD BOWL.
SO... WHY'D YOU COME HOME?
WHAT? I-- WELL, TRUTHFULLY, IT BECAME OBVIOUS THE TRIP WAS JUST A BOYS THING.
SO, I THOUGHT WHAT BETTER OPPORTUNITY FOR US GIRLS TO REALLY BOND.
NOW, STACEY...
...I WANT TO HEAR ALL THE JUICY GOSSIP YOUR SISTER'S TOO EMBARRASSED TO TELL.
WELL...VONNIE CAME OVER AND SHE WANTED TO SMOKE, BUT I SAID I'D TELL AND MIA THREATENED TO KILL ME.
THEN SHE INVITED SCOTT OVER. HE WAS VERY RUDE COMING OVER WITHOUT DADDY INVITING HIM.
VONNIE GOT JEALOUS AND CALLED HER A SLUT CUZ MIA WAS MAKING EYES WITH HIM.

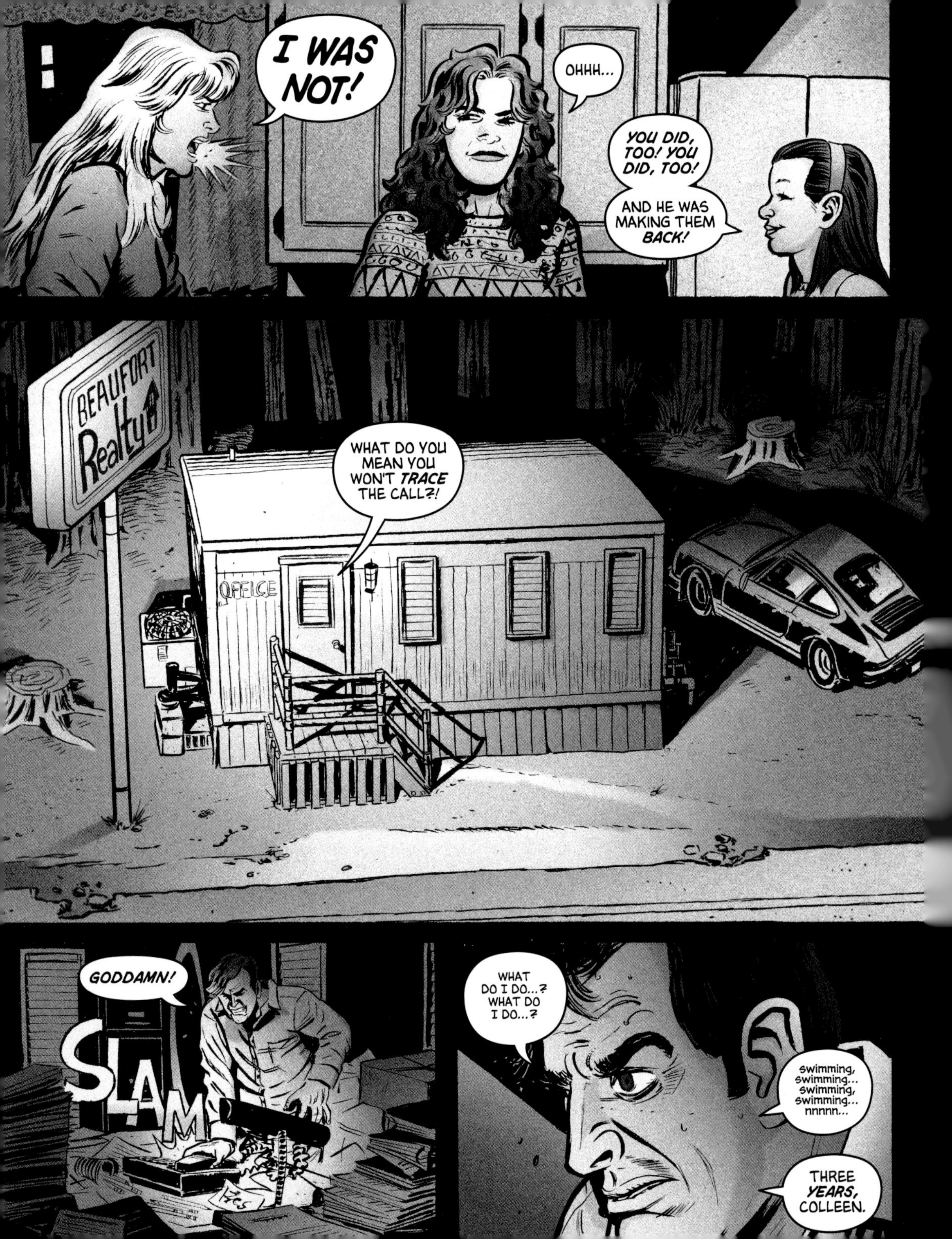
I WAS NOT!
OHHH...
YOU DID, TOO! YOU DID, TOO!
AND HE WAS MAKING THEM BACK!
BEAUFORT Realty
WHAT DO YOU MEAN YOU WON'T TRACE THE CALL?!
OFFICE
GODDAMN!
SLAM
WHAT DO I DO...? WHAT DO I DO...?
swimming, swimming... swimming, swimming... nnnnn...
THREE YEARS, COLLEEN.

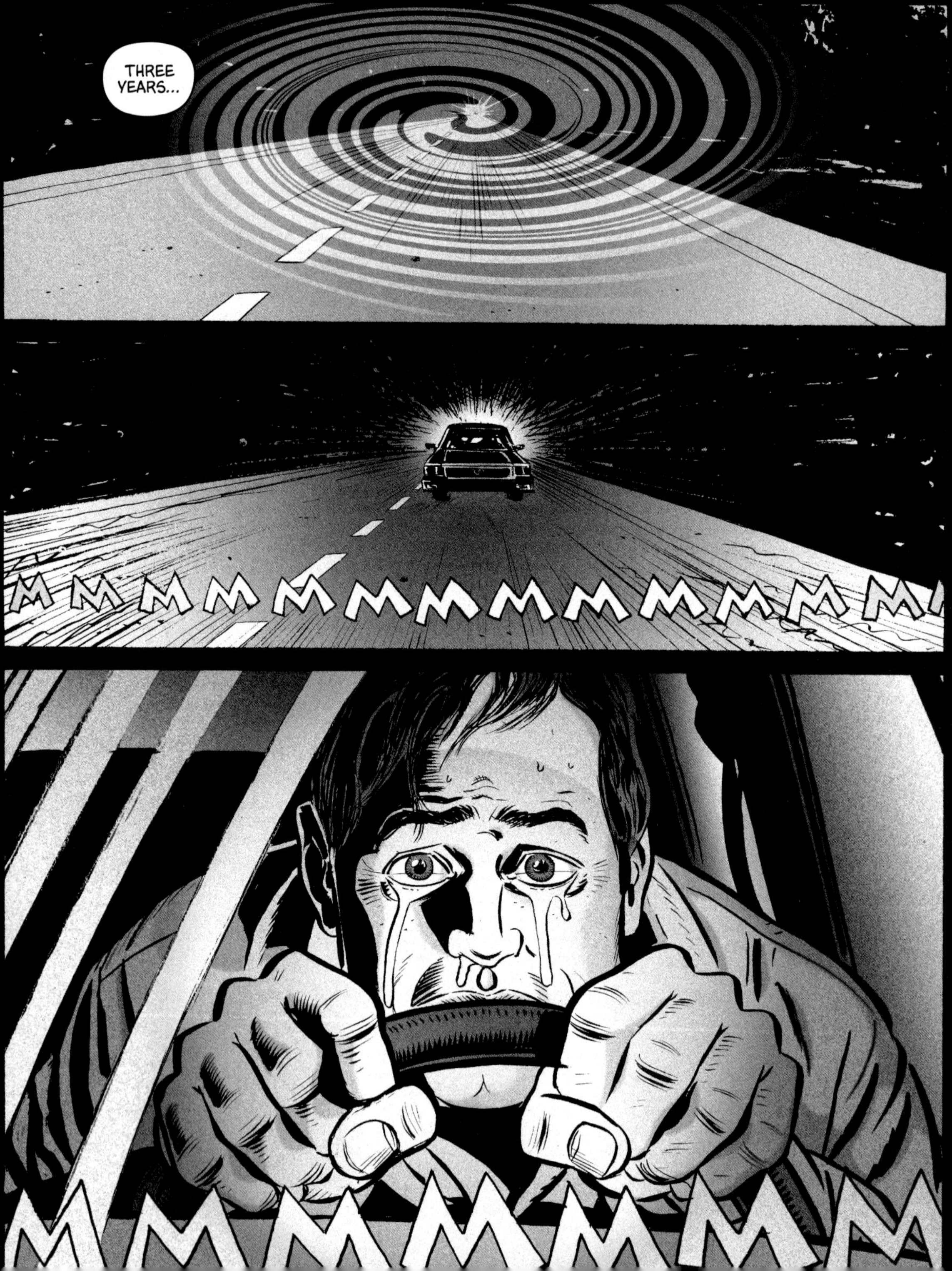

THREE YEARS...
MMMMMMMMMMMMM
MMMMMMM

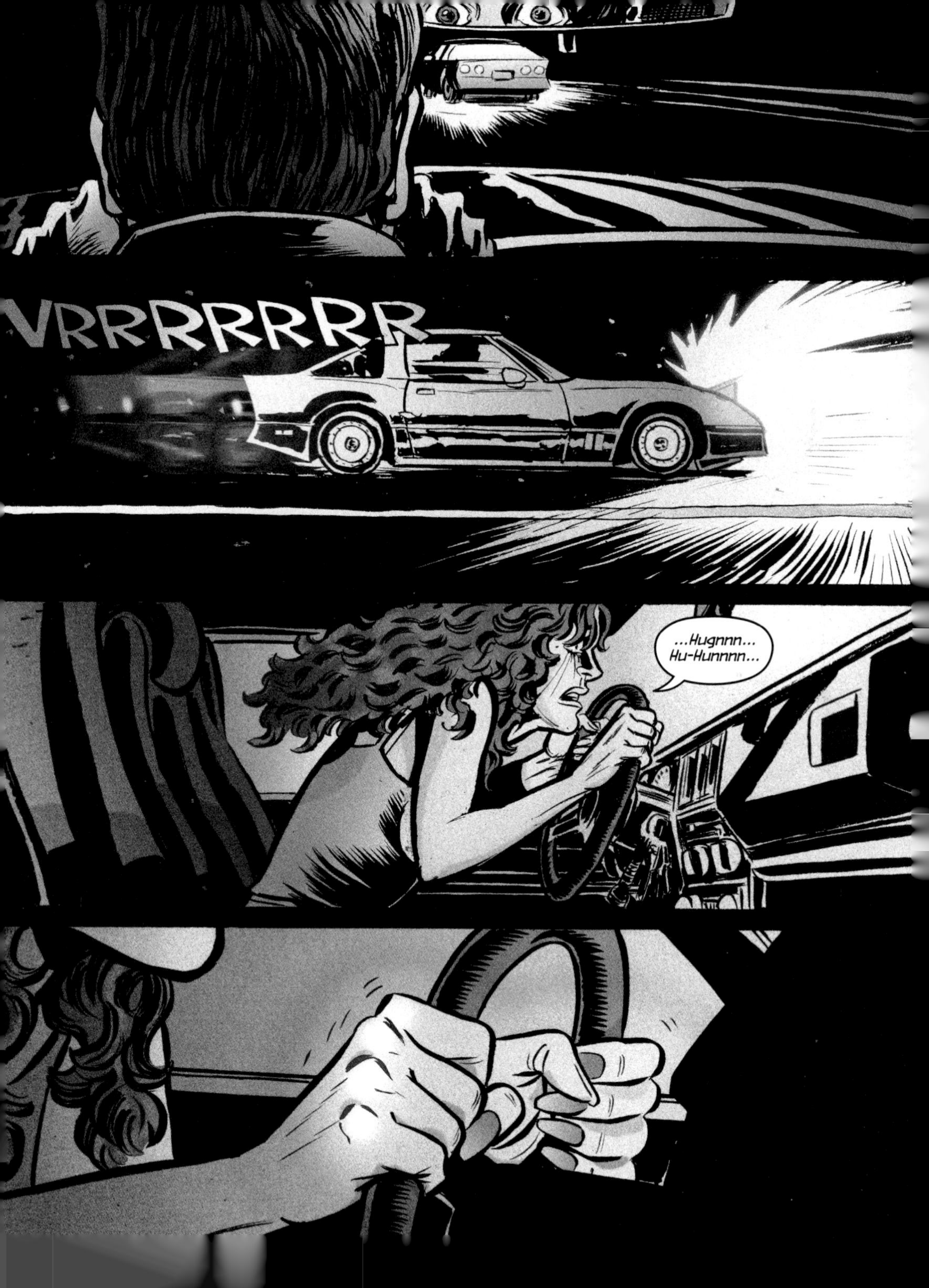
VRRRRRRR
...Hugnnn...
Hu-Hunnnn...

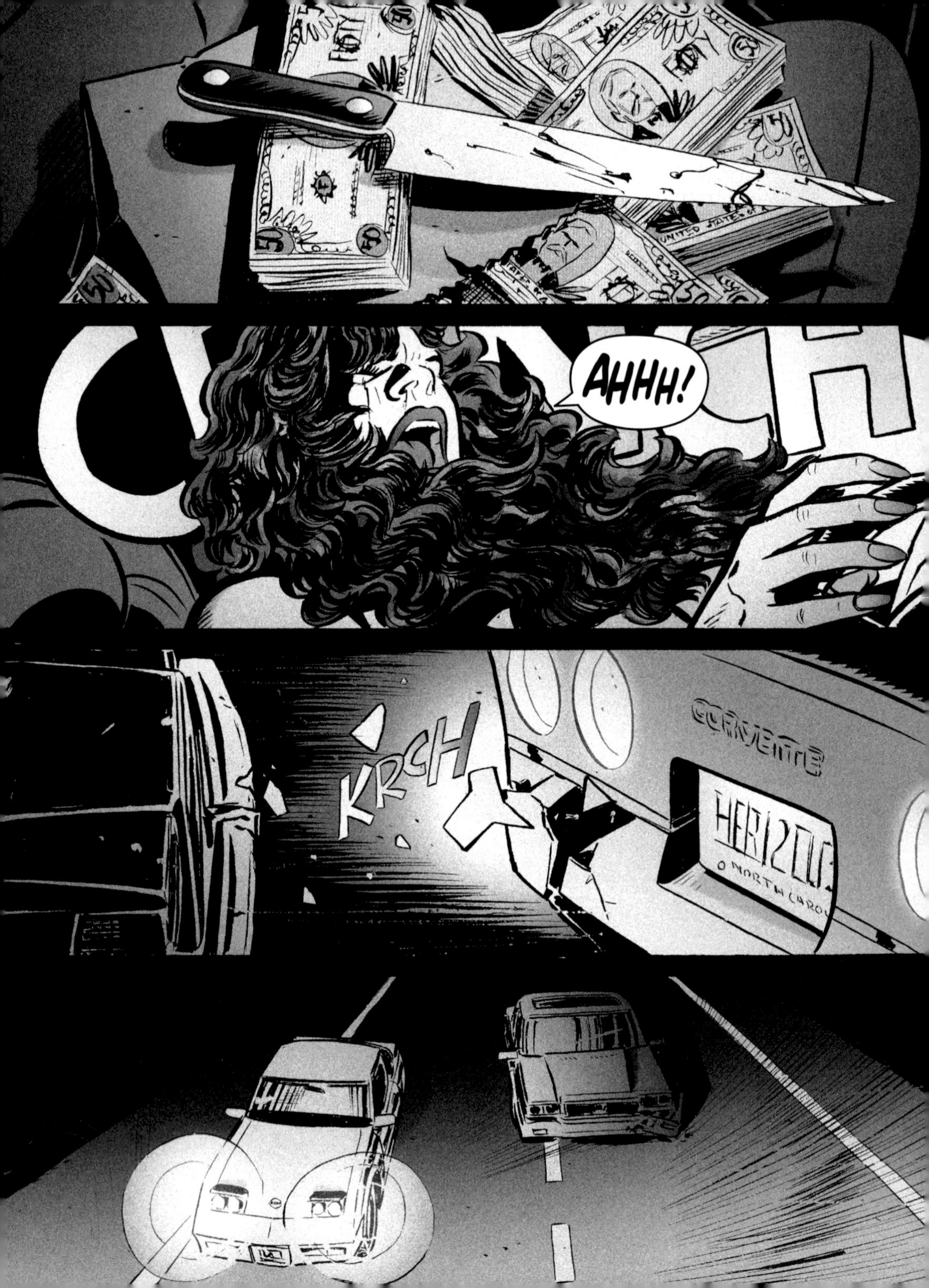
AHHH!
KRCH

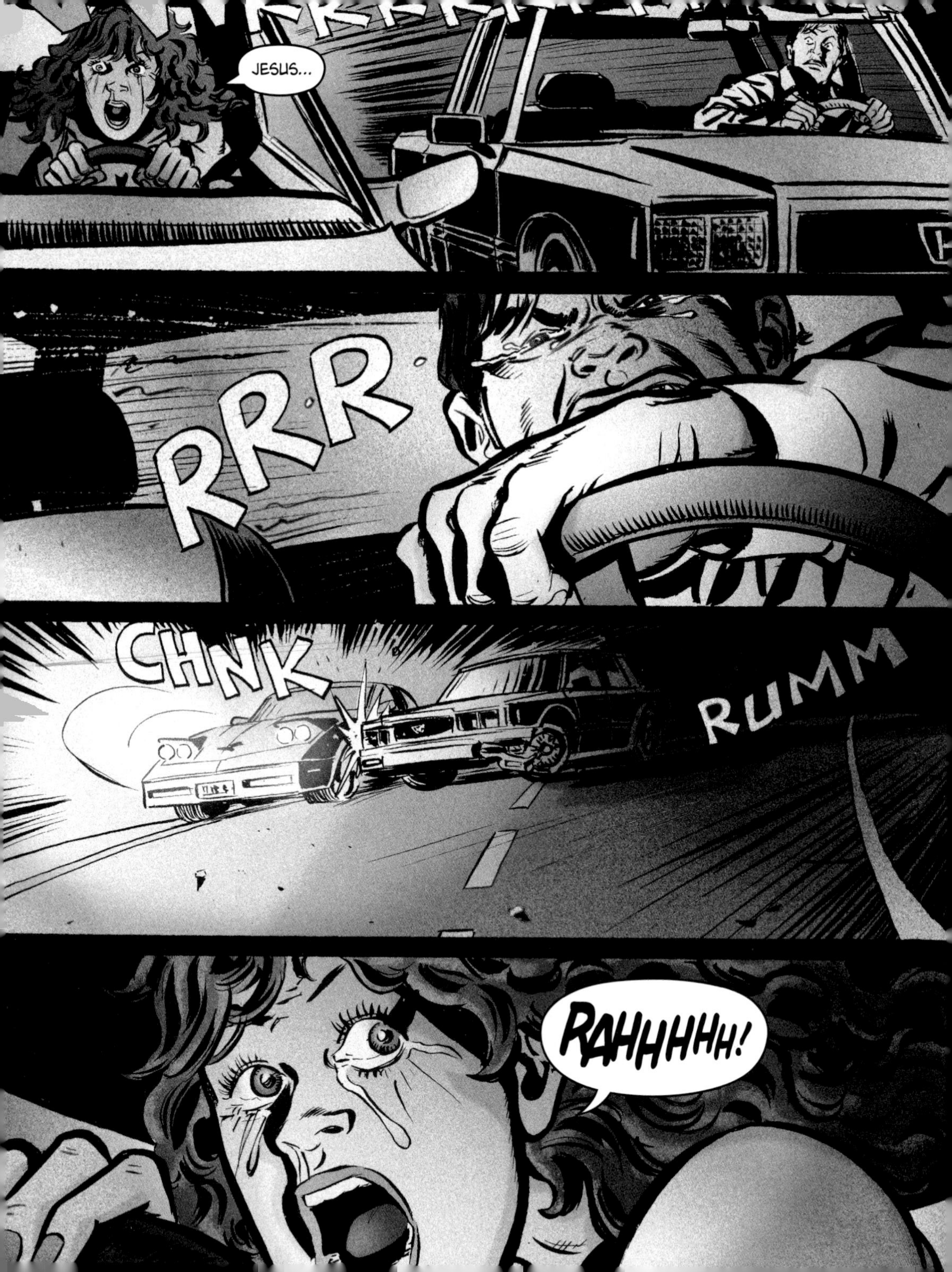
JESUS...
RRR
CHNK
RUMM
RAHHHHH!

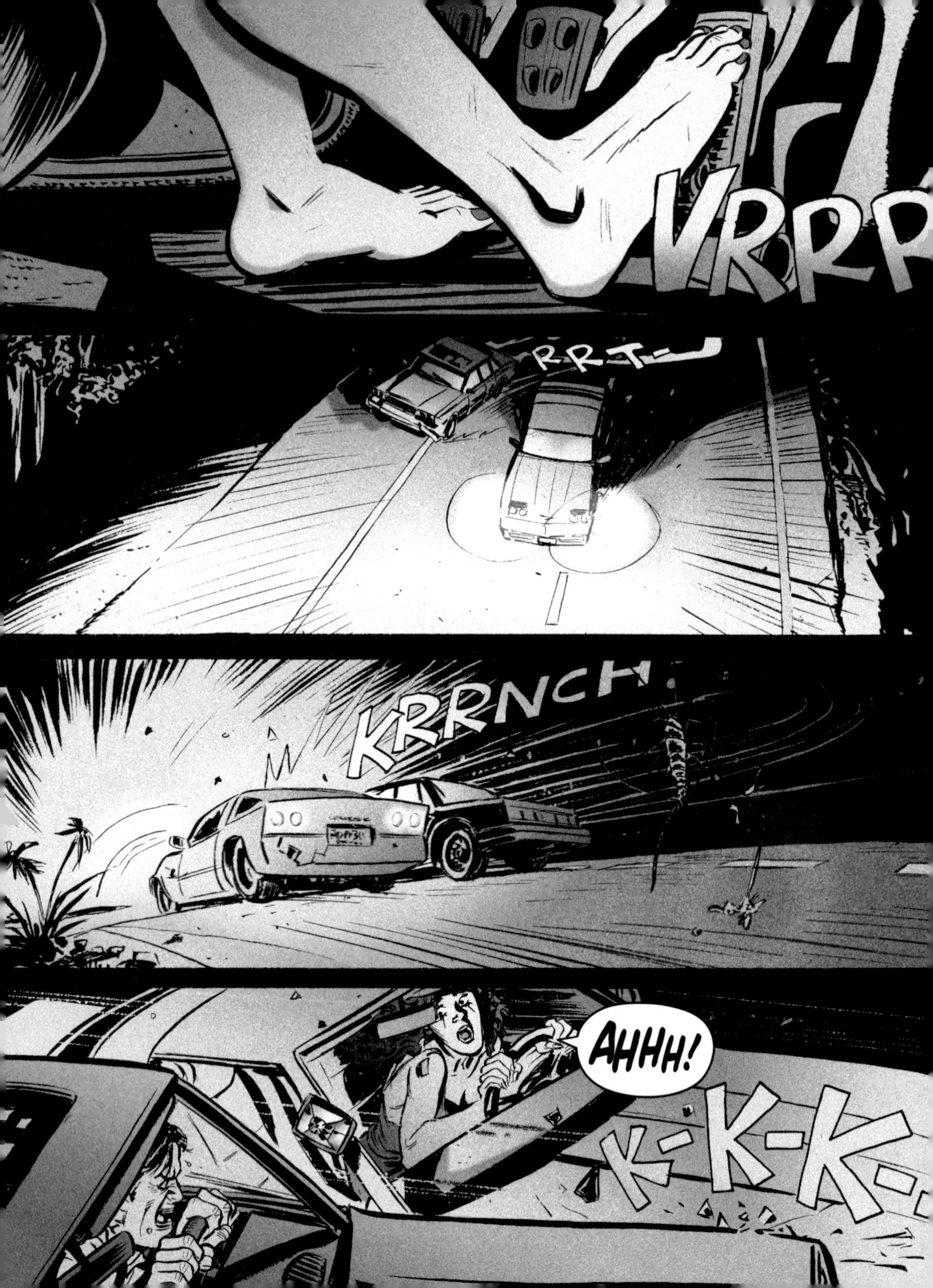
VRRR
RRT
KRRNCH
AHHH!
K-K-K-

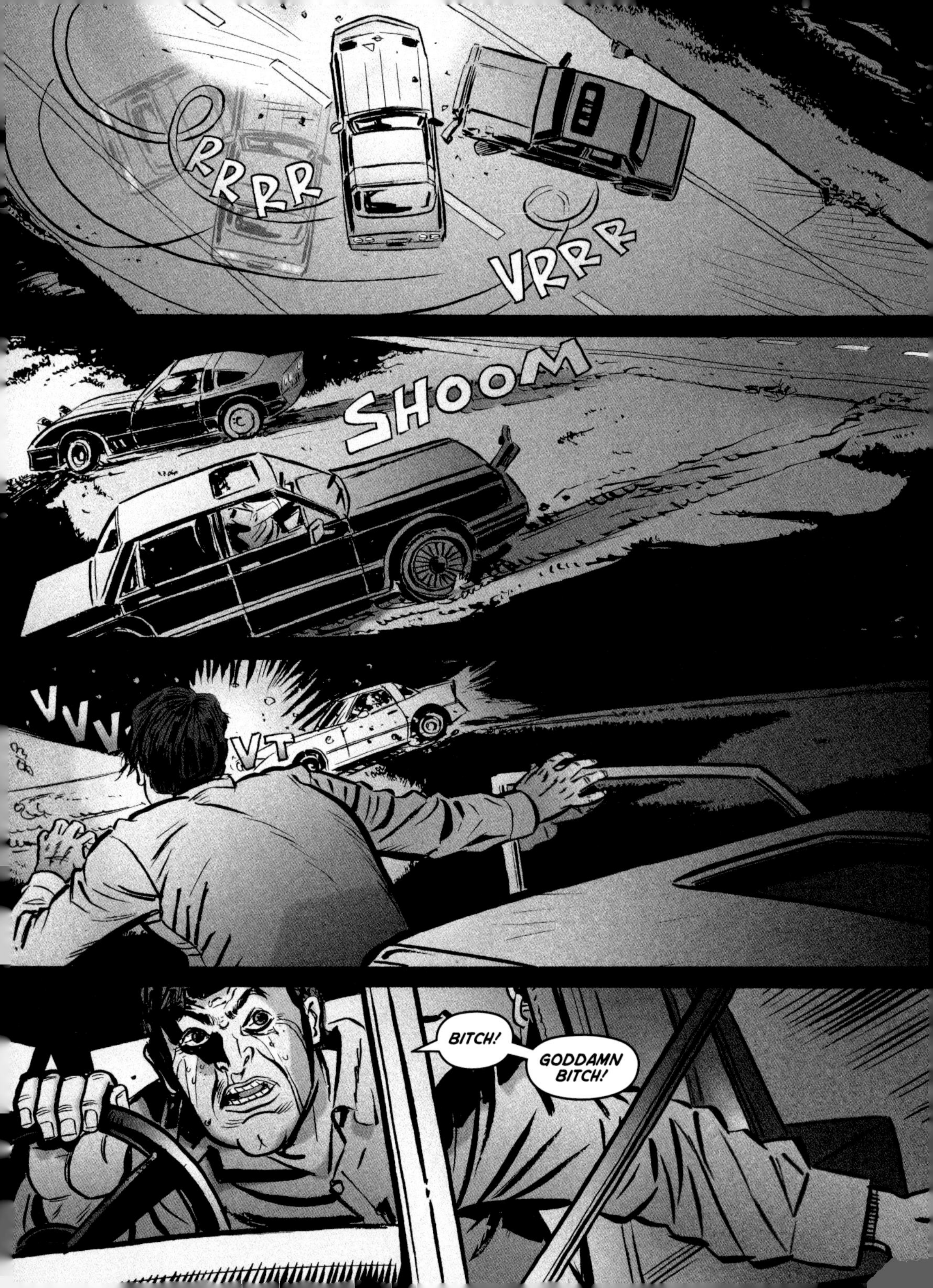
RRRR
VRRR
SHOOM
VVVVVT
BITCH!
GODDAMN BITCH!

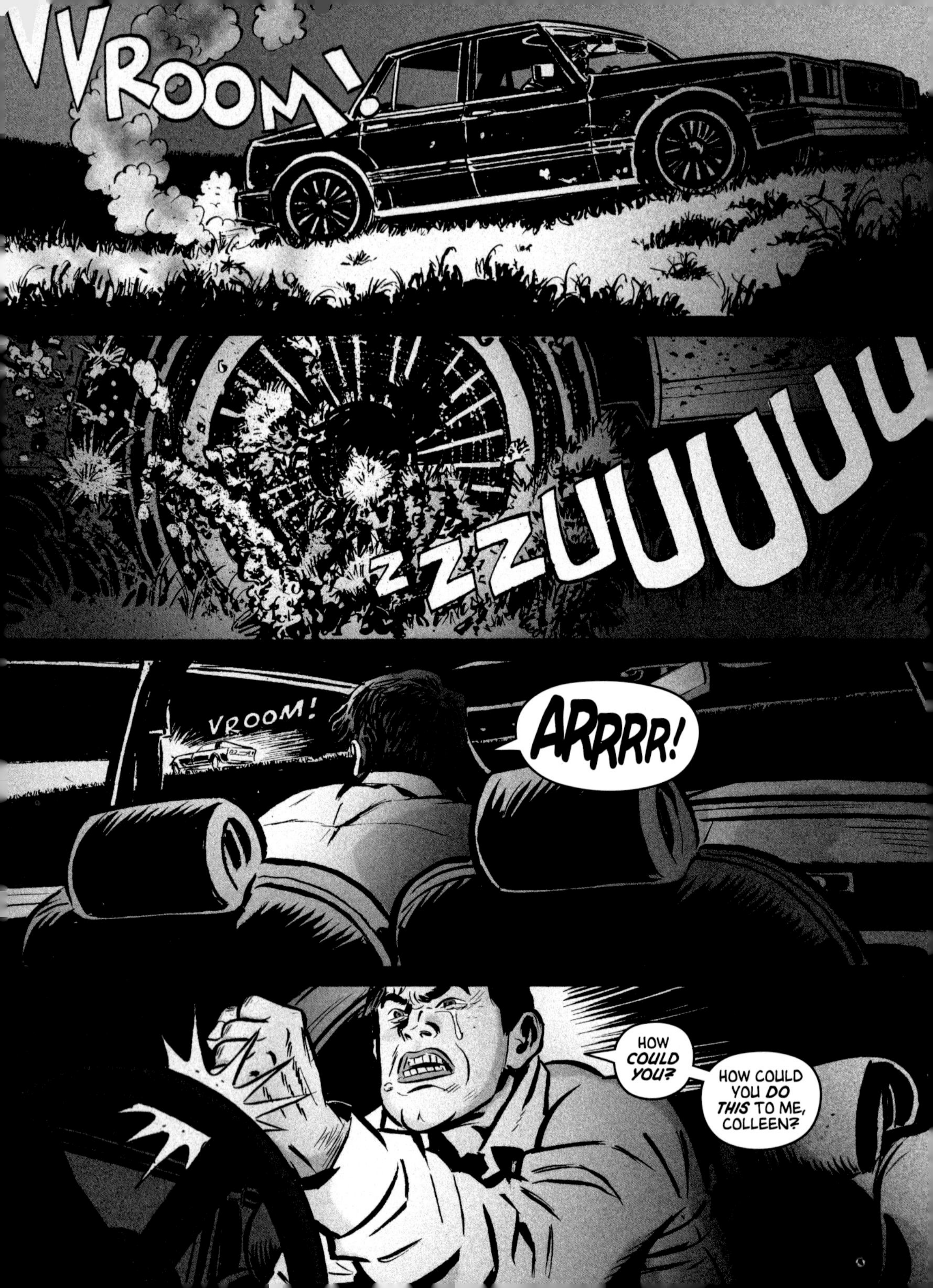
VVROOM!
ZZZUUUUUU
VROOM!
ARRRR!
HOW COULD YOU?
HOW COULD YOU DO THIS TO ME, COLLEEN?

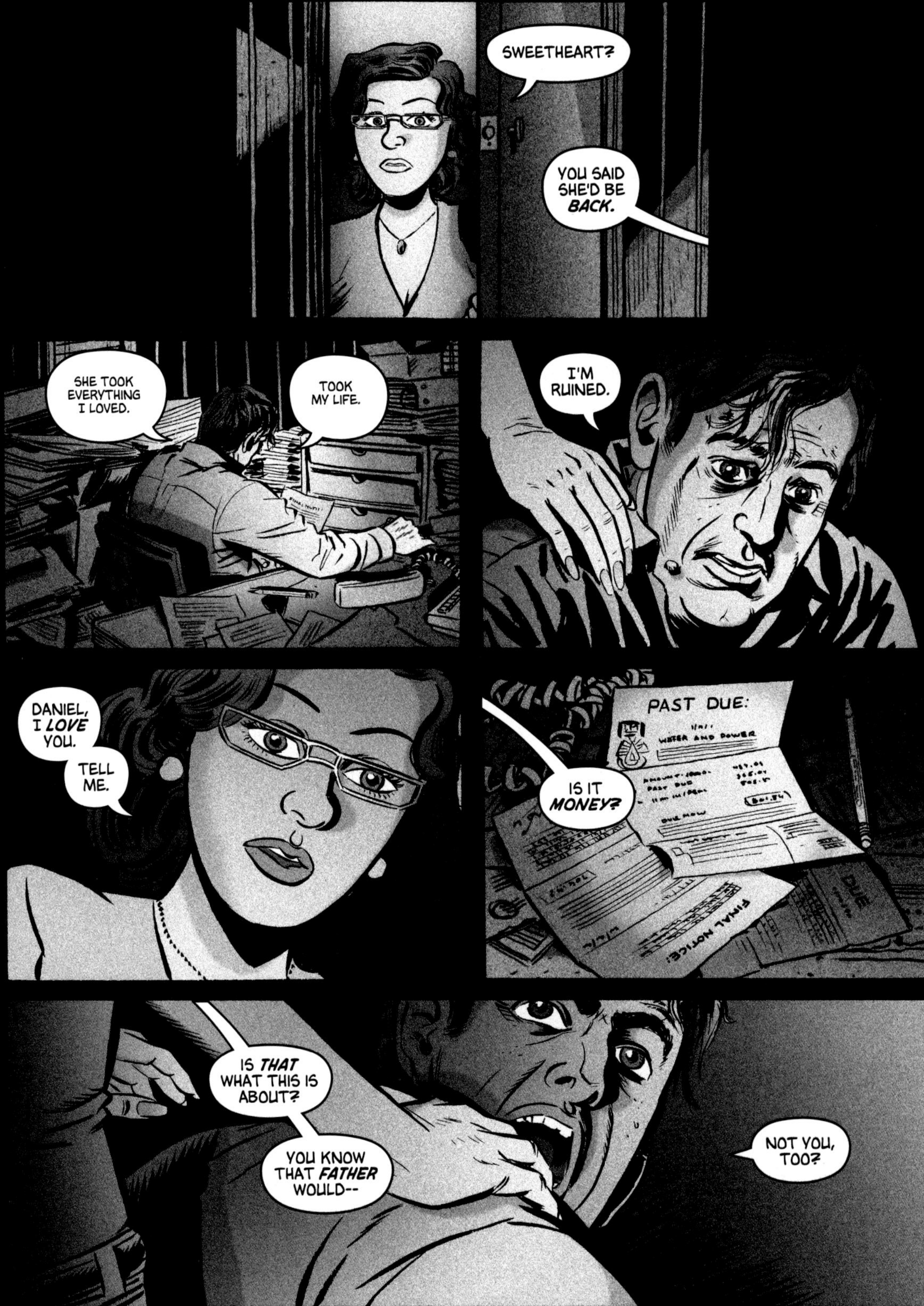
SWEETHEART?
YOU SAID SHE'D BE *BACK.*
SHE TOOK EVERYTHING I LOVED.
TOOK MY LIFE.
I'M RUINED.
DANIEL, I *LOVE* YOU.
TELL ME.
PAST DUE:
WATER AND POWER
IS IT *MONEY?*
FINAL NOTICE:
IS *THAT* WHAT THIS IS ABOUT?
YOU KNOW THAT *FATHER* WOULD--
NOT YOU, TOO?

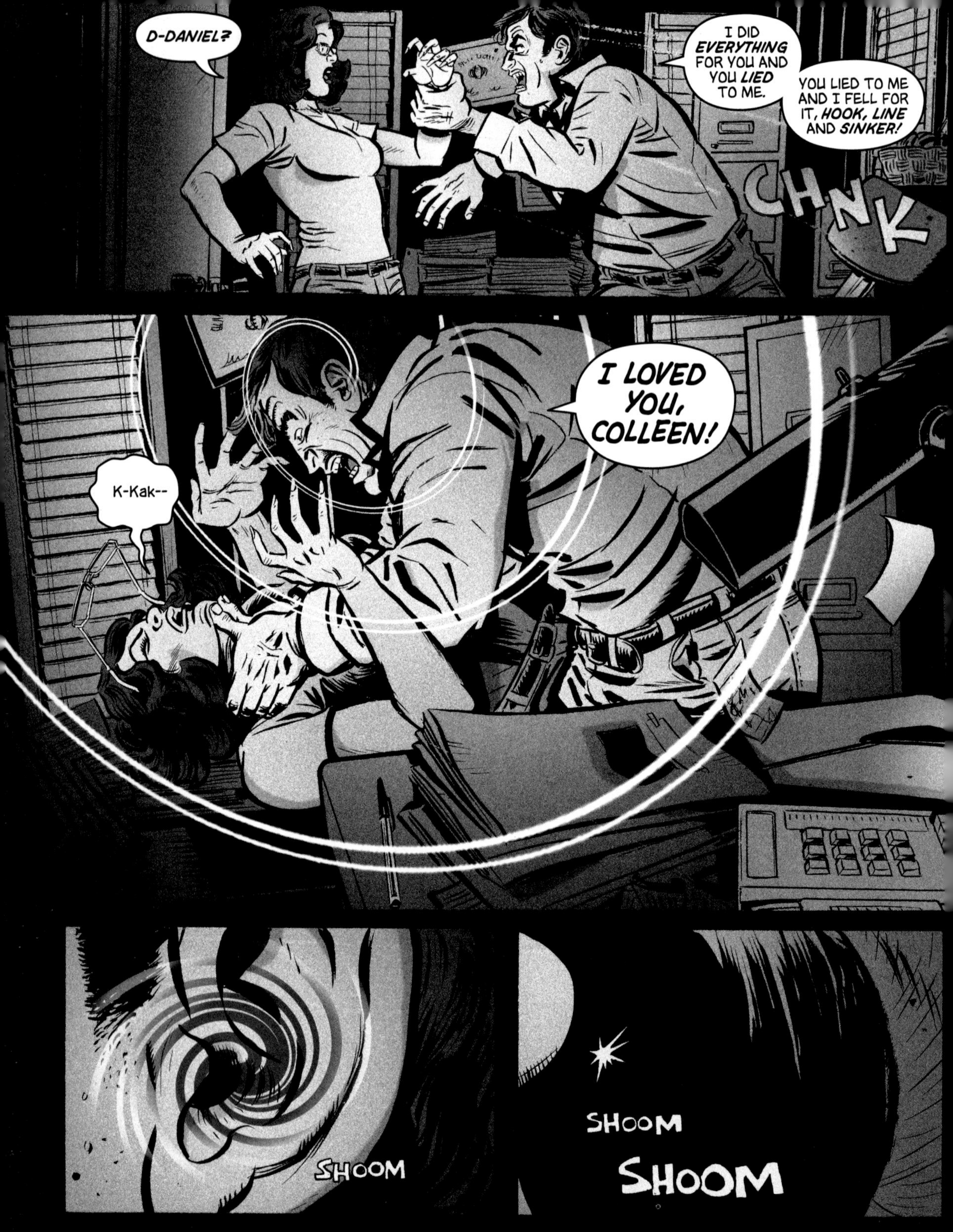
D-DANIEL?
I DID EVERYTHING FOR YOU AND YOU LIED TO ME.
YOU LIED TO ME AND I FELL FOR IT, HOOK, LINE AND SINKER!
CHNK
I LOVED YOU, COLLEEN!
K-Kak--
SHOOM
SHOOM
SHOOM

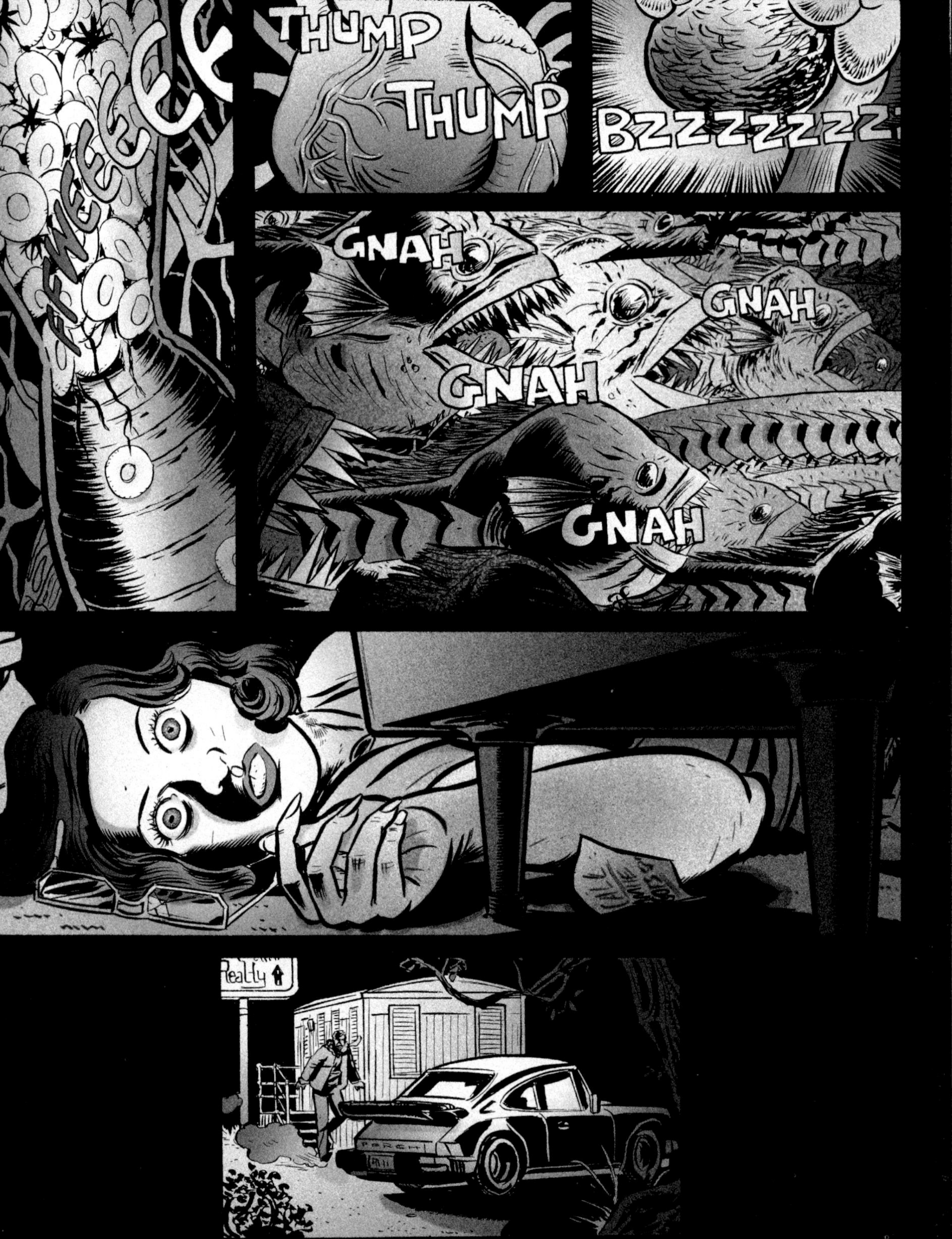
FFWEEEEE
THUMP
THUMP
BZZZZZZZZ
GNAH
GNAH
GNAH
GNAH
Realty

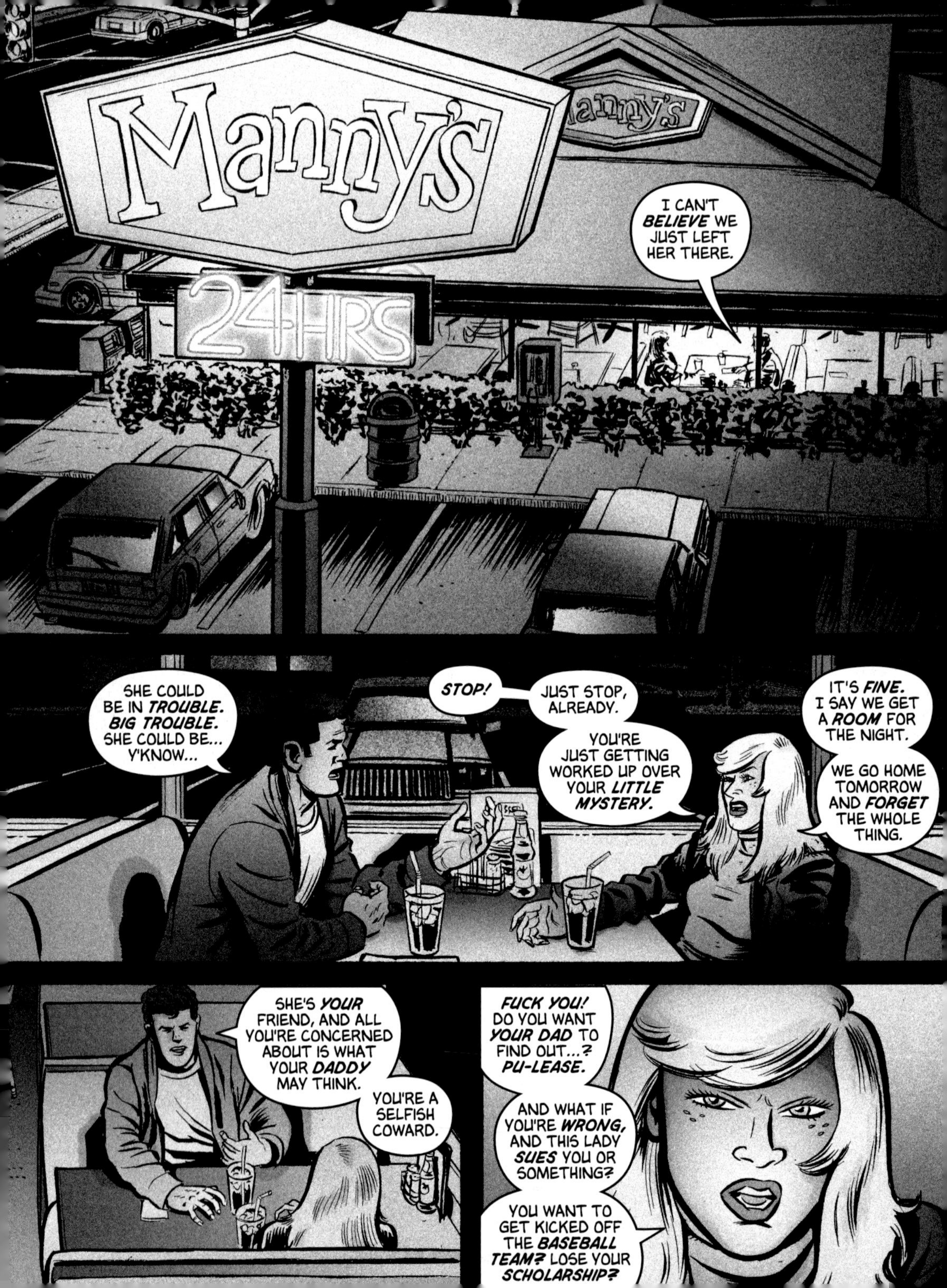
Manny's
Manny's
24HRS
I CAN'T BELIEVE WE JUST LEFT HER THERE.
SHE COULD BE IN TROUBLE. BIG TROUBLE. SHE COULD BE... Y'KNOW...
STOP!
JUST STOP, ALREADY.
YOU'RE JUST GETTING WORKED UP OVER YOUR LITTLE MYSTERY.
IT'S FINE. I SAY WE GET A ROOM FOR THE NIGHT.
WE GO HOME TOMORROW AND FORGET THE WHOLE THING.
SHE'S YOUR FRIEND, AND ALL YOU'RE CONCERNED ABOUT IS WHAT YOUR DADDY MAY THINK.
YOU'RE A SELFISH COWARD.
FUCK YOU! DO YOU WANT YOUR DAD TO FIND OUT...? PU-LEASE.
AND WHAT IF YOU'RE WRONG, AND THIS LADY SUES YOU OR SOMETHING?
YOU WANT TO GET KICKED OFF THE BASEBALL TEAM? LOSE YOUR SCHOLARSHIP?

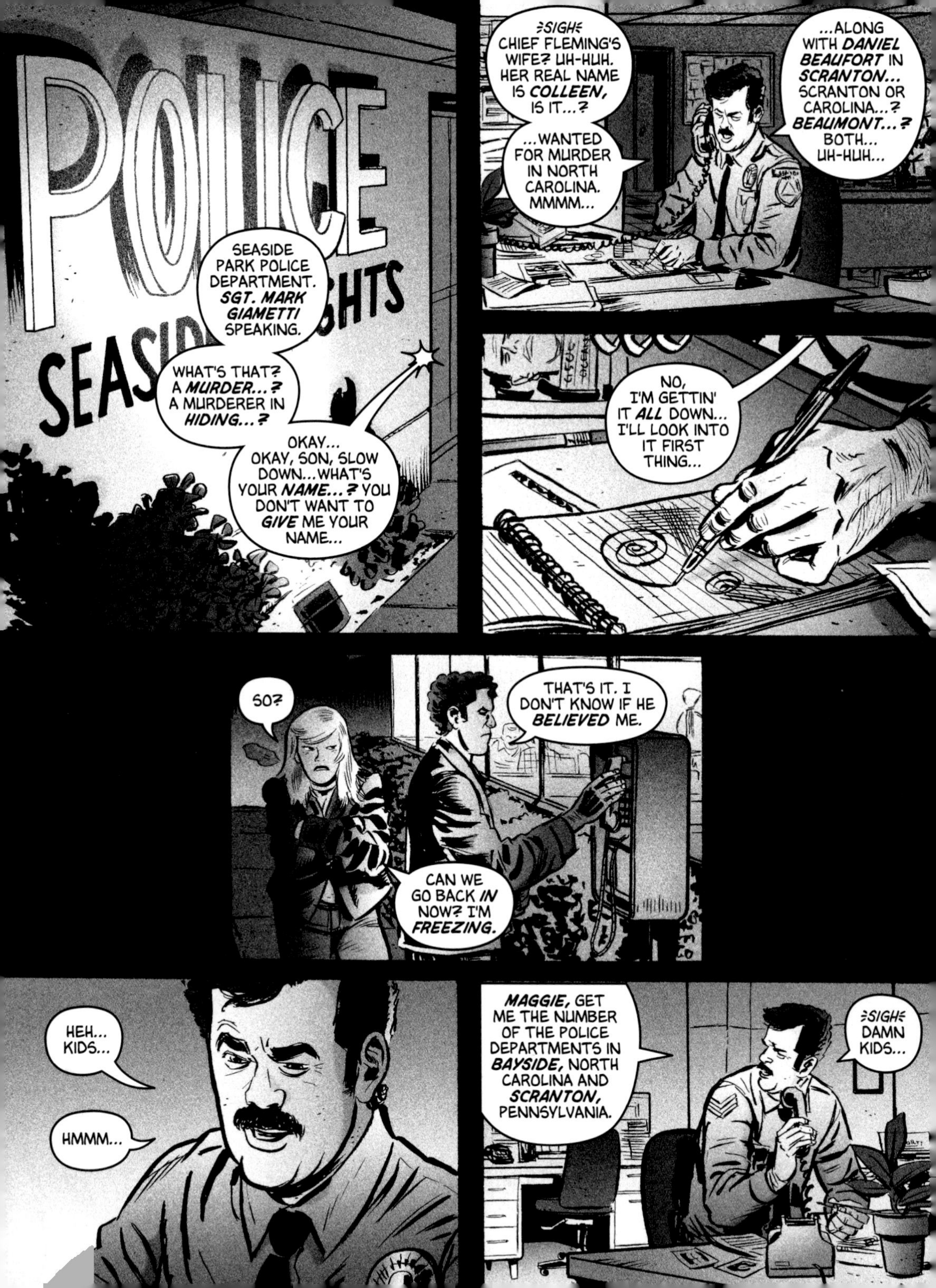
POLICE
SEASIDE HEIGHTS
SEASIDE PARK POLICE DEPARTMENT. SGT. MARK GIAMETTI SPEAKING.
WHAT'S THAT? A MURDER...? A MURDERER IN HIDING...?
OKAY... OKAY, SON, SLOW DOWN...WHAT'S YOUR NAME...? YOU DON'T WANT TO GIVE ME YOUR NAME...
SIGH CHIEF FLEMING'S WIFE? UH-HUH. HER REAL NAME IS COLLEEN, IS IT...?
...WANTED FOR MURDER IN NORTH CAROLINA. MMMM...
...ALONG WITH DANIEL BEAUFORT IN SCRANTON... SCRANTON OR CAROLINA...? BEAUMONT...? BOTH... UH-HUH...
NO, I'M GETTIN' IT ALL DOWN... I'LL LOOK INTO IT FIRST THING...
SO?
THAT'S IT. I DON'T KNOW IF HE BELIEVED ME.
CAN WE GO BACK IN NOW? I'M FREEZING.
HEH... KIDS...
HMMM...
MAGGIE, GET ME THE NUMBER OF THE POLICE DEPARTMENTS IN BAYSIDE, NORTH CAROLINA AND SCRANTON, PENNSYLVANIA.
SIGH DAMN KIDS...

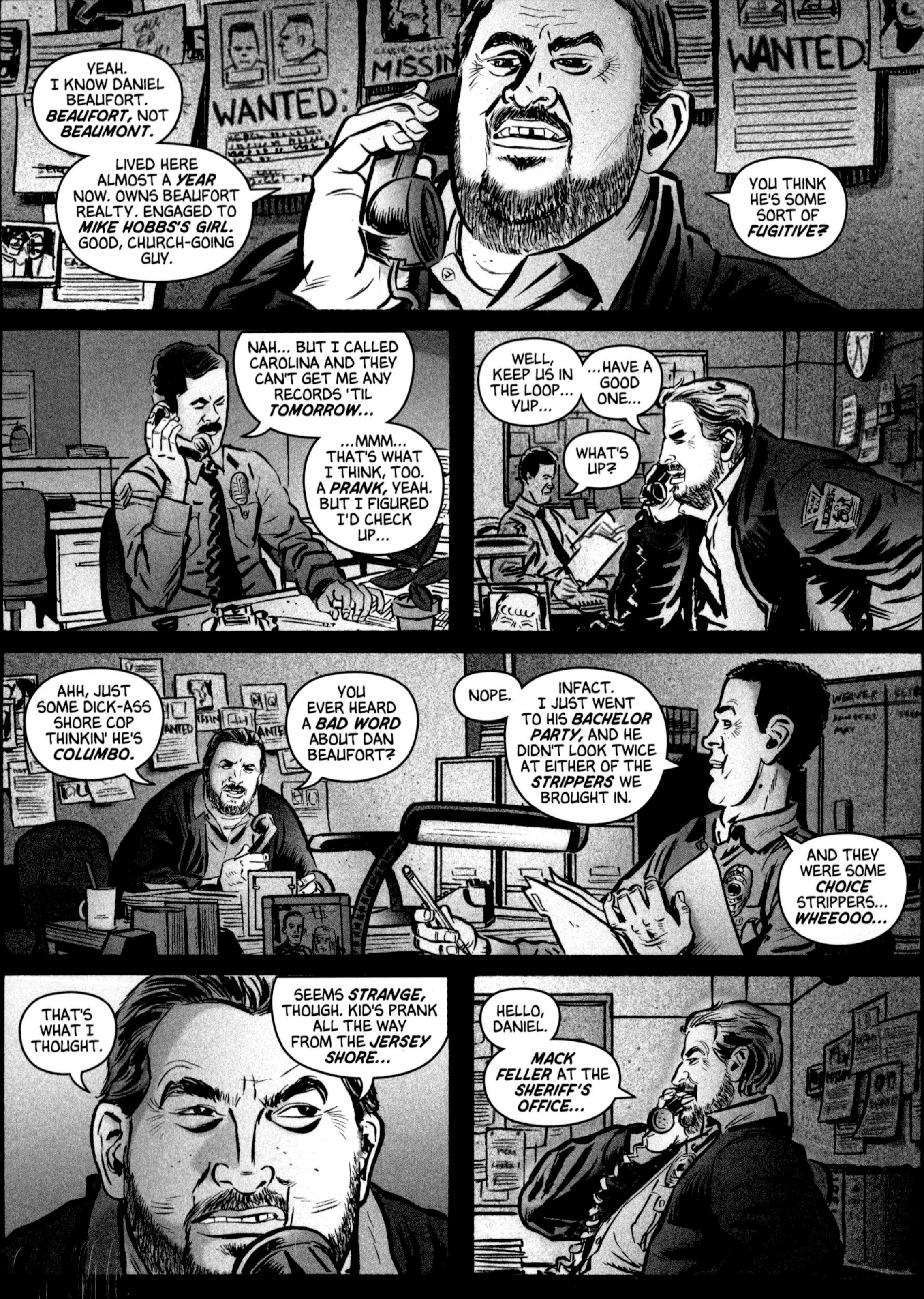
YEAH. I KNOW DANIEL BEAUFORT. **BEAUFORT,** NOT **BEAUMONT.**
LIVED HERE ALMOST A **YEAR** NOW. OWNS BEAUFORT REALTY. ENGAGED TO **MIKE HOBBS'S GIRL.** GOOD, CHURCH-GOING GUY.
YOU THINK HE'S SOME SORT OF **FUGITIVE?**
NAH... BUT I CALLED CAROLINA AND THEY CAN'T GET ME ANY RECORDS 'TIL **TOMORROW...**
...MMM... THAT'S WHAT I THINK, TOO. A **PRANK,** YEAH. BUT I FIGURED I'D CHECK UP...
WELL, KEEP US IN THE LOOP... YUP...
...HAVE A GOOD ONE...
WHAT'S UP?
AHH, JUST SOME DICK-ASS SHORE COP THINKIN' HE'S **COLUMBO.**
YOU EVER HEARD A **BAD WORD** ABOUT DAN BEAUFORT?
NOPE.
INFACT. I JUST WENT TO HIS **BACHELOR PARTY,** AND HE DIDN'T LOOK TWICE AT EITHER OF THE **STRIPPERS** WE BROUGHT IN.
AND THEY WERE SOME **CHOICE** STRIPPERS... **WHEEOOO...**
THAT'S WHAT I THOUGHT.
SEEMS **STRANGE,** THOUGH. KID'S PRANK ALL THE WAY FROM THE **JERSEY SHORE...**
HELLO, DANIEL.
MACK FELLER AT THE **SHERIFF'S OFFICE...**

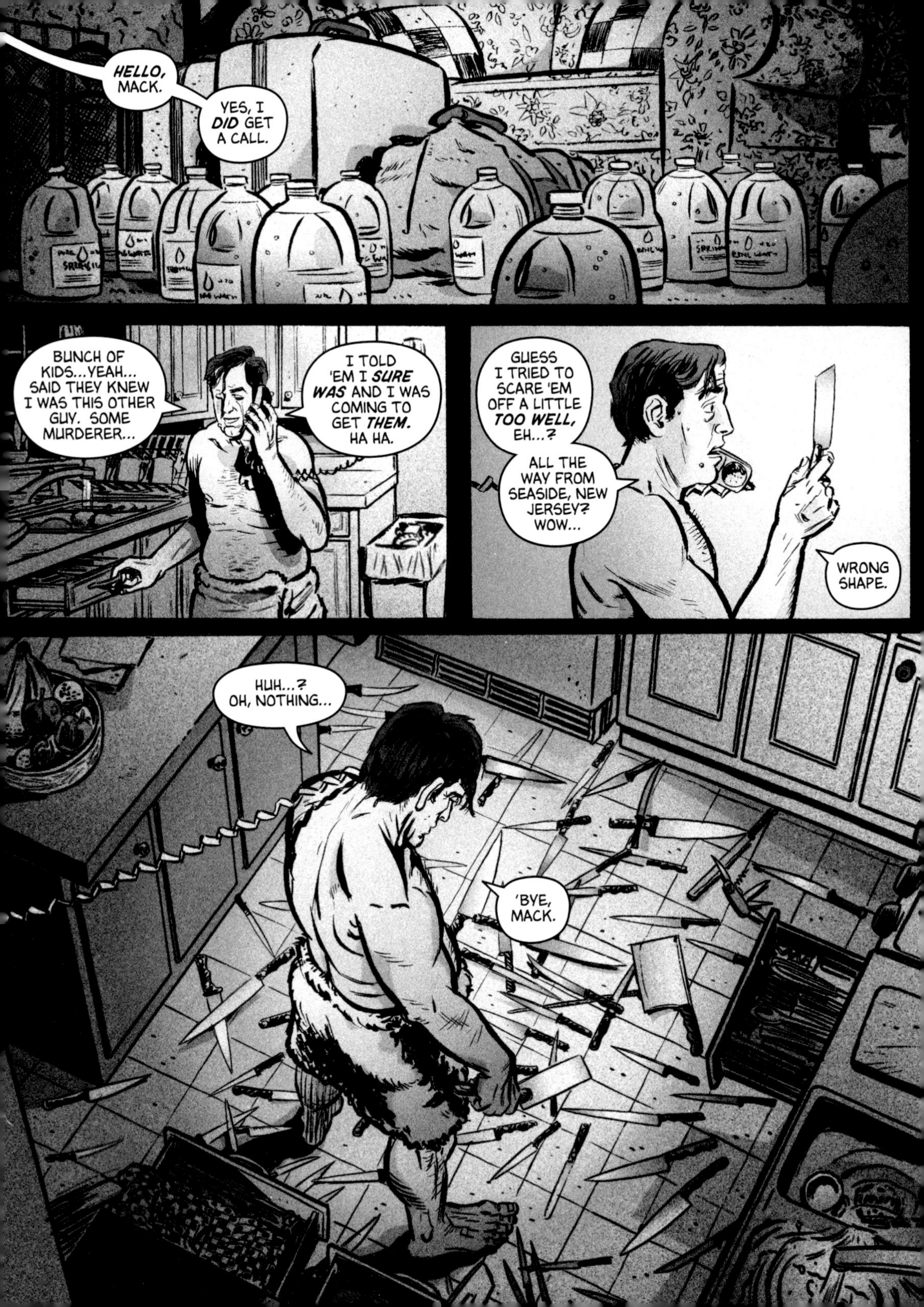
HELLO, MACK.
YES, I DID GET A CALL.
BUNCH OF KIDS...YEAH... SAID THEY KNEW I WAS THIS OTHER GUY. SOME MURDERER...
I TOLD 'EM I SURE WAS AND I WAS COMING TO GET THEM. HA HA.
GUESS I TRIED TO SCARE 'EM OFF A LITTLE TOO WELL, EH...?
ALL THE WAY FROM SEASIDE, NEW JERSEY? WOW...
WRONG SHAPE.
HUH...? OH, NOTHING...
'BYE, MACK.

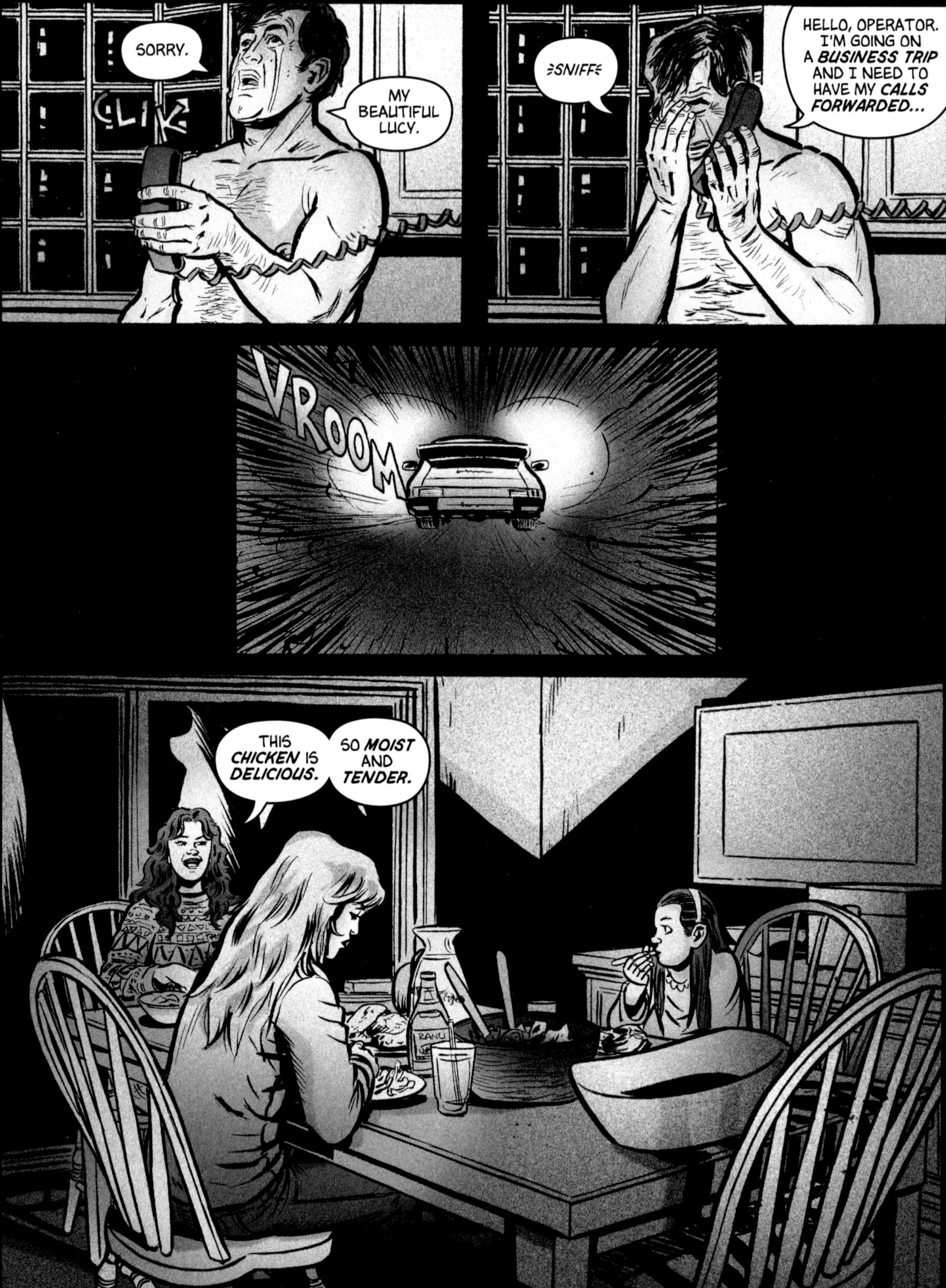
CLIK
SORRY.
MY BEAUTIFUL LUCY.
≡SNIFF≡
HELLO, OPERATOR. I'M GOING ON A BUSINESS TRIP AND I NEED TO HAVE MY CALLS FORWARDED...
VROOM
THIS CHICKEN IS DELICIOUS.
SO MOIST AND TENDER.
RANCH

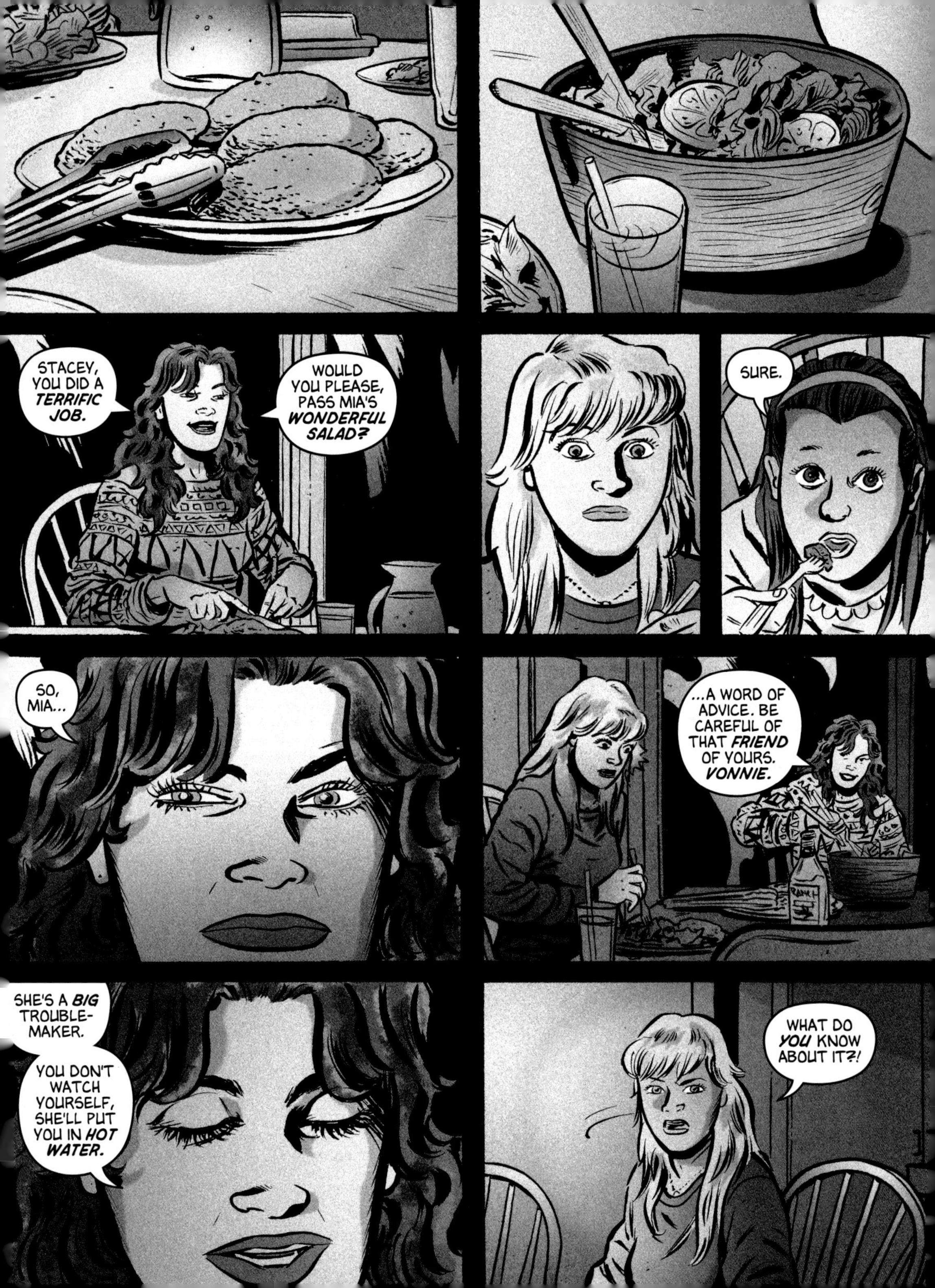
STACEY, YOU DID A *TERRIFIC* *JOB.*
WOULD YOU PLEASE, PASS MIA'S *WONDERFUL SALAD?*
SURE.
SO, MIA...
...A WORD OF ADVICE. BE CAREFUL OF THAT *FRIEND* OF YOURS. *VONNIE.*
SHE'S A *BIG* TROUBLE-MAKER.
YOU DON'T WATCH YOURSELF, SHE'LL PUT YOU IN *HOT WATER.*
WHAT DO *YOU* KNOW ABOUT IT?!

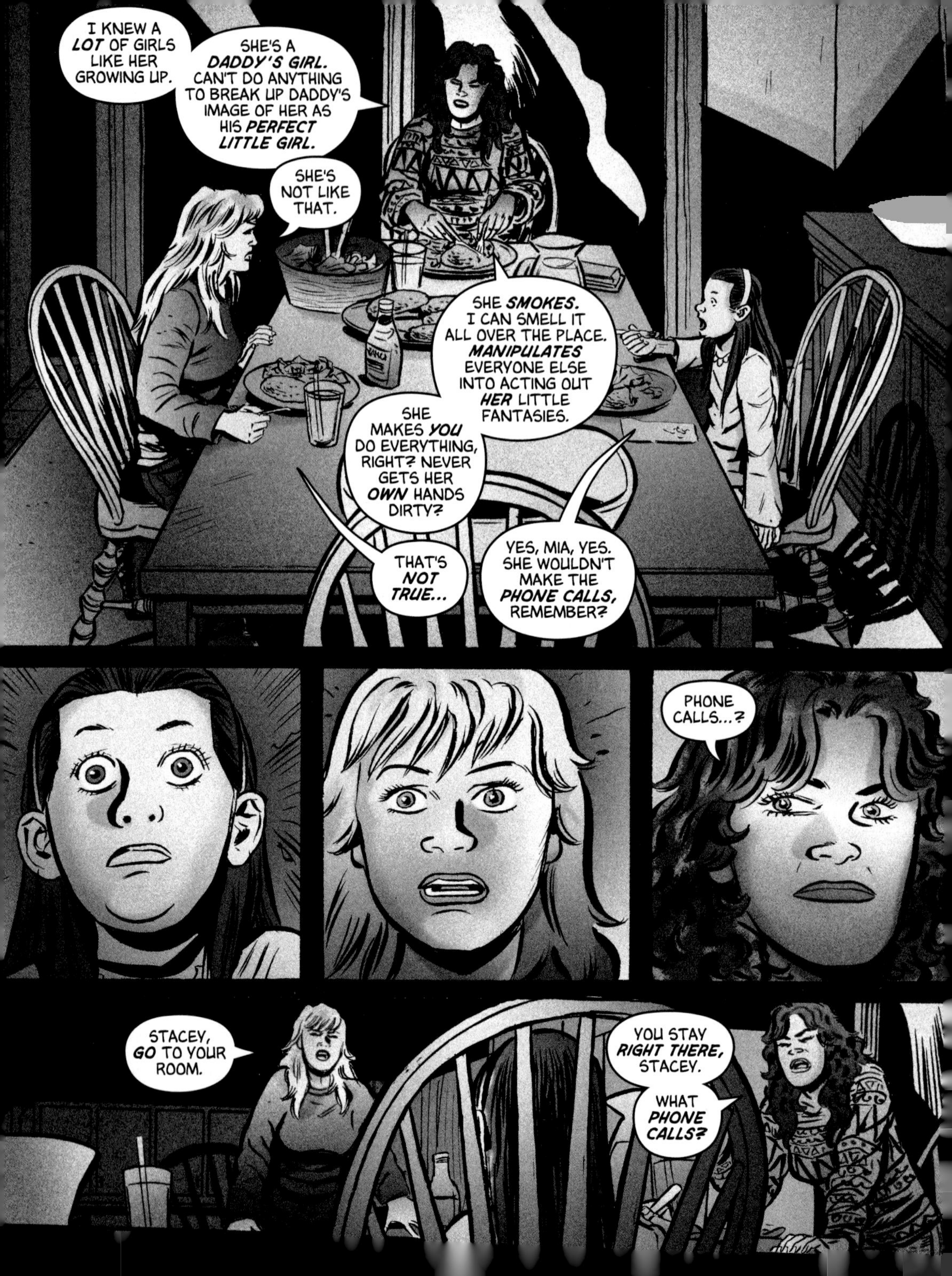
I KNEW A LOT OF GIRLS LIKE HER GROWING UP.
SHE'S A DADDY'S GIRL. CAN'T DO ANYTHING TO BREAK UP DADDY'S IMAGE OF HER AS HIS PERFECT LITTLE GIRL.
SHE'S NOT LIKE THAT.
SHE SMOKES. I CAN SMELL IT ALL OVER THE PLACE. MANIPULATES EVERYONE ELSE INTO ACTING OUT HER LITTLE FANTASIES.
SHE MAKES YOU DO EVERYTHING, RIGHT? NEVER GETS HER OWN HANDS DIRTY?
THAT'S NOT TRUE...
YES, MIA, YES. SHE WOULDN'T MAKE THE PHONE CALLS, REMEMBER?
PHONE CALLS...?
STACEY, GO TO YOUR ROOM.
YOU STAY RIGHT THERE, STACEY.
WHAT PHONE CALLS?

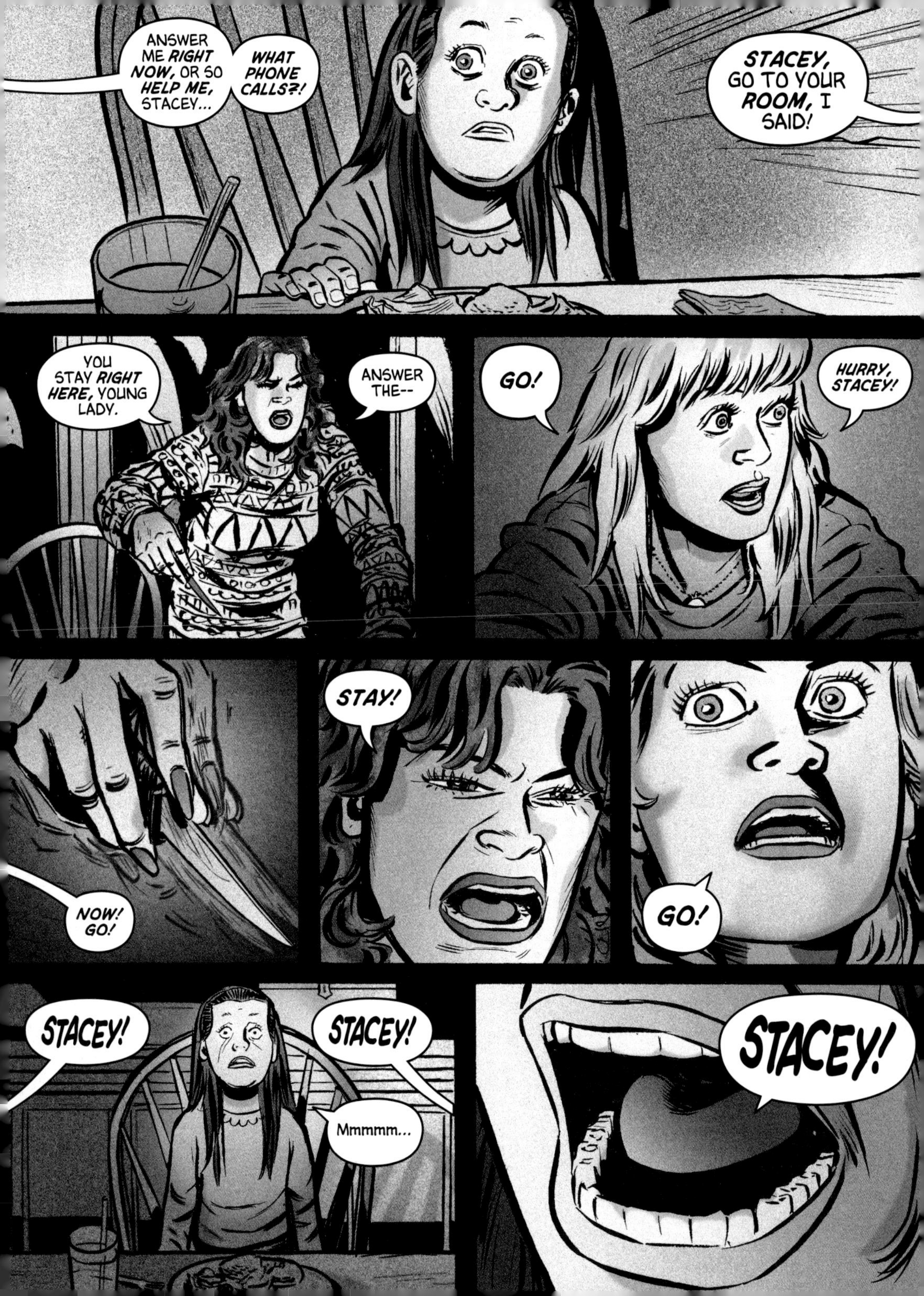
ANSWER ME RIGHT NOW, OR SO HELP ME, STACEY...
WHAT PHONE CALLS?!
STACEY, GO TO YOUR ROOM, I SAID!
YOU STAY RIGHT HERE, YOUNG LADY.
ANSWER THE--
GO!
HURRY, STACEY!
NOW! GO!
STAY!
GO!
STACEY!
STACEY!
Mmmmm...
STACEY!

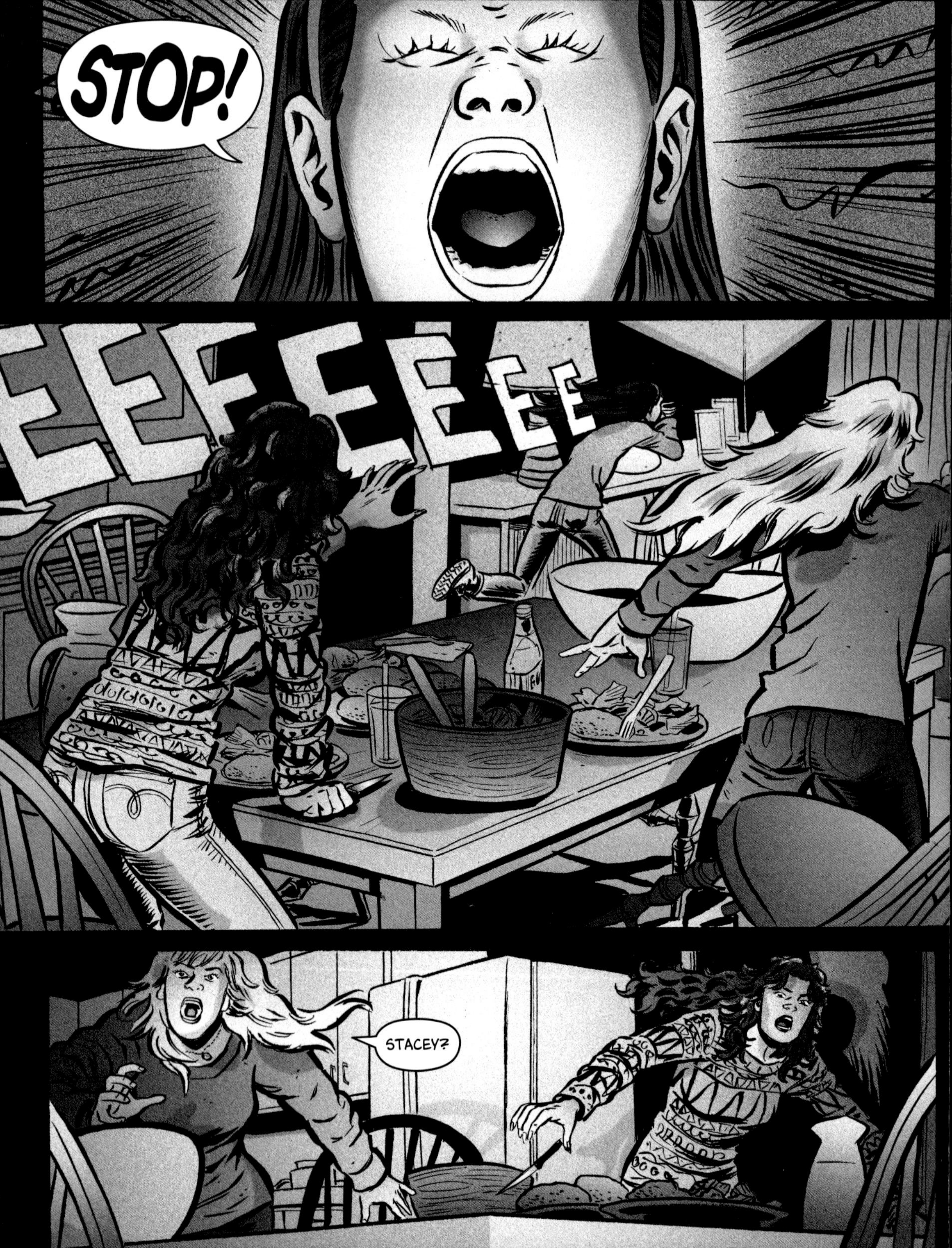
STOP!
EEEEEEEE
STACEY?

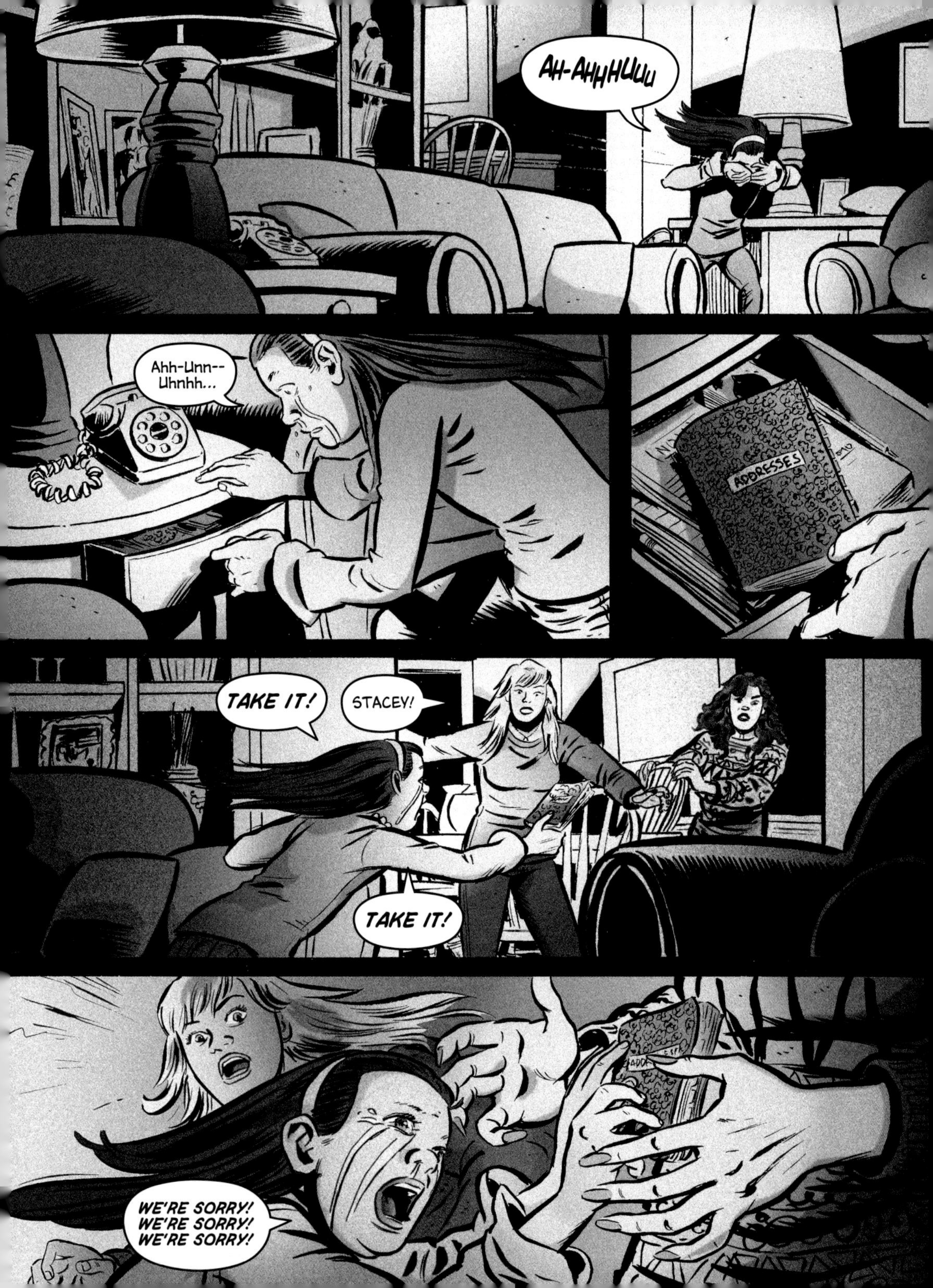
AH-AHHHUUU
Ahh-Unn--
Uhnhh...
ADDRESSES
TAKE IT!
STACEY!
TAKE IT!
WE'RE SORRY!
WE'RE SORRY!
WE'RE SORRY!

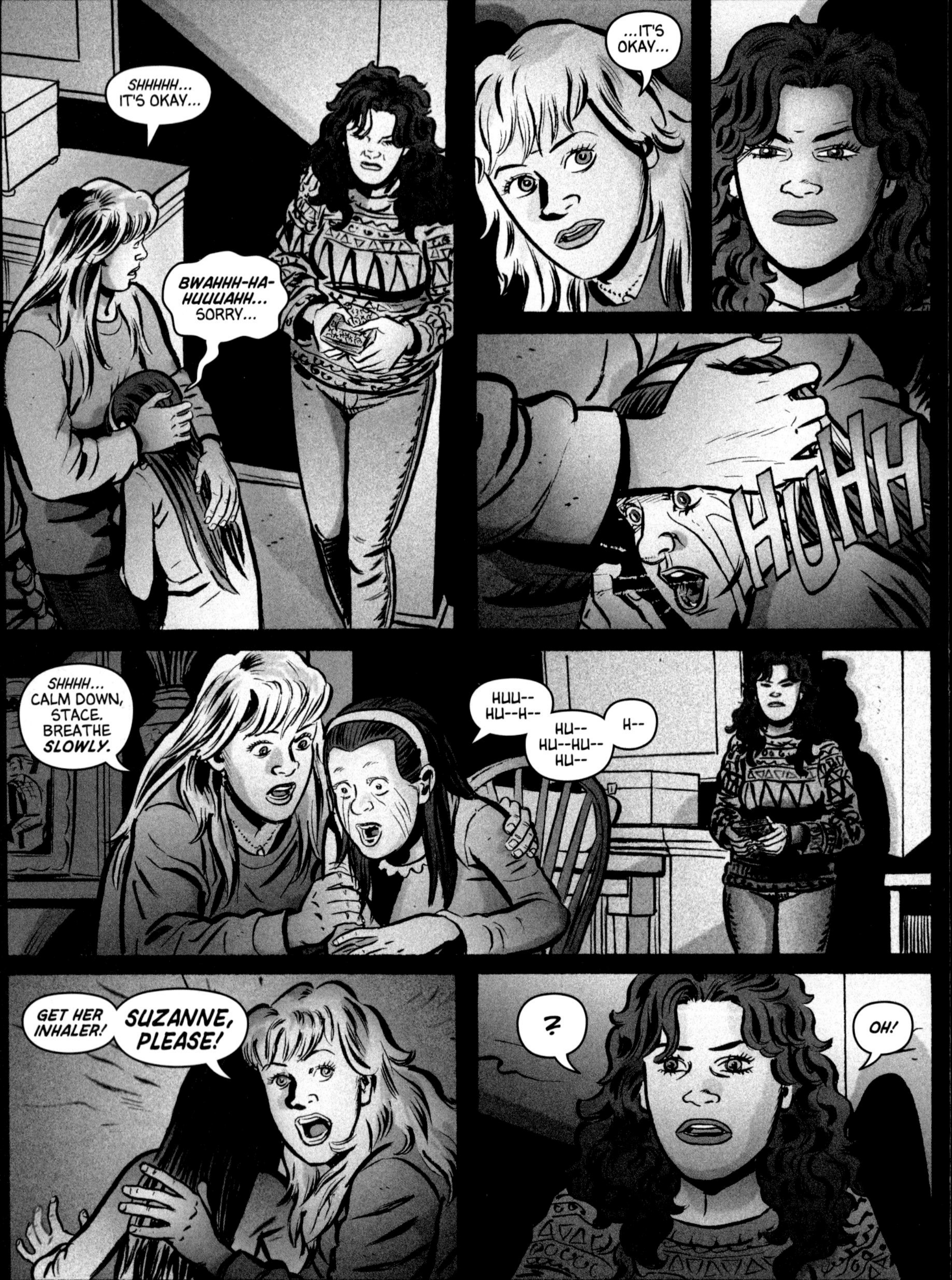
SHHHHH... IT'S OKAY...
BWAHHH-HA-HUUUAHH... SORRY...
...IT'S OKAY...
HUHH
SHHHH... CALM DOWN, STACE. BREATHE SLOWLY.
HUU-- HU--H--
HU-- HU--HU-- HU--
H--
GET HER INHALER!
SUZANNE, PLEASE!
?
OH!

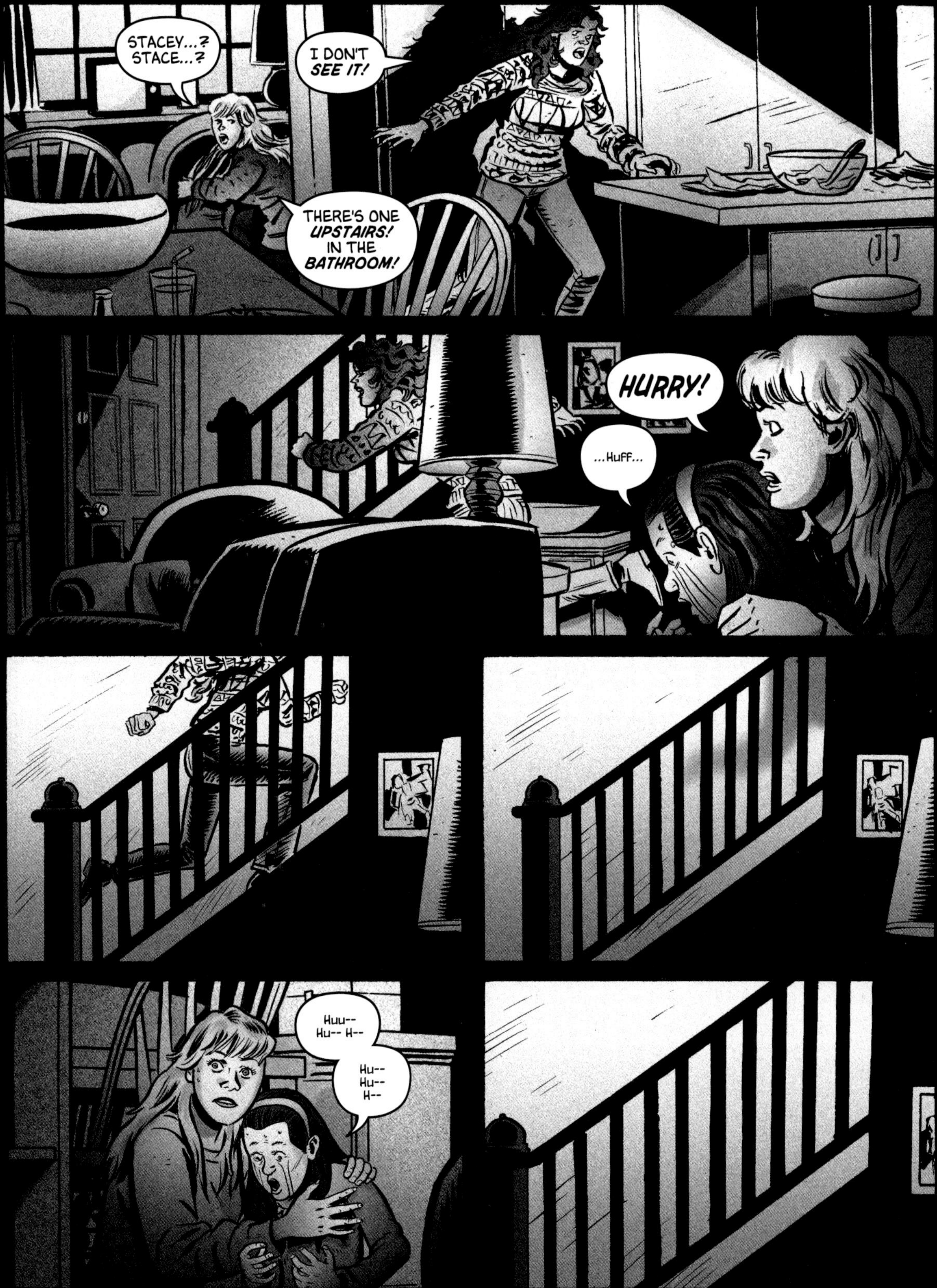
STACEY...? STACE...?
I DON'T SEE IT!
THERE'S ONE UPSTAIRS! IN THE BATHROOM!
HURRY!
...Huff...
Huu-- Hu-- H--
Hu-- Hu-- H--

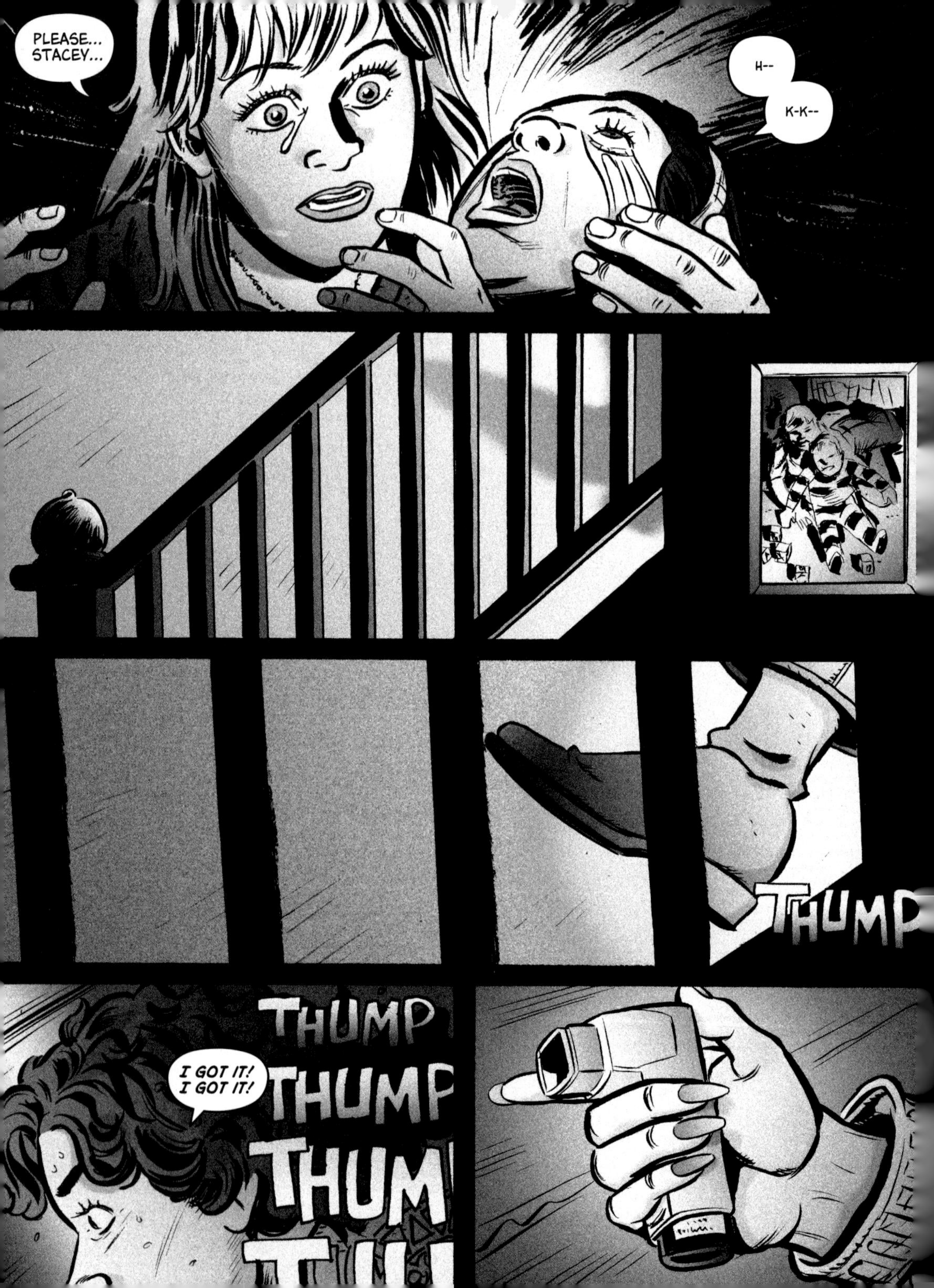

PLEASE... STACEY...
H--
K-K--
THUMP
THUMP
I GOT IT! I GOT IT!
THUMP
THUM

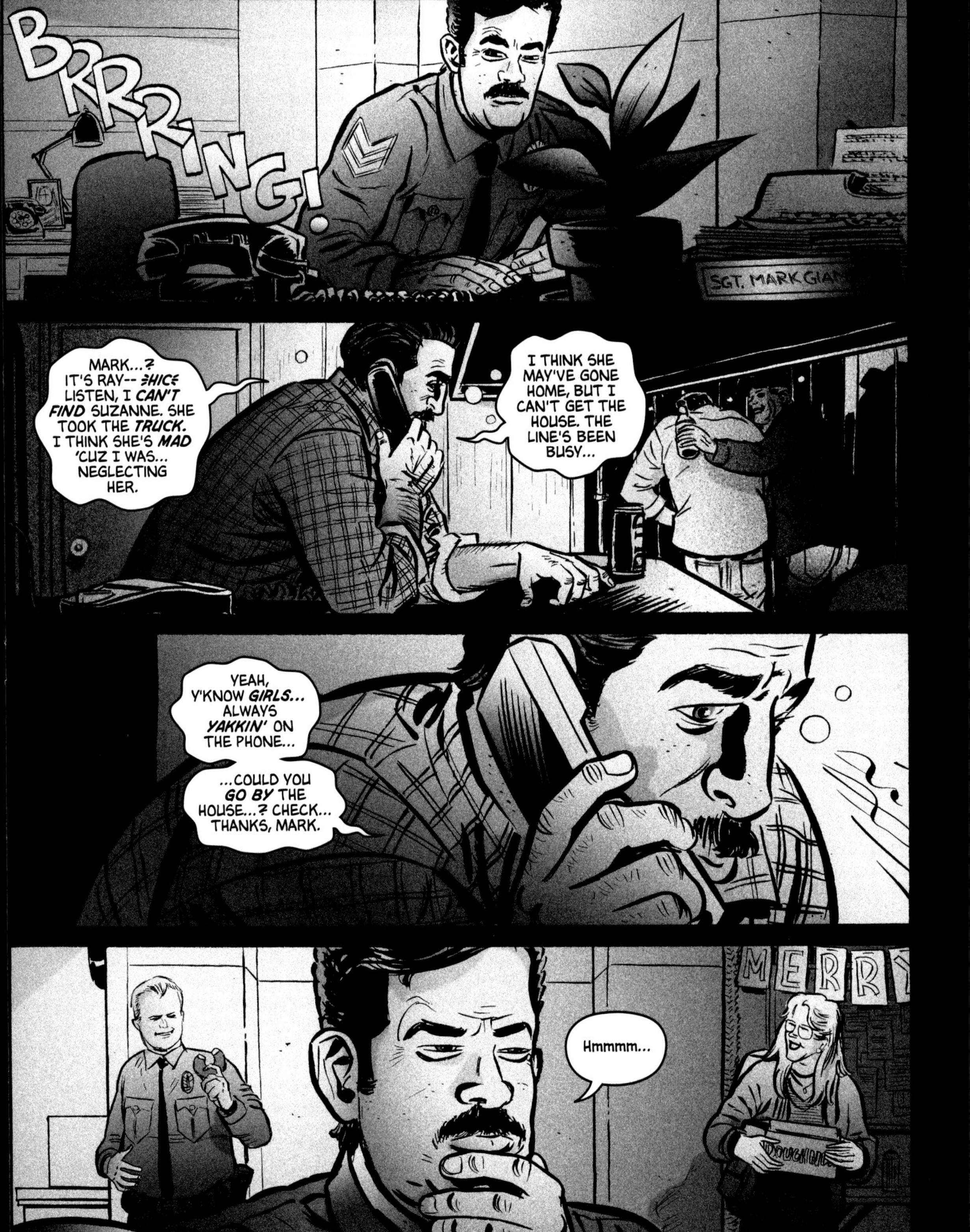
BRRRING!
SGT. MARK GIAN
MARK...? IT'S RAY-- *HIC* LISTEN, I CAN'T FIND SUZANNE. SHE TOOK THE TRUCK. I THINK SHE'S MAD 'CUZ I WAS... NEGLECTING HER.
I THINK SHE MAY'VE GONE HOME, BUT I CAN'T GET THE HOUSE. THE LINE'S BEEN BUSY...
YEAH, Y'KNOW GIRLS... ALWAYS YAKKIN' ON THE PHONE...
...COULD YOU GO BY THE HOUSE...? CHECK... THANKS, MARK.
MERRY
Hmmmm...

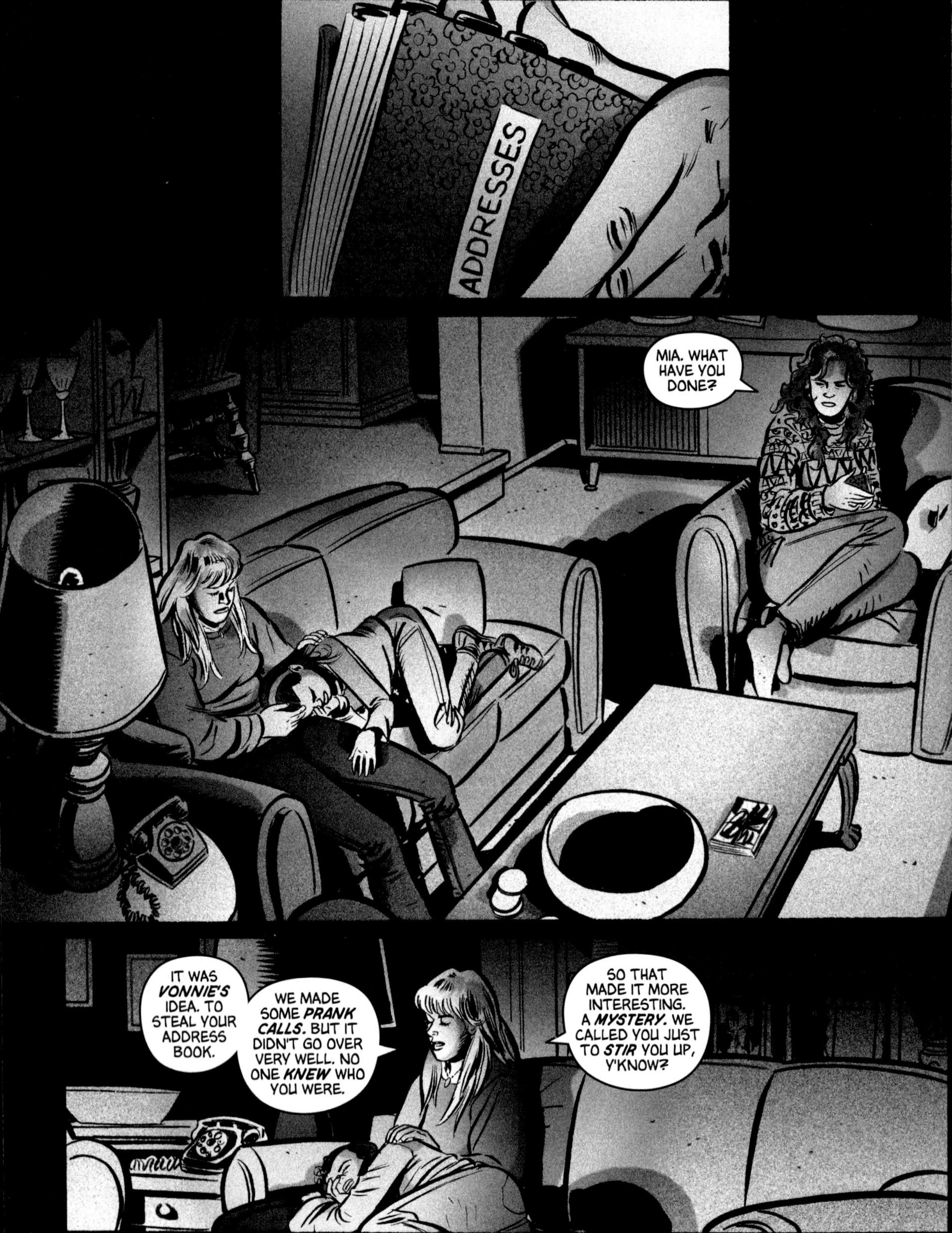
ADDRESSES
MIA. WHAT HAVE YOU DONE?
IT WAS VONNIE'S IDEA. TO STEAL YOUR ADDRESS BOOK.
WE MADE SOME PRANK CALLS. BUT IT DIDN'T GO OVER VERY WELL. NO ONE KNEW WHO YOU WERE.
SO THAT MADE IT MORE INTERESTING. A MYSTERY. WE CALLED YOU JUST TO STIR YOU UP, Y'KNOW?

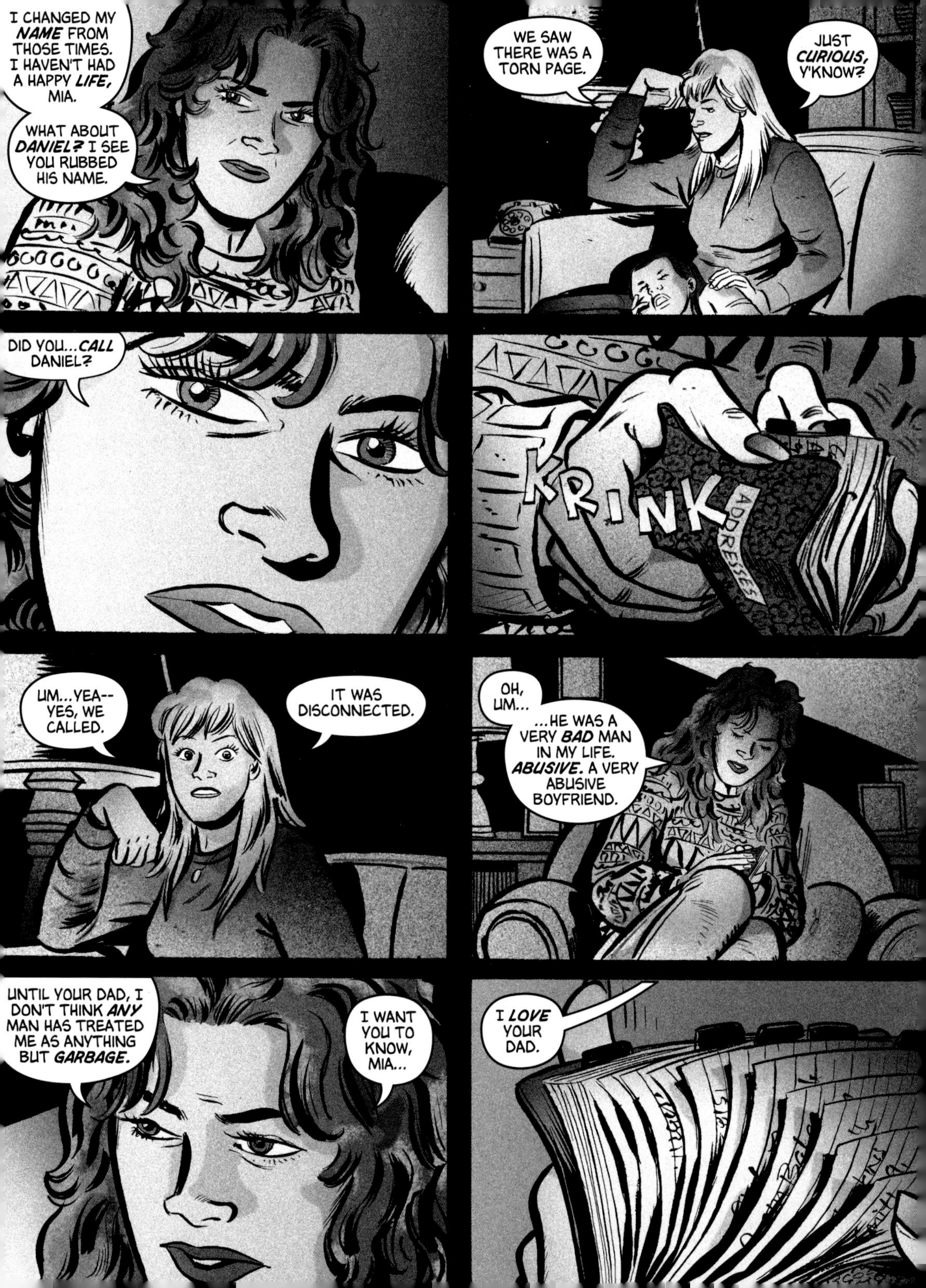
I CHANGED MY NAME FROM THOSE TIMES. I HAVEN'T HAD A HAPPY LIFE, MIA.
WHAT ABOUT DANIEL? I SEE YOU RUBBED HIS NAME.
WE SAW THERE WAS A TORN PAGE.
JUST CURIOUS, Y'KNOW?
DID YOU...CALL DANIEL?
KRINK!
ADDRESSES
UM...YEA-- YES, WE CALLED.
IT WAS DISCONNECTED.
OH, UM...
...HE WAS A VERY BAD MAN IN MY LIFE. ABUSIVE. A VERY ABUSIVE BOYFRIEND.
UNTIL YOUR DAD, I DON'T THINK ANY MAN HAS TREATED ME AS ANYTHING BUT GARBAGE.
I WANT YOU TO KNOW, MIA...
I LOVE YOUR DAD.

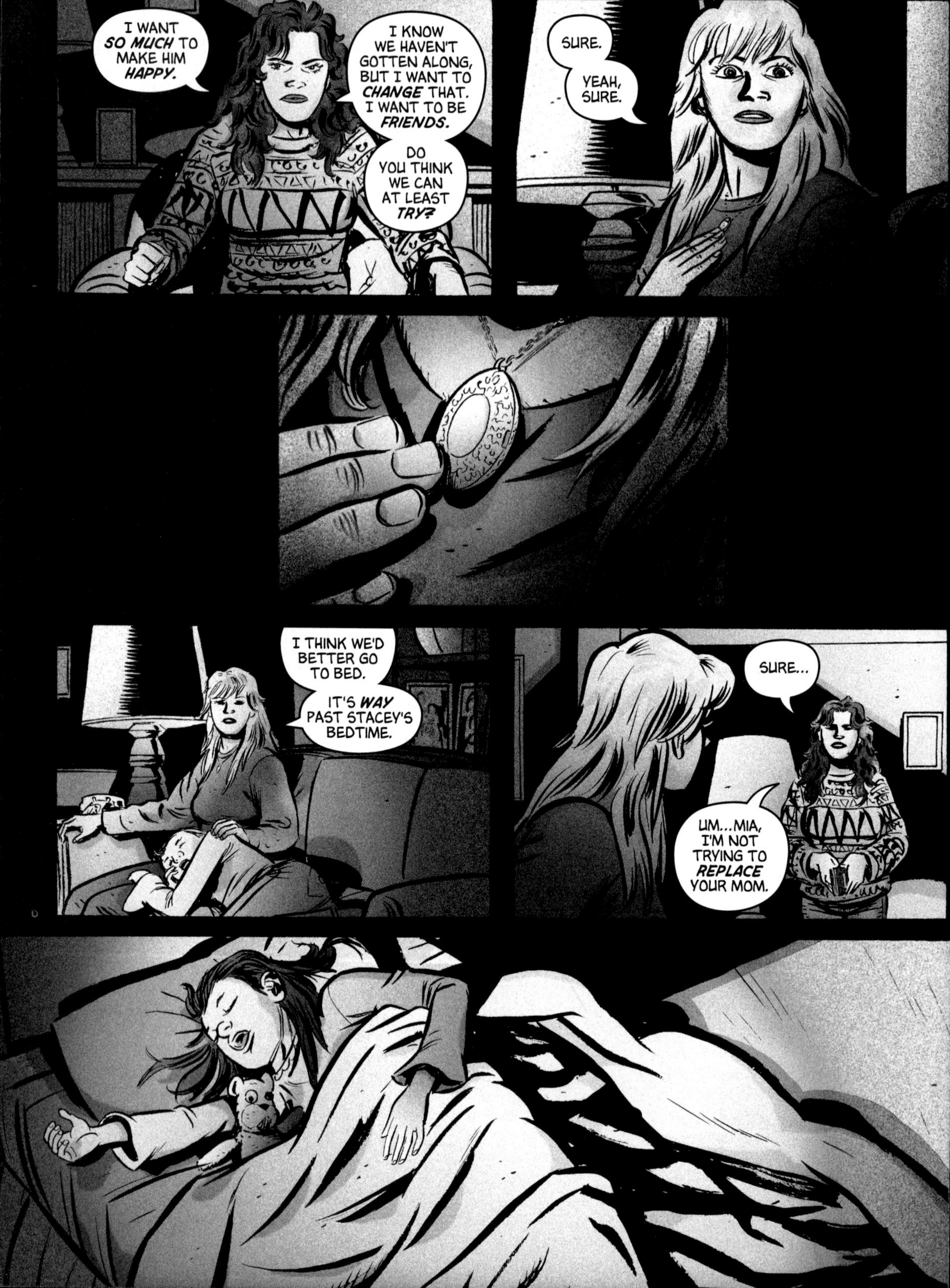
I WANT SO MUCH TO MAKE HIM HAPPY.
I KNOW WE HAVEN'T GOTTEN ALONG, BUT I WANT TO CHANGE THAT. I WANT TO BE FRIENDS.
DO YOU THINK WE CAN AT LEAST TRY?
SURE.
YEAH, SURE.
I THINK WE'D BETTER GO TO BED.
IT'S WAY PAST STACEY'S BEDTIME.
SURE...
UM...MIA, I'M NOT TRYING TO REPLACE YOUR MOM.

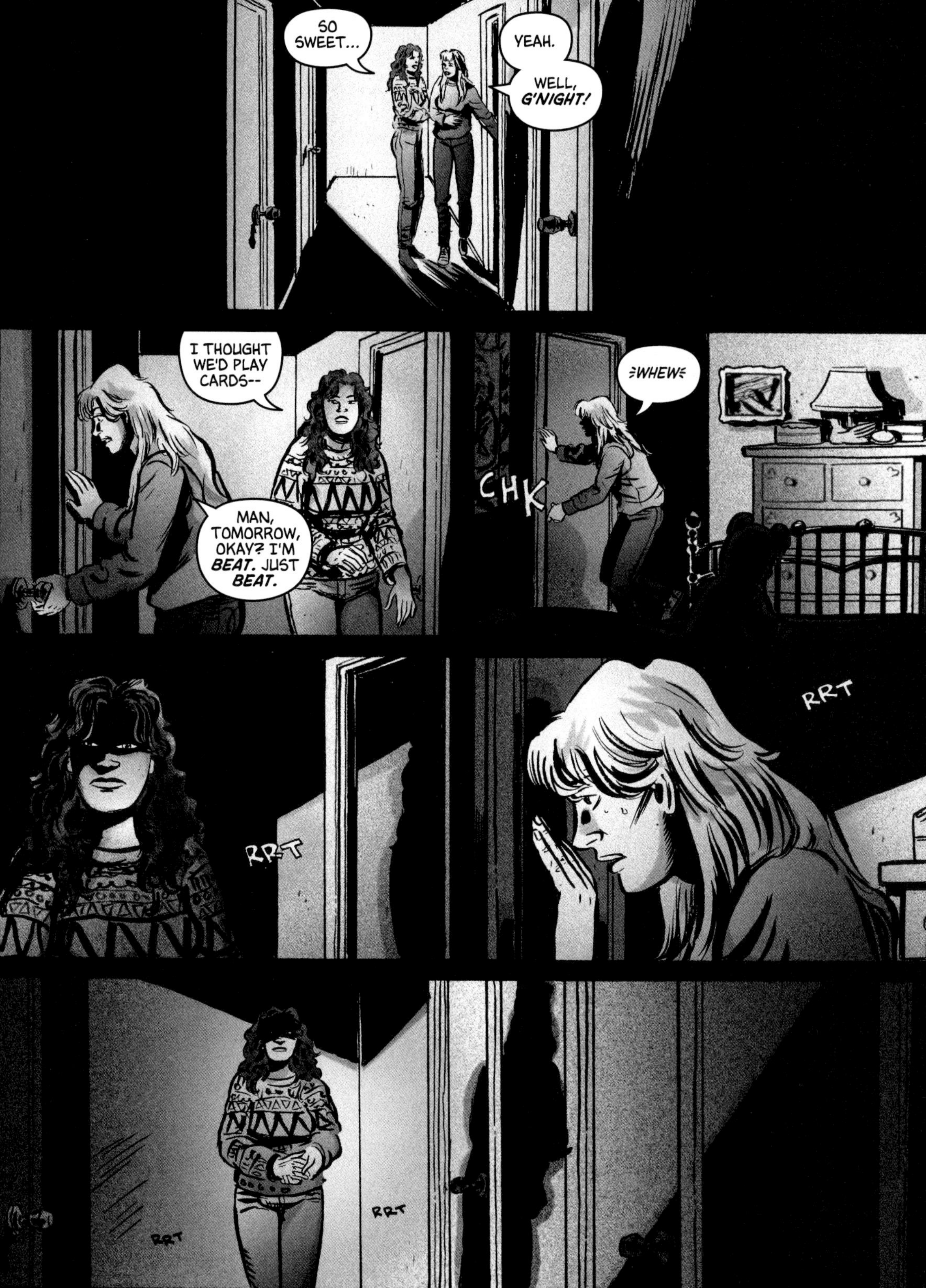
SO SWEET...
YEAH.
WELL, G'NIGHT!
I THOUGHT WE'D PLAY CARDS--
MAN, TOMORROW, OKAY? I'M BEAT. JUST BEAT.
CHK
WHEW
RRT
RRT
RRT
RRT

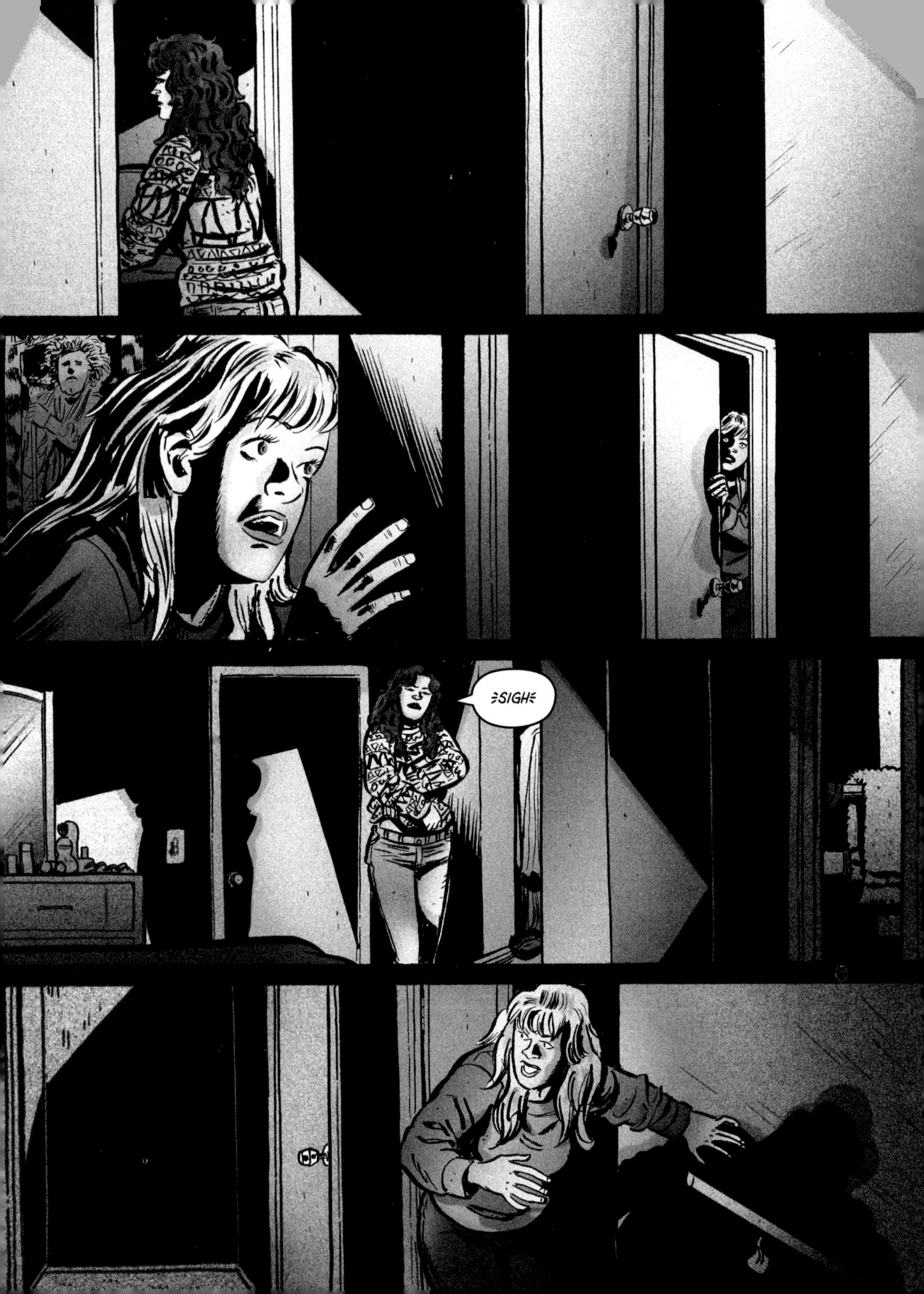
SIGH

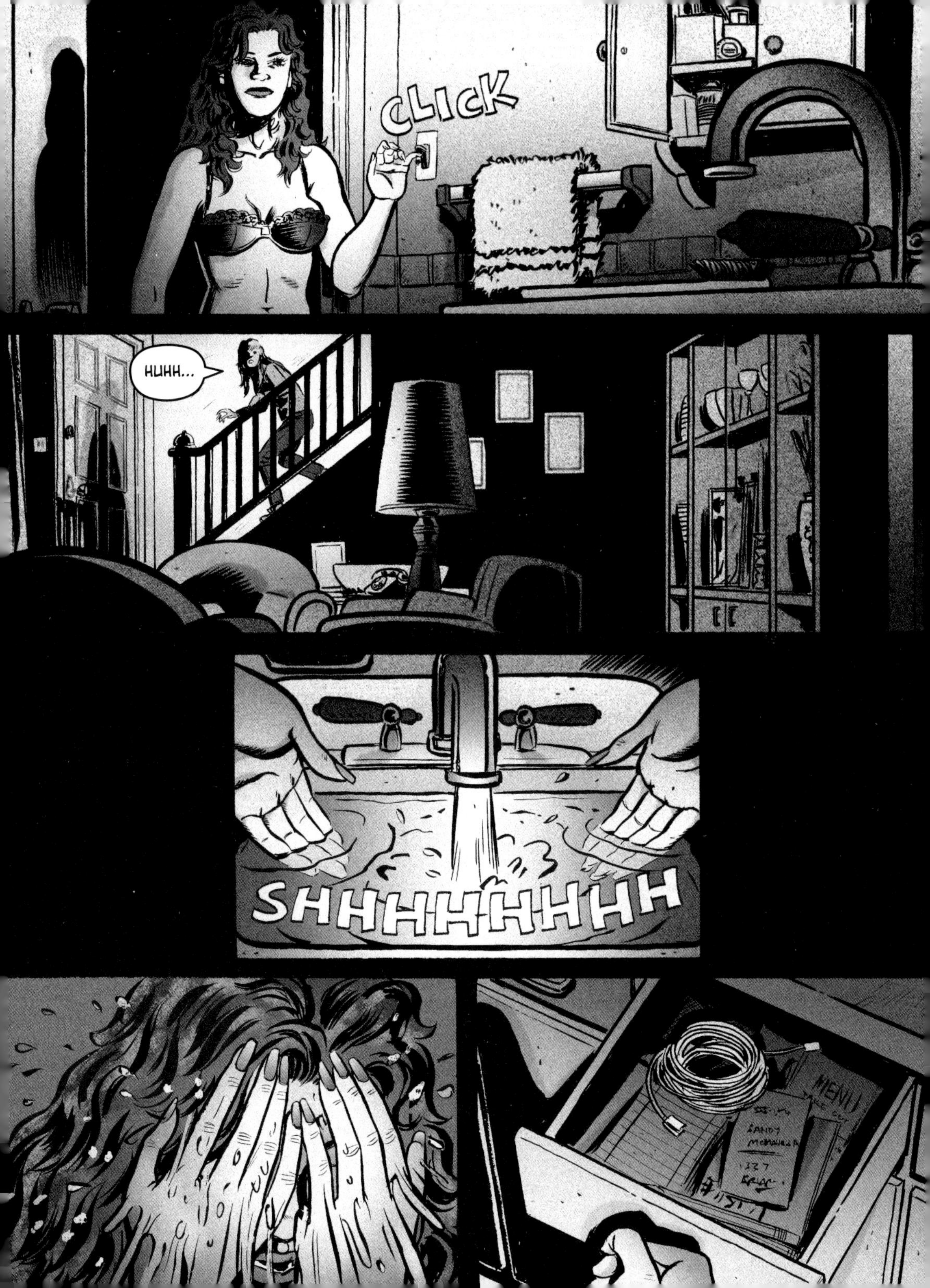
CLICK
HUHH...
SHHHHHHHHH
MENU
SANDY
1327

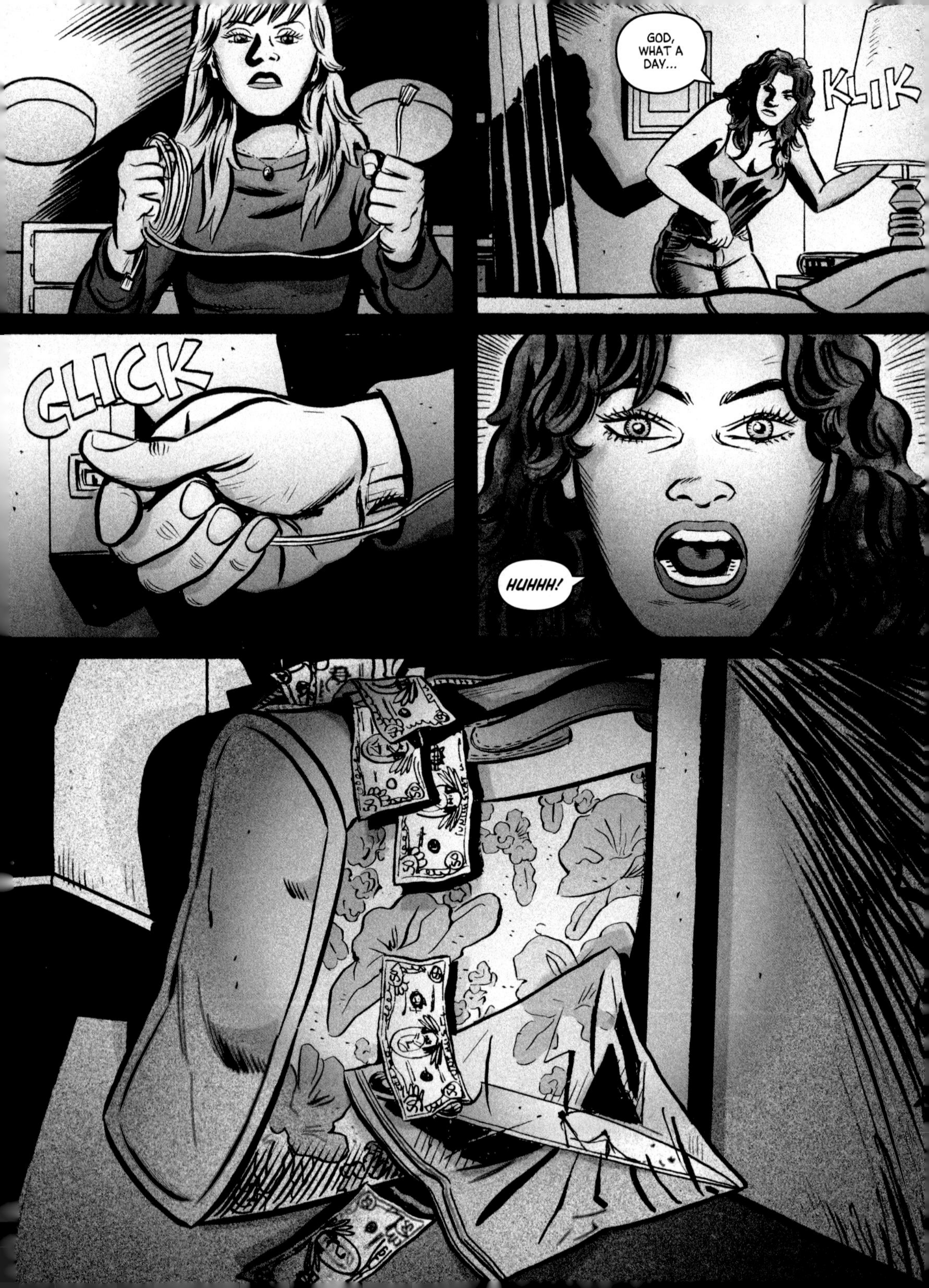
GOD, WHAT A DAY...
KLIK
CLICK
HUHHH!

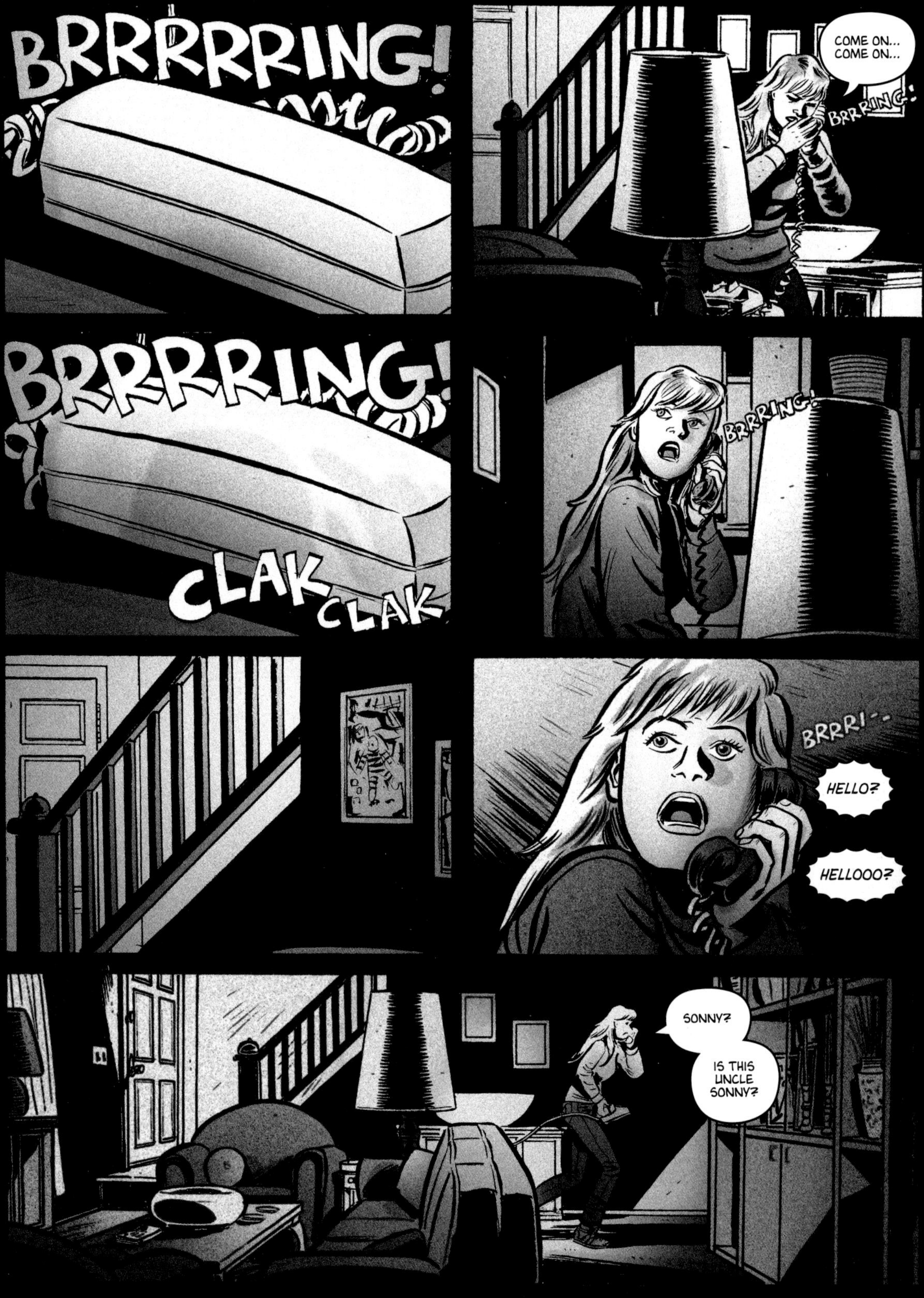
BRRRRRING!
COME ON...
COME ON...
BRRRING!
BRRRRING!
CLAK
CLAK
BRRRING!
BRRRI--
HELLO?
HELLOOO?
SONNY?
IS THIS
UNCLE
SONNY?

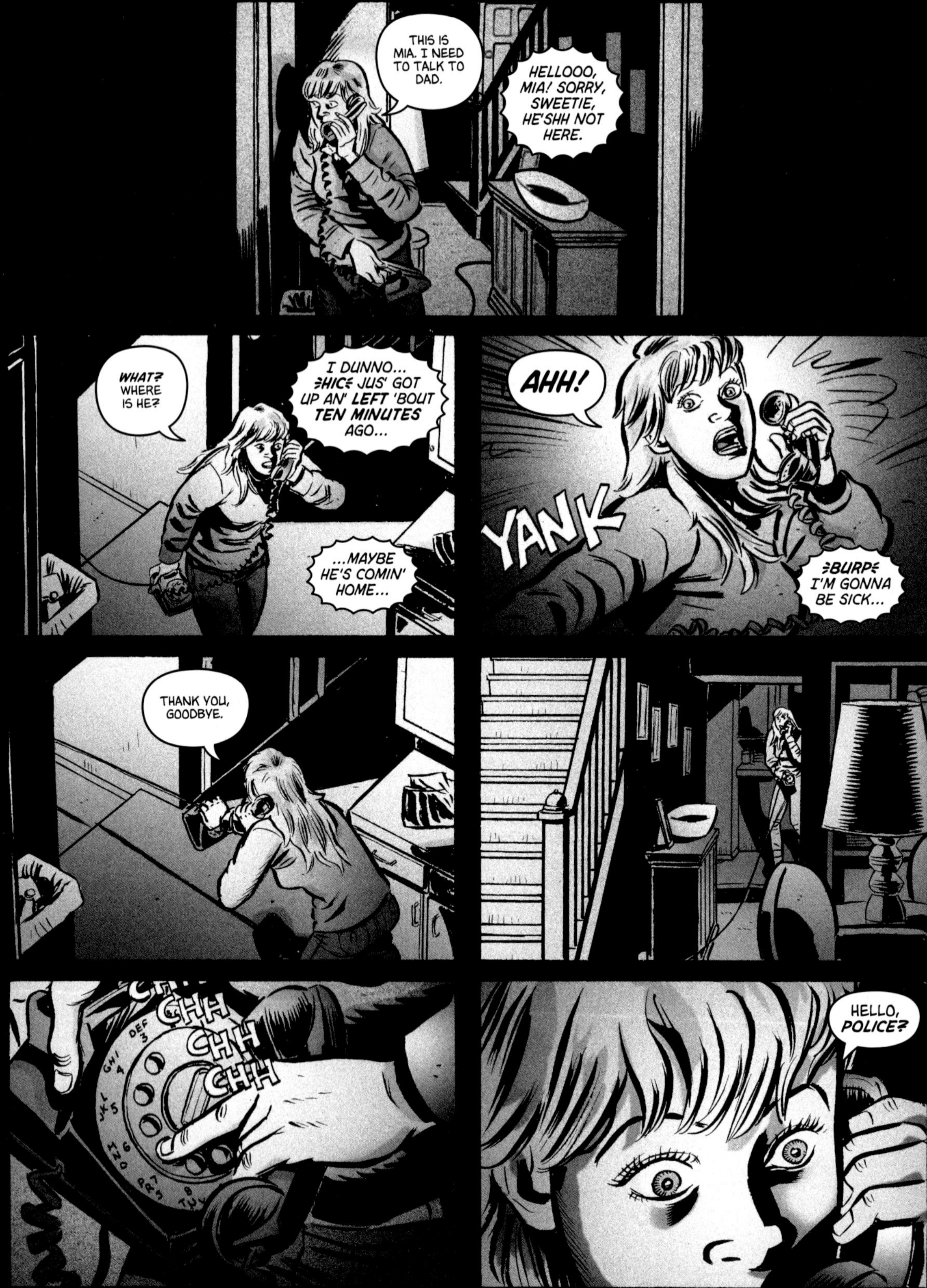
THIS IS MIA. I NEED TO TALK TO DAD.
HELLOOO, MIA! SORRY, SWEETIE, HE'SHH NOT HERE.
WHAT? WHERE IS HE?
I DUNNO... *HIC* JUS' GOT UP AN' LEFT 'BOUT TEN MINUTES AGO...
...MAYBE HE'S COMIN' HOME...
AHH!
YANK
BURP I'M GONNA BE SICK...
THANK YOU, GOODBYE.
CHH CHH CHH CHH
HELLO, POLICE?

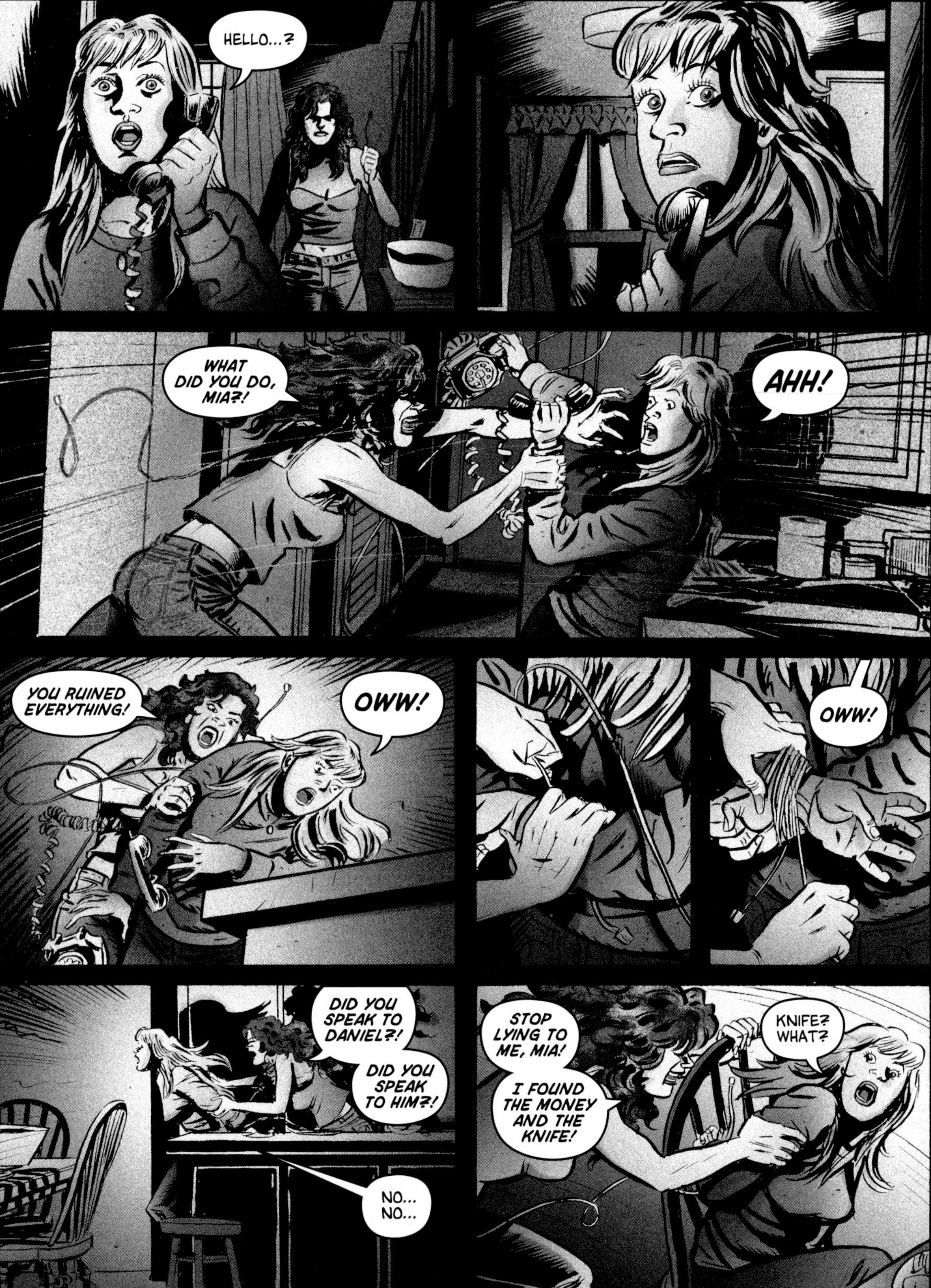
HELLO...?
WHAT DID YOU DO, MIA?!
AHH!
YOU RUINED EVERYTHING!
OWW!
OWW!
DID YOU SPEAK TO DANIEL?!
DID YOU SPEAK TO HIM?!
NO... NO...
STOP LYING TO ME, MIA!
I FOUND THE MONEY AND THE KNIFE!
KNIFE? WHAT?

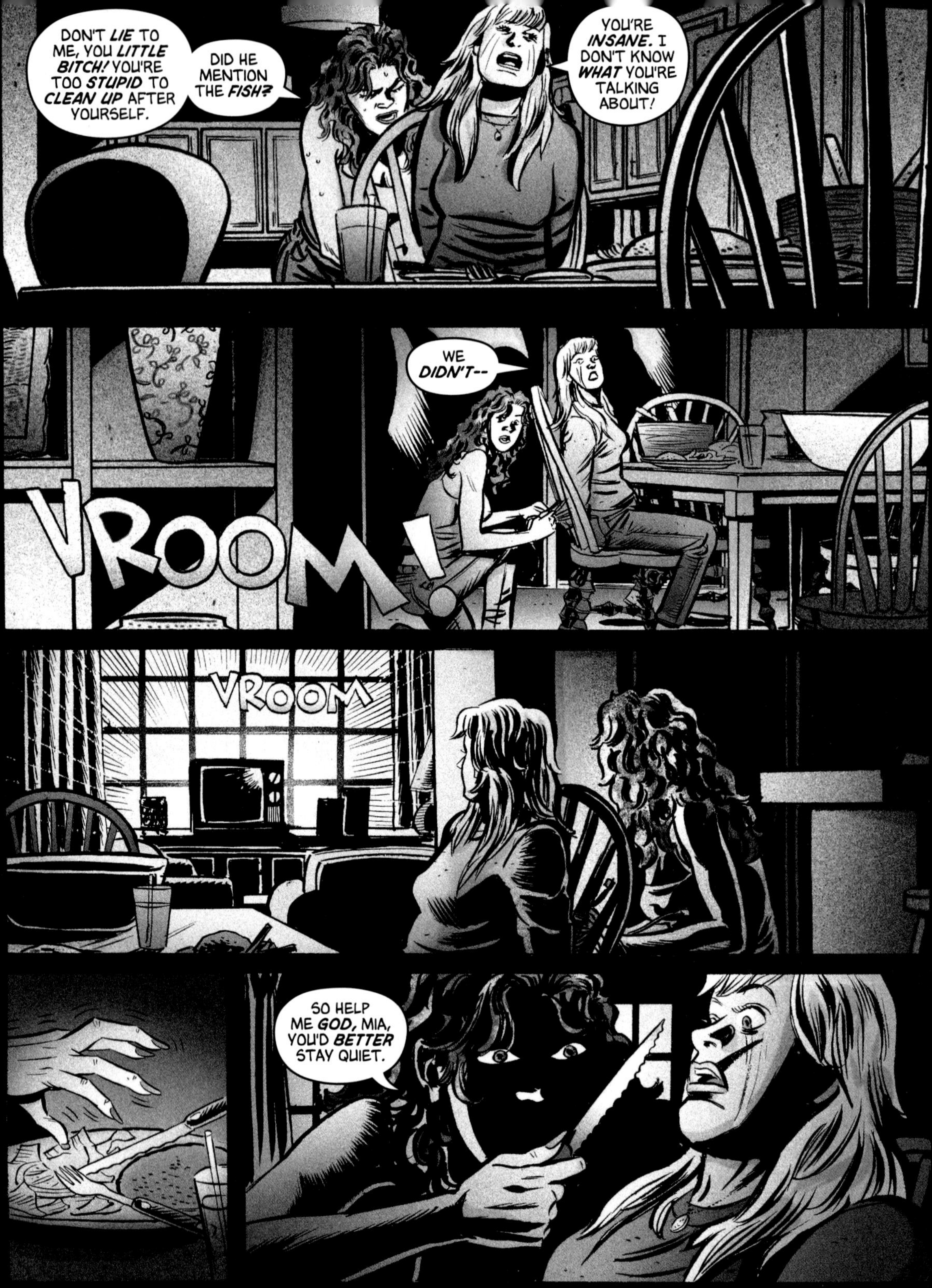
DON'T LIE TO ME, YOU LITTLE BITCH! YOU'RE TOO STUPID TO CLEAN UP AFTER YOURSELF.
DID HE MENTION THE FISH?
YOU'RE INSANE. I DON'T KNOW WHAT YOU'RE TALKING ABOUT!
WE DIDN'T--
VROOM!
VROOM
SO HELP ME GOD, MIA, YOU'D BETTER STAY QUIET.

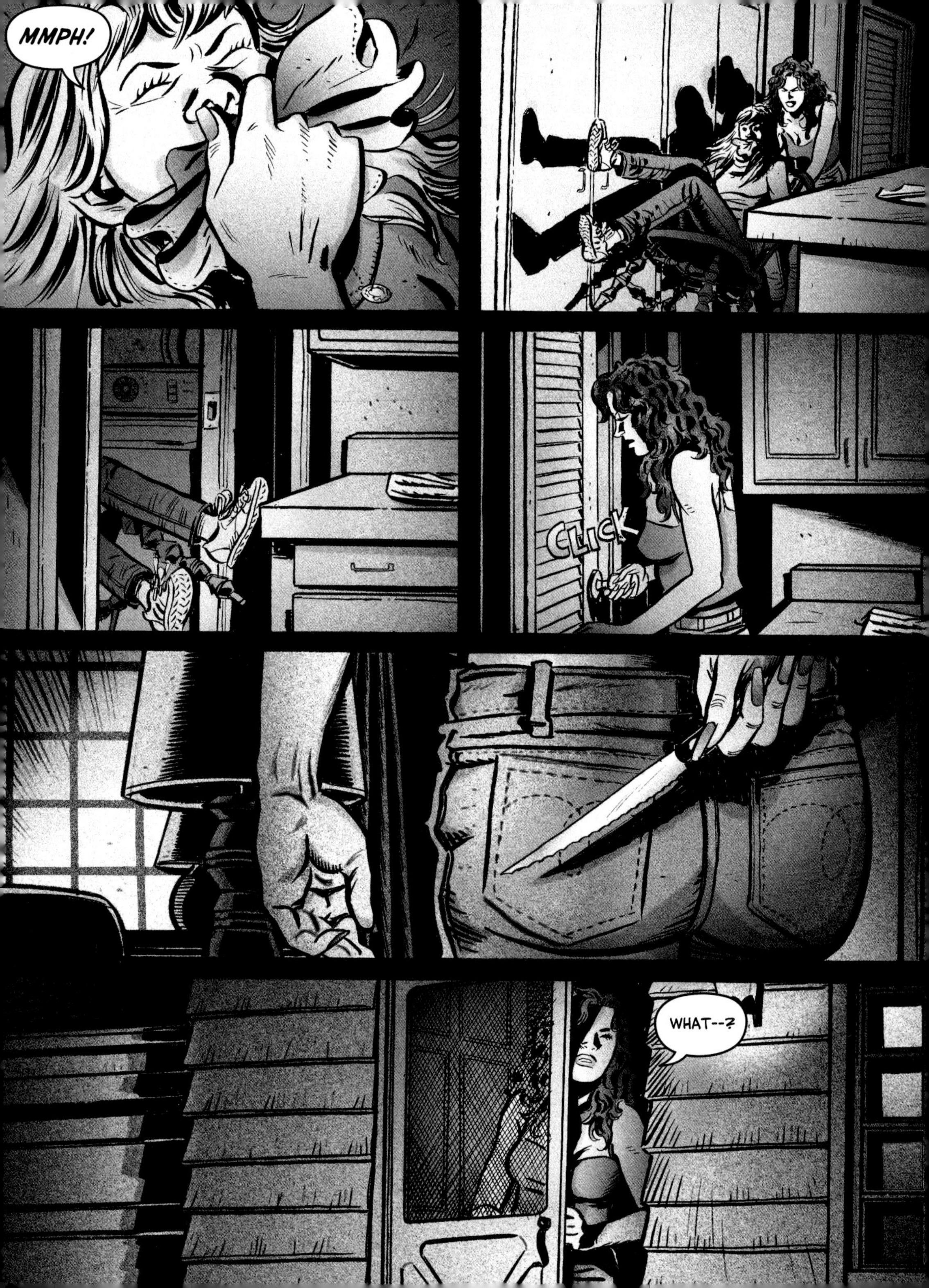
MMPH!
CLICK
WHAT--?

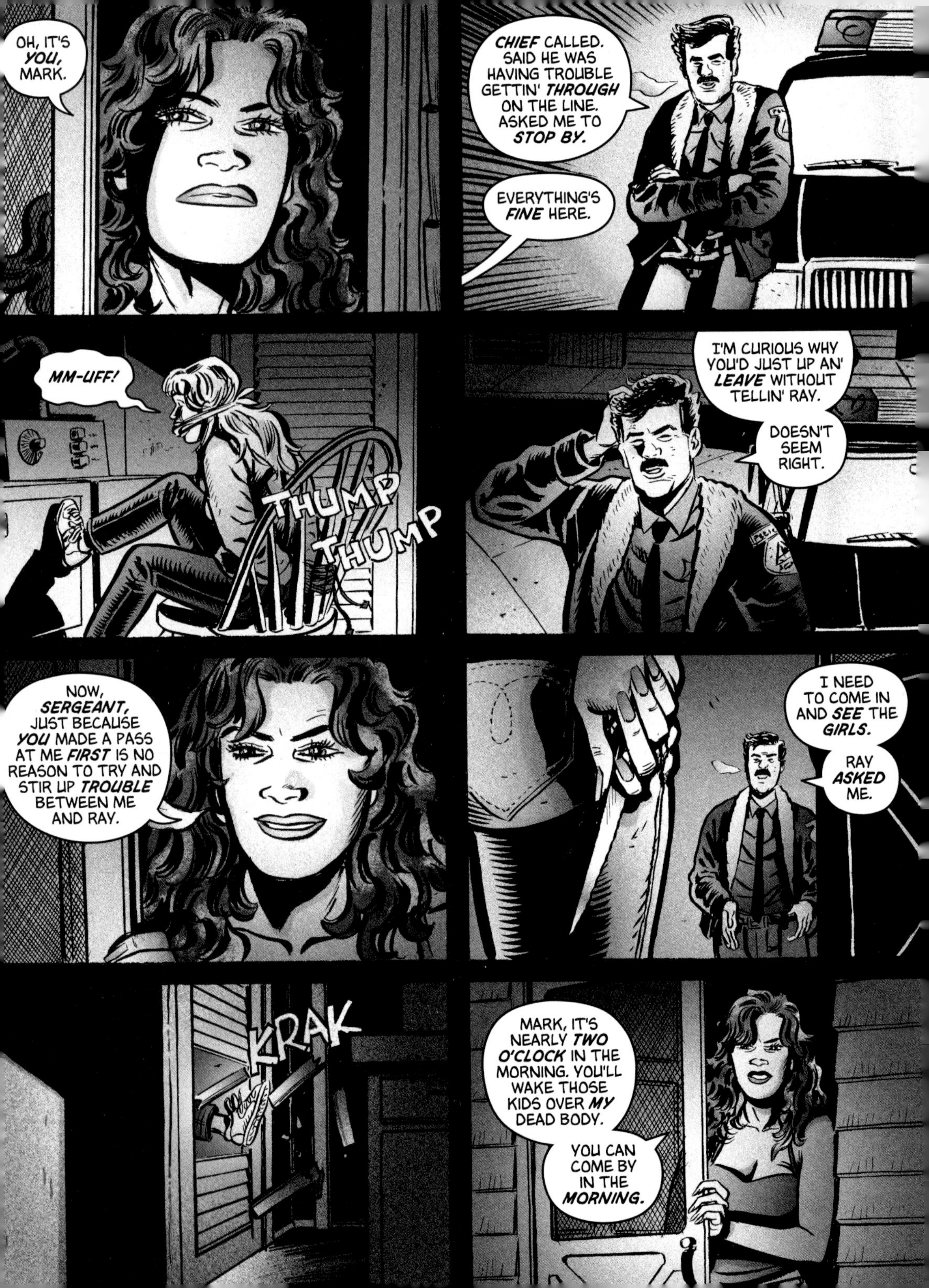
OH, IT'S *YOU,* MARK.
CHIEF CALLED. SAID HE WAS HAVING TROUBLE GETTIN' *THROUGH* ON THE LINE. ASKED ME TO *STOP BY.*
EVERYTHING'S *FINE* HERE.
MM-UFF!
THUMP THUMP
I'M CURIOUS WHY YOU'D JUST UP AN' *LEAVE* WITHOUT TELLIN' RAY.
DOESN'T SEEM RIGHT.
NOW, *SERGEANT,* JUST BECAUSE *YOU* MADE A PASS AT ME *FIRST* IS NO REASON TO TRY AND STIR UP *TROUBLE* BETWEEN ME AND RAY.
I NEED TO COME IN AND *SEE* THE *GIRLS.*
RAY *ASKED* ME.
KRAK
MARK, IT'S NEARLY *TWO O'CLOCK* IN THE MORNING. YOU'LL WAKE THOSE KIDS OVER *MY* DEAD BODY.
YOU CAN COME BY IN THE *MORNING.*

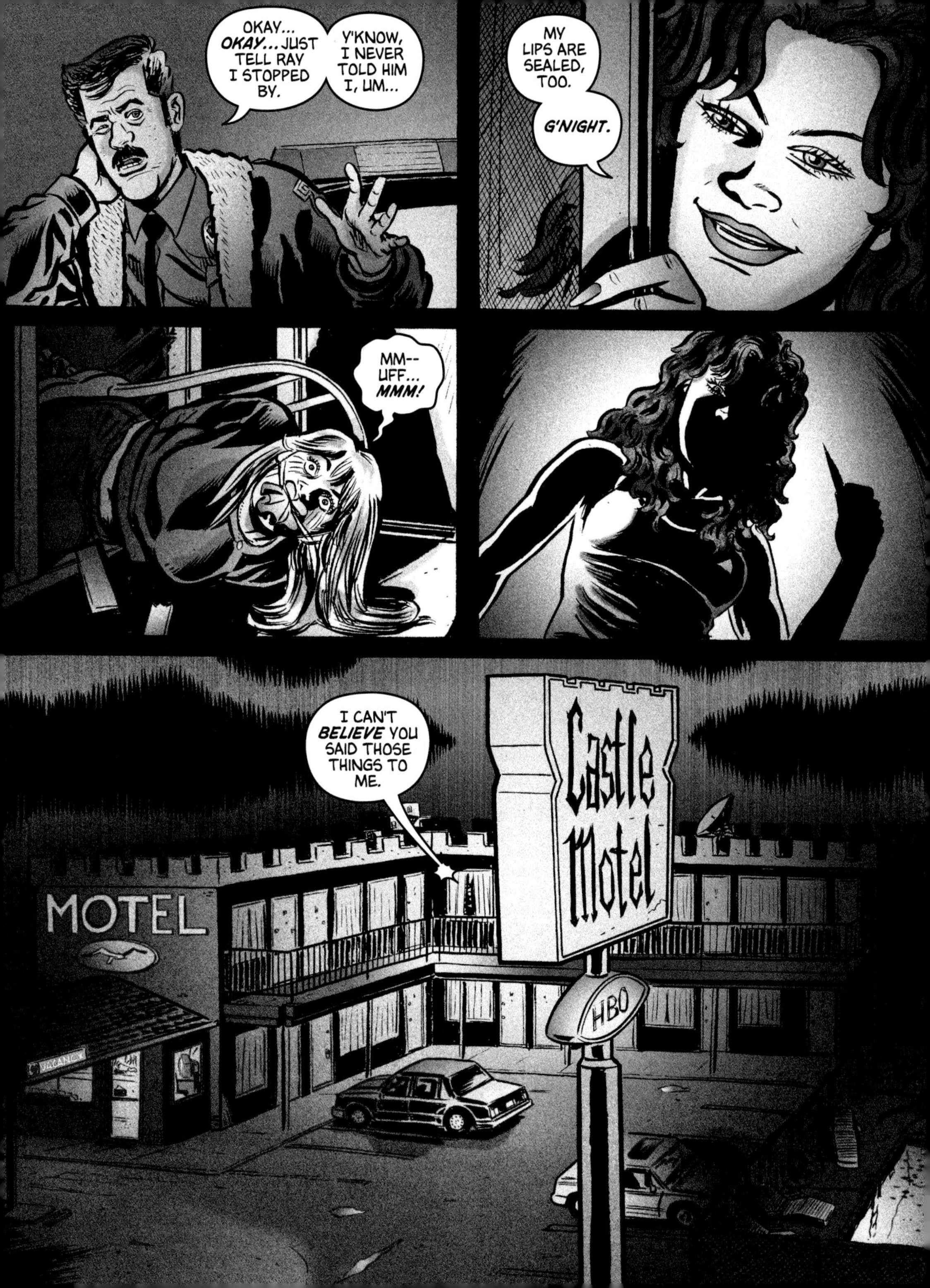
OKAY... **OKAY...** JUST TELL RAY I STOPPED BY.
Y'KNOW, I NEVER TOLD HIM I, UM...
MY LIPS ARE SEALED, TOO.
G'NIGHT.
MM-- UFF... **MMM!**
I CAN'T **BELIEVE** YOU SAID THOSE THINGS TO ME.
Castle Motel
MOTEL
HBO

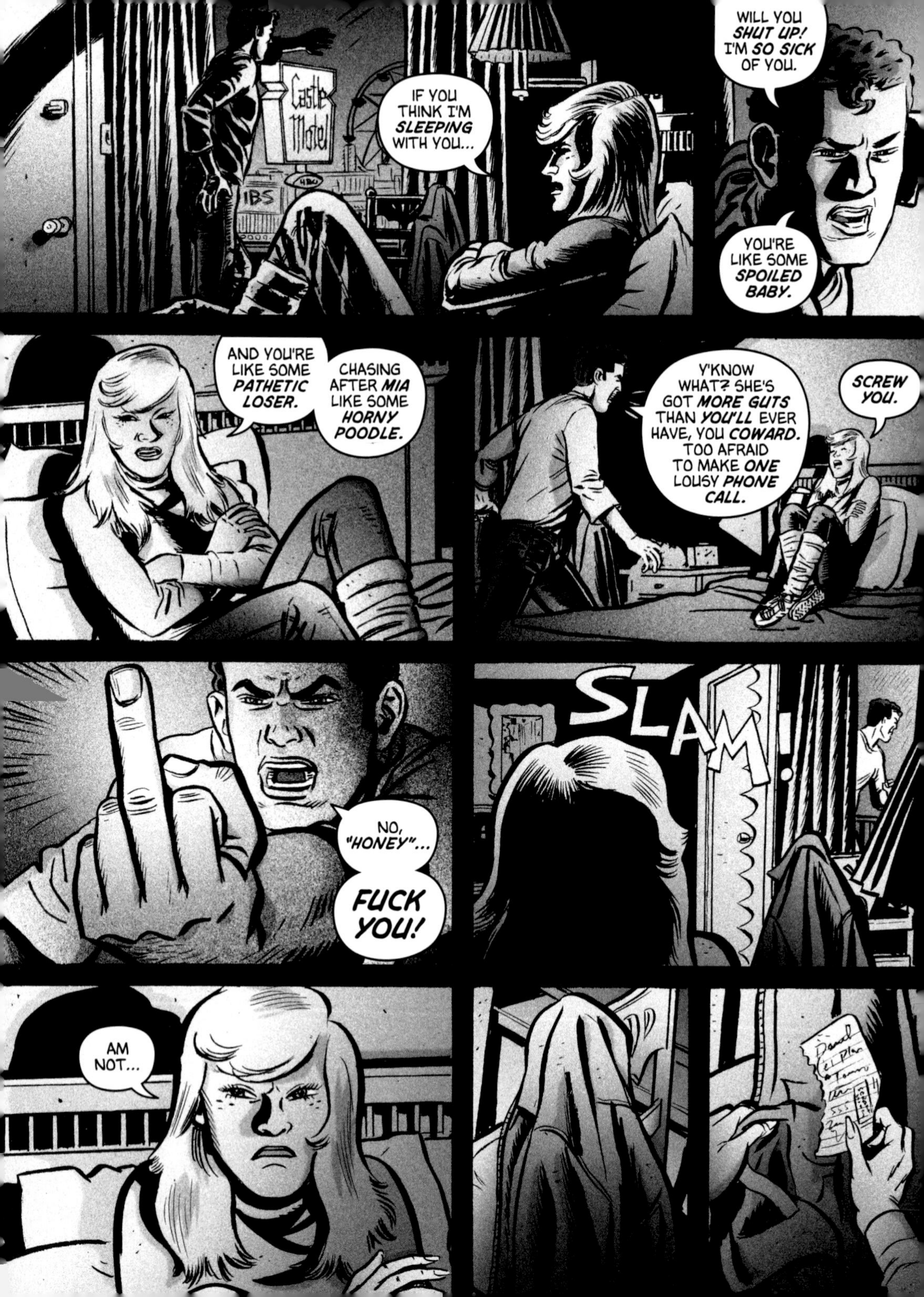

IF YOU THINK I'M SLEEPING WITH YOU...
WILL YOU SHUT UP! I'M SO SICK OF YOU.
YOU'RE LIKE SOME SPOILED BABY.
AND YOU'RE LIKE SOME PATHETIC LOSER.
CHASING AFTER MIA LIKE SOME HORNY POODLE.
Y'KNOW WHAT? SHE'S GOT MORE GUTS THAN YOU'LL EVER HAVE, YOU COWARD. TOO AFRAID TO MAKE ONE LOUSY PHONE CALL.
SCREW YOU.
NO, "HONEY"...
FUCK YOU!
SLAM!
AM NOT...

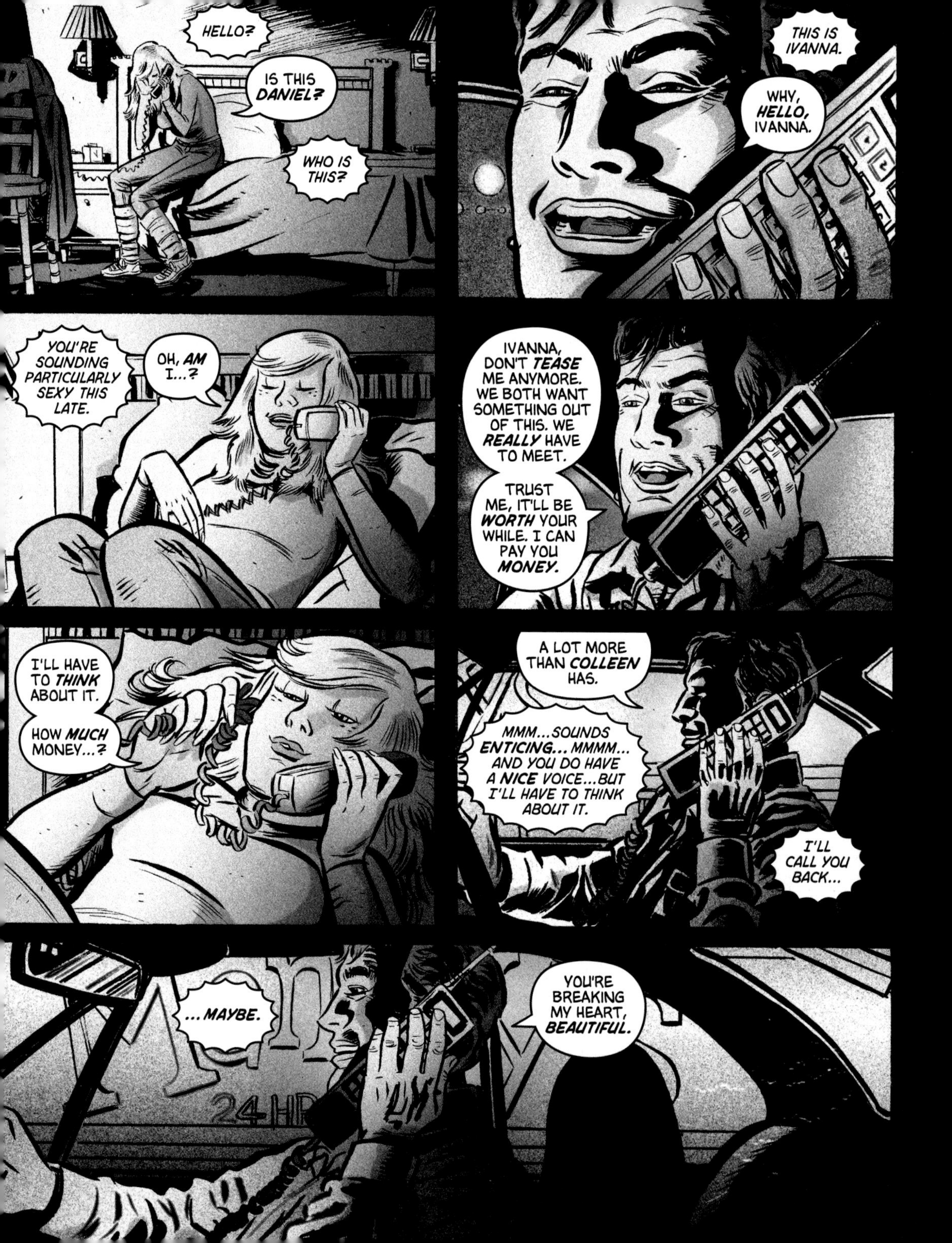
HELLO?
THIS IS IVANNA.
IS THIS DANIEL?
WHY, HELLO, IVANNA.
WHO IS THIS?
YOU'RE SOUNDING PARTICULARLY SEXY THIS LATE.
OH, AM I...?
IVANNA, DON'T TEASE ME ANYMORE. WE BOTH WANT SOMETHING OUT OF THIS. WE REALLY HAVE TO MEET.
TRUST ME, IT'LL BE WORTH YOUR WHILE. I CAN PAY YOU MONEY.
I'LL HAVE TO THINK ABOUT IT.
HOW MUCH MONEY...?
A LOT MORE THAN COLLEEN HAS.
MMM...SOUNDS ENTICING...MMMM... AND YOU DO HAVE A NICE VOICE...BUT I'LL HAVE TO THINK ABOUT IT.
I'LL CALL YOU BACK...
...MAYBE.
YOU'RE BREAKING MY HEART, BEAUTIFUL.

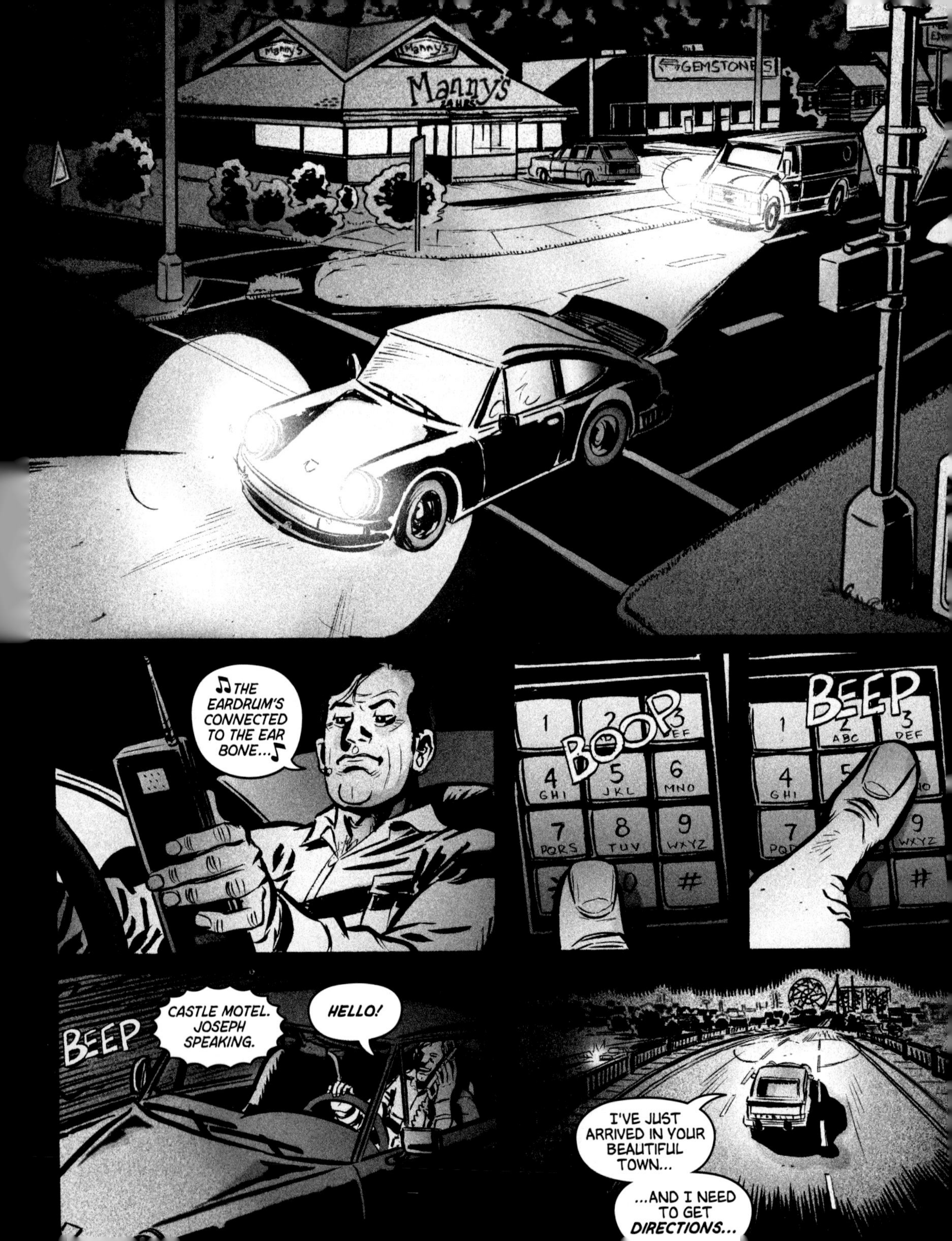

MANNY'S
MANNY'S
MANNY'S 24 HRS.
GEMSTONES
♫THE EARDRUM'S CONNECTED TO THE EAR BONE...♫
BOOP
BEEP
BEEP
CASTLE MOTEL. JOSEPH SPEAKING.
HELLO!
I'VE JUST ARRIVED IN YOUR BEAUTIFUL TOWN...
...AND I NEED TO GET DIRECTIONS...

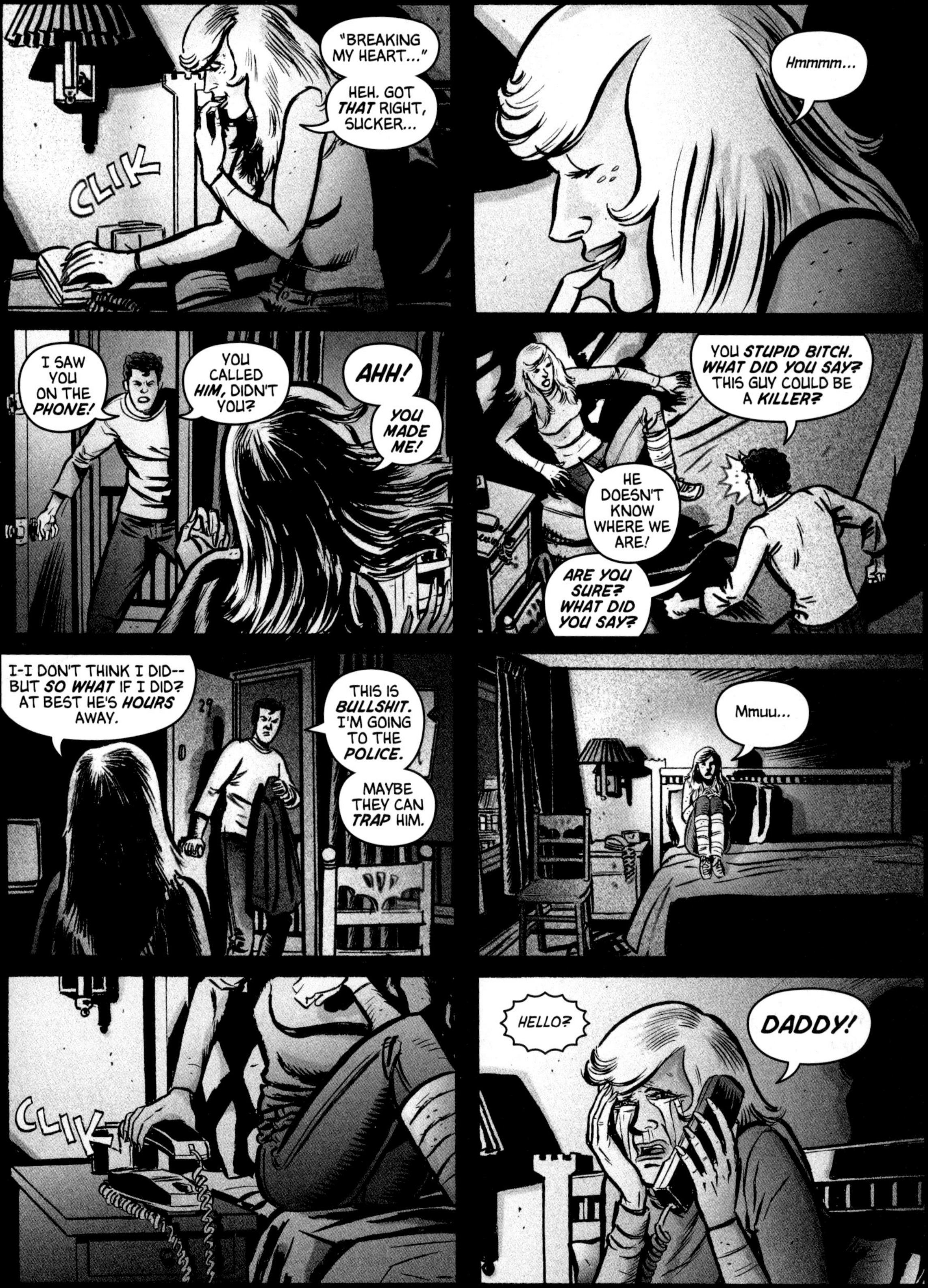

"BREAKING MY HEART..."
HEH. GOT THAT RIGHT, SUCKER...
CLIK
Hmmmm...
I SAW YOU ON THE PHONE!
YOU CALLED HIM, DIDN'T YOU?
AHH!
YOU MADE ME!
YOU STUPID BITCH. WHAT DID YOU SAY? THIS GUY COULD BE A KILLER?
HE DOESN'T KNOW WHERE WE ARE!
ARE YOU SURE? WHAT DID YOU SAY?
I-I DON'T THINK I DID-- BUT SO WHAT IF I DID? AT BEST HE'S HOURS AWAY.
THIS IS BULLSHIT. I'M GOING TO THE POLICE.
MAYBE THEY CAN TRAP HIM.
Mmuu...
CLIK
HELLO?
DADDY!

TINK
KLANK
CHAK

YOU HAVE *NO IDEA* WHAT YOU'VE DONE, MIA.

YOU'RE A STUPID, *STUPID* GIRL.

HE WAS SO *SOPHISTICATED.* SO *BEYOND* ME.

I WAS SO *IN LOVE* WITH HIM. I SAID I'D DO *ANYTHING* FOR HIM.

CHINK

TINK

I *STOLE* FOR HIM!

DANIEL'S A *DANGEROUS* MAN.

YOU HAVE *NO IDEA* WHAT HE'S *CAPABLE OF.*

I DON'T KNOW WHAT TO DO, MIA.

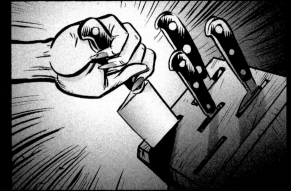

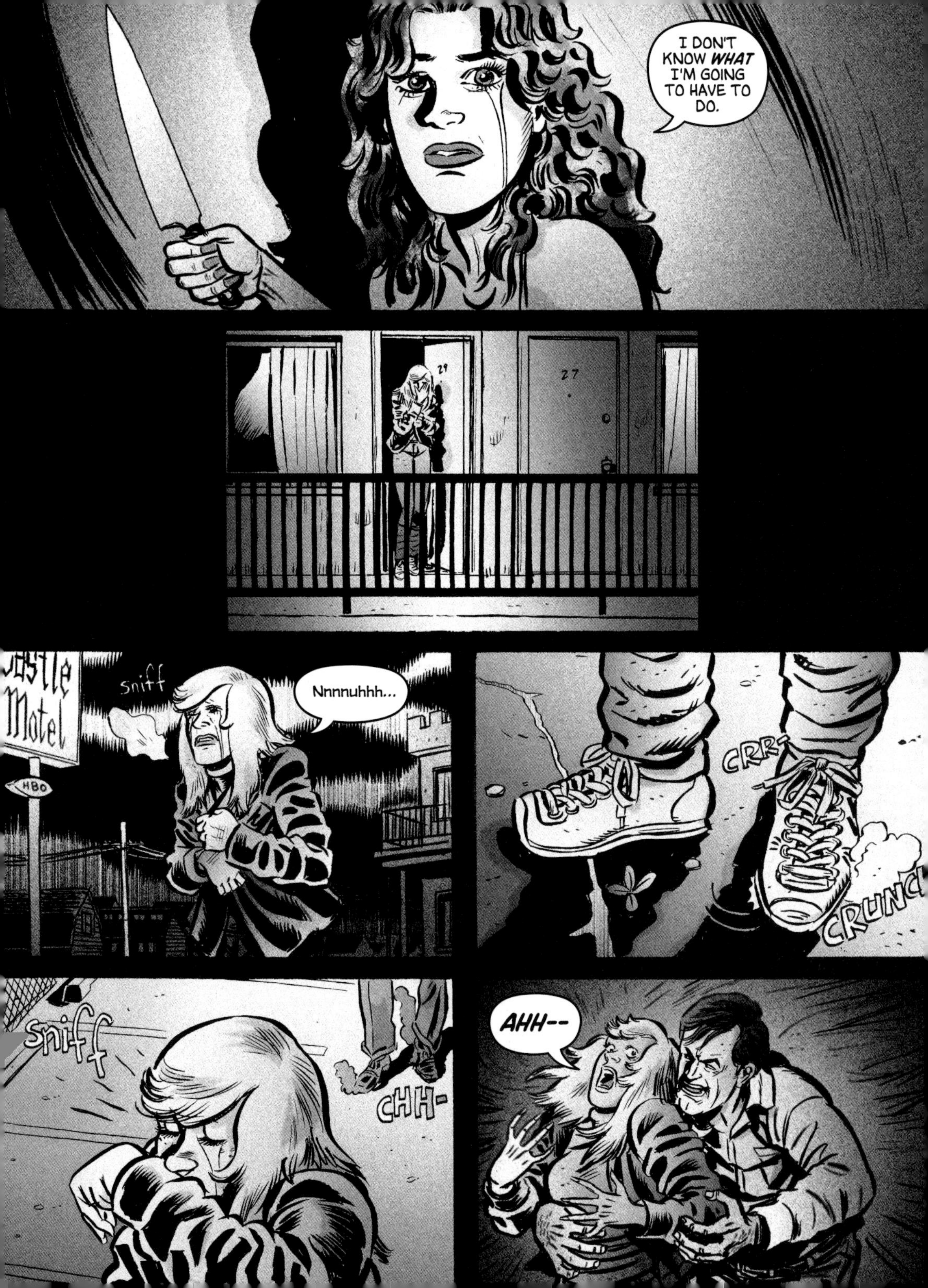
I DON'T KNOW WHAT I'M GOING TO HAVE TO DO.
29
27
sniff
Nnnnuhhh...
HBO
CRR-
CRUNCH
sniff
CHH-
AHH--

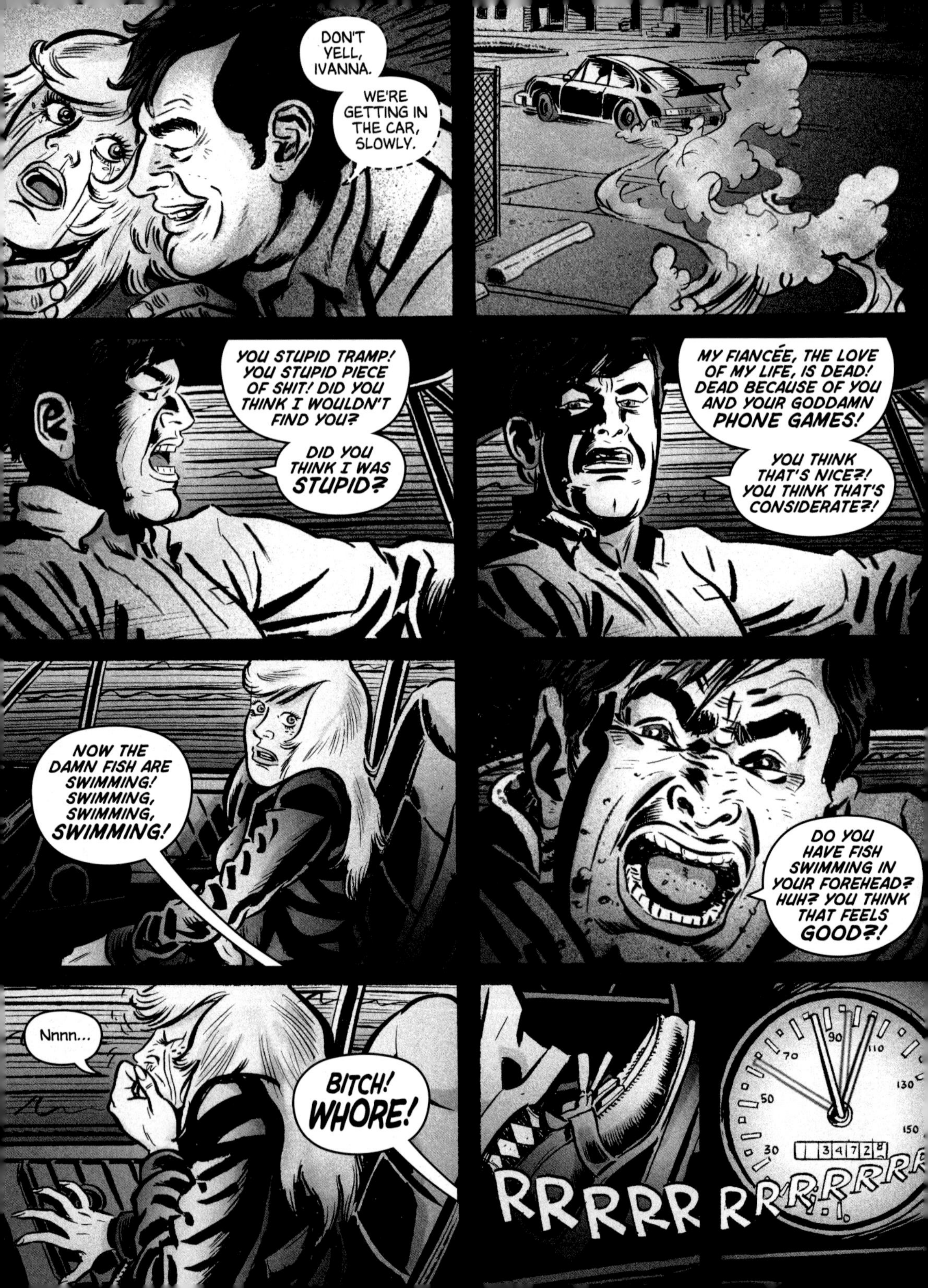
DON'T YELL, IVANNA.
WE'RE GETTING IN THE CAR, SLOWLY.
YOU STUPID TRAMP! YOU STUPID PIECE OF SHIT! DID YOU THINK I WOULDN'T FIND YOU?
DID YOU THINK I WAS STUPID?
MY FIANCÉE, THE LOVE OF MY LIFE, IS DEAD! DEAD BECAUSE OF YOU AND YOUR GODDAMN PHONE GAMES!
YOU THINK THAT'S NICE?! YOU THINK THAT'S CONSIDERATE?!
NOW THE DAMN FISH ARE SWIMMING! SWIMMING, SWIMMING, SWIMMING!
DO YOU HAVE FISH SWIMMING IN YOUR FOREHEAD? HUH? YOU THINK THAT FEELS GOOD?!
Nnnn...
BITCH! WHORE!
RRRRR RRRRRRR

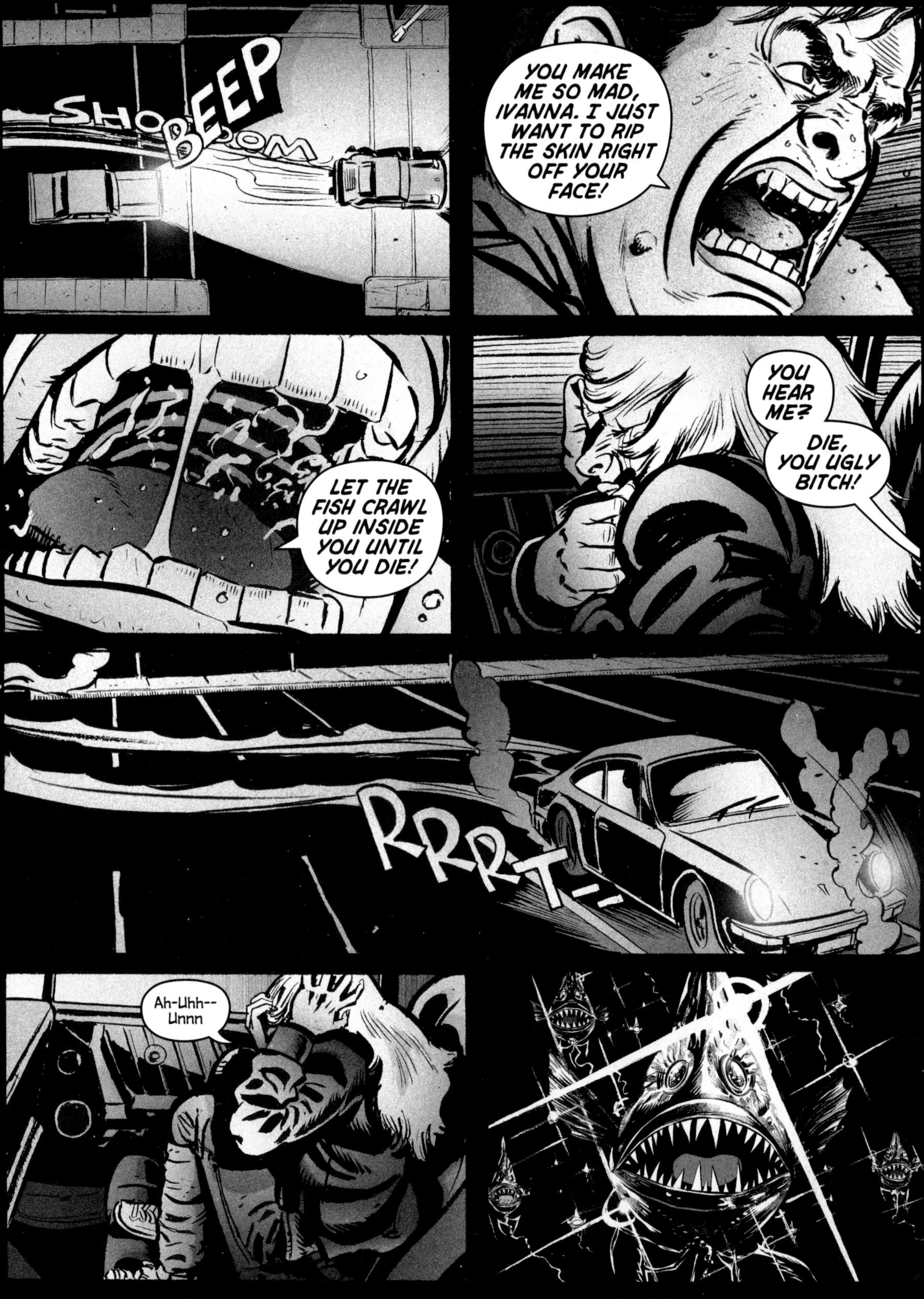
SHOBEEP
SHOBOOM
YOU MAKE ME SO MAD, IVANNA. I JUST WANT TO RIP THE SKIN RIGHT OFF YOUR FACE!
LET THE FISH CRAWL UP INSIDE YOU UNTIL YOU DIE!
YOU HEAR ME?
DIE, YOU UGLY BITCH!
RRRT--
Ah-Uhh-- Unnn

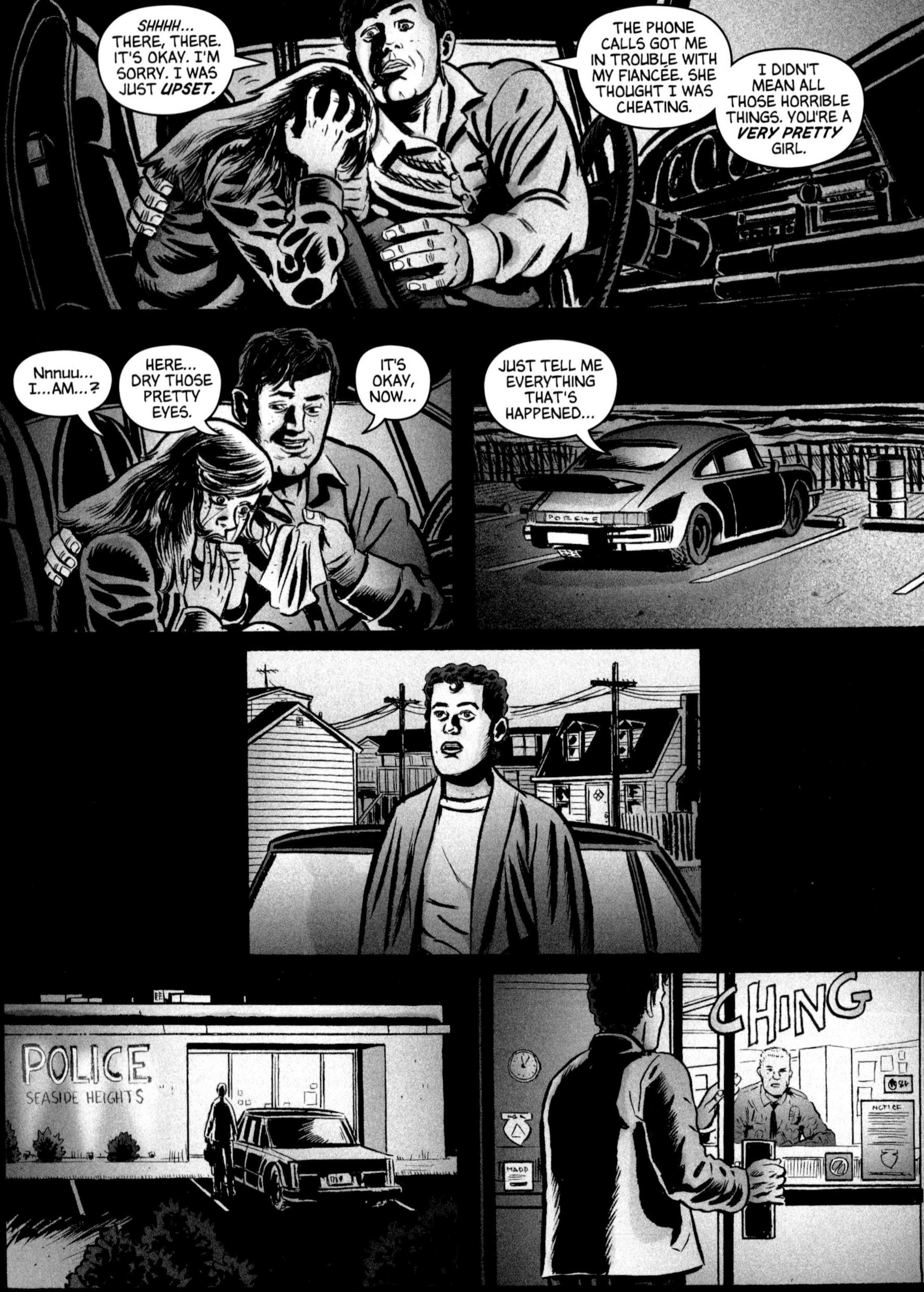
SHHHH... THERE, THERE. IT'S OKAY. I'M SORRY. I WAS JUST UPSET.
THE PHONE CALLS GOT ME IN TROUBLE WITH MY FIANCÉE. SHE THOUGHT I WAS CHEATING.
I DIDN'T MEAN ALL THOSE HORRIBLE THINGS. YOU'RE A VERY PRETTY GIRL.
Nnnuu... I...AM...?
HERE... DRY THOSE PRETTY EYES.
IT'S OKAY, NOW...
JUST TELL ME EVERYTHING THAT'S HAPPENED...
PORSCHE
POLICE
SEASIDE HEIGHTS
CHING
MADD
NOTICE

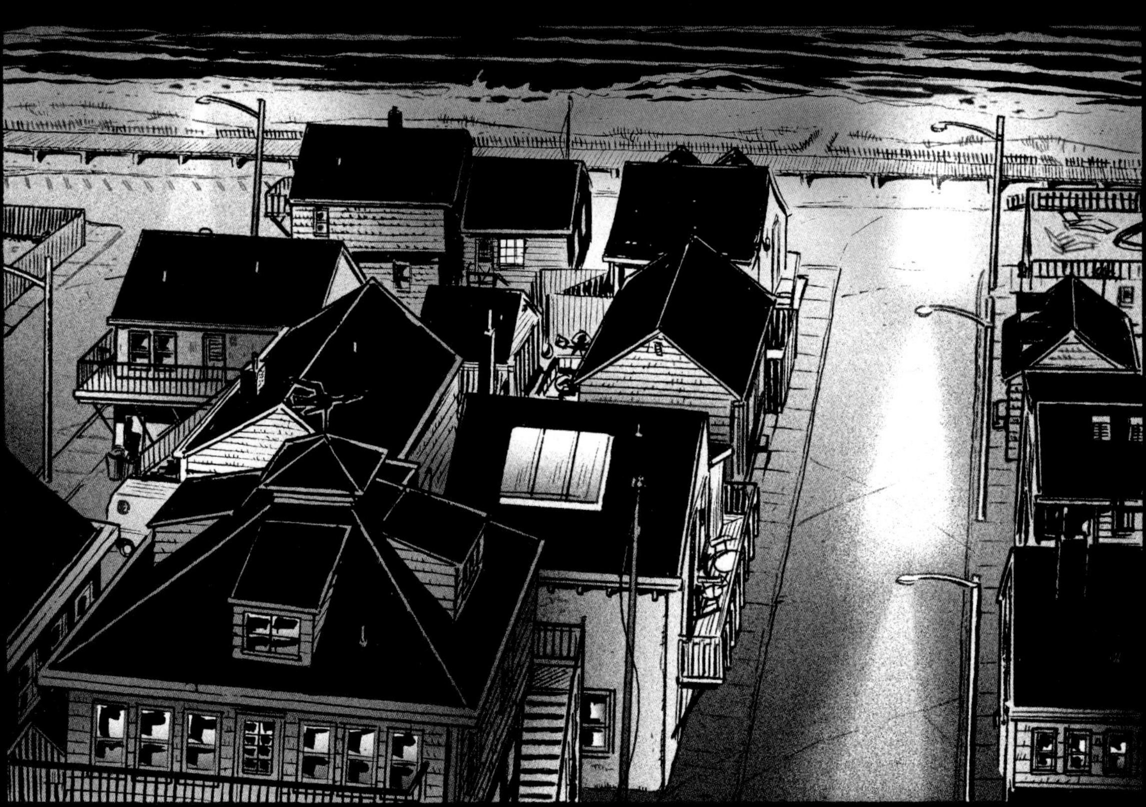

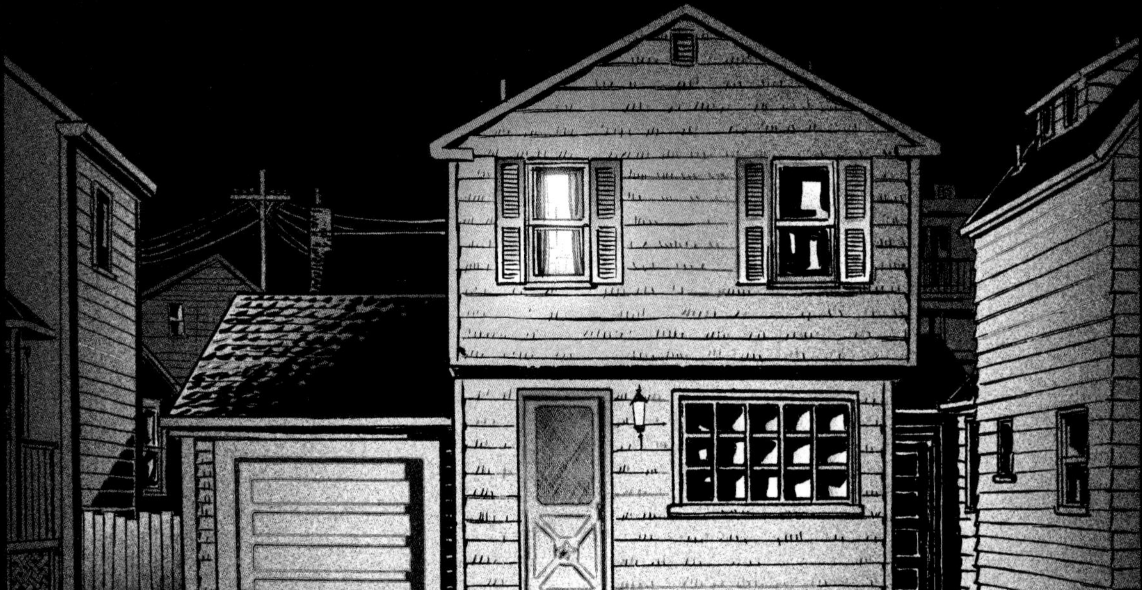

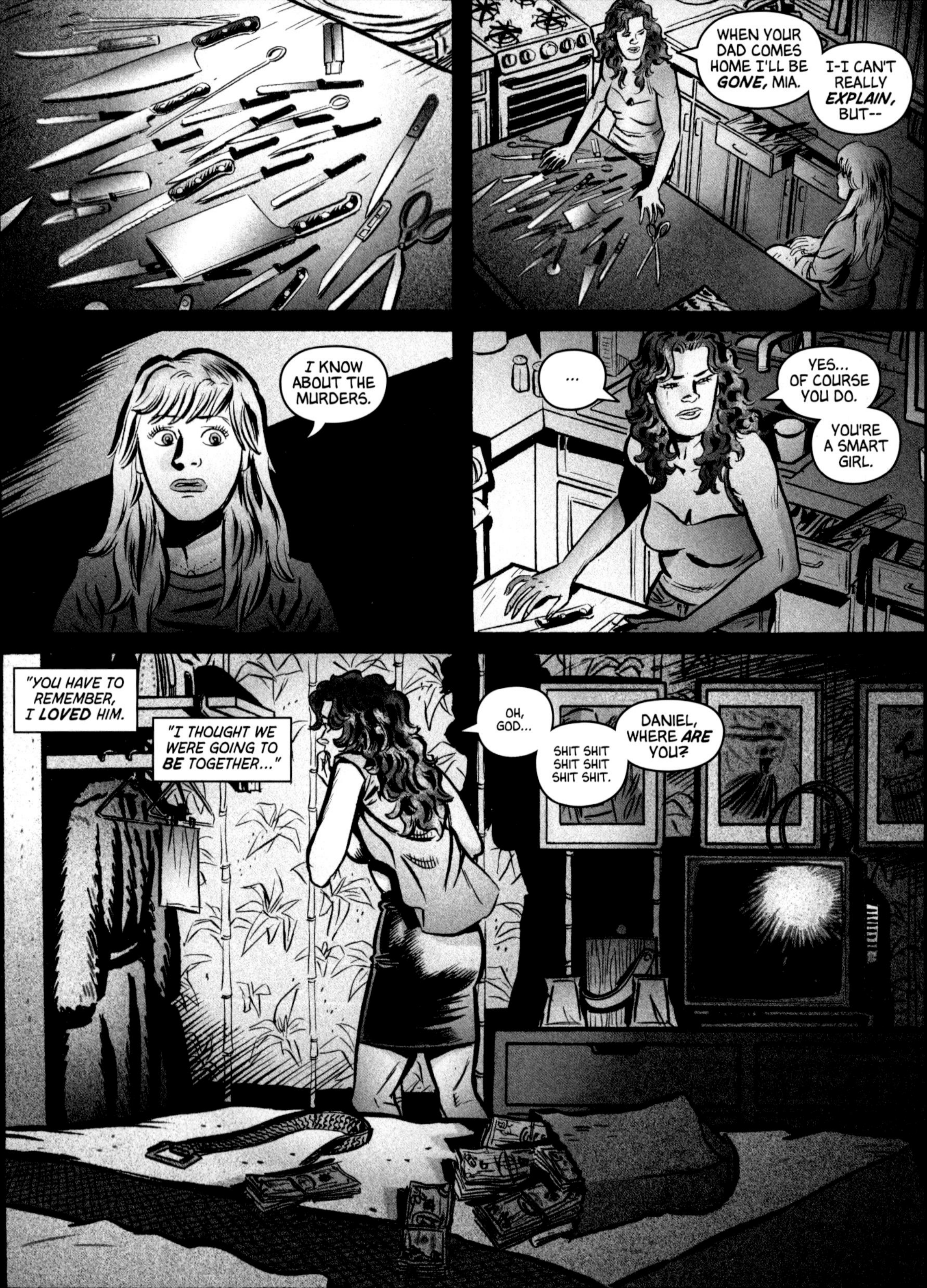
WHEN YOUR DAD COMES HOME I'LL BE GONE, MIA.
I-I CAN'T REALLY EXPLAIN, BUT--
I KNOW ABOUT THE MURDERS.
...
YES... OF COURSE YOU DO.
YOU'RE A SMART GIRL.
"YOU HAVE TO REMEMBER, I LOVED HIM.
"I THOUGHT WE WERE GOING TO BE TOGETHER..."
OH, GOD...
SHIT SHIT SHIT SHIT SHIT SHIT.
DANIEL, WHERE ARE YOU?

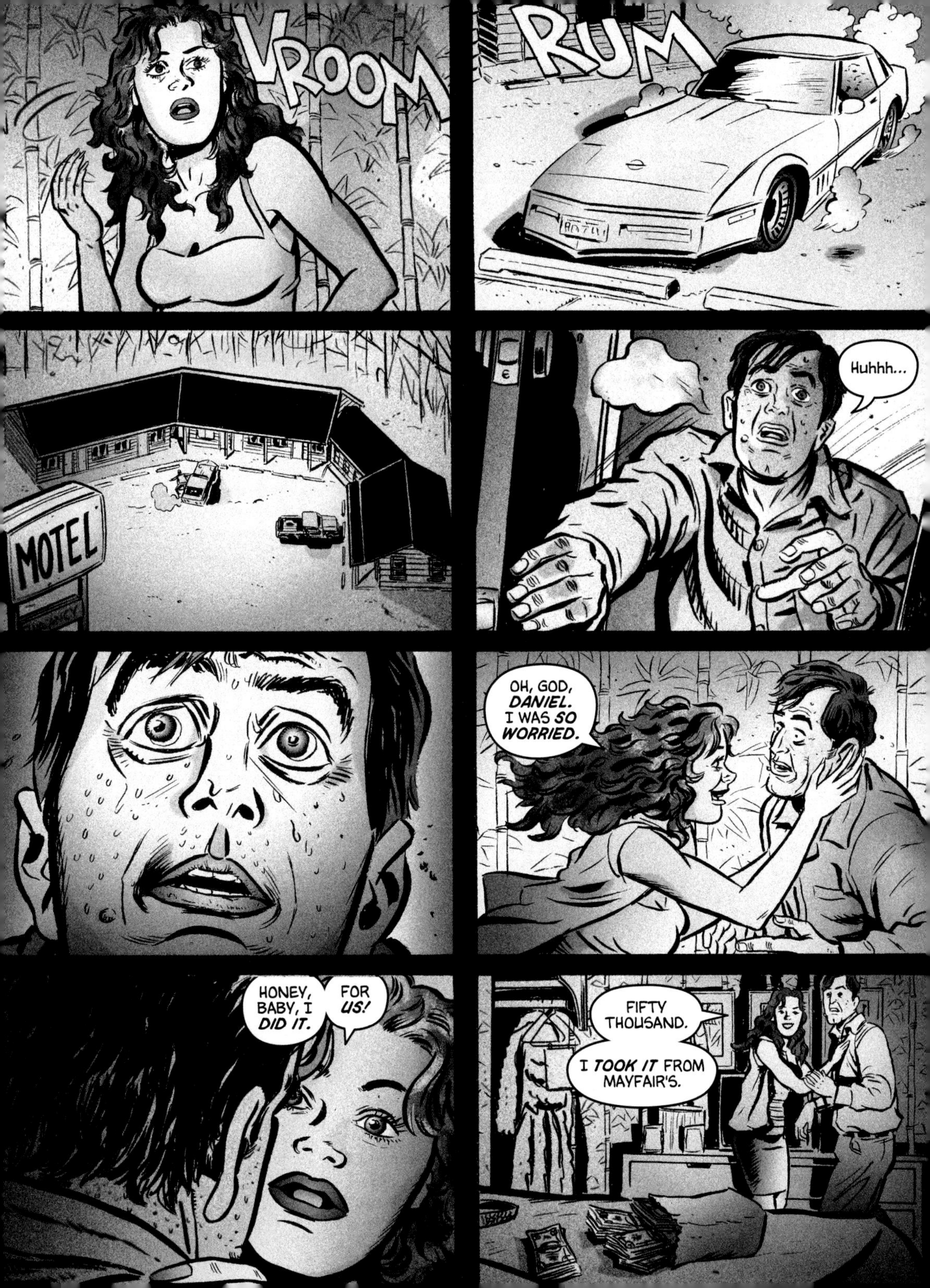
VROOM
RUM
MOTEL
Huhhh...
OH, GOD, DANIEL. I WAS SO WORRIED.
HONEY, BABY, I DID IT.
FOR US!
FIFTY THOUSAND.
I TOOK IT FROM MAYFAIR'S.

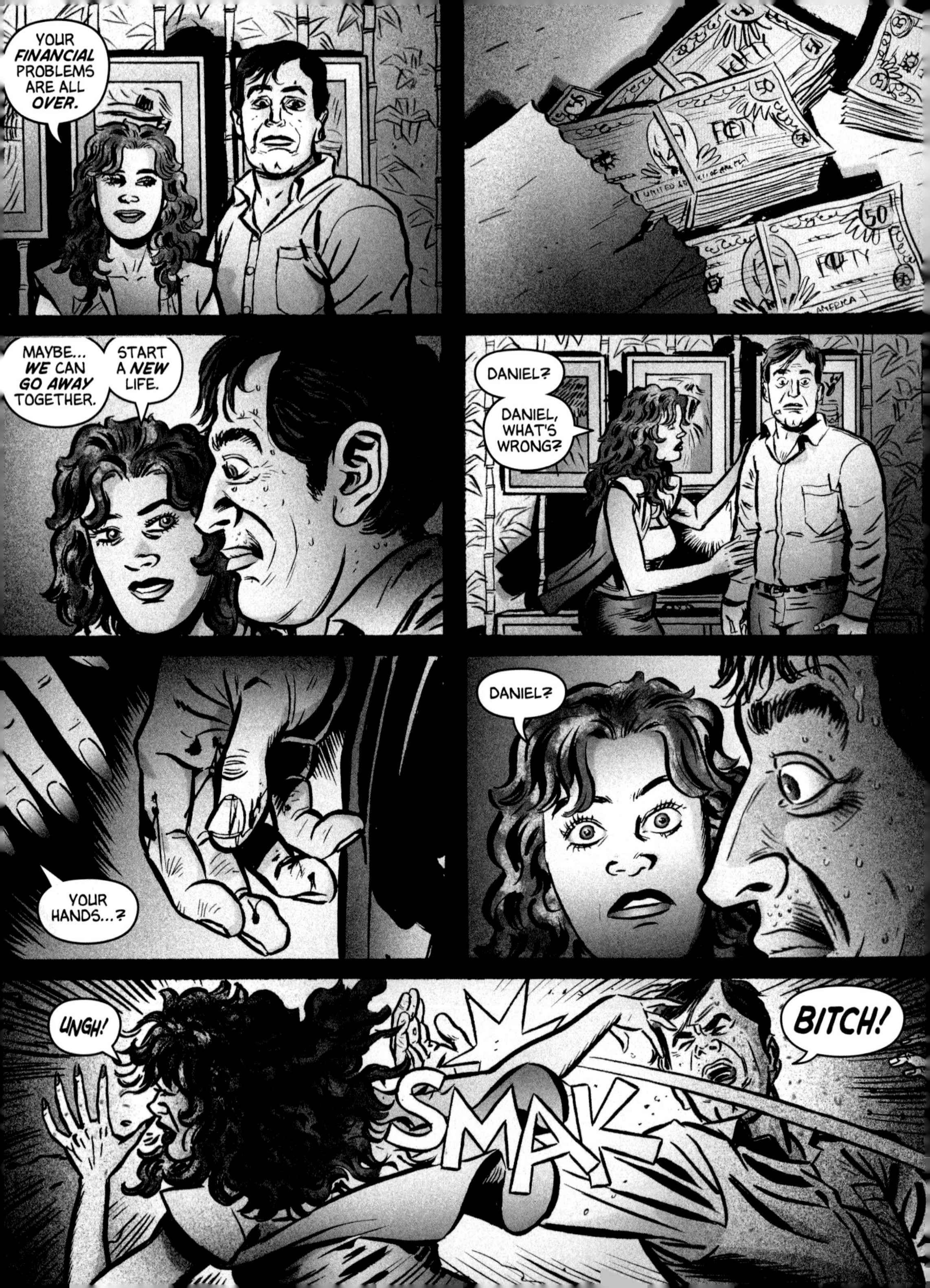
YOUR *FINANCIAL* PROBLEMS ARE ALL *OVER.*
MAYBE... *WE* CAN *GO AWAY* TOGETHER.
START A *NEW* LIFE.
DANIEL?
DANIEL, WHAT'S WRONG?
YOUR HANDS...?
DANIEL?
UNGH!
SMAK
BITCH!

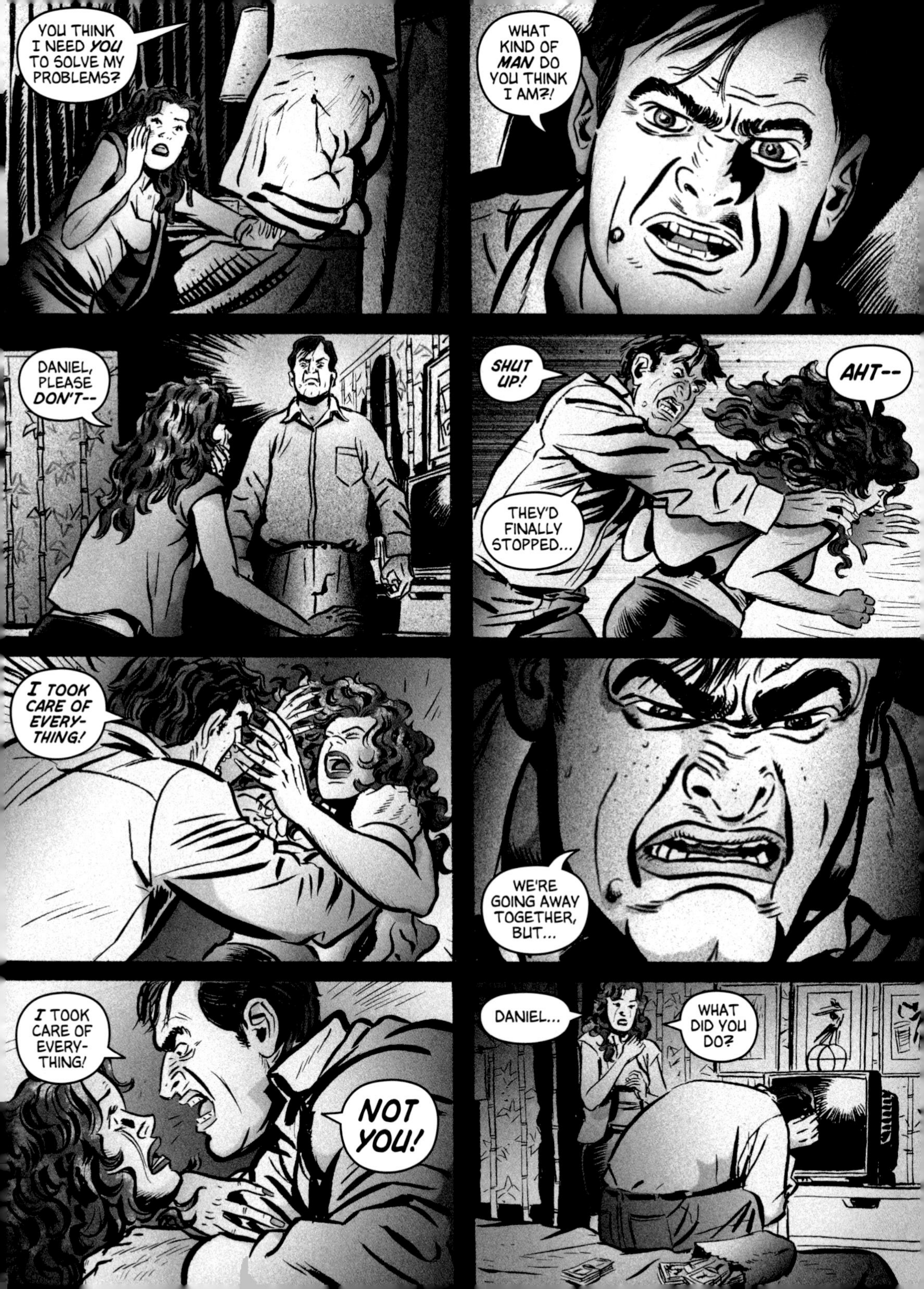
YOU THINK I NEED *YOU* TO SOLVE MY PROBLEMS?
WHAT KIND OF *MAN* DO YOU THINK I AM?!
DANIEL, PLEASE *DON'T*--
SHUT UP!
AHT--
THEY'D FINALLY STOPPED...
I TOOK CARE OF EVERY-THING!
WE'RE GOING AWAY TOGETHER, BUT...
I TOOK CARE OF EVERY-THING!
NOT YOU!
DANIEL...
WHAT DID YOU DO?

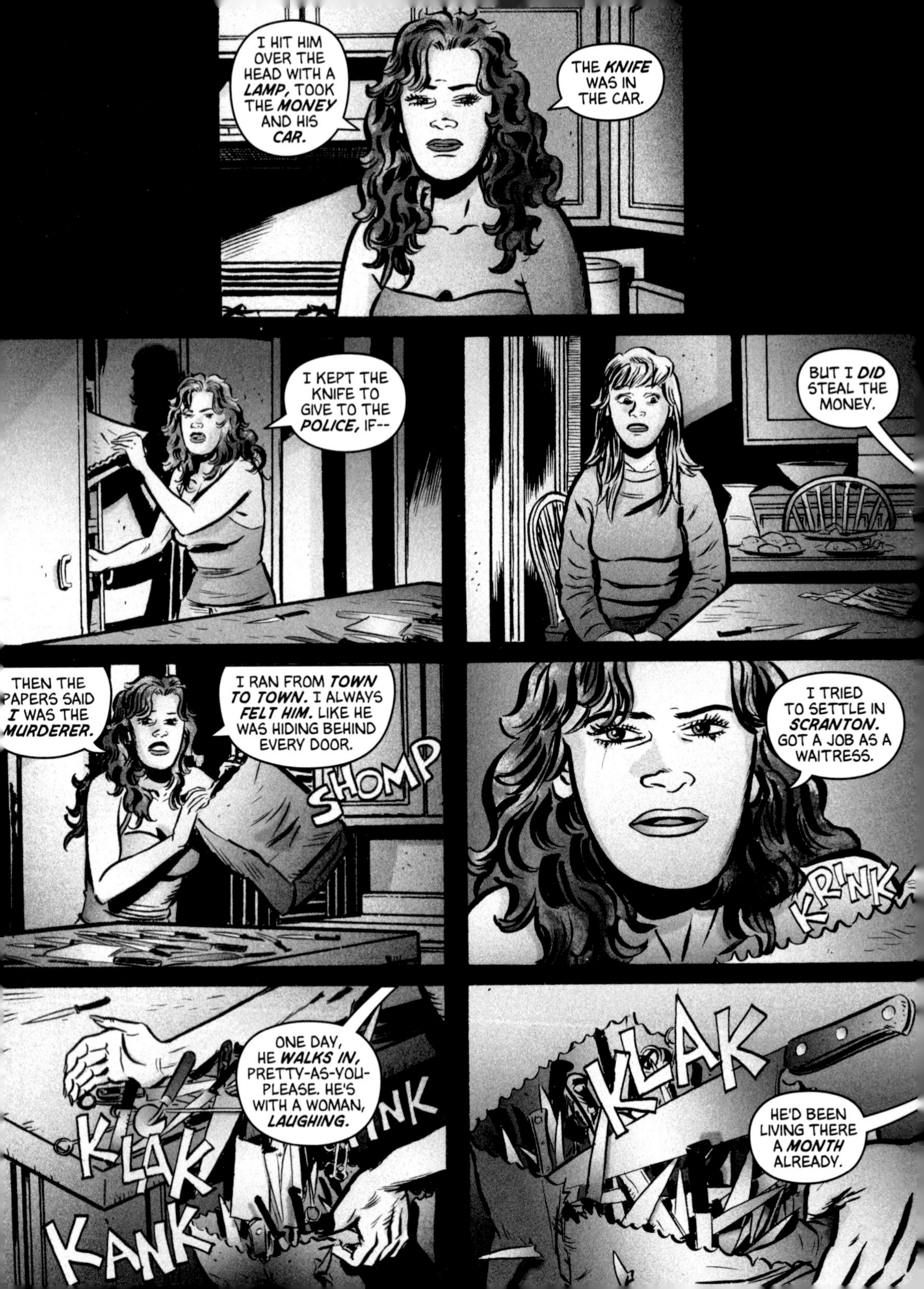
I HIT HIM OVER THE HEAD WITH A LAMP, TOOK THE MONEY AND HIS CAR.
THE KNIFE WAS IN THE CAR.
I KEPT THE KNIFE TO GIVE TO THE POLICE, IF--
BUT I DID STEAL THE MONEY.
THEN THE PAPERS SAID I WAS THE MURDERER.
I RAN FROM TOWN TO TOWN. I ALWAYS FELT HIM. LIKE HE WAS HIDING BEHIND EVERY DOOR.
SHOMP
I TRIED TO SETTLE IN SCRANTON. GOT A JOB AS A WAITRESS.
KRINK
ONE DAY, HE WALKS IN, PRETTY-AS-YOU-PLEASE. HE'S WITH A WOMAN, LAUGHING.
KLAK
KANK
TINK
KLAK
HE'D BEEN LIVING THERE A MONTH ALREADY.

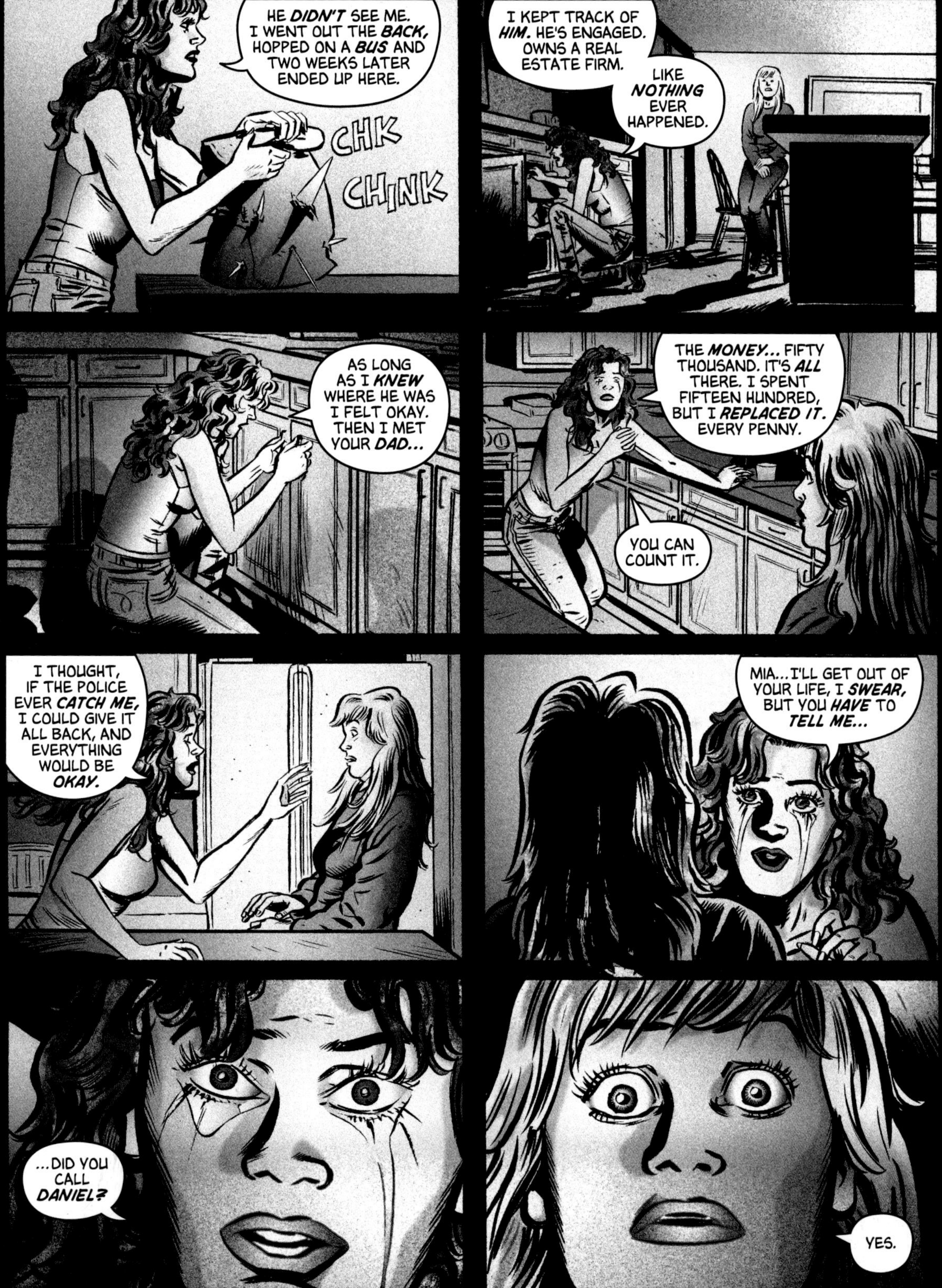
HE DIDN'T SEE ME. I WENT OUT THE BACK, HOPPED ON A BUS AND TWO WEEKS LATER ENDED UP HERE.
CHK
CHINK
I KEPT TRACK OF HIM. HE'S ENGAGED. OWNS A REAL ESTATE FIRM.
LIKE NOTHING EVER HAPPENED.
AS LONG AS I KNEW WHERE HE WAS I FELT OKAY. THEN I MET YOUR DAD...
THE MONEY... FIFTY THOUSAND. IT'S ALL THERE. I SPENT FIFTEEN HUNDRED, BUT I REPLACED IT. EVERY PENNY.
YOU CAN COUNT IT.
I THOUGHT, IF THE POLICE EVER CATCH ME, I COULD GIVE IT ALL BACK, AND EVERYTHING WOULD BE OKAY.
MIA...I'LL GET OUT OF YOUR LIFE, I SWEAR, BUT YOU HAVE TO TELL ME...
...DID YOU CALL DANIEL?
YES.

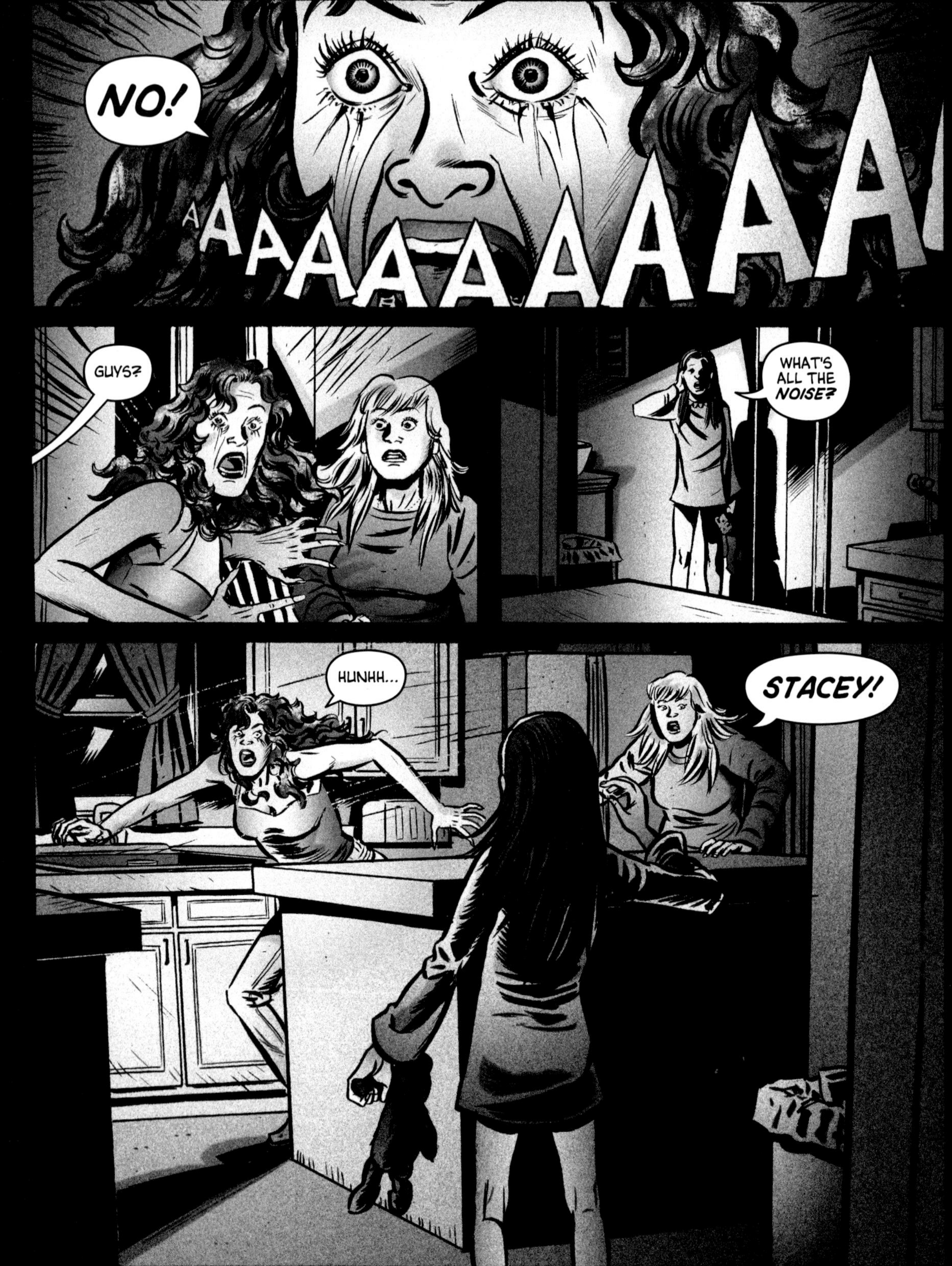
NO!
AAAAAAAAAAAA
GUYS?
WHAT'S ALL THE NOISE?
HUNHH...
STACEY!

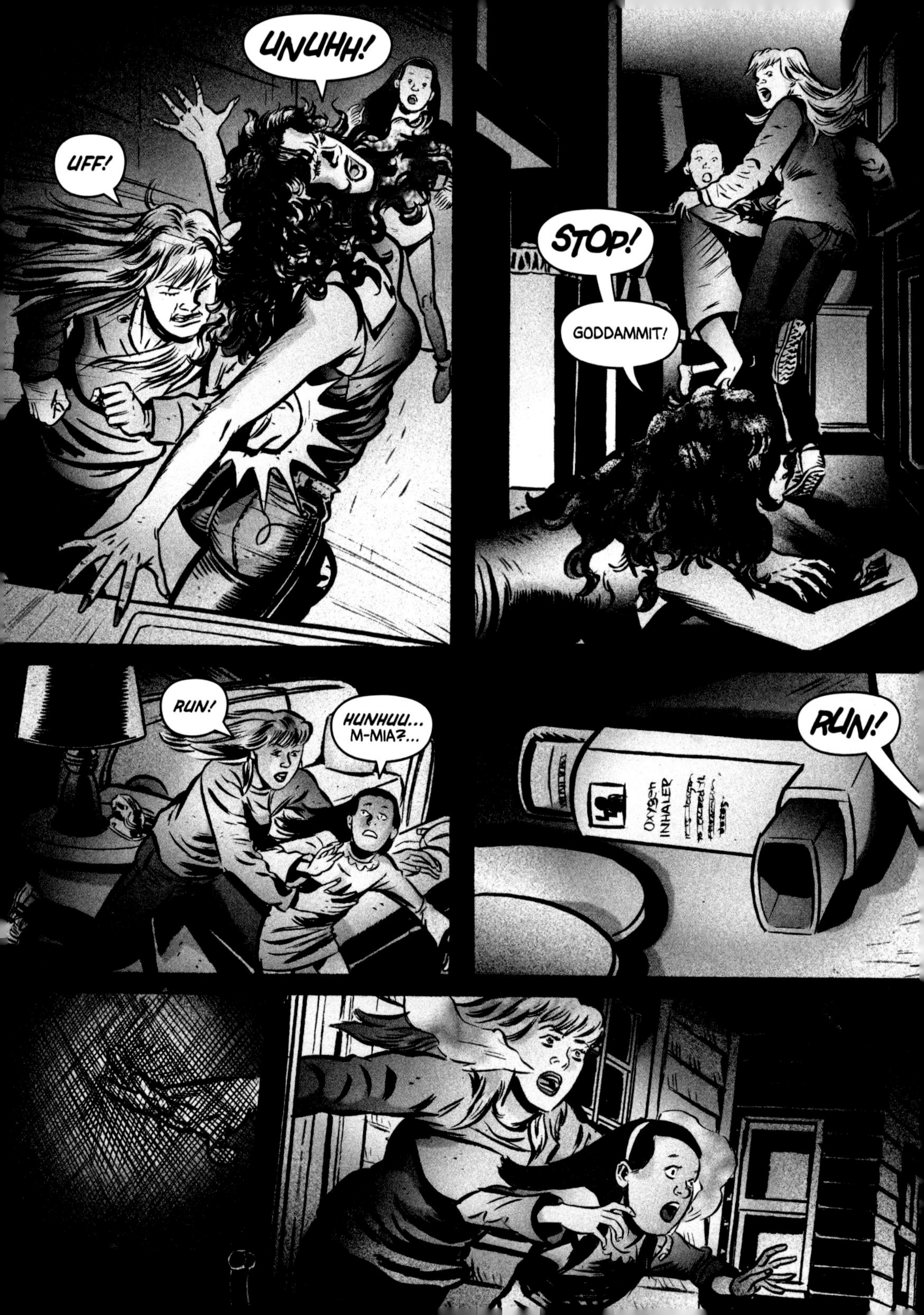
UNUHH!
UFF!
STOP!
GODDAMMIT!
RUN!
HUNHUU... M-MIA?...
Oxygen INHALER
RUN!

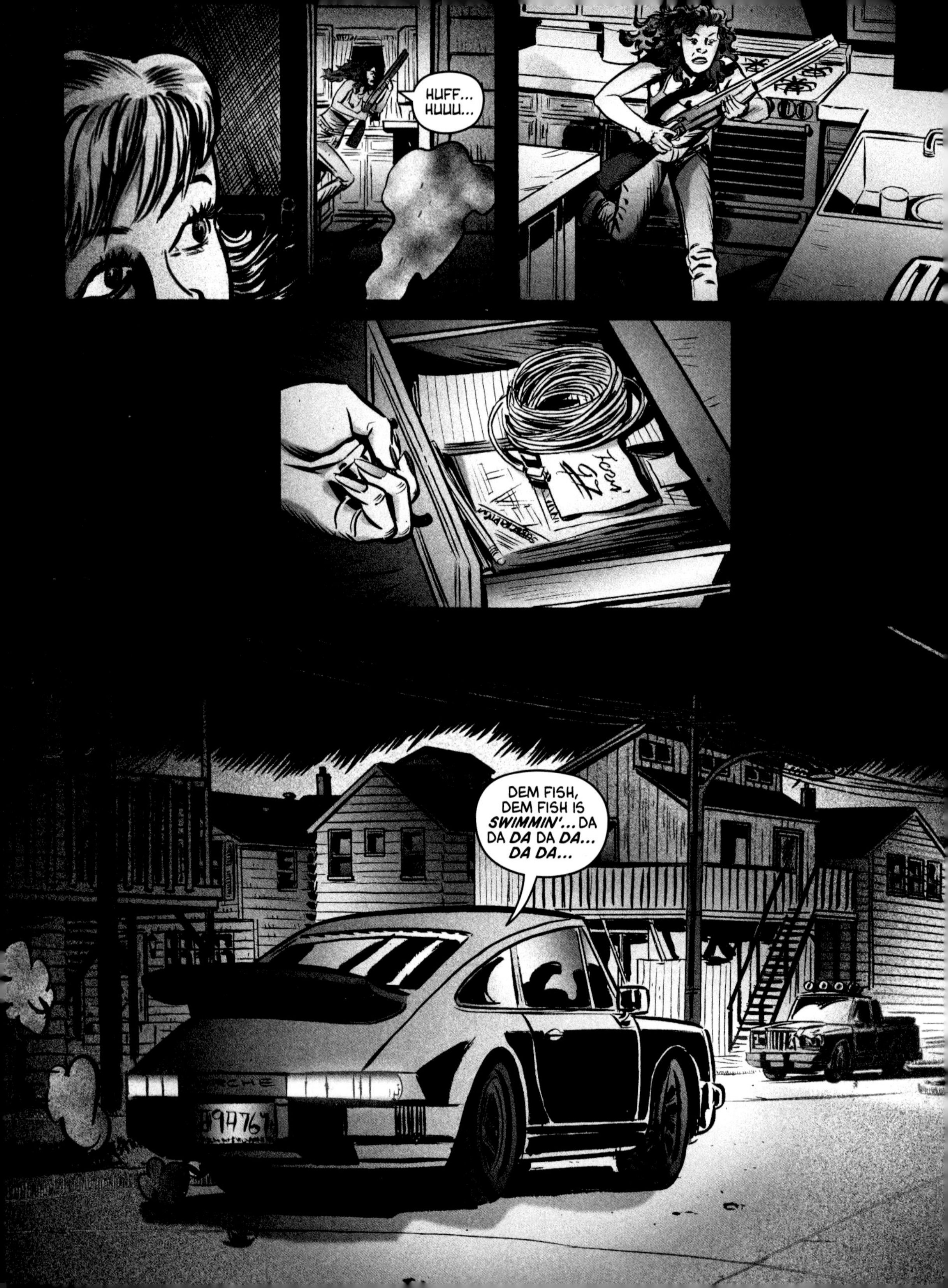
HUFF... HUUU...
DEM FISH, DEM FISH IS SWIMMIN'... DA DA DA DA DA... DA DA...

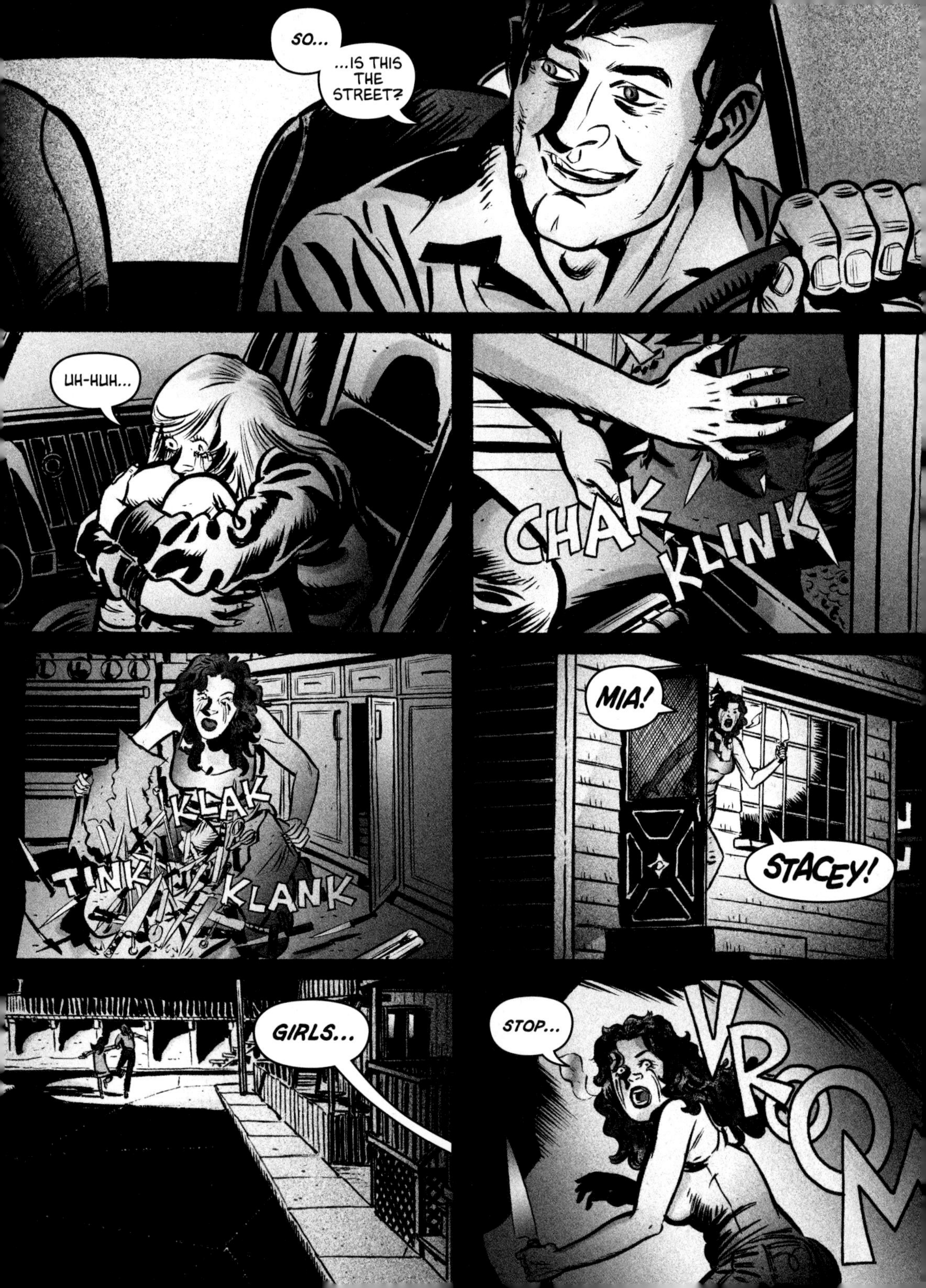
SO...
...IS THIS THE STREET?
UH-HUH...
CHAK
KLINK
KLAK
TINK
KLANK
MIA!
STACEY!
GIRLS...
STOP...
VROOM

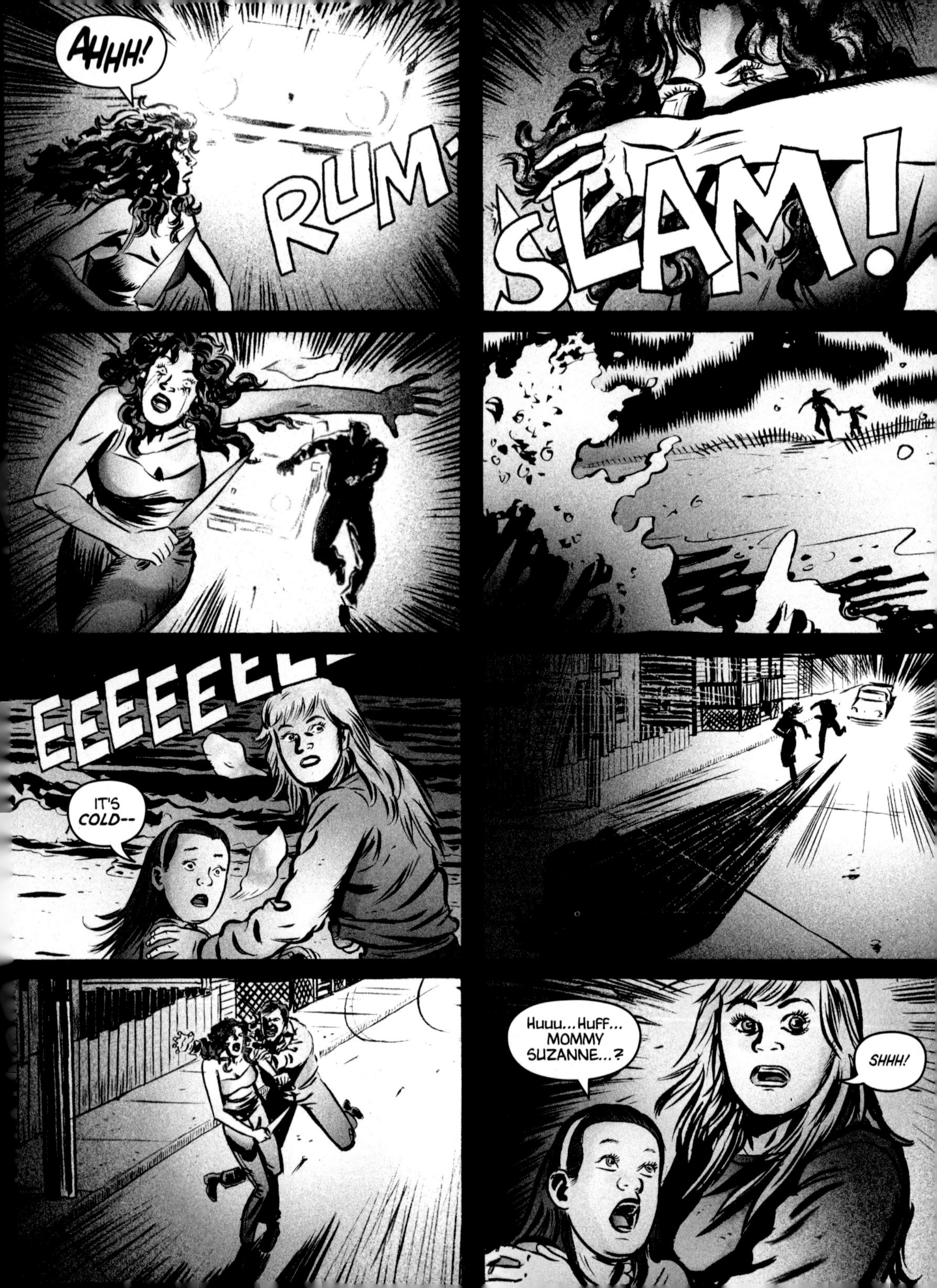
AHHH!
RUM-
SLAM!
EEEEEEE
IT'S COLD--
Huuu... Huff... MOMMY SUZANNE...?
SHHH!

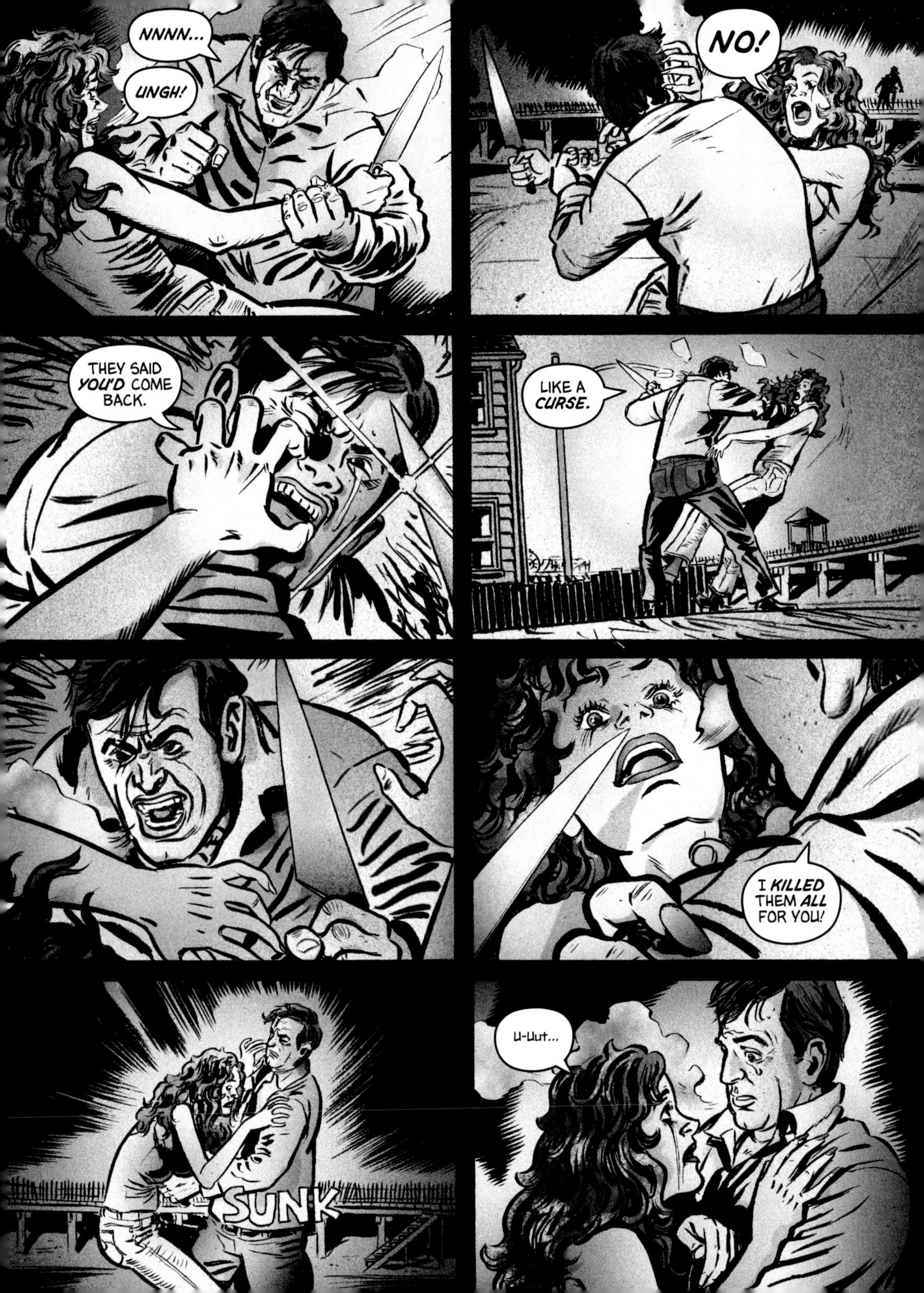
NNNN...
UNGH!
NO!
THEY SAID YOU'D COME BACK.
LIKE A CURSE.
I KILLED THEM ALL FOR YOU!
SUNK
U-Uut...

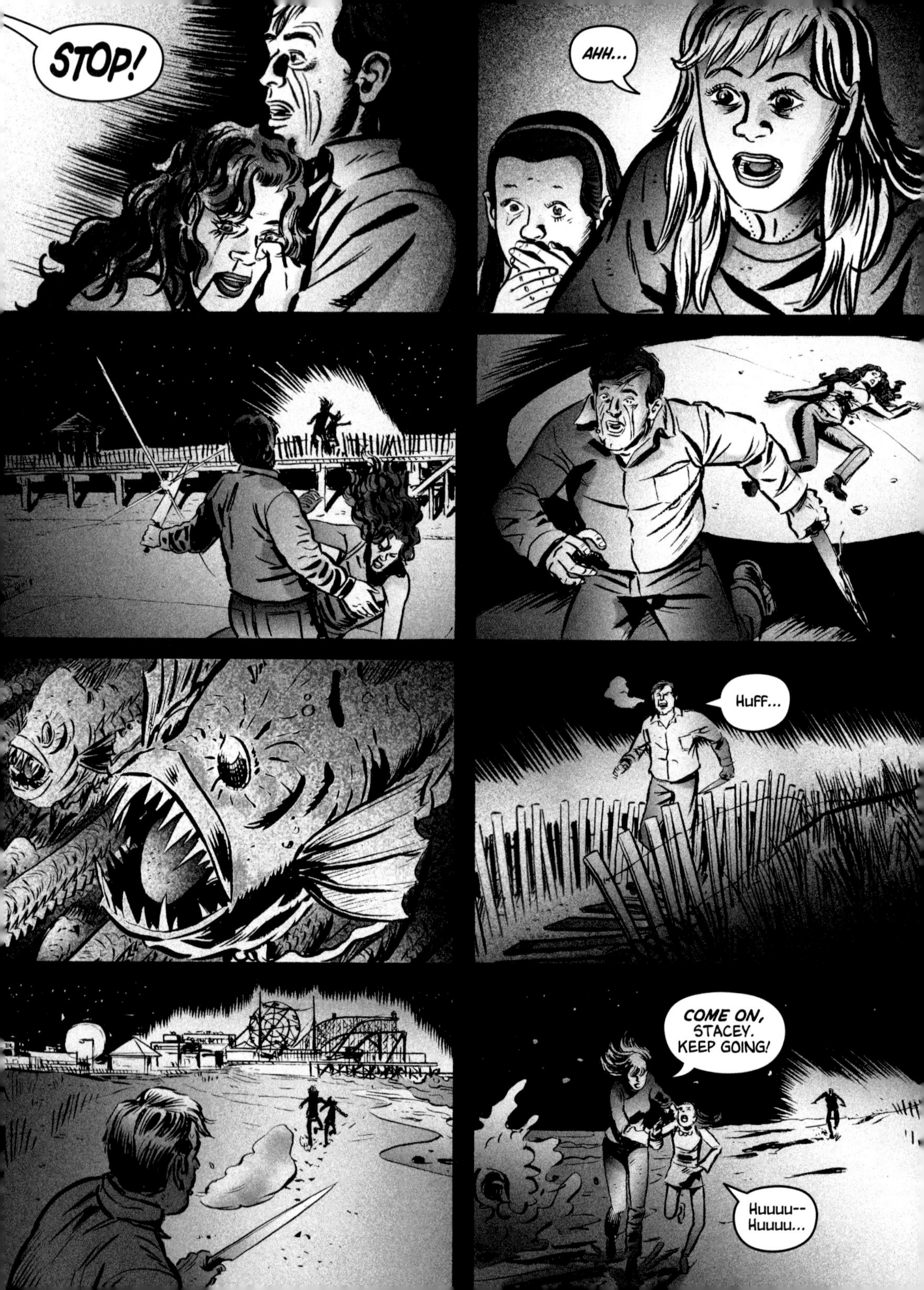
STOP!
AHH...
Huff...
COME ON, STACEY. KEEP GOING!
Huuuu--
Huuuu...

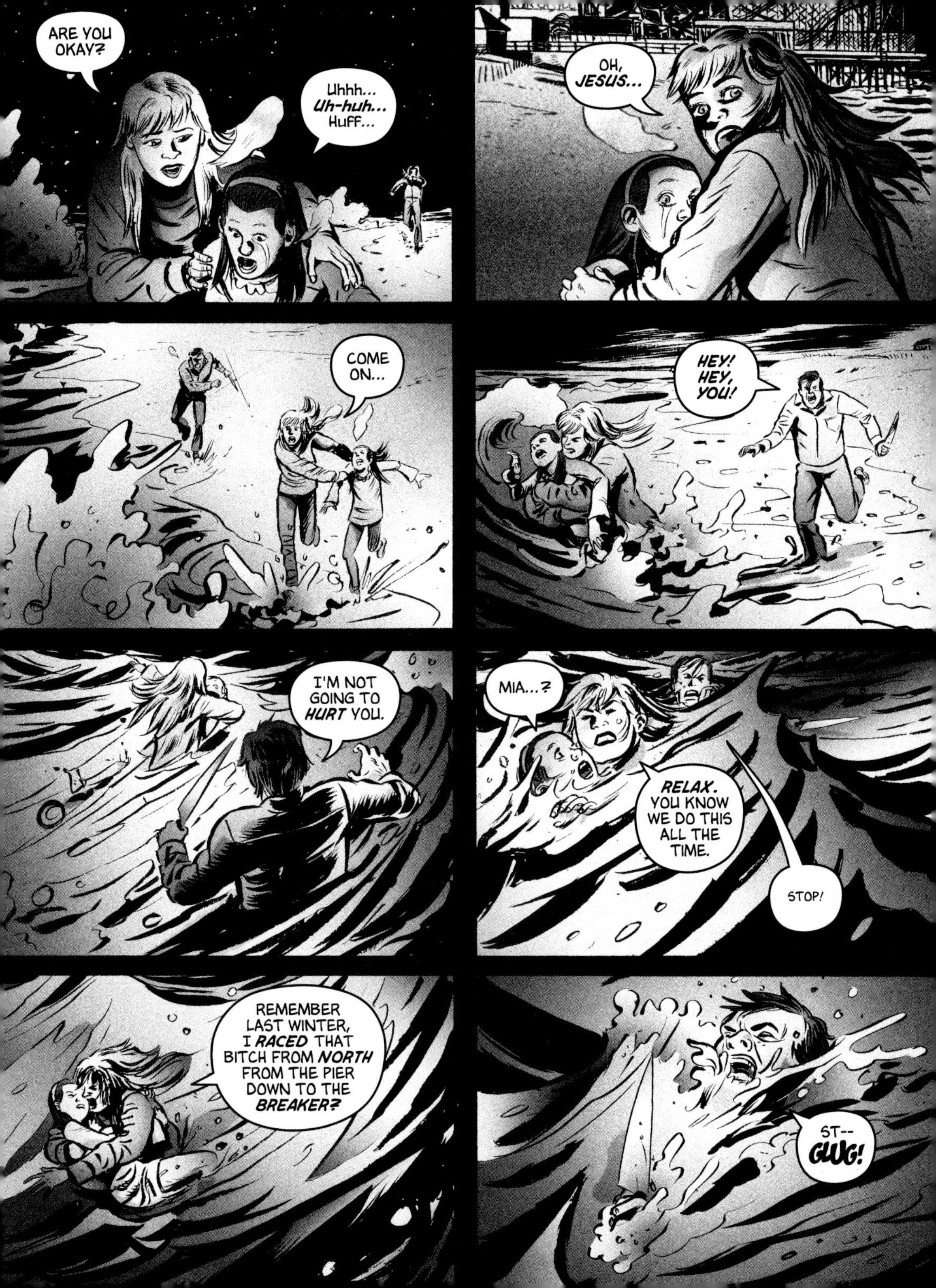
ARE YOU OKAY?
Uhhh... Uh-huh... Huff...
OH, JESUS...
COME ON...
HEY! HEY, YOU!
I'M NOT GOING TO HURT YOU.
MIA...?
RELAX. YOU KNOW WE DO THIS ALL THE TIME.
STOP!
REMEMBER LAST WINTER, I RACED THAT BITCH FROM NORTH FROM THE PIER DOWN TO THE BREAKER?
ST-- GLUG!

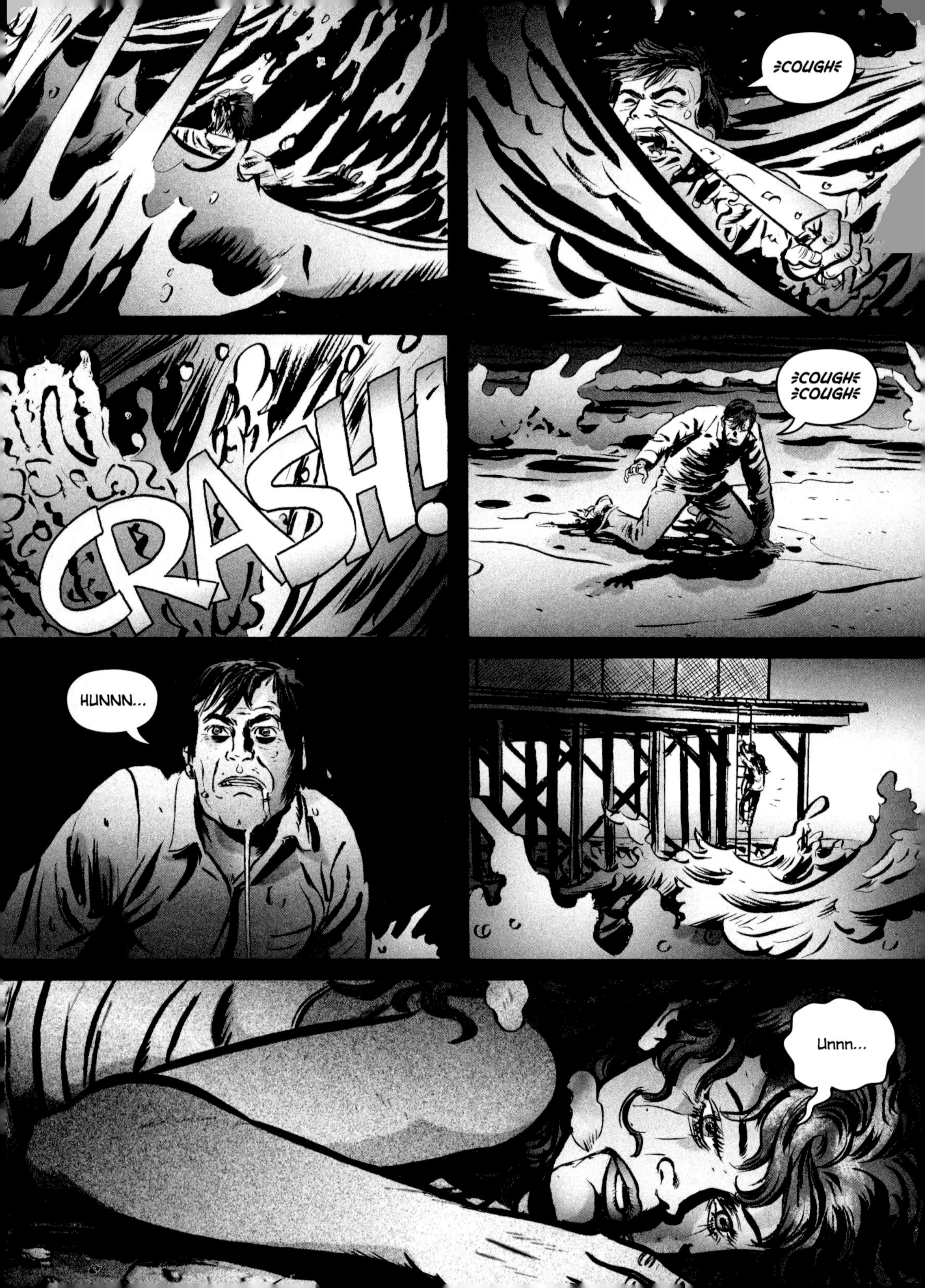
COUGH
CRASH!
COUGH COUGH
HUNNN...
Unnn...

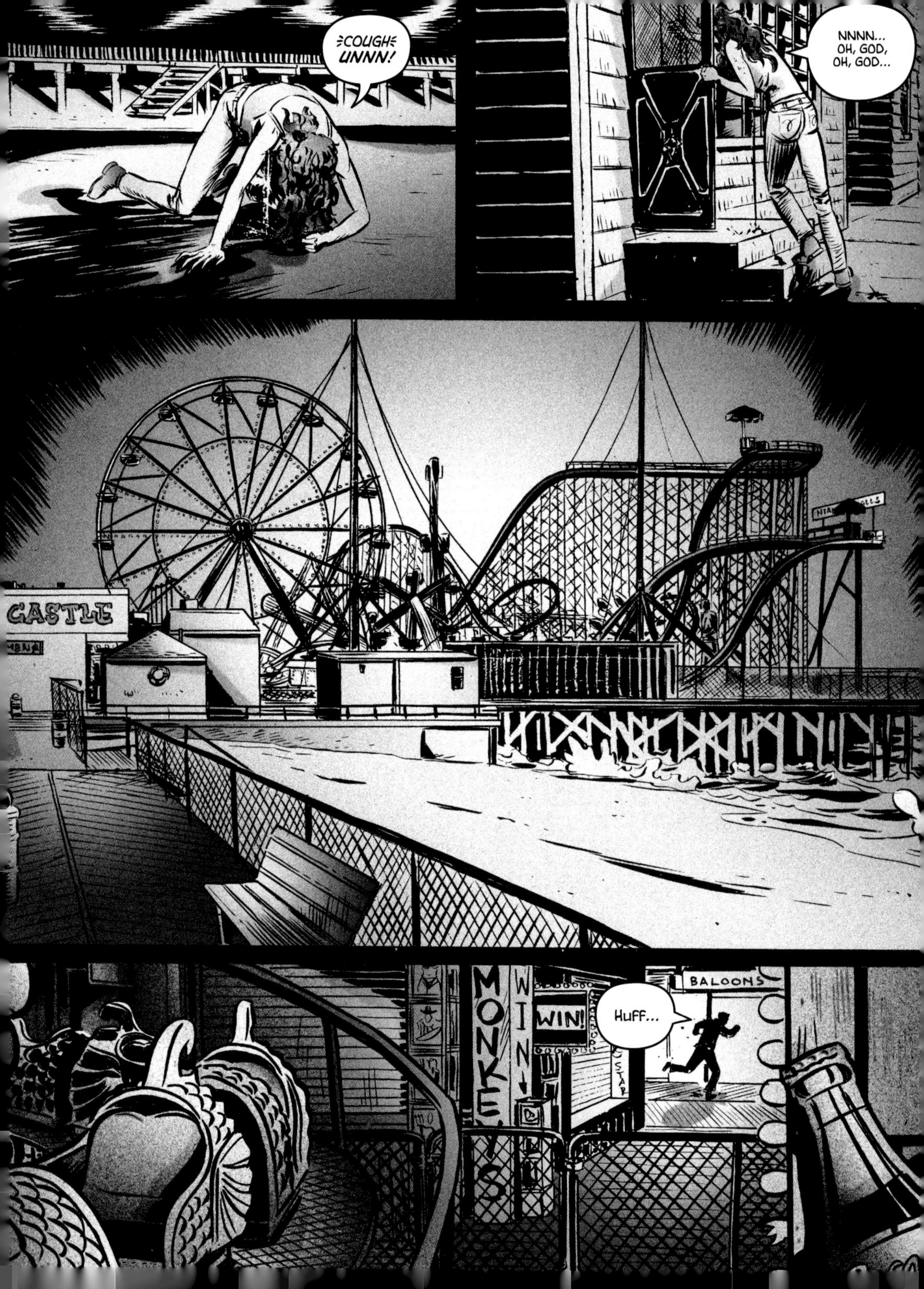

COUGH UNNN!
NNNN... OH, GOD, OH, GOD...
CASTLE
BALOONS
MONKEY'S
WIN!
Huff...

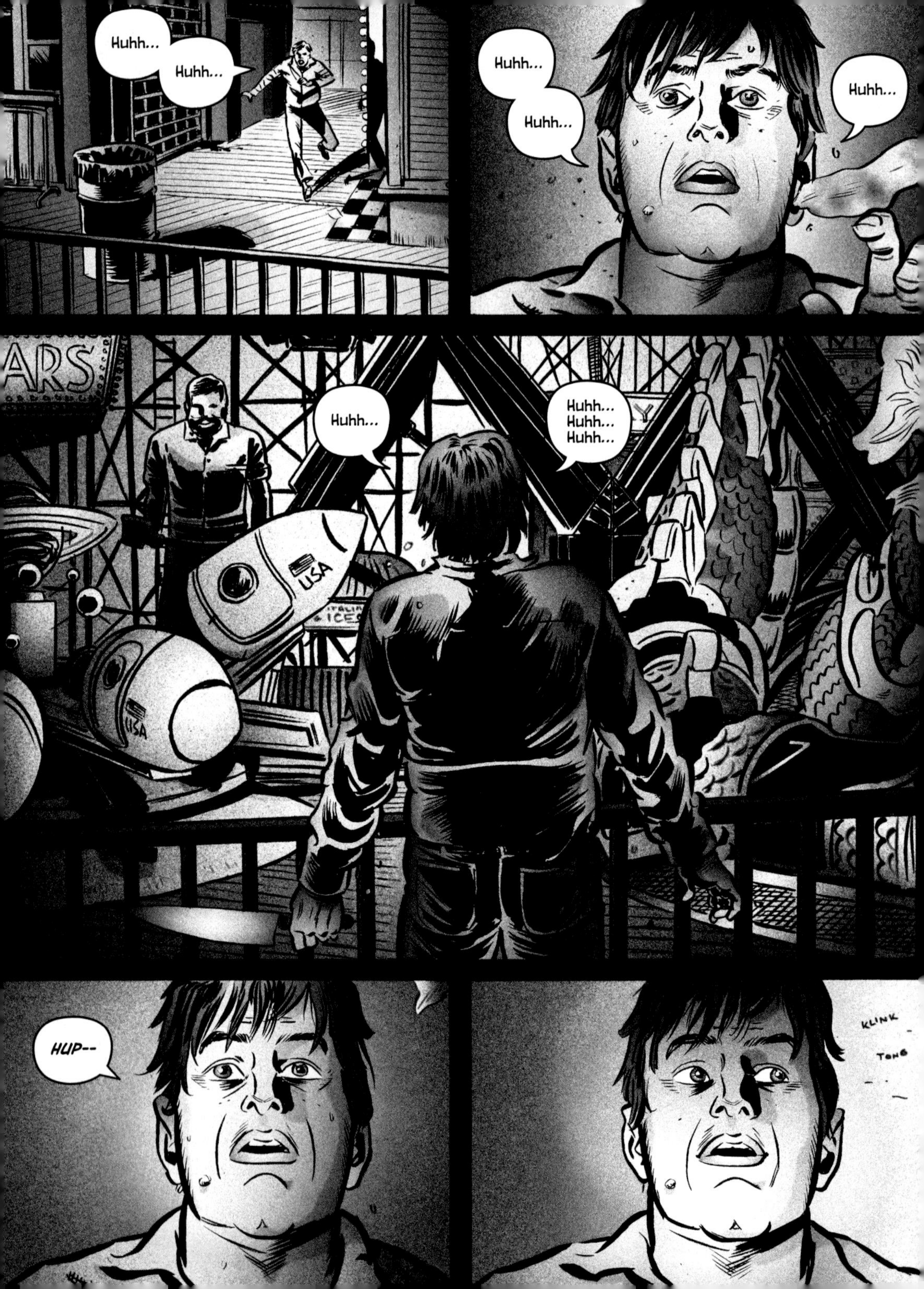
Huhh...
Huhh...
Huhh...
Huhh...
Huhh...
Huhh...
Huhh...
Huhh...
Huhh...
HUP--
KLINK
TONG

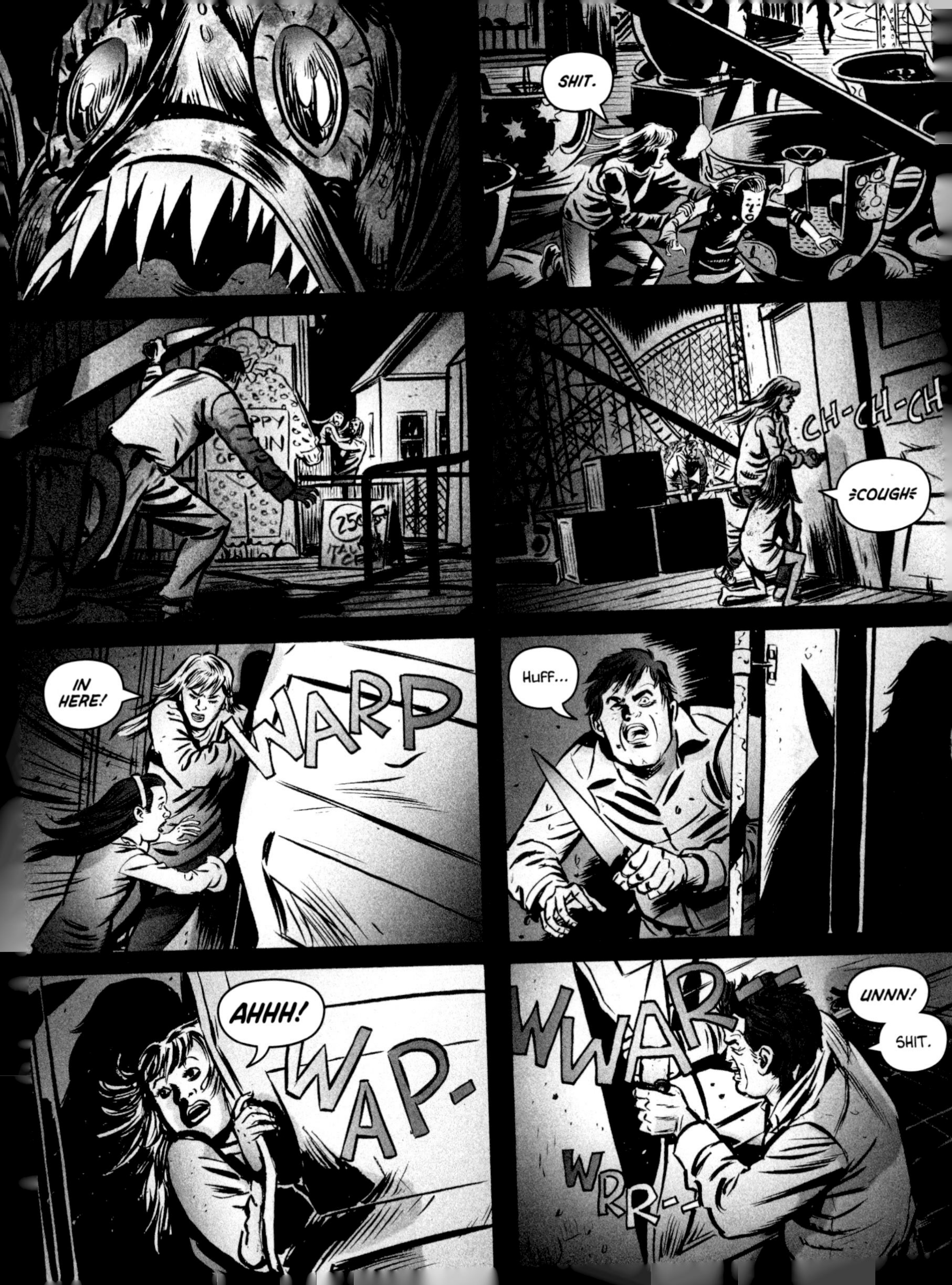
SHIT.
CH-CH-CH
COUGH
IN HERE!
WARP
HUFF...
AHHH!
WAP-
WWAR-
UNNN!
SHIT.
WRR--

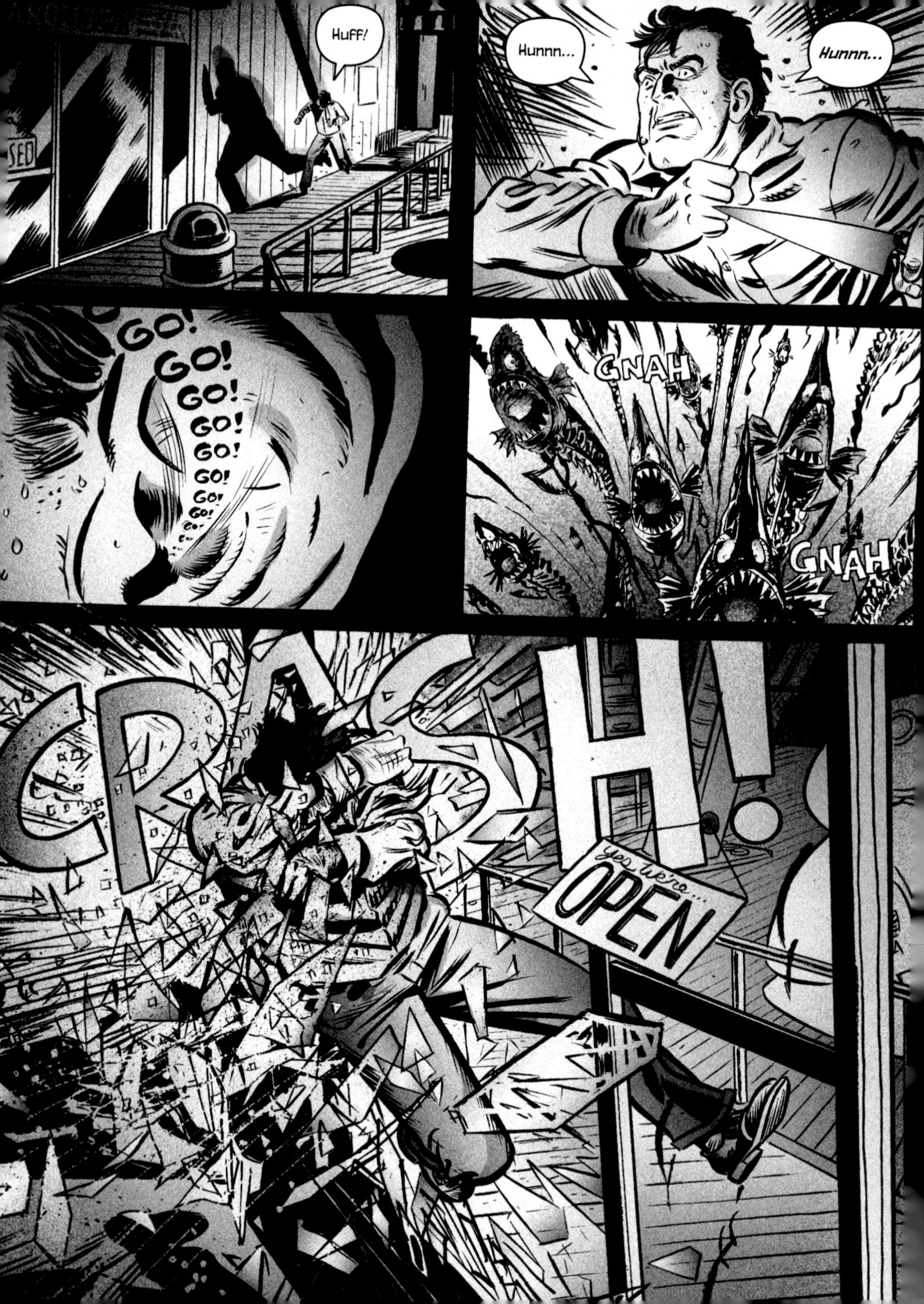
Huff!
Hunnn...
Hunnn...
GO!
GO!
GO!
GO!
GO!
GO!
GO!
GNAH
GNAH
CRASH!
yes we're...
OPEN

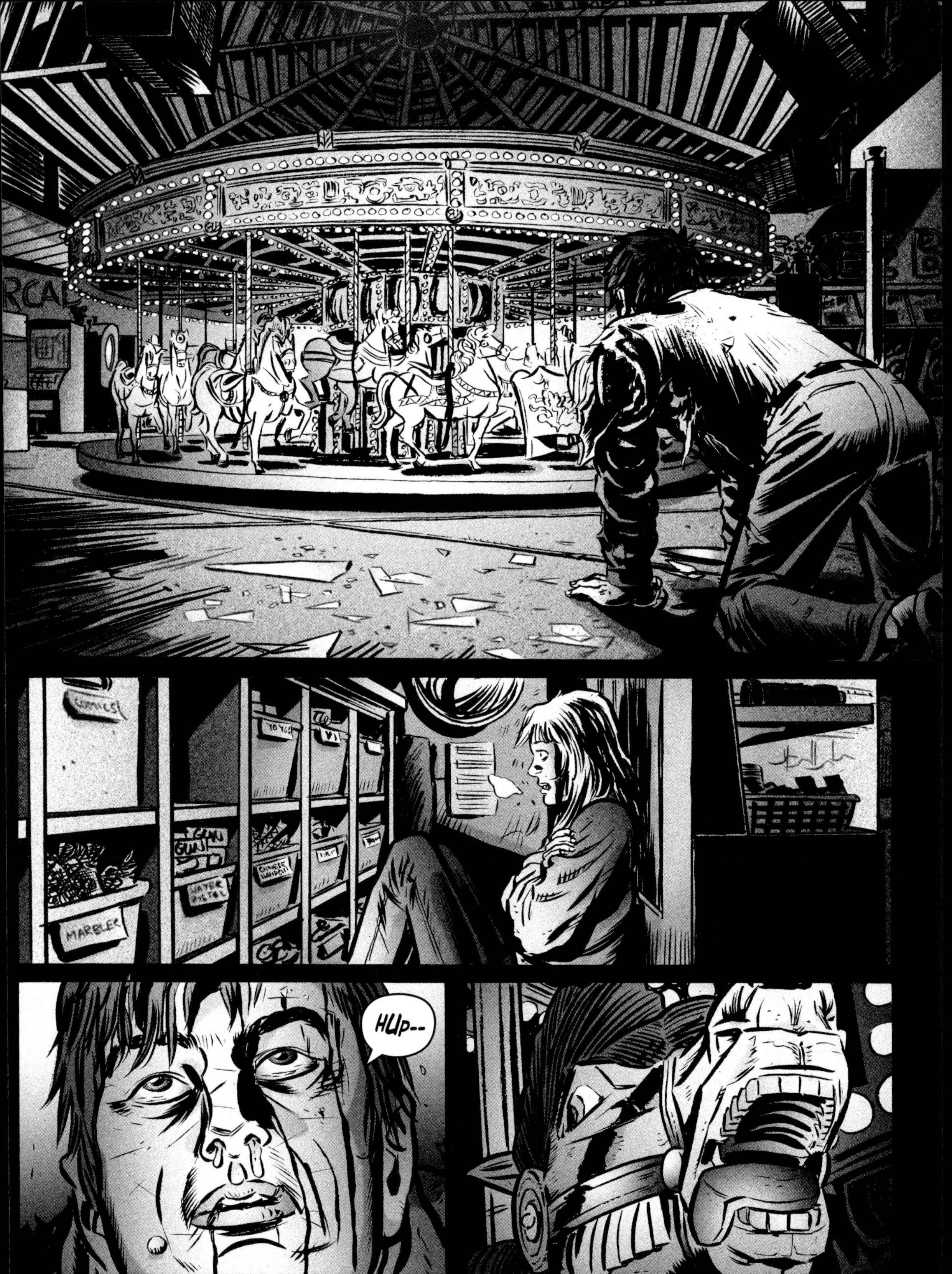
COMICS
MARBLES
HUp--

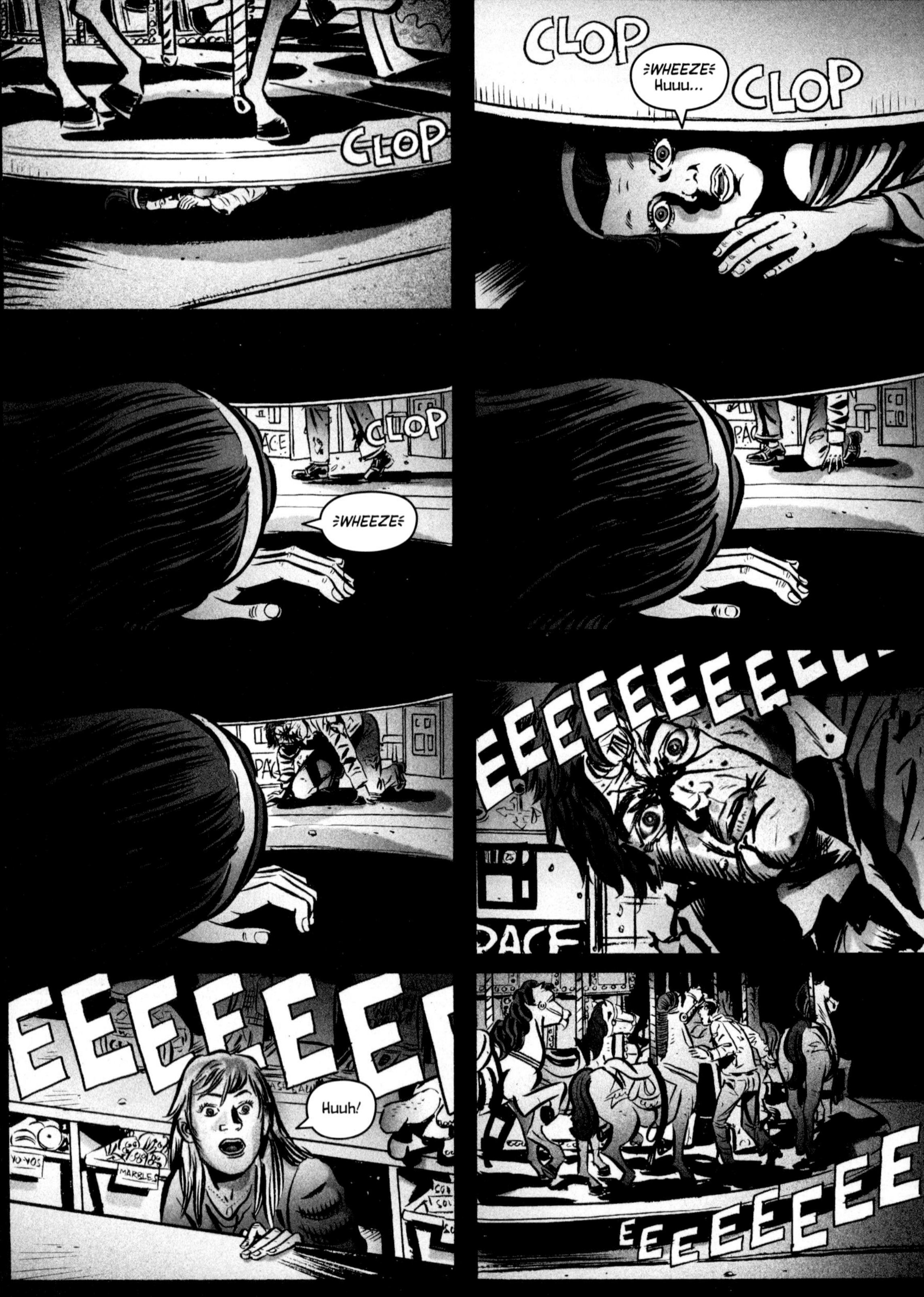

CLOP
CLOP
WHEEZE Huuu...
CLOP
CLOP
WHEEZE
EEEEEEEEEE
EEEEEE
Huuh!
YO-YOS
MARBLES
EEEEEEEEE

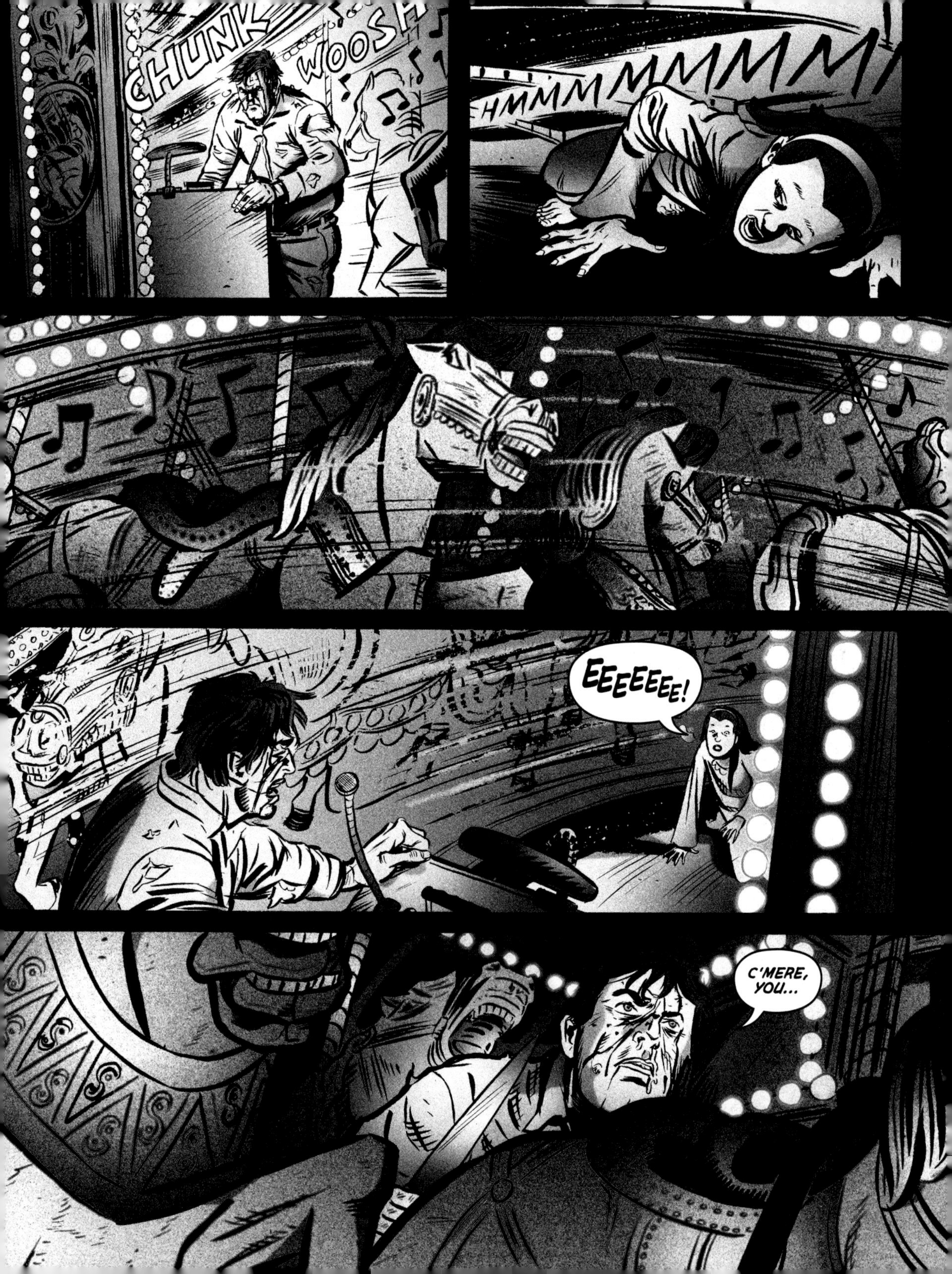
CHUNK
WOOSH
HMMMMMMMMM
EEEEEEE!
C'MERE, YOU...

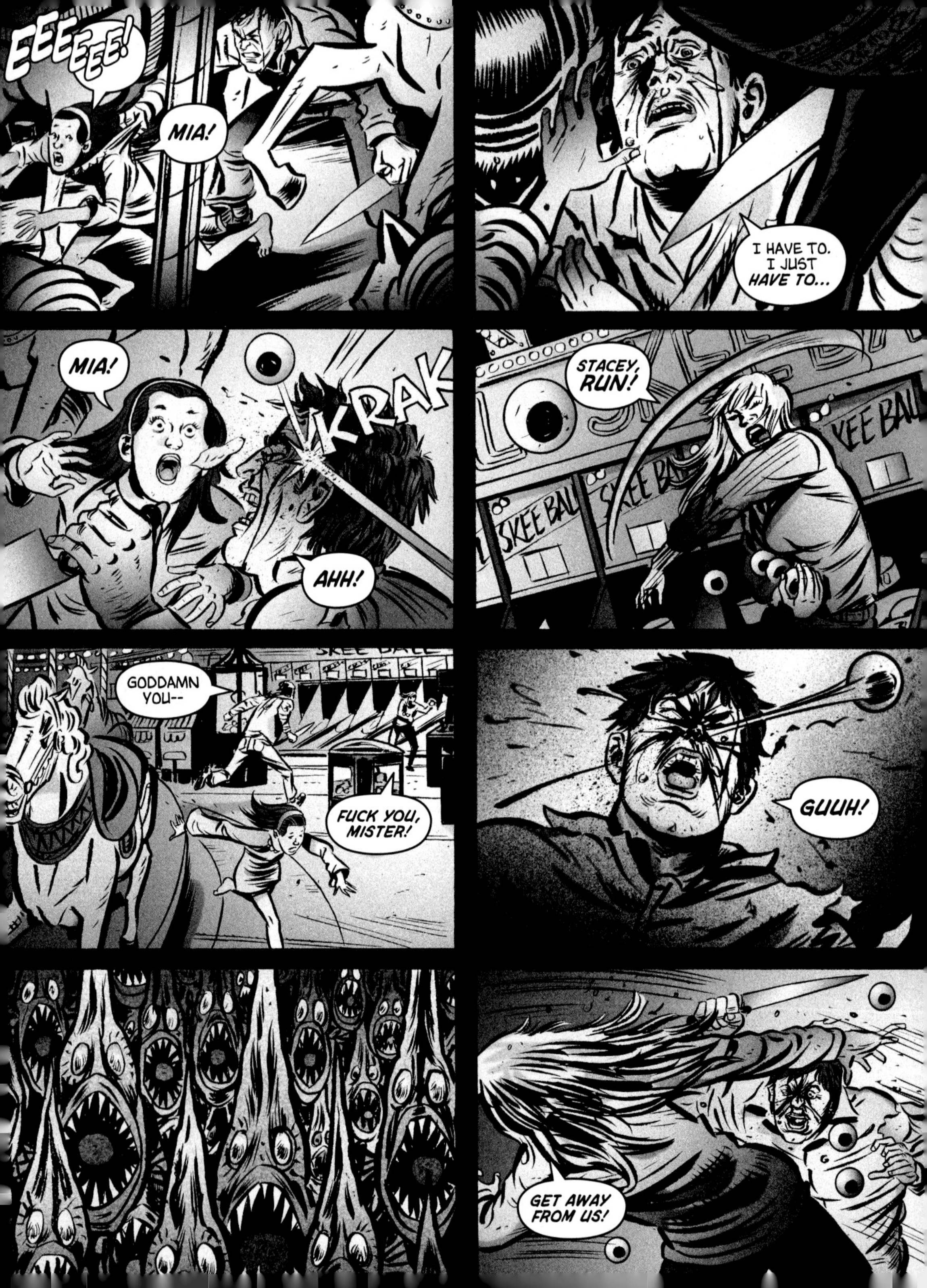

EEEEEE!
MIA!
I HAVE TO. I JUST HAVE TO...
MIA!
KRAK
AHH!
STACEY, RUN!
SKEE BALL
GODDAMN YOU--
FUCK YOU, MISTER!
GUUH!
GET AWAY FROM US!

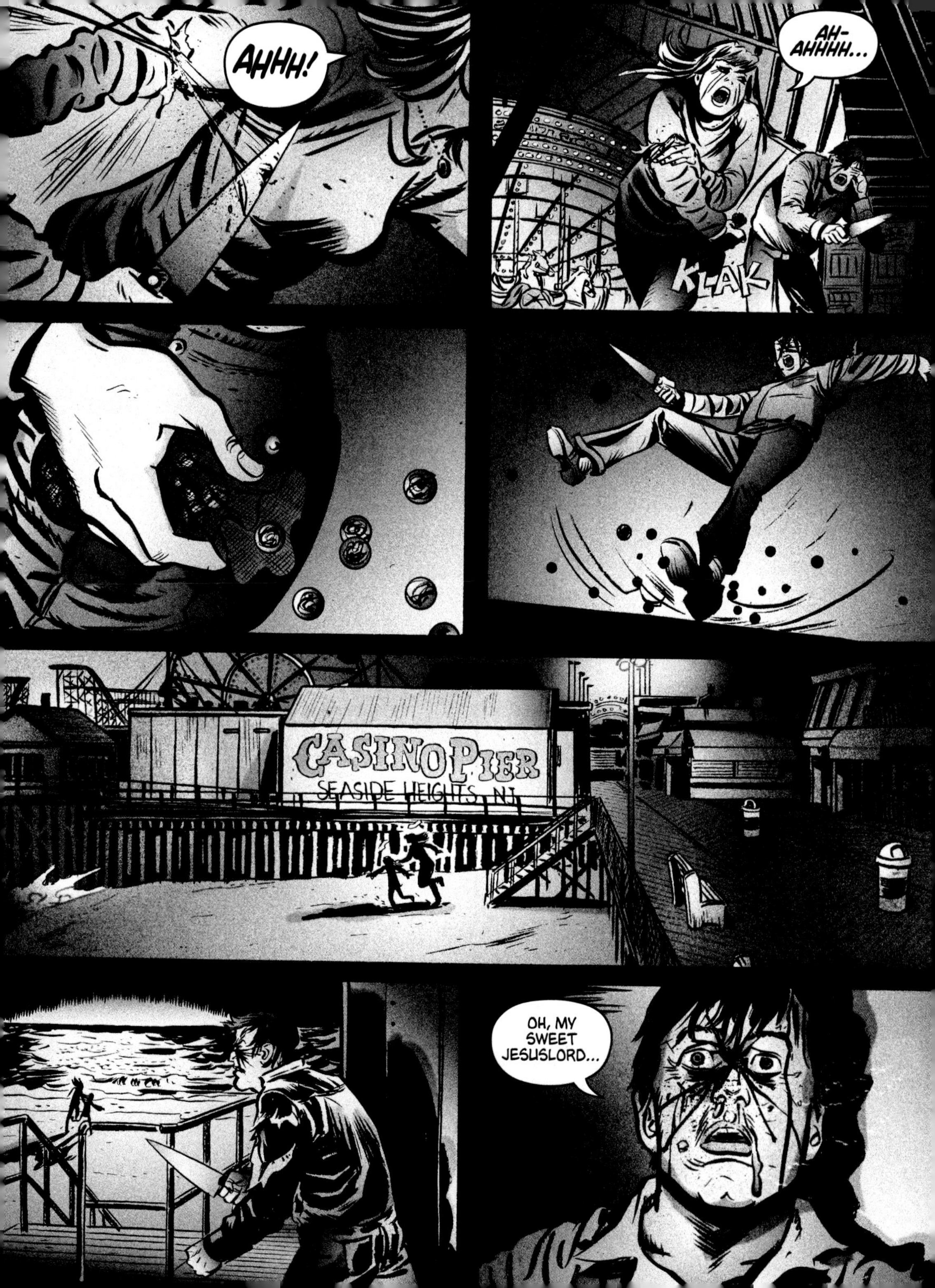
AHHH!
AH-
AHHHH...
KLAK
CASINO PIER
SEASIDE HEIGHTS, NJ
OH, MY
SWEET
JESUSLORD...

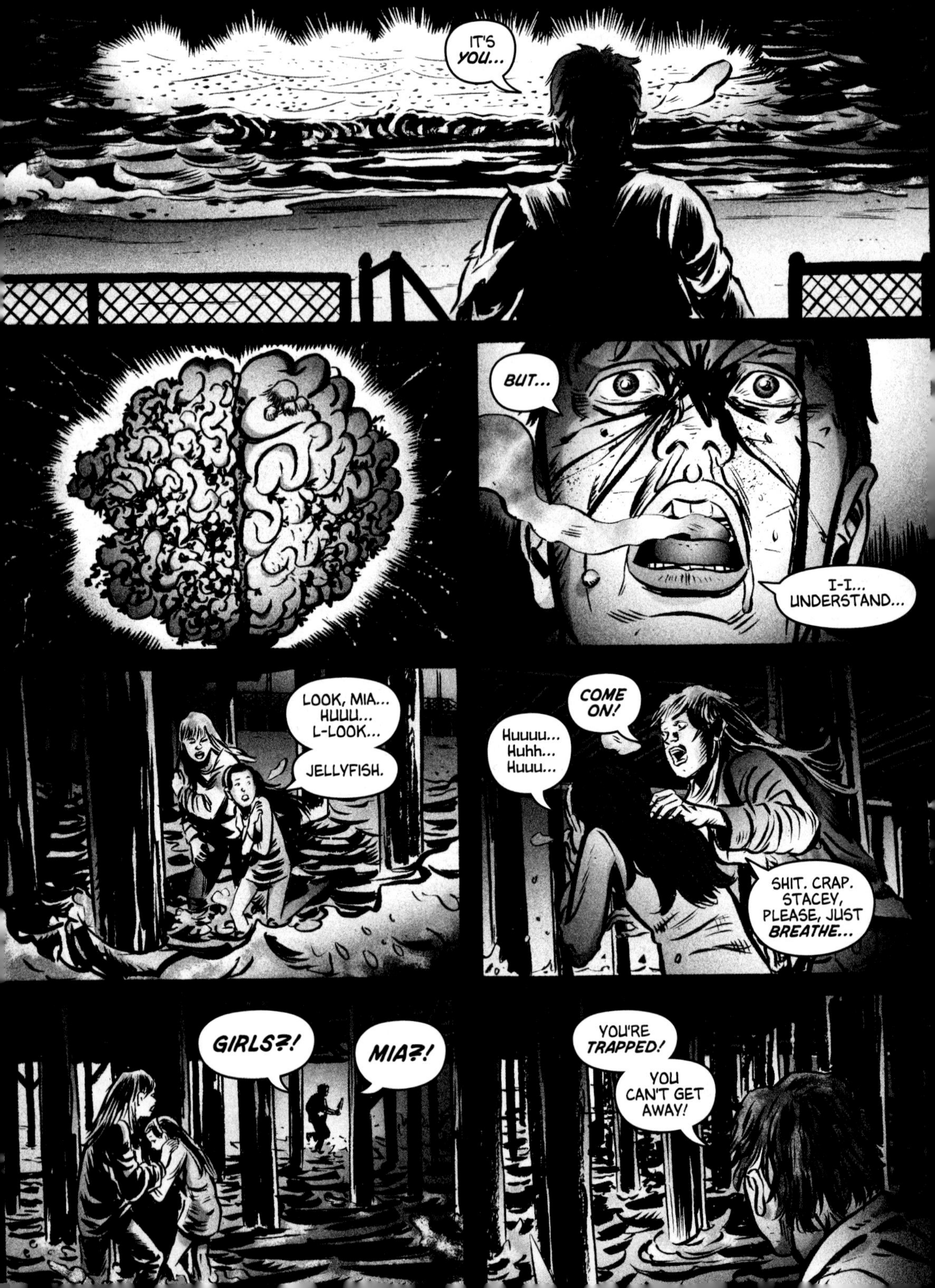

IT'S YOU...
BUT...
I-I... UNDERSTAND...
LOOK, MIA... HUUU... L-LOOK...
JELLYFISH.
COME ON!
Huuuu... Huhh... Huuu...
SHIT. CRAP. STACEY, PLEASE, JUST BREATHE...
GIRLS?!
MIA?!
YOU'RE TRAPPED!
YOU CAN'T GET AWAY!

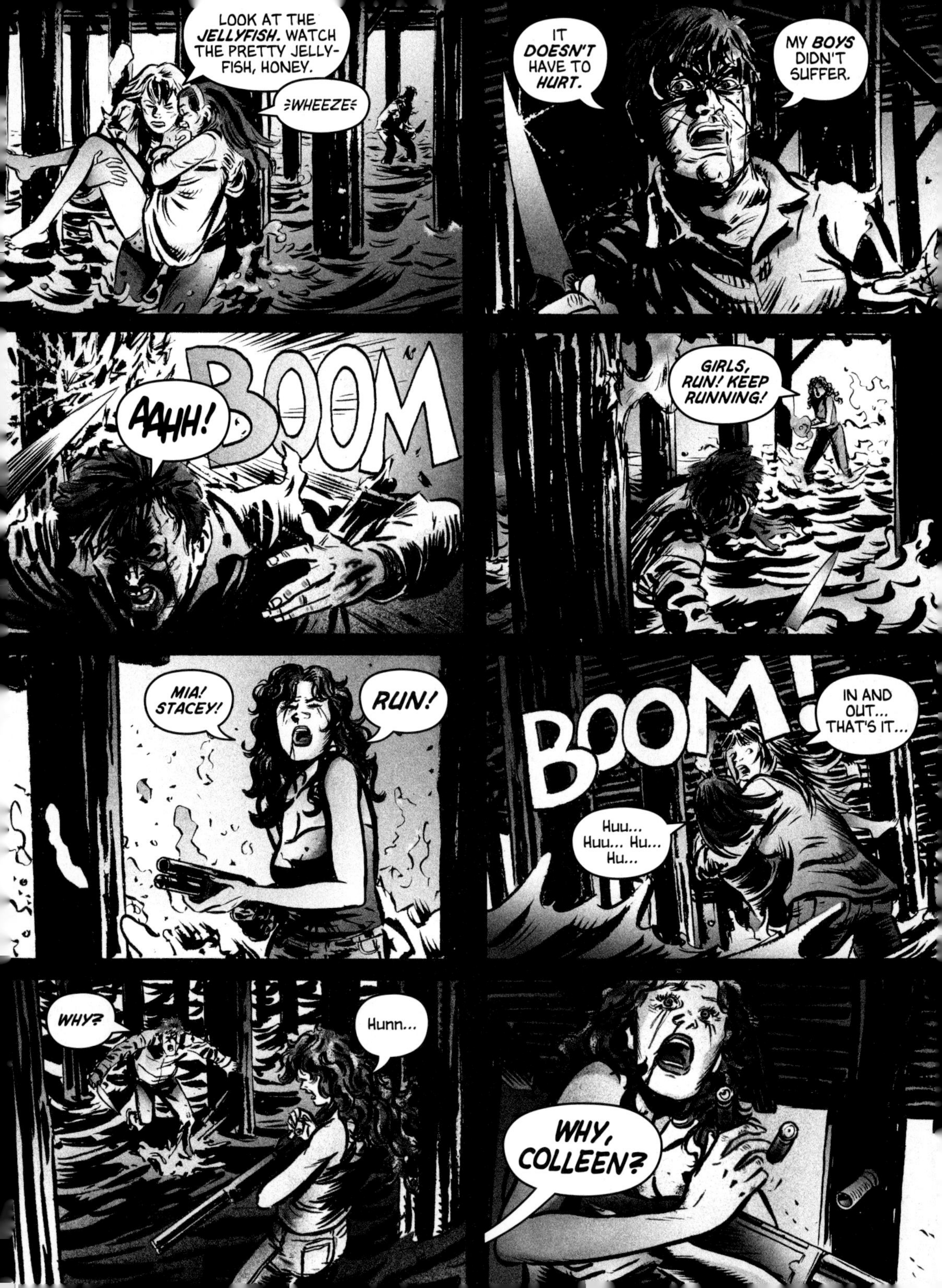
LOOK AT THE JELLYFISH. WATCH THE PRETTY JELLY-FISH, HONEY.
WHEEZE
IT DOESN'T HAVE TO HURT.
MY BOYS DIDN'T SUFFER.
BOOM
AAHH!
GIRLS, RUN! KEEP RUNNING!
MIA! STACEY!
RUN!
BOOM!
IN AND OUT... THAT'S IT...
Huu... Huu... Hu... Hu...
WHY?
Hunn...
WHY, COLLEEN?

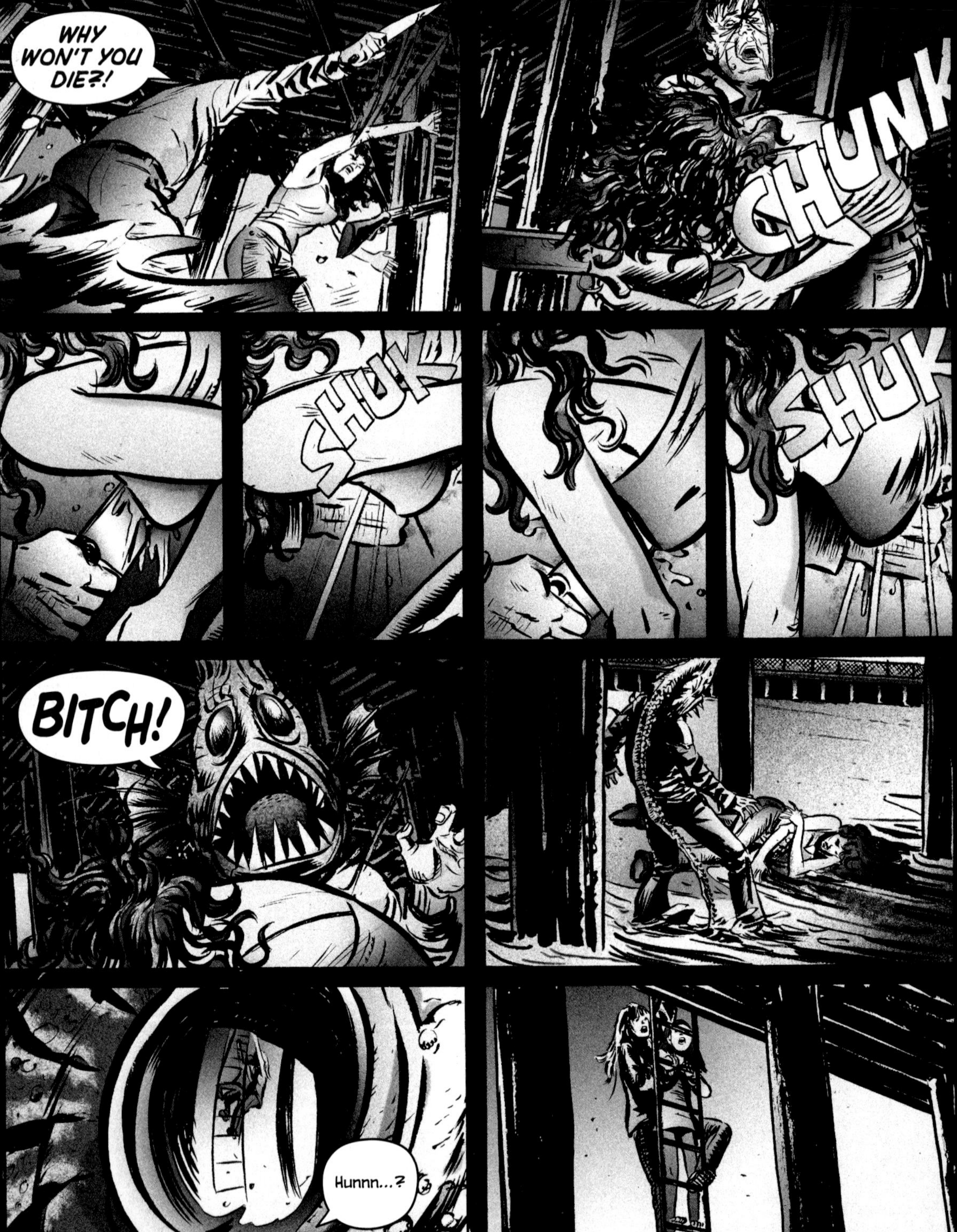
WHY WON'T YOU DIE?!
CHUNK
SHUK
SHUK
BITCH!
Hunnn...?

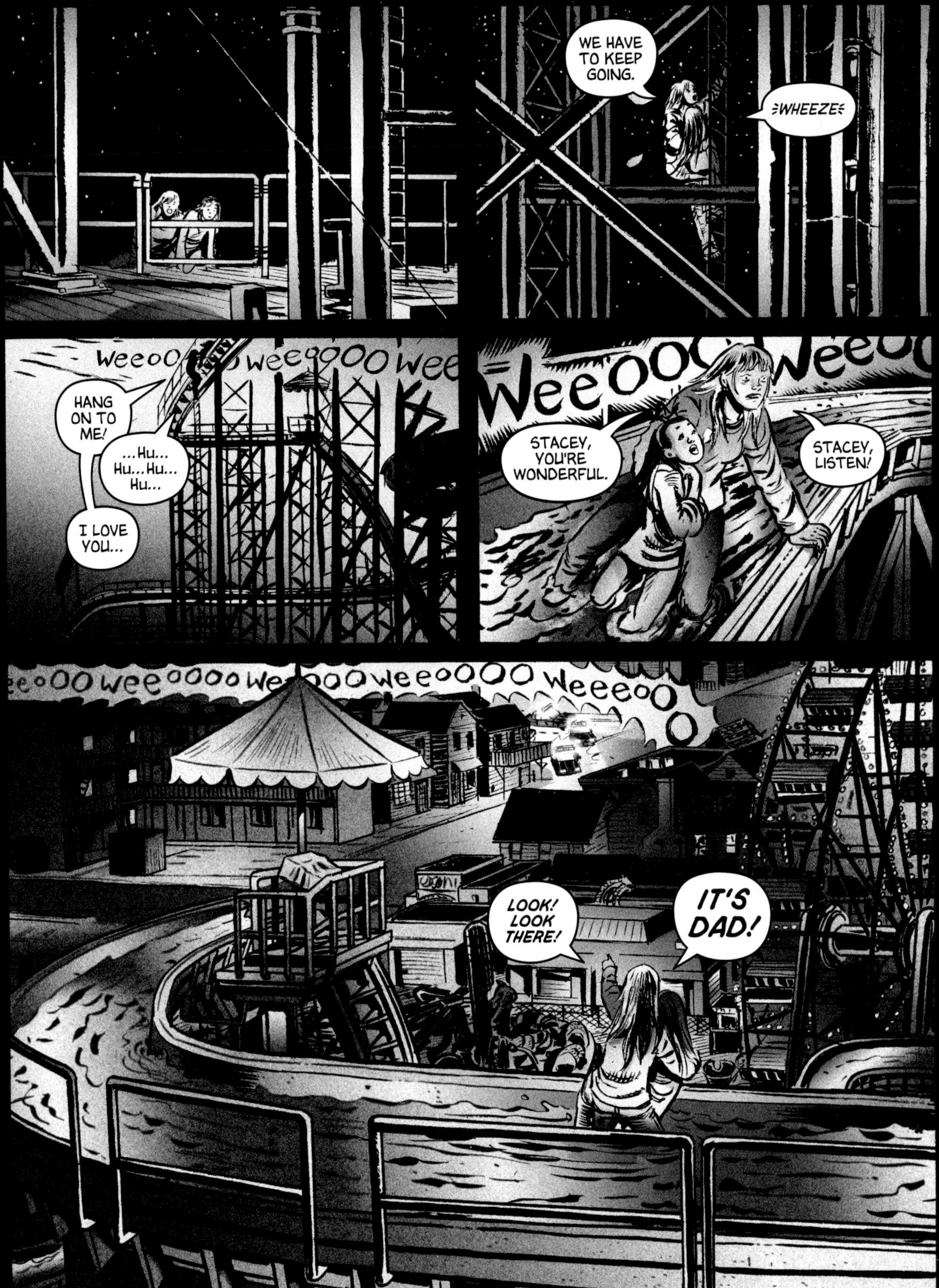
WE HAVE TO KEEP GOING.
WHEEZE
Weeoo weeoooo wee
HANG ON TO ME!
...Hu... Hu...Hu... Hu...
I LOVE YOU...
Weeooo weeo
STACEY, YOU'RE WONDERFUL.
STACEY, LISTEN!
eeoOO weeoooo weeoOO weeoOOO weeeoOO
LOOK! LOOK THERE!
IT'S DAD!

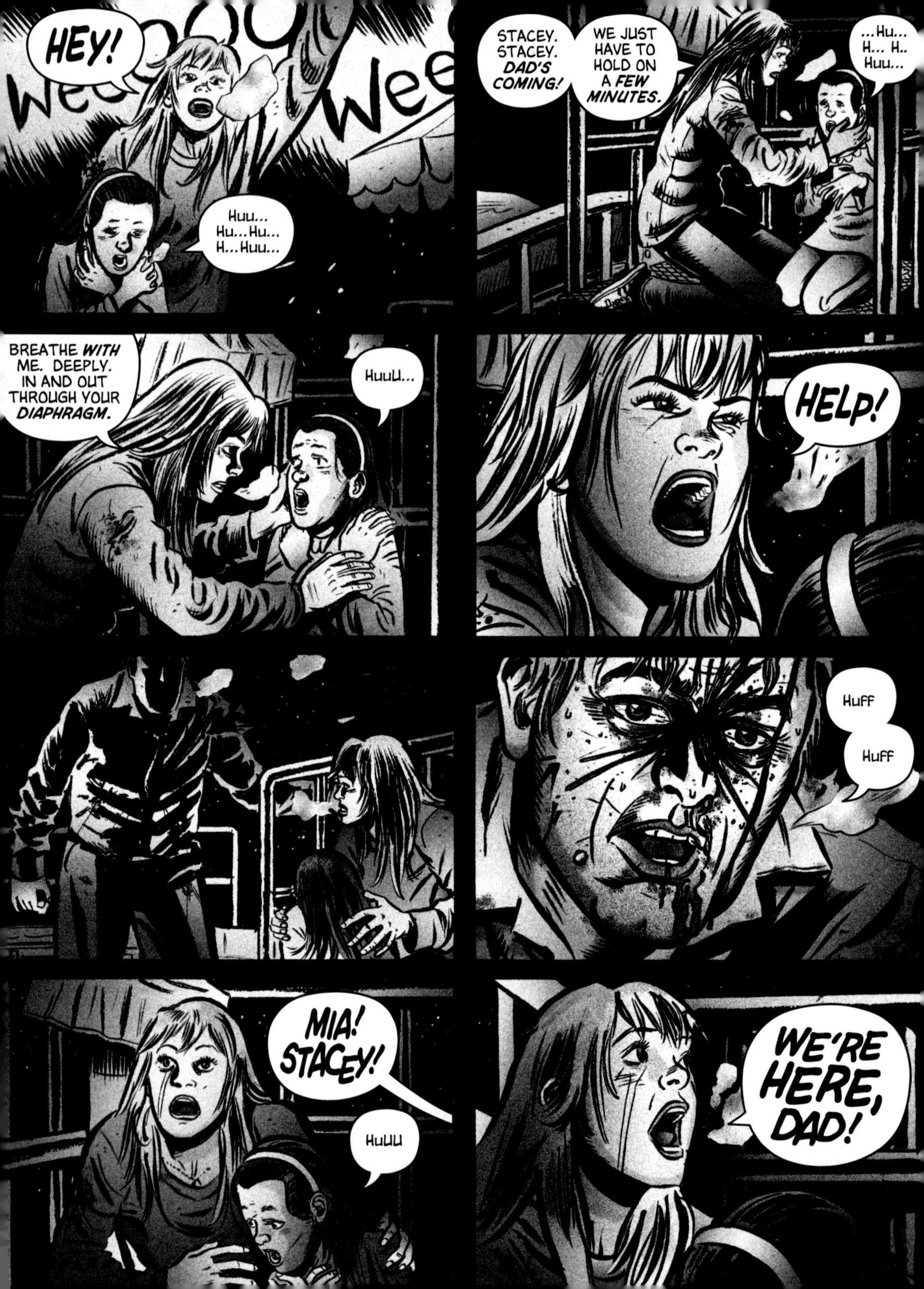
HEY!
Weeooo Weeoo
Huu...
Hu...Hu...
H...Huu...
STACEY. STACEY. DAD'S COMING!
WE JUST HAVE TO HOLD ON A FEW MINUTES.
...Hu... H... H.. Huu...
BREATHE WITH ME. DEEPLY. IN AND OUT THROUGH YOUR DIAPHRAGM.
Huuu...
HELP!
Huff
Huff
MIA! STACEY!
Huuu
WE'RE HERE, DAD!

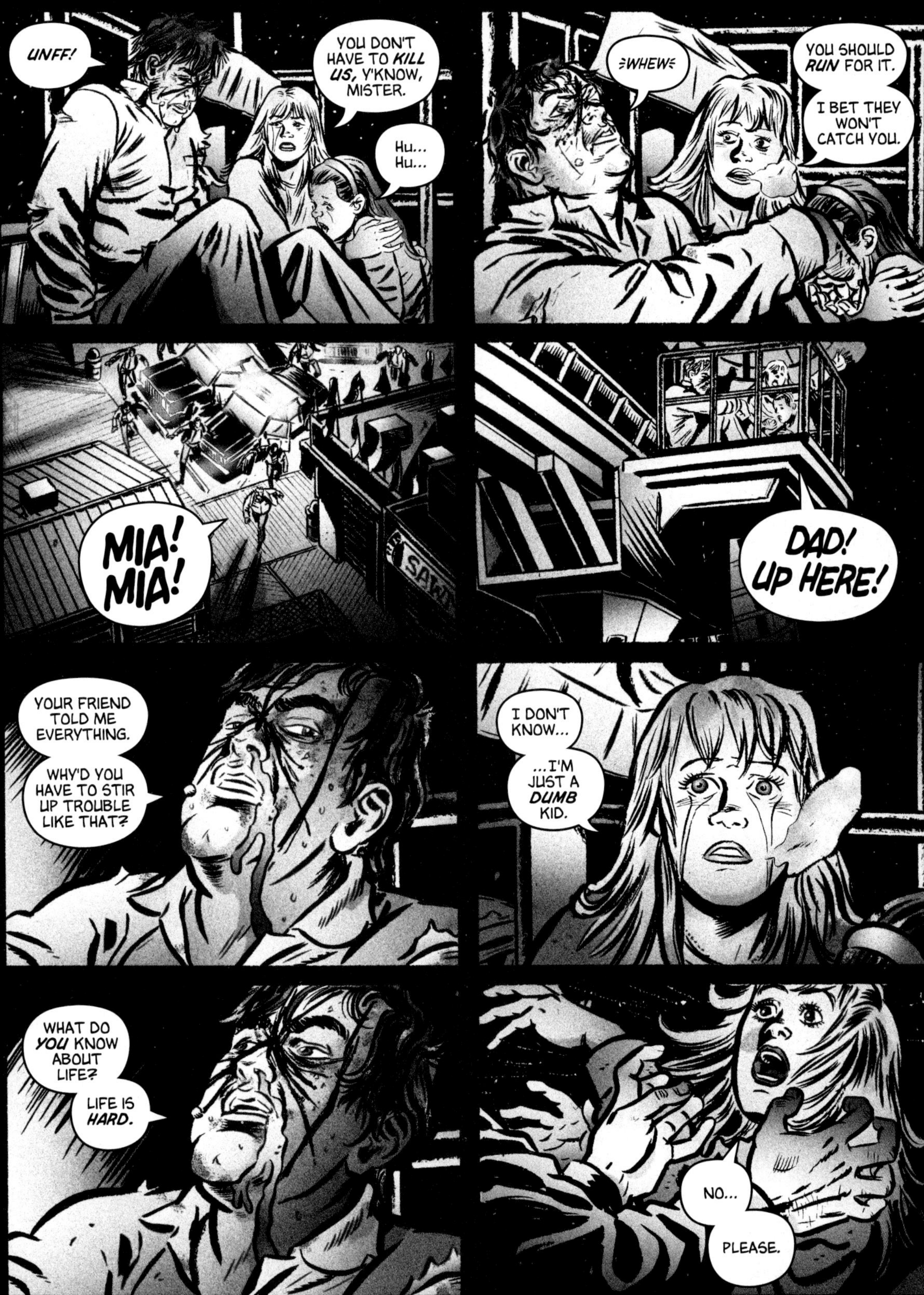
UNFF!
YOU DON'T HAVE TO KILL US, Y'KNOW, MISTER.
Hu... Hu...
WHEW
YOU SHOULD RUN FOR IT.
I BET THEY WON'T CATCH YOU.
MIA! MIA!
DAD! UP HERE!
YOUR FRIEND TOLD ME EVERYTHING.
WHY'D YOU HAVE TO STIR UP TROUBLE LIKE THAT?
I DON'T KNOW...
...I'M JUST A DUMB KID.
WHAT DO YOU KNOW ABOUT LIFE?
LIFE IS HARD.
NO...
PLEASE.

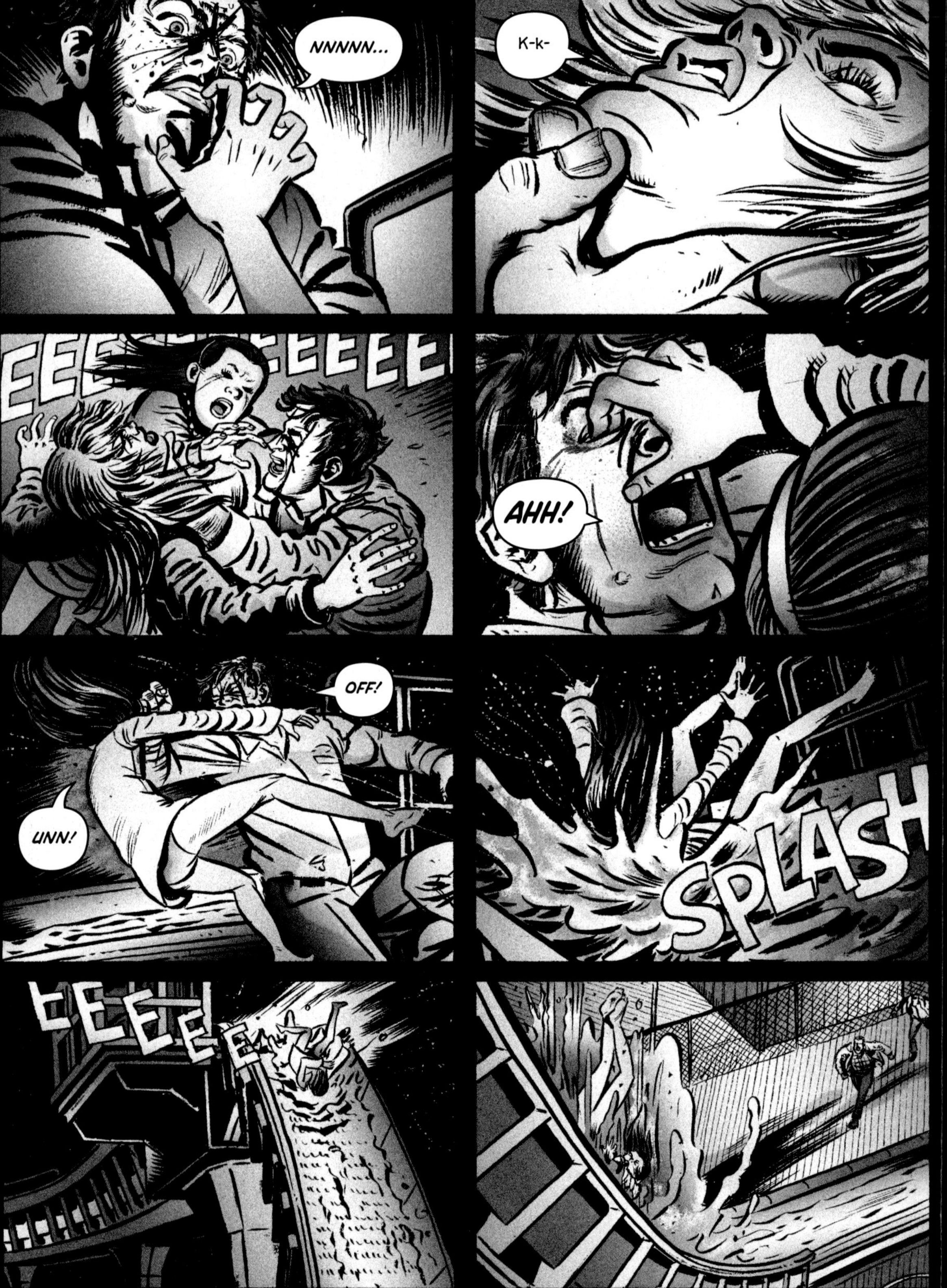
NNNNN...
K-k-
EEEEEEEEEEE
AHH!
OFF!
UNN!
SPLASH
EEEEEE

GET HER TO THE AMBULANCE!

CHIEF...

...I CAN'T GET A SHOT!

RAHH!

NN--NN-N!

?

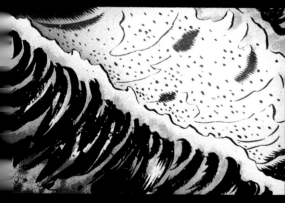

W-WHAT? WHAT HAVE I DONE WRONG...?

WHAT...?

TELL ME WHAT TO DO.

JUMP!

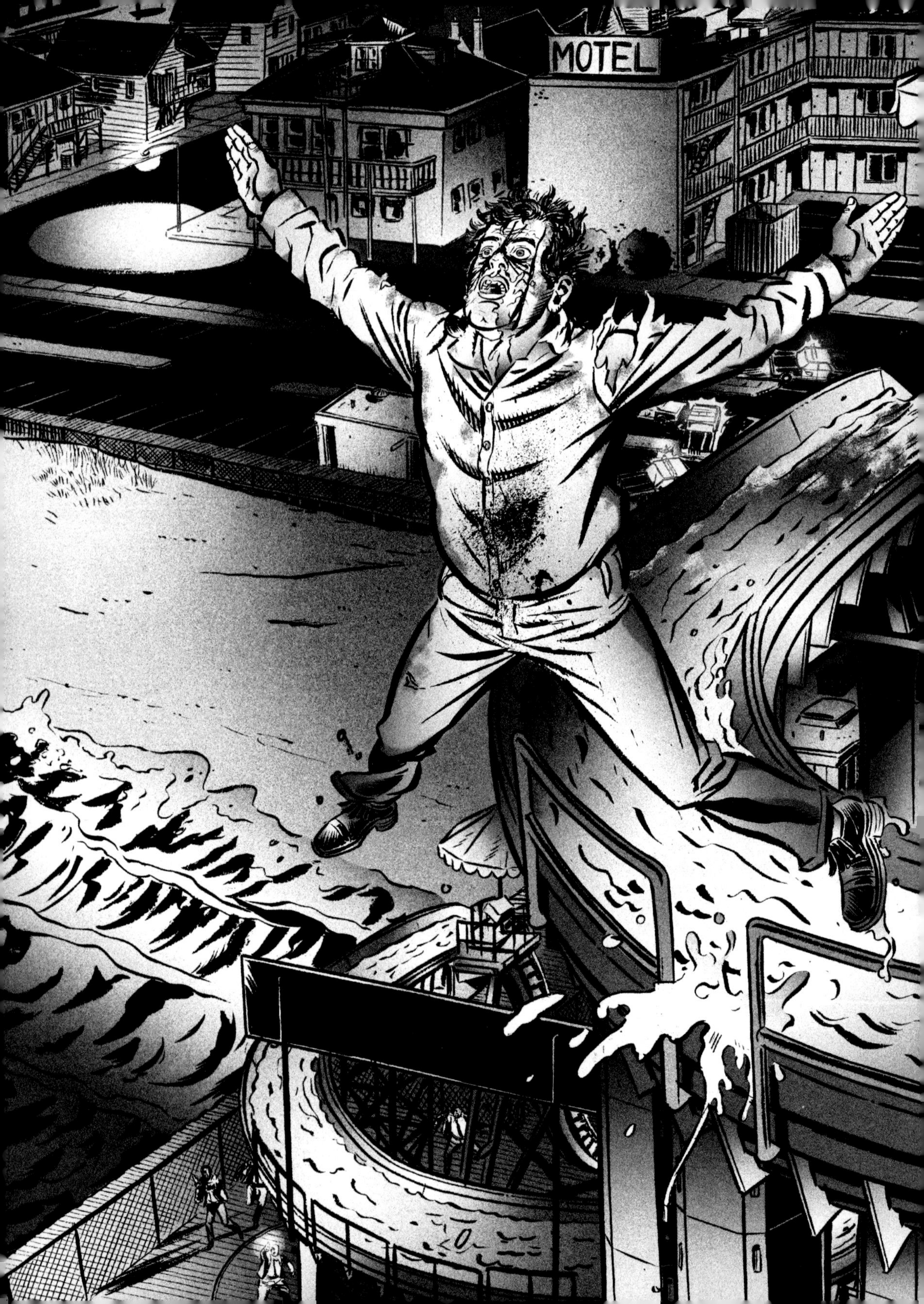
MOTEL

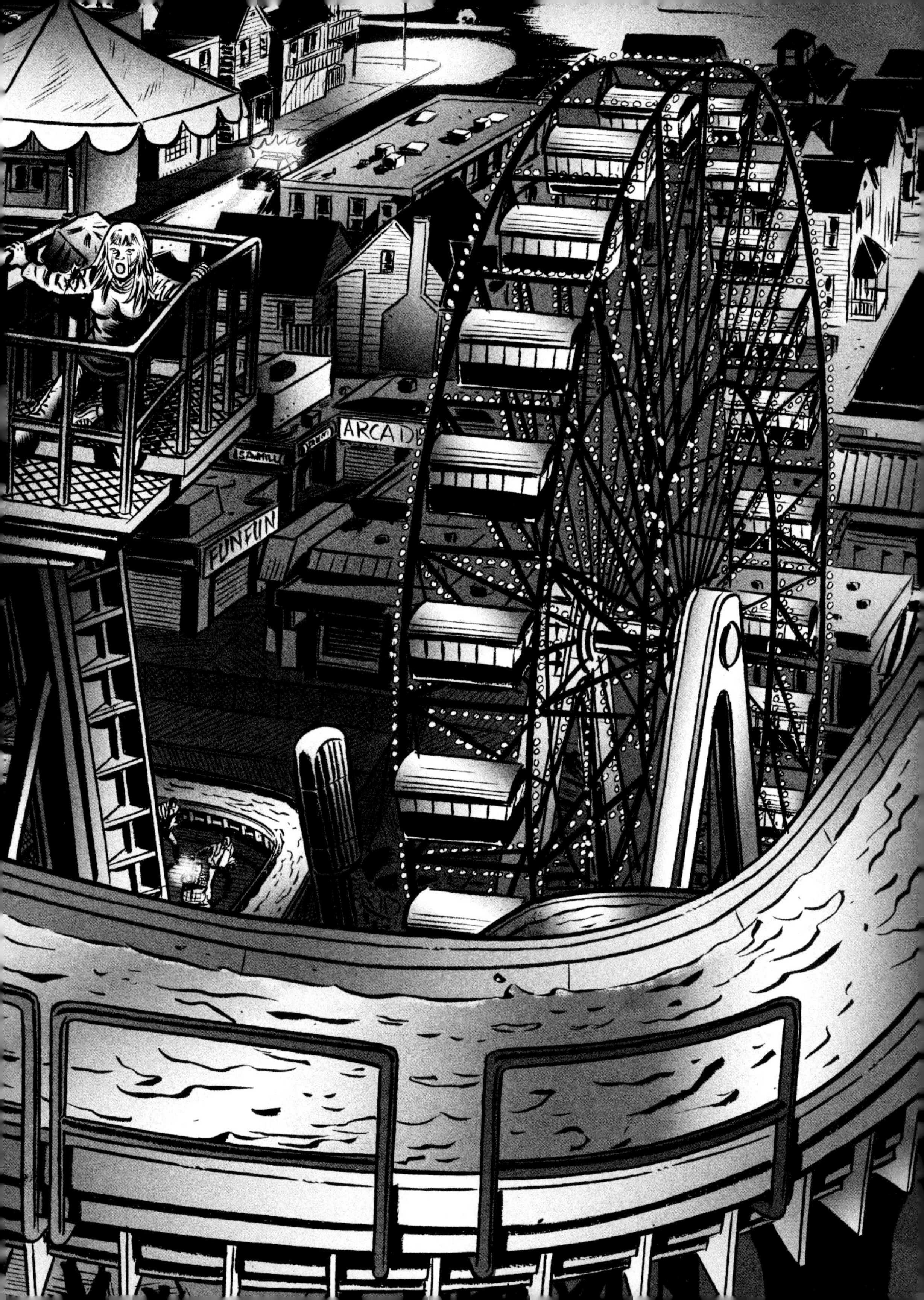
ARCAD
FUNFUN

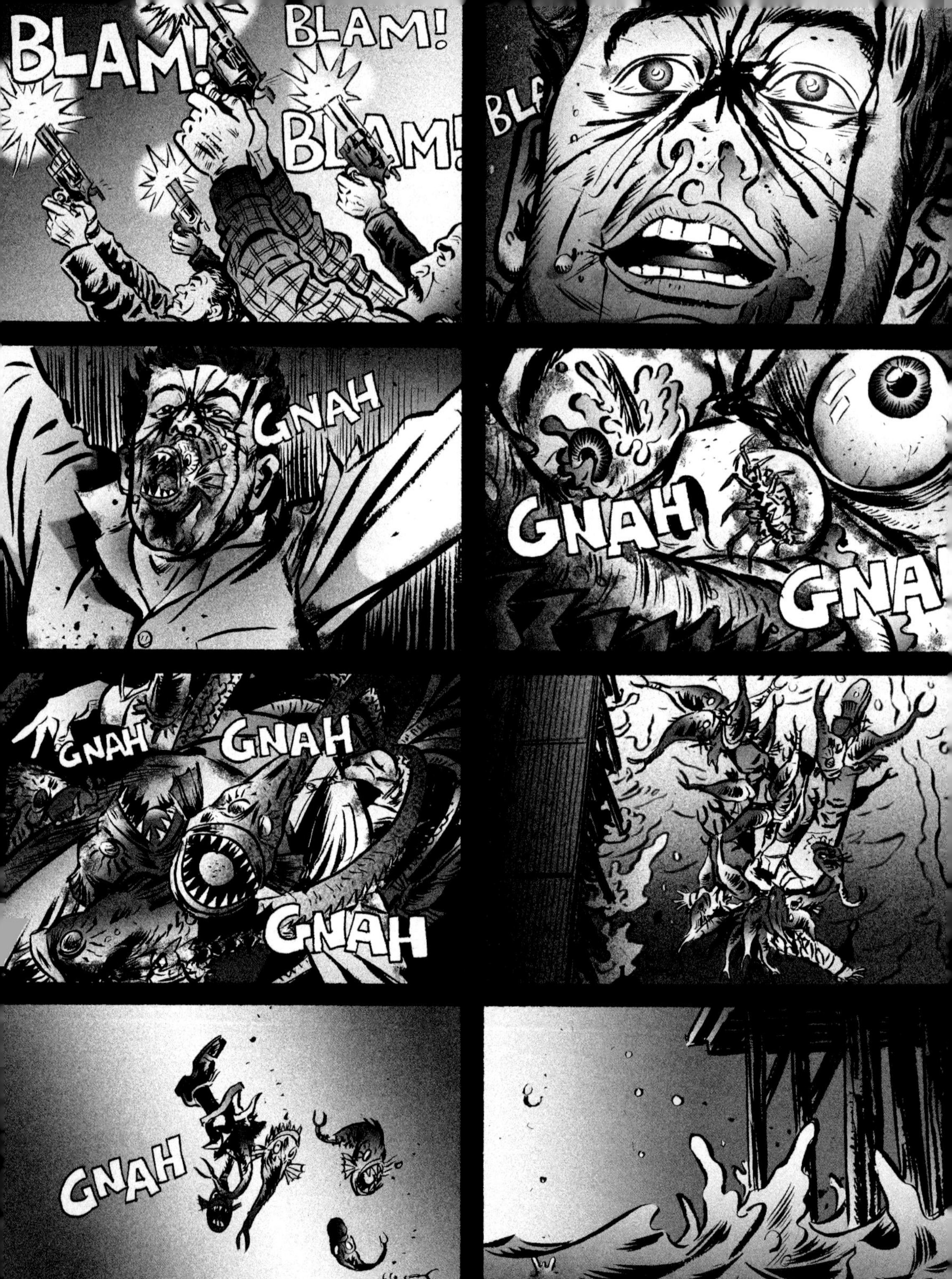
BLAM!
BLAM!
BLAM!
BLA
GNAH
GNAH
GNA
GNAH
GNAH
GNAH
GNAH

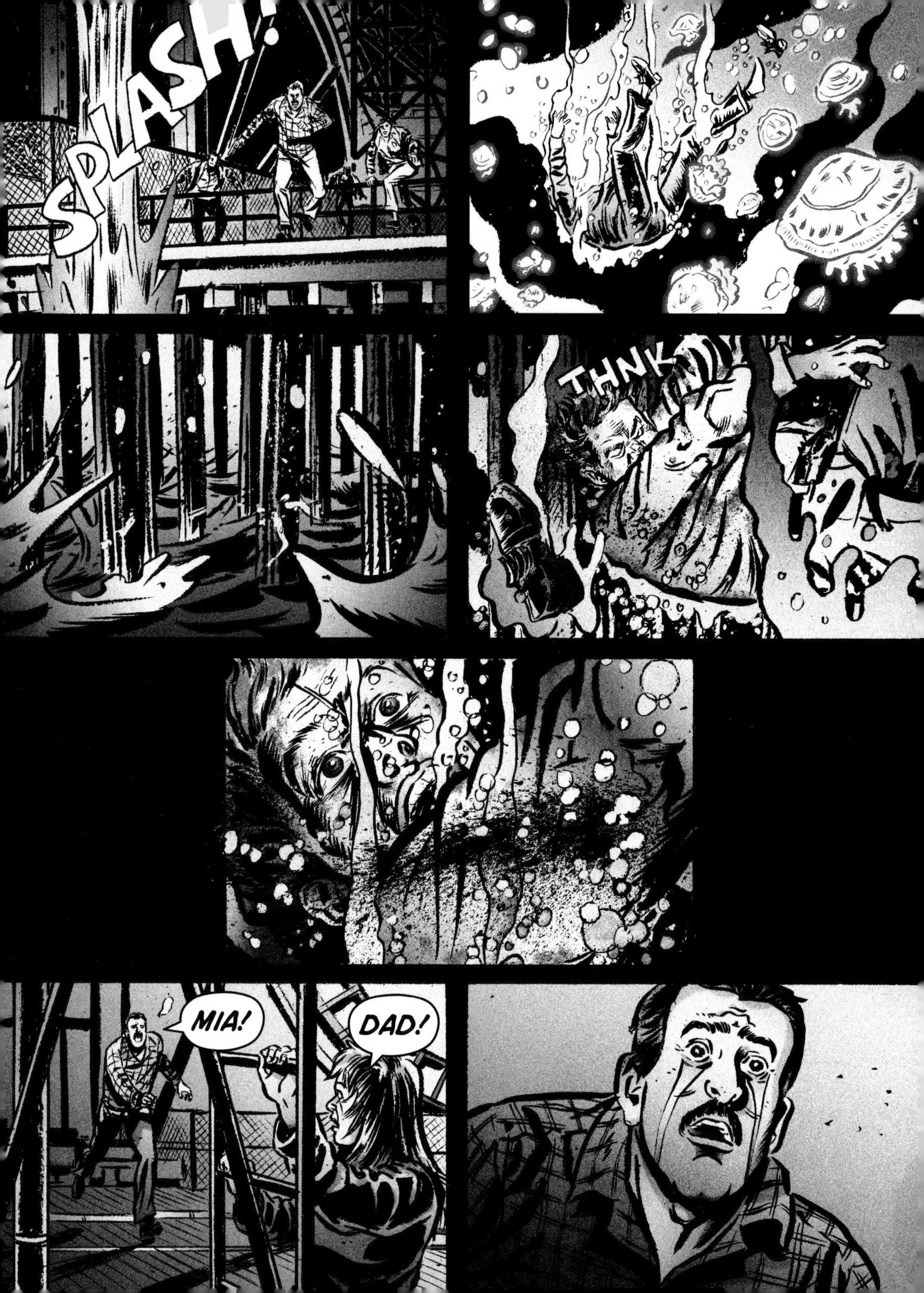
SPLASH!
THNK
MIA!
DAD!

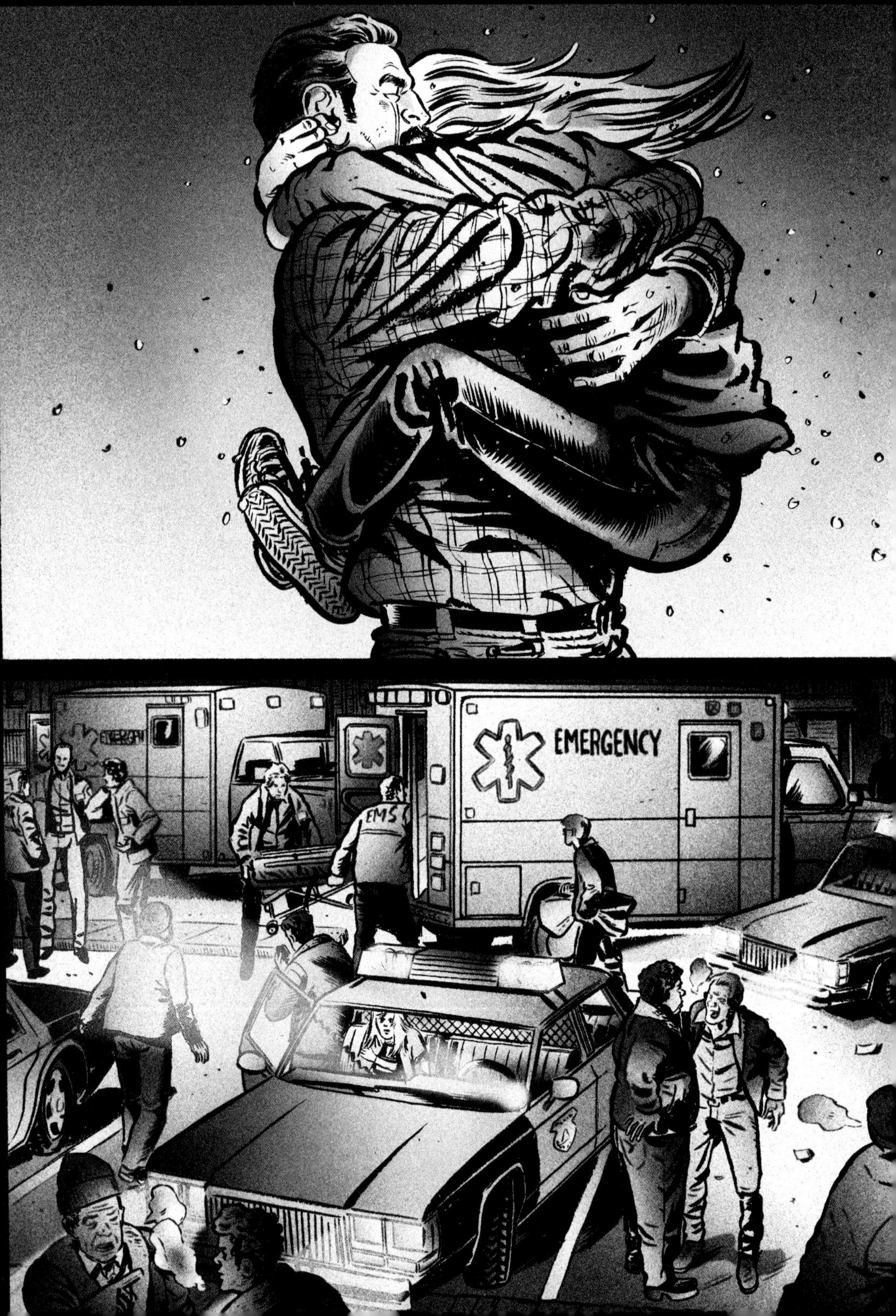
EMERGENCY
EMS

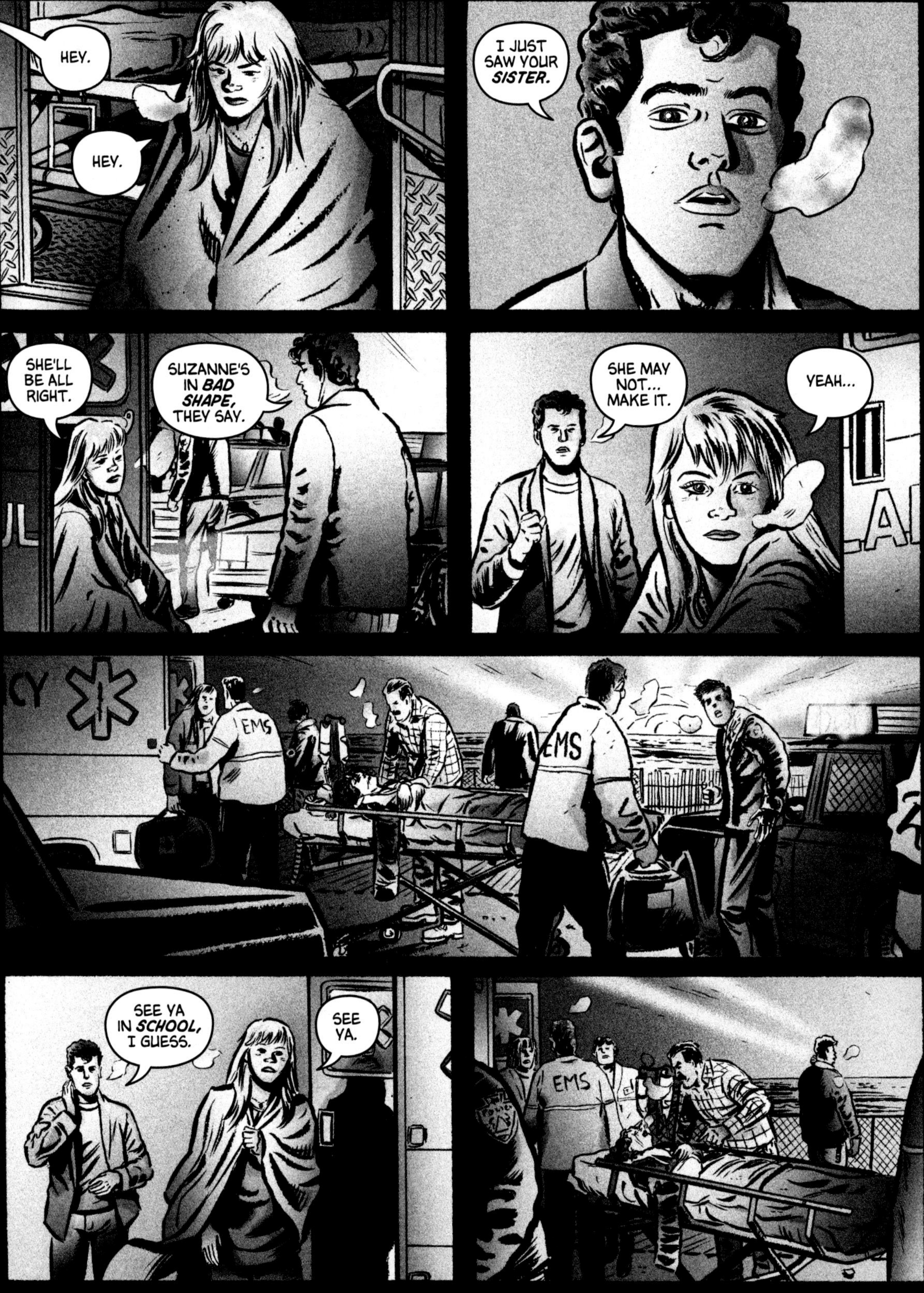
HEY.
HEY.
I JUST SAW YOUR SISTER.
SHE'LL BE ALL RIGHT.
SUZANNE'S IN BAD SHAPE, THEY SAY.
SHE MAY NOT... MAKE IT.
YEAH...
EMS
EMS
SEE YA IN SCHOOL, I GUESS.
SEE YA.
EMS

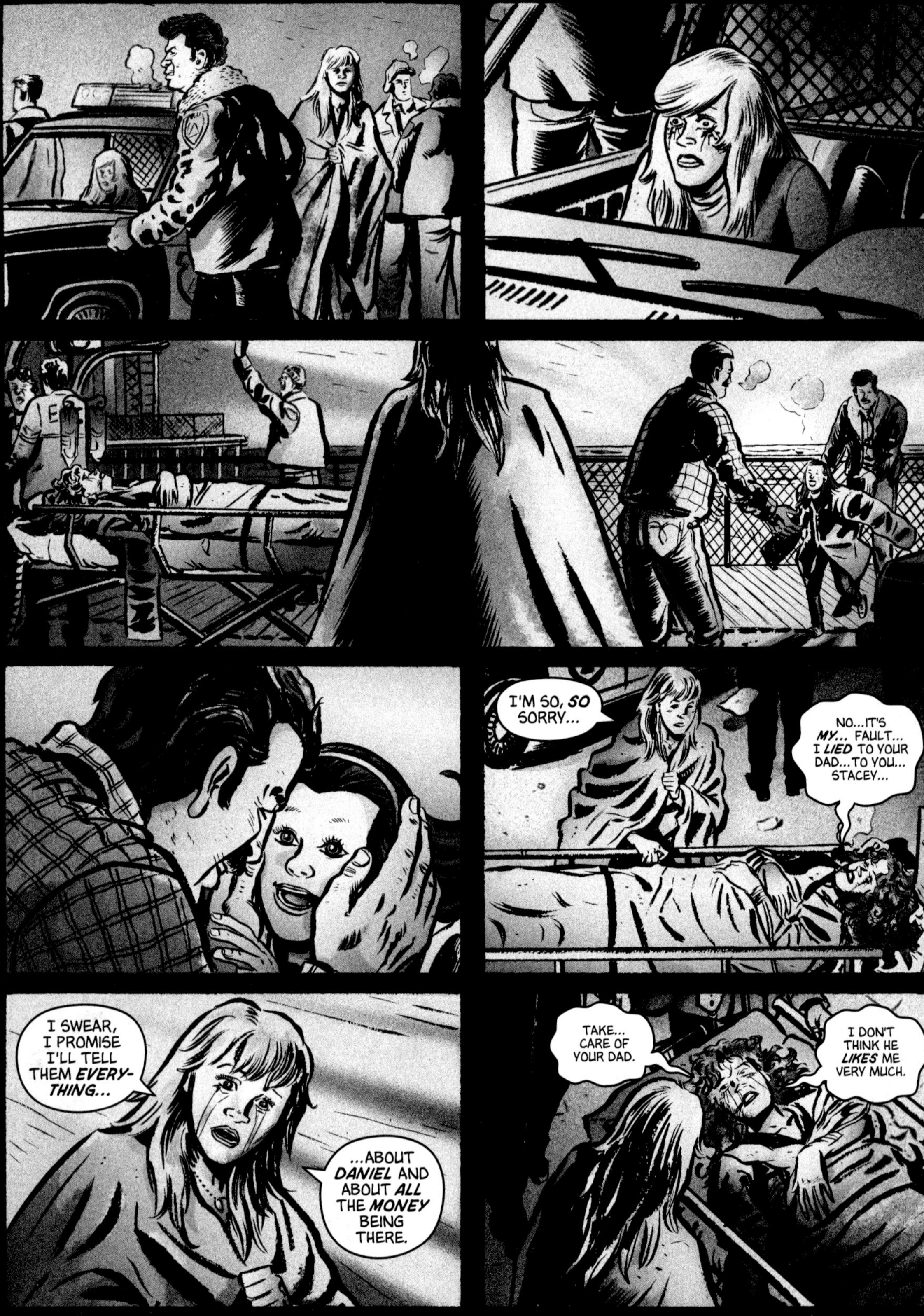
I'M SO, *SO* SORRY...
NO...IT'S *MY*... FAULT... I *LIED* TO YOUR DAD...TO YOU... STACEY...
I SWEAR, I PROMISE I'LL TELL THEM *EVERY-THING...*
...ABOUT *DANIEL* AND ABOUT *ALL* THE *MONEY* BEING THERE.
TAKE... CARE OF YOUR DAD.
I DON'T THINK HE *LIKES* ME VERY MUCH.